Irrational Exuberance

Irrational Exuberance

REVISED AND EXPANDED THIRD EDITION

Robert J. Shiller

Princeton University Press
Princeton and Oxford

Published by Princeton University Press, 41 William Street, Princeton, New Jersey 08540
In the United Kingdom: Princeton University Press, 6 Oxford Street, Woodstock, Oxfordshire OX20 1TW

press.princeton.edu

Jacket design by Steve Attardo / NINETYNORTH

Library of Congress Cataloging-in-Publication Data

Shiller, Robert J.
    Irrational exuberance / Robert J. Shiller.—Revised and expanded third edition.
        pages   cm
    Includes bibliographical references and index.
    ISBN 978-0-691-16626-1 (hardcover : alk. paper)
    1. Stocks—United States.   2. Stock exchanges—United States.   3. Stocks—Prices—United States.   4. Real property—Prices—United States.   5. Risk.
6. Dow Jones industrial average.   I. Title.
HG4910.S457   2015
332.63'2220973—dc23   2014036705

This book has been composed in Adobe Palatino and Berkeley Old Style Book and Black by Princeton Editorial Associates Inc., Scottsdale, Arizona

Printed on acid-free paper. ∞

Printed in the United States of America

10 9 8 7 6 5 4 3 2 1

To Ben and Derek

Contents

Figures and Tables

Figures

Tables

Preface to the Third Edition

One might think that years after the bursting of the speculative bubbles that led to the 2007–9 world financial crisis, we should be living in a distinctly different post-bubble world. One might think people would have "learned their lesson" and would not again pile into expanding markets, as so many did before the crisis, thereby worsening incipient bubbles. But evidence of bubbles has accelerated since the crisis. Valuations in the stock and bond markets have reached high levels in the United States and some other countries, and valuations in the housing market have been increasing rapidly in many countries. All this has been occurring despite a disappointing world recovery from the financial crisis, an increasingly tense international situation—with deadly wars in Gaza, Iraq, Israel, Syria, and Ukraine—and a wave of potentially disruptive nationalist sentiment and political polarization in the United States, Europe, and Asia.

As of this writing, the International Monetary Fund has just put out a warning of overheated housing markets in Asia, Europe, Latin America, and in Australia, Canada, and Israel.[1] A similar warning has been issued by the Bank for International Settlements.[2]

The bubbly and apparently unstable situation warrants some concern, although not yet generally as extreme as when the first edition of this book issued a warning about the overpriced and vulnerable stock market (see the reprinted 2000 Preface below), or when the second edition of this book issued a warning about the overpriced and vulnerable housing market as well (see the reprinted 2005 Preface below).

By the time this book finds its way into the hands of readers, the markets may be in a very different situation. Markets can change very rapidly, and the optimistic pricing we see at the time of this writing (in October 2014) is hard to predict. Current pricing may not last long when compared with publication lag and the time needed for an issue to become part of readers' agendas. But I am writing for future readers, years hence, who will read about the markets in the mid–second decade of the twenty-first century as just one of many examples described in the book—examples of broader tendencies and uncertainties.

Hence, the themes of the first edition of this book, with some updating, remain relevant today and probably always will be relevant. When the first edition of this book came out in 2000, I took pains to assert that the stock market bubble of that time, while exceptionally large, was really nothing fundamentally new. Chapter 8 in this edition, "New Eras and Bubbles around the World," details how many times we have had similar, if smaller or more localized, stock market booms and crashes. There *was* something relatively new then: the stock market boom that we now know peaked in early 2000 was worldwide in scope. In the first edition, I called it the Millennium Boom, because it came just before the dawn of the new millennium. We might also confidently call it the Millennium Bubble now, after it is over. But this boom or bubble was not really bigger in its collapse than its counterpart, which peaked in 1929. These really large bubbles are rare events, but the Millennium Bubble was not unique in history.

In the second edition (2005), I made much of the fact that for the United States as a whole, the boom in home prices nationwide that had begun in the late 1990s was the biggest ever, or biggest at least since 1890, when my data began. But, at the same time, the new chapter that was added to that edition also recounted earlier housing bubbles, and, if you look at centuries past, land price bubbles. Centuries ago, real estate speculation would have been more likely an investment in land—a farm or a town lot for building a home. Another big change in the second half of the twentieth century was a massive decline in lending standards for home mortgages. That decline, and the magnitude of the housing boom around the world (which we might now, after the collapse of home prices in many areas after 2006, confidently call a bubble) was unique. We might call this the Ownership-Society Boom, associated as it was with a slogan used by George W. Bush in his 2004 U.S. presidential campaign to describe his plan to promote widespread ownership of homes, stocks, and other investments. (I will call the current stock market boom, from 2009 to the time of this writing in 2014, the New-Normal Boom, after a term popularized by Bill Gross [then of PIMCO] in 2009.)

But there is really nothing new about these bubbles—not fundamentally new. They are repeats of approximately the same phenomenon, of new era stories proliferating by word-of-mouth contagion, of the distinct feel of mass enthusiasm for one kind of investment.

Improving information technology may accelerate their dynamics. Changing patterns of investing are also a factor. The rising impact of international investors and of institutional investors in single-family homes has been much noted in recent years. But the basic bubble phenomenon is the same. In the future, we will surely have even bigger such bubbles, each built up around its new and different new era story, and we will have to invent new names for them.

I was not expecting to hear about housing bubbles when I visited Colombia in mid-2013. Yet over and over again I heard about their amazing real estate boom. While taking me through the seaside resort town of Cartagena, my limousine driver pointed out a number of ordinary-looking homes that had recently sold for millions of U.S. dollars.

The Banco de la República, Colombia's central bank, has on their website a home price index for three major cities: Bogotá, Medellín, and Cali. The index shows home price increases of 69% in real (inflation-adjusted) terms since 2004. That rate of price growth recalls the U.S. experience, with the S&P/ Case-Shiller Ten-City Home Price Index for the United States rising 131% in real terms from its bottom in 1997 to its peak in 2006.

The vulnerability we have to bubbles in Colombia and all over the world reveals our continuing lack of understanding of these phenomena. Just what is a speculative bubble? The *Oxford English Dictionary* defines a bubble as "anything fragile, unsubstantial, empty, or worthless; a deceptive show. From 17th c. onwards often applied to delusive commercial or financial schemes." The problem is that words like *show* and *scheme* suggest a deliberate creation, rather than a widespread social phenomenon that is not directed by any central impresario.

Maybe the word *bubble* is used too carelessly. Eugene Fama certainly thinks so. Fama, the most important proponent of the "efficient markets hypothesis," denies that speculative bubbles exist. In his 2014 Nobel lecture, Fama states that the word *bubble* refers to "an irrational strong price increase that implies a predictable strong decline."[3] If that is what *bubble* means, and if *predictable* means that we can specify the date when a bubble bursts, then I agree with him that there may be little solid evidence that bubbles exist. But that is not my definition of a bubble, for speculative markets are just not so predictable.

In the second edition of this book, I tried to give a better definition of a bubble that accords with more enlightened usage of that term. The definition, given in Chapter 1, describes a situation in which news of price increases spurs investor enthusiasm, in a sort of psychological epidemic. That seems to be the core of the meaning of the word as it is most consistently used.

Implicit in this definition is a suggestion about why it is so difficult for "smart money" to profit by betting against bubbles: the psychological contagion promotes a mindset that justifies the price increases, so that participation in the bubble might be called almost rational. But it is not rational.

The story in every country is different, reflecting its own news, which does not always jibe with news in other countries. For example, the current story in Colombia appears to be that the country's government, now under the well-regarded management of President Juan Manuel Santos Calderón, has brought down inflation and interest rates to developed-country levels while all but eliminating the threat posed by the FARC rebels, thereby injecting new vitality into the Colombian economy. That is a good enough story to drive a housing bubble.

New era stories drive high expectations for investing returns but not necessarily high confidence. The high expectations during the upswing of a bubble may be more in the form of a sort of wishful thinking rather than an expression of confidence. In bubble times, there seems to be a tendency for complacency, as an aspect of social psychology, even if people haven't individually concluded that there is no risk.

Indeed, once you draw their attention to the risks, people are not so confident during a growing bubble. Figure 5.4, which plots investor valuation confidence, was actually exceptionally low at the all-time U.S. stock market peak in early 2000. People were certainly aware at some level of risks. Moreover, in a survey of homebuyers that Karl Case and I have been conducting over the years, we pose the following question to recent homebuyers directly: "Buying a house in this area today involves: 1. A great deal of risk; 2. Some risk; 3. Little or no risk." The answers are puzzling. In 2004, when the housing market was showing its fastest price increases, only 19% said "little or no risk." It is not as if everyone thought that "home prices can never fall" during the bubble, though they are often accused of having thought that. In the 2009 survey, at the depths of the worst recession since the Great Depression of the 1930s, the percentage of respondents choosing that option was actually lower, at 17.2%.[4]

During bubbles, it seems that the psychological ambience is rather one of public inattention to the thought that prices could fall, rather than firm belief that they can never fall. The new era stories are not new strongly held convictions—they are merely ideas foremost in people's minds that serve as justification both for the actions of others and of themselves.

Because bubbles are essentially subtle social-psychological phenomena, they are, by their very nature, difficult to control. Regulatory action since the financial crisis might diminish bubbles in the future, but it is yet to be seen whether such actions will be sufficient.

Liquid public markets for home prices do not exist that would allow skeptics of housing bubbles to take short positions against these bubbles, which would, if it were possible, have the effect of incorporating their doubts into the market prices. As we discuss in Chapter 11, if it is difficult to short the market, then a basic premise of the efficient markets theory is not met. The so-called "smart money" can stop investing in homes altogether, but afterward will not be able to take actions to stop others from bidding prices even further up and up. Any large group of investors, from anywhere in the world, for example, could bid local home prices up to crazy levels if they get the idea to do so, or any large institutional investors, playing some kind of game, could do so too. There is no reputable theory to say that, in the absence of the possibility of short sales, they cannot. Many have tried to make such short sales for single-family homes possible, so far with little success.

In the past few years, some high-tech institutional players, such as the Blackstone Group, have begun to invest in single-family homes, and the presence of these players might tend to alter the dynamics of home price bubbles, reducing month-to-month momentum in these markets. But high short-term momentum in home prices, as well as the longer-term real estate bubbles, are surely still with us.

The word *bubble* creates a mental picture of an expanding soap bubble, which is destined to pop suddenly and irrevocably. But speculative bubbles are not so easily ended; indeed, they may deflate somewhat, as the story changes, and then reflate.

It would seem more accurate to refer to these episodes as speculative epidemics. We know that a new epidemic can suddenly appear just as an older one is fading if a new form of the virus appears, or if some environmental factor increases the contagion rate. Similarly, a new speculative bubble can appear anywhere if a new story about the economy appears and if it has enough narrative strength to spark a new contagion of investor thinking.

This is what happened in the bull market of the 1920s in the United States, with its peak in 1929. We have distorted that history by thinking of bubbles as a period of dramatic price growth, followed by a sudden turning point and a major and definitive crash. In fact, a major boom in real stock prices in the United States after "Black Tuesday" brought them halfway back to 1929 levels by 1930. This was followed by a second crash, another boom from 1932 to 1937, and a third crash.

Since the second edition of this book, there has been much discussion of the price-earnings ratio that John Campbell of Harvard University and I had developed and that this book featured from its first edition: real price divided by the ten-year average of real earnings. The press has seemed to adopt the name I had sometimes given it, the CAPE (for Cyclically Adjusted

Price-Earnings ratio), so now I regularly call it that, too. This ratio has appeared as the third figure of the first chapter of this book in all editions, though the name "CAPE" did not appear in the earlier editions of this book. The ratio may be regarded as adjusting the usual price-earnings ratio, which is based on one-year earnings, for the business cycle, correcting for the sudden spikes in the price-earnings ratio that occur after business recessions when earnings may be very low, by averaging earnings over a long period of time.

As of this writing, the CAPE for the United States stands at 26, higher than ever before except for the times around 1929, 2000, and 2007, all major market peaks. But this book is not primarily about the current situation in asset markets but about getting a sense of reality about the nature and dynamics of these markets.

The current edition of this book is partly motivated by work I did with George Akerlof for our 2009 book *Animal Spirits*, a book whose title correctly suggests some overlap of topics with *Irrational Exuberance*. The ancient term "animal spirits" (in Latin, *spiritus animalis*) refers to the fluctuations in the basic driving force in human actions; it is a term that was resurrected by the economist John Maynard Keynes, who gives a view of the economy as involving fundamental psychological instabilities. Both fluctuations in irrational exuberance and animal spirits are still very much a part of our lives. We must still summon our whole arsenal of social sciences to try to understand them.

Outline of This Book

Reproduced here are the Prefaces for the 2005 and 2000 editions of the book, to give a sense how this book has evolved over the financial ups and downs. The 2005 Preface was issued just before the peak of the Ownership-Society Bubble. The 2000 Preface appeared with the first edition, just as the market was reaching the peak of the Millennium Bubble.

The book proper begins with three introductory chapters that place in historical context the ups and downs of the three major markets for investors: the stock market, the bond market, and the real estate market. Chapter 2 is new to this third edition of the book, added in response to widespread concern about a possible bond market bubble. The three chapters allow us to see how remarkable fluctuations in these markets have been, and to gain overall perspectives on trends in the markets.

Part One discusses the structural factors that drive market bubbles. This part begins, in Chapter 4, with a discussion of the precipitating factors that cause market fluctuations: events outside the markets, such as politics, technology, and demography. The chapter lists precipitating factors that are ultimately, largely through their effects on investor psychology, behind three recent stock market booms: the Millennium Boom, 1982–2000; the Ownership-Society Boom, 2003–7; and the New-Normal Boom, 2009 to the present. It is important even today to go through the precipitating factors of past booms to help us appreciate the diverse kinds of things that may drive booms of the future.

Part Two considers cultural factors that further reinforce the structure of the speculative bubble. The news media, discussed in Chapter 6, are critical, since they amplify stories that have resonance with investors, often regardless of their validity. Chapter 7 analyzes the "new era" theories that tend to arise spontaneously from time to time. In this edition, the analysis applies to both the stock market and the real estate market. The popularity of these theories is seen to derive from activity in the markets themselves, not from disinterested analysis of the true merit of these stories. Chapter 8 looks at the major stock market booms around the world in the past half century and describes the kind of new era theories that arose in association with many of them.

Part Three considers psychological factors that underlie market behavior. Chapter 9 argues that, with the true value of the markets so poorly defined by economic and financial theory, and so difficult to compute, the public relies on some largely psychological anchors for market value. Chapter 10 describes some important results from social psychology and sociology that help us understand why so many different people change their opinions at the same time.

Part Four investigates attempts on the part of academic and popular thinkers to rationalize market bubbles. Chapter 11 considers the efficient markets theory. Chapter 12 discusses the theory, often advanced during a bubble, that the public has just learned some important fact—even though the "fact" either is questionable or has already been widely known for some time.

Part Five, Chapter 13, considers the implications of speculative bubbles for individual investors, institutions, and governments. Several prescriptions for urgently needed policy changes are offered at this time of vulnerability in both the stock market and the real estate market, as are suggestions for ways in which individual investors can lower their exposure to the consequences of a "burst" bubble.

This edition of the book has also added, as an appendix, the revised version of the Nobel lecture I gave at the Nobel Prize events in Stockholm in December 2013. The Nobel lecture puts many of the arguments of the book into a broader context, with additional references to academic discussions of some of the basic conclusions here.

I have created a website, irrationalexuberance.com, which will present new information related to the topics in this book and will provide regular updates for some of the data and charts shown in this book.

Preface to the Second Edition, 2005

I n the preface to the first edition of this book, reproduced following this one, I described this book as a study of the millennium stock market boom, the boom that afflicted much of the world in the years leading up to 2000. A number of those who read the book have told me they think this book addressed a much broader subject. They are right: this book is really about the behavior of all speculative markets, about human vulnerability to error, and about the instabilities of the capitalist system.

When I was writing the first edition, mostly in 1999, the stock market boom seemed invincible. The S&P 500 index had gone up 34% in 1995, 20% in 1996, 31% in 1997, 26% in 1998, and 20% in 1999. Similar strings of stock market price increases had occurred in many other countries. So many years in a row of such spectacular increases could not be the result of mere chance, or so it seemed to many people then—and to the experts who encouraged this view. The stock market boom was widely viewed as the harbinger of a new economic era. But my book took a very different, and much dimmer, view of this stock market boom.

When the book appeared on store shelves in March 2000, I was on sabbatical from Yale, and I embarked on an extended ten-country book tour. Obviously, at that point in history, no one knew that March 2000 was to represent the peak of the market. Talking with so many people about the errors I thought they were making led me to ideas about how to strengthen the arguments presented in this new edition.

A few memories still strike me today, years later, about the kind of human errors that I encountered on my tour. I remember appearing on a radio talk show and hearing a woman tell me that she just *knew* I was wrong: the stock market has a pronounced uptrend; it *has* to go up generally. The tremor in her voice made me wonder what accounted for her emotions.

I also recall seeing a man who came to *two* of my book talks, each time sitting in the back and looking agitated. Why did he come back a second time, and what was upsetting him so?

I remember giving a talk presenting my bearish view of the market to a group of institutional investors, and then listening as a major institutional portfolio manager told me that he agreed with me, but was nevertheless going to ignore everything I had just said as he managed his portfolio. He believed that the views I expressed ultimately did not have enough authority to be taken seriously by his clients and colleagues, and that he could not alter his portfolio allocation based solely on what might seem to be one person's idiosyncratic opinion—even if he himself agreed with it.

But most of what I remember is people cheerfully and with apparent interest listening to my talk and then blithely telling me that they did not particularly believe me. Some kind of collective conclusion had been reached about the stock market—and it had a powerful hold on people's minds.

After 2000, the stock market boom abruptly ended; the U.S. stock market, and the markets in the same countries whose stock prices had also soared, came down substantially from their peaks in 2000. By the time the S&P 500 reached bottom in March 2003 it had fallen by half in real (inflation-corrected) terms. This outcome led to a change in investor psychology.

I remember having breakfast with a woman and her husband at the very end of 2000, when the market was down substantially from its peak, the tech stocks down more than 50%. She said she did the investing for the family, and in the 1990s she had been a genius. He agreed. Now, she confided, her self-esteem had collapsed. Her perception of the market was all an illusion, a dream, she said. Her husband did not disagree.

But, as profound as the psychological reaction to this stock market drop has been for some people, it appears that collective enthusiasm for stocks is more enduring than one might think; it seems, in large measure, that the enthusiasm is still not over. The stock market has not seen as big a drop as would have been predicted by the extreme overpricing of the market in 2000—at least not yet—and this intense psychological correction has not been experienced by most people.

The stock market has not come down to historical levels: the stock market price-earnings ratio as I define it in this book is still, at this writing, in the mid-20s, far higher than the historical average. Moreover, the market for homes has produced a situation in which median home prices are sometimes ten times buyers' per capita income or more. Irrational exuberance really is still with us.

In a broad sense, this book, from its first edition in 2000, has been about trying to understand the change in thinking of the people whose actions ultimately drive the markets. It is about the psychology of speculation, about the feedback mechanism that intensifies this psychology, about herd behavior that can spread through millions or even billions of people, and about the implications of such behavior for the economy and for our lives. Although the book originally focused directly on current economic events, it was, and is, about how errors of human judgment can infect even the smartest people, thanks to overconfidence, lack of attention to details, and excessive trust in the judgments of others, stemming from a failure to understand that others are not making independent judgments but are themselves following still others—the blind leading the blind.

The presumed enlightened opinion that people tend to rely on for economic judgments is often rather like the "man of smoke" in Aldo Palazzeschi's eponymous surrealistic 1911 novel. The protagonist is made only of smoke; he is virtually nothing at all, but he acquires a public persona and authority that is a construct of the collective imagination, until the public changes its mind, deciding he is not the font of truth, whereupon he disappears completely. Events such as that represented in Palazzeschi's novel are a reality: unsubstantiated belief systems, insubstantial wisps, do create bouts of irrational exuberance for significant periods of time, and these bouts ultimately drive the world economy.

I have revised the book in this second edition to try to extend its argument that variations caused by changing attitudes, irrational beliefs, and foci of attention are an important factor in our changing economic lives, and to examine the consequences for our economy and our future. I have recast the examples of these variations in terms of more recent events. Notably, I have added a chapter about the enormous home price boom that many countries have been experiencing since the late 1990s, and I have broadened the discussion throughout the book to consider speculation in real estate. Beyond that, this edition extends and improves the basic arguments in a number of directions. I have been thinking about the issues in this book for five more years since the first edition, and the research on behavioral economics, which I closely follow, has made substantial progress over that interval as well.

The issues that are treated in this book are serious, and of continuing relevance today. People in much of the world are still overconfident that the stock market, and in many places the housing market, will do extremely well, and this overconfidence can lead to instability. Significant further rises in these markets could lead, eventually, to even more significant declines. The bad outcome could be that eventual declines would result in a substantial increase in the rate of personal bankruptcies, which could lead to a secondary string of bankruptcies of financial institutions as well. Another long-run consequence could be a decline in consumer and business confidence, and another, possibly worldwide, recession. This extreme outcome—like the situation in Japan since 1990 writ large—is not inevitable, but it is a much more serious risk than is widely acknowledged.

Lest raising these possibilities seem alarmist, one should note that we are already living with some of the unpleasant repercussions of past over-confidence. The stock markets of many countries dropped by half from their 2000 peak by 2002, and have rebounded only a little. Overinvestment by corporations, encouraged by the booming stock market, led to a collapse of investment spending in the early years of the twenty-first century, and to a worldwide recession.

The boom years of the 1990s created a business atmosphere akin to a gold rush, and led many people to distort their business decisions, the results of which will weigh upon us for many years to come. Part of this change in busi-ness atmosphere was a decline in ethical standards, a decline in the belief in integrity, honesty, patience, and trust in business. A string of scandals affect-ing corporate boards, accounting firms, and mutual funds surfaced after the market dropped.

These extravagant years eventually led to severe budgetary problems for governments, both national and local. In the 1990s—with the stock market going up, investors reaping capital gains, and the economy booming—tax revenues rose, and many governments found it difficult to restrain increases in expenditures. After the stock market decline, tax revenues fell, throwing many governments into severe deficit crises. By 2002, the average government deficit among member countries in the Organization for Economic Cooperation and Development was 3% of gross domestic product. The government defi-cits have in turn led to troubled attempts to restrain spending, with uneven consequences for different constituencies.

An additional consequence of the intense stock market boom of the late 1990s was the home price boom, which began around 1997 or 1998 and then intensified after 2000 throughout many countries of the world. The home price boom appears to have begun around the time in 1997 that the stock market boom was engendering a proliferation of "new era" theories about the economy, and it is still going very strongly in many cities despite a stock market correction. We have yet to see the full consequences of these price changes.

Speculative instability appears to be increasingly important to the world economy. We are focusing more intently on the unpredictable markets. It is not that the existing stock markets are demonstrably becoming more volatile. There is no obvious long-run trend to greater stock market volatility. It is rather that the number of people participating in these markets is increasing, and that the scope of speculative markets, the kind of risks that are traded, is broadening. More and more electronic markets are being created every year, trading a wider and wider range of risks, and more and more people, in both advanced and emerging countries, are being drawn in to participate in these markets.

People will increasingly fear that their livelihoods really depend on their wealth, wealth that is highly unstable because of market changes. So, over the longer run, people will increasingly pay attention to market movements. There is an increasing perception that the price of assets matters very much to our lives. People increasingly believe that they must defend their private property and doubt that they can depend on social institutions to save them if things turn out badly. They see merciless capitalism as the wave of the future.

There is a name for this economic system—"the ownership society"—and President George W. Bush, among others, likes to use this term. People must take ownership of their own future, and plan for their future as property owners in many senses of the word. There is indeed much to be said for the ownership society in terms of its ability to promote economic growth. But by its very nature it also invites speculation, and, filtered through the vagaries of human psychology, it creates a horde of risks that we must somehow try to manage.

I do not know the future, and I cannot accurately predict the ups and downs of the markets. But I do know that, despite a significant slip in confidence since 2000, people still place too much confidence in the markets and have too strong a belief that paying attention to the gyrations in their investments will someday make them rich, and so they do not make conservative preparations for possible bad outcomes.

Preface to the First Edition, 2000

This book is a broad study, drawing on a wide range of published research and historical evidence, of the enormous recent stock market boom. Although it takes as its specific starting point the current situation, it places that situation in the context of stock market booms generally, and it also makes concrete suggestions regarding policy changes that should be initiated in response to this and other booms.

The need for such a book is particularly urgent today, in view of the widespread and quite fundamental disagreement about the stock market. When people disagree at such a basic level, it is usually because they possess only pieces of the overall picture. Yet meaningful consensus can only be achieved by laying out all the available facts. I have therefore tried in this book to present a much broader range of information than is usually considered in writings on the market, and I have tried to synthesize this information into a detailed picture of the market today.

Why did the U.S. stock market reach such high levels by the turn of the millennium? What changed to cause the market to become so highly priced? What do these changes mean for the market outlook in the opening decades of the new millennium? Are powerful fundamental factors at work to keep the market as high as it is now or to push it even higher, even if there is a downward correction? Or is the market high only because of some *irrational exuberance*—wishful thinking on the part of investors that blinds us to the truth of our situation?

The answers to these questions are critically important to private and public interests alike. How we value the stock market now and in the future influences major economic and social policy decisions that affect not only investors but also society at large, even the world. If we exaggerate the present and future value of the stock market, then as a society we may invest too much in business start-ups and expansions, and too little in infrastructure, education, and other forms of human capital. If we think the market is worth more than it really is, we may become complacent in funding our pension plans, in maintaining our savings rate, in legislating an improved Social Security system, and in providing other forms of social insurance. We might also lose the opportunity to use our expanding financial technology to devise new solutions to the genuine risks—to our homes, cities, and livelihoods—that we face.

To answer these questions about today's stock market, I harvest relevant information from diverse and, some would say, remote fields of inquiry. Insights from these fields too often go unnoticed by market analysts, but they have proved critical in defining similar market episodes throughout history, as well as in other markets around the world. These fields include economics, psychology, demography, sociology, and history. In addition to more conventional modes of financial analysis, they bring potent insights to bear on the issues at hand. Much of the evidence is drawn from the emerging field of behavioral finance, which, as the years go by, is looking less and less like a minor subfield of finance and more and more like a central pillar of serious finance theory.

I marshal the most important insights offered by researchers in these fields. Taken as a whole, they suggest that the present stock market displays the classic features of a *speculative bubble:* a situation in which temporarily high prices are sustained largely by investors' enthusiasm rather than by consistent estimation of real value. Under these conditions, even though the market could possibly maintain or even substantially increase its price level, the outlook for the stock market into the next ten or twenty years is likely to be rather poor—and perhaps even dangerous.

I do not purport to present a wholly new conception of financial market behavior. This book is a work neither of economic theory nor of econometrics, although it partakes in both. Rather, it is an attempt to characterize the complex nature of our real markets today, considering whether they conform or do not conform to our expectations and models. By assembling the most relevant evidence, economic and otherwise, on the state of the market, I hope to correct what I consider to be the perilous policy paths now being followed by legislators and economic leaders. I also hope to challenge financial thinkers to improve their theories by testing them against the impressive evidence that suggests that the price level is more than merely the sum of the available economic information, as is now generally thought to be the case.

Within the past generation the branch of financial theory that is derived from the assumption that all people are thoroughly rational and calculating has become the most influential analytical device to inform our mastery of the market. Those financial theorists who consider the market price to be a cunningly efficient processor of financial information have had a profound effect on the systematic management of the world's wealth, from the corner stockbroker right up to the Federal Reserve. But most of these scholars of finance and economics shrink from public statements about the level of the stock market (although they are often more loose-lipped in expressing their opinions at lunch and over beers) because they do not want to be caught saying things in public that they cannot prove. Assuming the mantle of scientific detachment, these financial economists tend to fall back on the simple but elegant model of market efficiency to justify their professional position.

However, there are serious risks inherent in relying too heavily on such pristine models as the basis for policy discussion, for these models deal only with problems that can be answered with scientific precision. If one tries too hard to be precise, one runs the risk of being so narrow as to be irrelevant. The evidence I present in the following chapters suggests that the reality of today's stock market is anything but test-tube clinical. If the theory of finance is to grow in its usefulness, all economists eventually will have to grapple with these messier aspects of market reality. Meanwhile, participants in public debate and economic policy formation must sort out this tangle of market factors now, before it is too late.

Among the unanticipated consequences of today's investment culture is that many of the tens of millions of adults now invested in the stock market act as if the price level is simply going to keep rising at its current rate. Even though the stock market appears based on some measures to be higher than it has ever been, investors behave as though it can never be too high, and it can never go down for long. Why would they behave this way? Their logic is apparently consistent with the free-rider argument. That is, if millions of researchers and investors are studying stock prices and confirming their apparent value, why waste one's time in trying to figure out reasonable prices? One might as well take the free ride at the expense of these other diligent investors who have investigated stock prices and do what they're doing—buy stocks!

But unknown to most investors is the troubling lack of credibility in the quality of research being done on the stock market, to say nothing of the clarity and accuracy with which it is communicated to the public. Some of this so-called research often seems no more rigorous than the reading of tea leaves. Arguments that the Dow is going to 36,000 or 40,000 or 100,000 hardly inspire trust. Certainly *some* researchers are thinking more realistically about the market's prospects and reaching better-informed positions on its future, but these are not the names that grab the headlines and thus influence public attitudes.

Instead the headlines reflect the news media's constant attention to trivial factoids and "celebrity" opinion about the market's price level. Driven as their authors are by competition for readers, listeners, and viewers, media accounts tend to be superficial and thus to encourage basic misconceptions about the market. A conventional wisdom of sorts, stressing the seemingly eternal durability of stocks, has emerged from these media accounts. The public has learned to accept this conventional—but in my view shallow—wisdom. To be fair to the Wall Street professionals whose views appear in the media, it is difficult for them to correct the conventional wisdom because they are limited by the blurbs and sound bites afforded them. One would need to write books to straighten these things out. This is such a book.

As noted earlier, the conventional wisdom holds that the stock market as a whole has always been the best investment, and always will be, even when the market is overpriced by historical standards. Small investors, in their retirement funds, are increasingly shifting their investments toward stocks, and the investment policy of 100% stocks in retirement funds is increasingly popular. They put their money where their mantra is. This attitude invites exploitation by companies who have an unlimited supply of equities to sell. "You want stocks? We'll give you stocks."

Most investors also seem to view the stock market as a force of nature unto itself. They do not fully realize that they themselves, as a group, determine the level of the market. And they underestimate how similar to their own thinking is that of other investors. Many individual investors think that institutional investors dominate the market and that these "smart money" investors have sophisticated models to understand prices—superior knowledge. Little do they know that most institutional investors are, by and large, equally clueless about the level of the market. In short, the price level is driven to a certain extent by a self-fulfilling prophecy based on similar hunches held by a vast cross-section of large and small investors and reinforced by news media that are often content to ratify this investor-induced conventional wisdom.

When the Dow Jones Industrial Average first surpassed 10,000 in March 1999, Merrill Lynch took out a full-page newspaper ad with a headline saying, "Even those with a disciplined long-term approach like ours have to sit back and say 'wow.'" In the bottom left corner of the page, next to a stock plot ending up at 10,000, appeared the words "HUMAN ACHIEVEMENT." If this is an achievement worth congratulating, then we should congratulate employees whenever they submit glowing self-evaluation reports.

At present there is a whiff of extravagant expectation, if not irrational exuberance, in the air. People are optimistic about the stock market. There is a lack of sobriety about its downside and the consequences that would ensue as a result. If the Dow were to drop to 6,000, the loss would represent something like the equivalent value of the entire housing stock of the United

States. There would be harmful and uneven effects on individuals, pension funds, college endowments, and charitable organizations.

We need to know if the price level of the stock market today, tomorrow, or on any other day is a sensible reflection of economic reality, just as we need to know as individuals what we have in our bank accounts. This valuation is the future food on our tables and clothes on our backs, and nearly every decision to spend money today ought to be influenced by it. We need a better understanding of the forces that shape the long-run outlook for the market—and it is such an understanding that this book is intended to provide.

Acknowledgments

Jeremy Siegel, while clearly not agreeing with me on all points, urged me to set down my ideas in this book. He is its real instigator. Jeremy has been a lifelong friend. Our families regularly vacation together, and I learned a distinctive approach to finance from him while strolling the beach together or watching our children fish. In the years since the first edition of this book appeared, he and I have frequently been cast as antagonists, he the bull and I the bear. But in fact we share a lot of the same worldview, and his new book *The Future for Investors* in many ways complements this book.

John Campbell, my former student, then co-author on a dozen scholarly papers on financial markets, and for years a close friend, has been my intellectual other half in formulating many of the ideas that led to this book. My original work on volatility in financial markets was refined and significantly advanced with his collaboration. He has also offered many helpful suggestions for this book and comments on the manuscript.

Peter Dougherty, my editor at Princeton University Press, has been an extremely important formative influence on the book, helping to define the fundamental aspects of its structure. He has been a great colleague and more—really almost a collaborator. Peter Strupp and his colleagues at Princeton Editorial Associates have as always been most helpful throughout the production process.

My assistants Carol Copeland, Minhua Wan, Sumithra Sudhir, and now Bonnie Blake have kept me going through difficult times with their steadfast support. I was fortunate to have a number of excellent student research assistants to help me during the writing: Eric Bair, Yigit Bora Bozkurt, Peter Fabrizio, Jon Fougner, Gerardo Garcia Lopez, Michael Gousgounis, William "Drew" Haluska, Erik Hjalmarsson, Yuanfeng Hou, Murad Jivraj, Leora Kelman, Alston E. Lambert II, Anthony Ling, Luis Mancilla, Steven Pawliczek, Stefan Schneeberger, and Kinde Wubneh.

I am also blessed with a number of friends and colleagues who read drafts of the manuscript and provided extensive comments: Stefano Athanasoulis, John Geanakoplos, William Konigsberg, Stephen Morris, Sharon Oster, Jay Ritter, Martin Shubik, and James Tobin.

My colleagues at the Cowles Foundation for Research in Economics at Yale University—Glena Ames, Donald Brown, Stefan Krieger, Stephen Morris, and William Nordhaus—have been a great help. I must also take this occasion to express gratitude to our late founder, Alfred Cowles III, an investment manager in the early part of this century and patron of mathematical economics, who tabulated the pre-1926 dividend and earnings data used in this book.

Help from my colleagues at the Yale International Center for Finance—its director, William Goetzmann, as well as Zhiwu Chen, Roger Ibbotson, Eli Levy, Jim Snyder, Ivo Welch, and Jeffrey Wurgler—is also acknowledged. Roger, who in 2000 was giving talks titled "Dow 100,000" and predicting a brilliant future for the stock market, was a willing foil for my ideas. The Dow has just surpassed 17,000, and so I think he will *eventually* be right.

My research with colleagues at Barclays Bank, who have collaborated in research on the dynamics of sector stock market indices, is another source of enlightenment for this book. Among the many collaborators I would mention Laurence Black, Oliver Bunn, Kenneth Crawford, Anthony Lazanas, Vytautas Martinaitis, Benedict Redmond, Richa Singh, Arne Staal, Cenk Ural, and Ji Zhuang.

Support from my colleague Prof. Karl E. Case of Wellesley College has also been most important. I met him after hearing about an article he wrote in 1986 that attempted to enumerate the reasons for the surge in home prices in the Boston area. We first did a questionnaire survey of attitudes of homebuyers in 1988. He has been working with me ever since to understand the psychology of real estate markets. Case and I continue to update the survey data with the support of the Yale School of Management, our latest work now joint with Anne Kinsella Thompson of McGraw Hill Construction.

I am grateful to Bracebridge Capital, Fuller and Thaler Asset Management, LSV Asset Management, and the Russell Sage Foundation for sponsoring the behavioral finance workshops that Richard Thaler and I have been organizing since 1991 at the National Bureau of Economic Research, and to the Russell Sage Foundation and the Federal Reserve Bank of Boston for sponsoring the behavioral macroeconomics workshops that George Akerlof and I organized there in 1994–2007. The term *behavioral economics* refers to research on markets

'ails of human behavior, including human
book benefits immeasurably from the work
emerging field of behavioral economics, which
a solid place in university economics and finance

al Science Foundation has supported much of my basic
ancial markets. Their continuing support of my work for over
rs enabled me to focus attention on issues independent of financial
res. Whitebox Advisors, under the leadership of Andrew Redleaf, has
en a grant to Yale University to support research on behavioral economics,
and this grant also helped support the revisions of this book for the second
edition.

I am also grateful to Brad Barber, Scott Boorman, David Colander, Robert
Ellickson, Ray Fair, Peter Garber, Jeffrey Garten, Christian Gollier, Sunil
Gottipati, Trevor Greetham, Stanley Hamilton, Anne Laferrere, Jonathan
Laing, Ricky Lam, Xindan Li, Yan Li, Justin Yifu Lin, Benoit Mercereau,
John Rey, Colin Robertson, Tsur Somerville, Nassim Taleb, Philippe Trainar,
Mark Warshawsky, Oleg Zamulin, Yong Zhang, and Ning Zhu for helpful
discussions. Yoshiro Tsutsui of Osaka University and Fumiko Kon-Ya of the
Japanese Securities Research Institute have collaborated with me for many
years on questionnaire survey research exploring investor attitudes in Japan
as well as the United States. Help from Josephine Rinaldi and Walt Smietana
at CompuMail has been much appreciated. I should certainly also thank the
numerous investors who have taken the time to fill out questionnaires for me.

To my wife, Virginia Shiller, who is a clinical psychologist at the Yale Child
Study Center, I owe fundamental gratitude for getting me really interested in
psychology and convincing me of its importance in economics. She has given
the most careful reading and criticism to the entire book and has helped me
greatly in articulating my ideas. She also kept the home fires burning while
I spent long days and nights working.

One

The Stock Market in
Historical Perspective

When Alan Greenspan, then Chair of the
Federal Reserve Board, used the term
irrational exuberance to describe the behavior of stock market investors, the
world fixated on those words.[1] He spoke at a black-tie dinner in Washington,
D.C., on December 5, 1996, and the televised speech was followed the world
over. As soon as he uttered these words, stock markets dropped precipitously.
In Japan, the Nikkei index dropped 3.2%; in Hong Kong, the Hang Seng
dropped 2.9%; and in Germany, the DAX dropped 4%. In London, the FTSE
100 was down 4% at one point during the day, and in the United States, the
next morning, the Dow Jones Industrial Average was down 2.3% near the
beginning of trading. The sharp reaction of the markets all over the world to
those two words in the middle of a staid and unremarkable speech seemed
absurd. This event made for an amusing story about the craziness of markets,
a story that was told for a time around the world.

The amusing story was forgotten as time went by, but not the words
irrational exuberance, which were referred to again and again. Greenspan did
not coin the phrase *irrational exuberance*, but he did cause it to be attached to a
view about the instability of speculative markets. The chain of stock market
events caused by his uttering these words made the words seem descriptive
of essential reality. Gradually they became Greenspan's most famous quote—
a catch phrase for everyone who follows the market.

Why do people still refer so much to *irrational exuberance* years later?
I believe that the words have become a useful name for the kind of social
phenomenon that perceptive people saw with their own eyes happening in

1

the 1990s, and that in fact, it appears, has happened again and again in history, when markets have been bid up to unusually high and unsustainable levels under the influence of market psychology.

Many perceptive people were remarking, as the great surge in the stock market of the 1990s continued, that there was something palpably irrational in the air, and yet the nature of the irrationality was subtle. There was not the kind of investor euphoria or madness described by some storytellers, who chronicled earlier speculative excesses like the stock market boom of the 1920s. Perhaps those storytellers were embellishing the story. Irrational exuberance is not *that* crazy. The once-popular terms *speculative mania* or *speculative orgy* seemed too strong to describe what we were going through in the 1990s. It was more like the kind of bad judgment we all remember having made at some point in our lives when our enthusiasm got the best of us. *Irrational exuberance* seems a very descriptive term for what happens in markets when they get out of line.

Irrational exuberance is the psychological basis of a speculative bubble. I define a speculative bubble as a situation in which news of price increases spurs investor enthusiasm, which spreads by psychological contagion from person to person, and, in the process, amplifies stories that might justify the price increase and brings in a larger and larger class of investors, who, despite doubts about the real value of the investment, are drawn to it partly through envy of others' successes and partly through a gambler's excitement. We will explore the various elements of this definition of a bubble throughout this book.

Greenspan's "irrational exuberance" speech in 1996 came during the biggest historical example to date of a speculative upsurge in the U.S. stock market. The Dow Jones Industrial Average (from here on, the Dow for short) stood at around 3,600 in early 1994. By March 1999, it passed 10,000 for the first time. The Dow peaked at 11,722.98 in January 14, 2000, just two weeks after the start of the new millennium. The market had tripled in five years. Other stock price indices peaked a couple of months later. The real (inflation-corrected) Dow did not reach this level again until 2014, and, as of this writing, the real Standard & Poor's 500 index has still not quite returned to its 2000 level. It is curious that this peak of the Dow (as well as other indices) occurred in close proximity to the end of the celebration of the new millennium—it was as if the celebration itself was part of what had propelled the market, and the hangover afterward had brought it back down.

Figure 1.1 shows the monthly real (corrected for inflation using the Consumer Price Index) Standard and Poor's (S&P) Composite Stock Price Index, a more comprehensive index of stock market prices than the Dow, based, since 1957, on 500 stocks rather than just the 30 stocks that are used to compute the Dow.[2] Inflation correction was used here because the overall

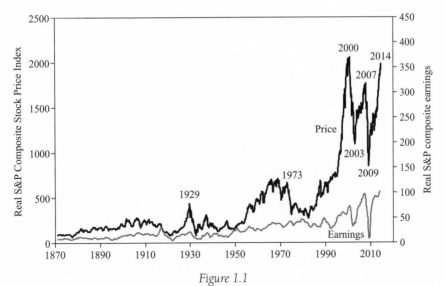

Figure 1.1
U.S. Stock Prices and Earnings, 1871–2014
Real (inflation-corrected) S&P Composite Stock Price Index, monthly, January
1871 through June 2014 (upper curve), and real S&P Composite earnings (lower
curve), January 1871 to March 2014. *Source:* Author's calculations using data from
S&P Statistical Service; U.S. Bureau of Labor Statistics; Cowles and associates,
Common Stock Indexes; and Warren and Pearson, *Gold and Prices.* See also note 3.

level of prices has been very unstable over parts of this period (the government printed a lot of money, which pushed all prices up) so that the un-
corrected numbers would give a misleading impression of the real increase in
the stock market. The stock prices are shown from 1871 through 2014 (upper
curve), along with the total earnings (corporate profits per share) that the
corporations that comprise the index made in doing their businesses (lower
curve) for the same years.[3]

This stock market chart is unusual: most long-term plots of stock prices
are not this long term, and most are done in nominal terms, without inflation
correction. On this chart, the magnitude of the boom beginning in 1982 and
peaking in 2000 stands out especially well. It is a unique event in history.

The 2000 Millennium Boom peak in world stock prices was followed by the
Ownership-Society Boom, 2003–7, which I have named after a slogan used by
George Bush in his 2004 presidential campaign. This peak was followed by
the world financial crisis in 2008–9. Starting in 2009, after the crisis lessened,
there was another major upswing in world stock markets, which I will call the
New-Normal Boom, after a phrase popularized by Bill Gross, then of PIMCO,
in 2009.[4] The news media have shown a tendency since 2000 to dramatize the

"new records" set in stock markets in 2007 and 2014. But, in fact, these post-2000 booms were not record setting. The biggest-ever upswing in the real (inflation-corrected) U.S. stock market was from July 1982 to August 2000, when the market went up 7.7-fold, dwarfing the 5.2-fold upswing from December 1920 to September 1929, and also dwarfing the 5.1-fold upswing from June 1949 to December 1968. The upswings from 2003 to 2007 (1.5-fold) and from 2009 to 2014 (2.3-fold) are mild by comparison. For the purpose of understanding irrational exuberance, I will emphasize the 1982–2000 Millennium Boom, particularly its later years, when this exuberance became most palpable.

The stock market increase from 1994 (when the real stock market had already more than doubled since 1982) to 2000 could not obviously be justified in any reasonable terms. Basic economic indicators did not come close to tripling. Over the same interval, U.S. gross domestic product rose less than 40%, and corporate profits rose less than 60%, and that from a temporary recession-depressed base. Viewed in the light of these figures, the stock price increase appears unwarranted.

Large stock price increases occurred in many countries at around the same time, and the peaks in the stock markets were often roughly simultaneous in many countries in early 2000. Figure 1.2 shows the paths of stock prices for ten countries and for the world as a whole from 1995 to 2014. As can be seen from Figure 1.2, between 1995 and 2000 the real stock market valuations of Brazil, France, China, and Germany roughly tripled, while that of the United Kingdom roughly doubled. In 1999, the year before the peak, real stock price increases averaged 58% over the ten countries shown in Figure 1.2. The prices of all countries went up sharply in 1999; in fact, the smallest increase, occurring in the United Kingdom, was still an impressive 16%. Stock markets in Asia (Hong Kong, Indonesia, Japan, Malaysia, Singapore, and South Korea) and Latin America (Chile and Mexico) also made astounding gains in 1999. It was a truly spectacular worldwide stock market boom.

The end of the 2000 boom brought stock markets down across much of the world by 2003, as can be seen in Figure 1.2. Once again, the next boom, peaking in late 2007 or early 2008, had huge impacts over much of the world. After that, the world slipped into the most serious recession since the Great Depression of the 1930s, economic growth rates faltered, and the post-bubble weakness of the world economy continued for years after. Despite the weakness of the world economy, the third stock market boom that began around 2009 affected many countries.

Looking back to Figure 1.1, which shows a longer history for the S&P Index, we can see how differently the market behaved up to 2000 compared with the long past. The spiking of prices in the years 1982 through 2000 was most remarkable: the price index looks like a rocket taking off through the top of

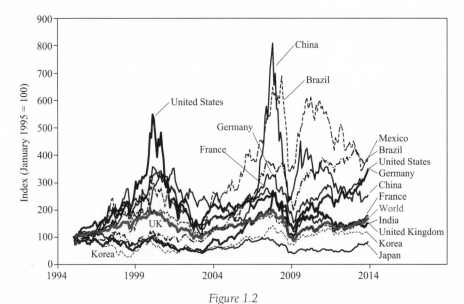

Figure 1.2
Real Stock Prices in Ten Countries and the World,
January 1995–July 2014
Monthly closing prices in Brazil (Bovespa), China (SE Shang Composite), France
(CAC), Germany (DAX), India (Sensex), Japan (Nikkei), Korea (KOSPI), Mexico
(Mexbol), United Kingdom (FTSE 100), the United States (NASDAQ Composite),
and the Morgan-Stanley Capital International All Country World Index, all
deflated by the monthly Consumer Price Index for the currency, all rescaled to
January 1995 = 100. *Source:* Bloomberg and International Monetary Fund *Inter-*
national Financial Statistics (1999).

the chart, only to sputter and crash. This—the largest stock market boom
ever—may be referred to as the *Millennium Boom* or, now that it is over, the
Millennium Bubble.[5]

The boom and crash in the stock market in the years after 1994 are clearly
related to the behavior of earnings. As can be seen in Figure 1.1, S&P Composite
earnings grew very fast in the late 1990s before they crashed after 2000, rose
again until 2007, utterly crashed in 2009, and then rose with the market.
Earnings seem to have been oscillating around a slow, steady growth path
that has persisted for over a century.

Inspection of Figure 1.1 should make it clear that nothing like the
Millennium Boom had ever happened before in the entire stock market history since 1871. There was of course the famous stock run-up of the 1920s,
culminating in the 1929 crash. Figure 1.1 reveals this boom as a cusp-shaped
price pattern for those years. If one corrects for the market's smaller scale then,

one recognizes that this episode in the 1920s does somewhat resemble the recent stock market increase, but it is the only historical episode that comes even close to being comparable.

Price Relative to Earnings

Figure 1.3 shows the cyclically adjusted price-earnings ratio (CAPE), that is, the real (inflation-corrected) S&P Composite Index divided by the ten-year moving average of real earnings on the index. The points shown reflect monthly data from January 1881 to June 2014.[6] The price-earnings ratio is a measure of how expensive the market is relative to an objective measure of the ability of corporations to earn profits. John Campbell and I originally defined CAPE using the ten-year average, along lines proposed by Benjamin Graham and David Dodd in 1934.[7]

The ten-year average smooths out such events as the temporary burst of earnings during World War I, the temporary decline in earnings during World War II, and the frequent boosts and declines that we see due to the business cycle.[8] Note again that there was an enormous spike after 1997, when the ratio rose until it hit 47.2 intraday on March 24, 2000. Price-earnings ratios by this measure had never been so high. The closest parallel was September 1929, when the ratio hit 32.6.

In 2000 earnings were quite high in comparison with the Graham and Dodd measure of long-run earnings, but nothing here was startlingly out of the ordinary. What was extraordinary in 2000 was the behavior of price (as also seen in Figure 1.1), not earnings.

Part of the explanation for the remarkable price behavior between 1990 and 2000 may have to do with the unusual behavior of corporations' profits as reflected in their earnings reports. Many observers remarked then that earnings growth in the five-year period ending in 1997 was extraordinary: real S&P Composite earnings more than doubled over this interval, and such a rapid five-year growth of real earnings had not occurred for nearly half a century. But 1992 marked the end of a recession during which earnings were temporarily depressed.[9] Similar increases in earnings growth following periods of depressed earnings from recession or depression have happened before. In fact, there was more than a quadrupling of real earnings from 1921 to 1926 as the economy emerged from the severe recession of 1921 into the prosperous Roaring Twenties. Real earnings doubled during the five-year periods following the depression of the 1890s, the Great Depression of the 1930s, and World War II.

It was tempting for observers in 2000, at the peak of the market, to extrapolate this earnings growth and to believe that some fundamental changes in the economy had produced a new higher growth trend in earnings.

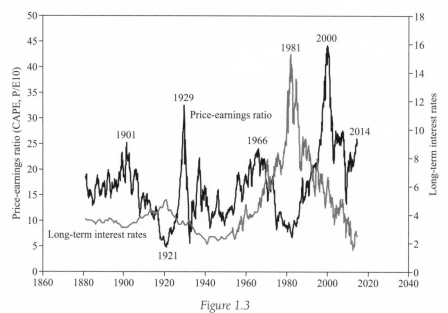

Figure 1.3
U.S. Cyclically Adjusted Price-Earnings Ratio (CAPE) and Interest Rates, 1881–2014

Price-earnings ratio, monthly, January 1881 to June 2014. Numerator: real (inflation-corrected) S&P Composite Stock Price Index. Denominator: moving average over preceding ten years of real S&P Composite earnings. Years of peaks are indicated. *Source:* Author's calculations using data shown in Figure 1.1. Interest rate is the yield of long-term U.S. government bonds (nominal), January 1881 to June 2014 (author's splicing of two historical long-term interest rate series). See also note 7.

Certainly, expansive talk about the new millennium at the time encouraged such a story. But it would have been more reasonable, judging from the cyclical behavior of earnings throughout history, to predict a reversal of such earnings growth.

The bust in corporate profits between 2000 and 2001, the biggest drop in profits in percentage terms since 1920–21, is certainly part of the story about the drop in the market. This drop certainly diminished support for the notion that the new high-tech economy was infallible. But there is a question of how to interpret the drop in earnings. As we shall discuss in Chapter 5, the drop in earnings could be seen in many dimensions, and in part, as just an indirect consequence of the changes in investor psychology that produced the decline in the market. Part of the crash in earnings after 2000 was also just a technical accounting reaction to the stock price decline, since companies were required by accounting rules to deduct from earnings the impairment in value of some of their stock market holdings, holdings that were far reduced in value after the crash in the stock market.

Other Periods of High Price Relative to Earnings

There have been three earlier times when the price-earnings ratio as shown in Figure 1.3 attained high values, though never as high as the 2000 value. The first time was in June 1901, when the price-earnings ratio reached a high of 25.2. This might be called the "Twentieth Century Peak," since it came around the time of the celebration of the new century. (The advent of the twentieth century was celebrated on January 1, 1901, not January 1, 1900.)[10] This peak occurred as the aftermath of a doubling of real earnings within five years, following the U.S. economy's emergence from the depression of the 1890s.[11] The 1901 peak in the price-earnings ratio occurred after a sudden spike in the ratio, which took place between July 1900 and June 1901, an increase of 43% in eleven months. A turn-of-the-century optimism appeared—associated with expansive talk about a prosperous and high-tech future.

After 1901, there was no pronounced immediate downtrend in real prices, but for the next decade, prices bounced around or just below the 1901 level and then fell. By June 1920, the stock market had lost 67% of its June 1901 real value. The average real return in the stock market (including dividends) was 3.4% a year in the five years following June 1901, barely above the real interest rate. The average real return (including dividends) was 4.4% a year in the ten years following June 1901, 3.1% a year in the fifteen years following June 1901, and −0.2% a year in the twenty years following June 1901.[12] These returns are lower than we generally expect from the stock market, though had one held on into the 1920s, returns would have improved dramatically.

The second instance of a high price-earnings ratio occurred in September 1929, the high point of the market in the 1920s and the second-highest ratio of all time. After the spectacular bull market of the 1920s, the ratio attained a value of 32.6. As we all know, the market tumbled from this high, with a real drop in the S&P Index of 80.6% by June 1932. The decline in real value was profound and long-lasting. The real S&P Composite Index did not return to its September 1929 value until December 1958. The average real return in the stock market (including dividends) was −13.1% a year for the five years following September 1929, −1.4% a year for the next ten years, −0.5% a year for the next fifteen years, and 0.4% a year for the next twenty years.[13]

The third instance of a high price-earnings ratio occurred in January 1966, when the ratio as shown in Figure 1.3 reached a local maximum of 24.1. We might call this the "Kennedy-Johnson Peak," drawing as it did on the prestige and charisma of President John Kennedy and the help of his vice-president and successor, Lyndon Johnson. This peak came after a dramatic bull market and after a five-year real price surge of 52% from May 1960. This surge, which took the price-earnings ratio to its local maximum, corresponded to a surge in real earnings of 36%. The market reacted to this earnings growth as if it expected the growth to continue, but of course it did not. Real earnings increased little in the next decade. Real prices bounced around near their January 1966 peak, surpassing it somewhat in 1968, then falling sharply back after 1973. Real stock prices were down 56% from their January 1966 value by December 1974 and would not be back up to the January 1966 level until May 1992. The average real return in the stock market (including dividends) was –2.6% a year for the five years following January 1966, –1.8% a year for the next ten years, –0.5% a year for the next fifteen years, and 1.9% a year for the next twenty years.

We see evidence in these past episodes of temporarily high price that irrational exuberance is not a new thing, and that such episodes do not end well. The high CAPE—higher than any peaks save 1929, 2000, and 2007 as of this writing in 2014—warrants some concern, though we do not yet know the aftermath of this time. We will return to a discussion of the predictive power of the price-earnings ratio in Chapter 11.

Worries about Irrational Exuberance

As reflected in the first edition of this book, in 2000 I thought that most people I met, from all walks of life, were puzzled over the apparently high levels of the stock market. It seemed that they were unsure whether the market levels made any sense, or whether they were indeed the result of some human tendency that might be called *irrational exuberance.* They wondered whether the high levels of the stock market might have reflected unjustified optimism, an optimism that might have pervaded our thinking and affected many of our life decisions. They seemed unsure what to make of any small market downturn, wondering whether the previous market psychology could ever return.

Even Alan Greenspan seemed unsure. He made his "irrational exuberance" speech two days after I had testified before him and the Federal Reserve Board that market levels were irrational, but a mere seven months later he reportedly took an optimistic "new era" position on the economy and the stock market. In fact, Greenspan has always been very cautious in his public statements, and did not commit himself to either view. A modern version of the prophets who spoke in riddles, Greenspan likes to pose questions rather than make pronouncements. In the public exegesis of his remarks it was often forgotten that, when it comes to such questions, even he did not know the answers.

Years after its 2000 peak, the market is back up near its peak levels in real terms. The news media in 2007 and 2014 seemed to relish trumpeting new records set (in nominal terms) by the stock market. And yet, deep down, people know that the market was then and is now highly priced, and they are uncomfortable with this fact.

Lacking answers from our wisest experts, many are inclined to turn to the wisdom of the markets to answer our questions, to use the turns of the stock market as fortune tellers use tea leaves. But before we begin assuming that the market is revealing some truth about this new era, it behooves us to reflect on the *real* determinants of market moves and how these market moves, in their effects, filter through the economy and our lives.

Many of those real determinants are in our minds. They are the "animal spirits" that John Maynard Keynes thought drove the economy, and that were the subject of my 2009 book *Animal Spirits* with George Akerlof.[14] These same animal spirits drive other markets, such as the bond market and the real estate market, to which we now turn as other case studies of speculative behavior, before we begin our analysis of the causes of such behavior in Part One of this book.

Two

The Bond Market in Historical Perspective

The path of interest rates through time has been a matter of intense public concern, for interest rates are viewed as central to everything in the economy. Interest rates are viewed as something abstract and fundamental, the price of time itself. And yet they show fluctuations through time that reveal a speculative and human component, not entirely unlike that of the stock market, discussed in the previous chapter.

There are both short-term interest rates, rates on loans or bills for a year or less, and long-term interest rates, rates on bonds, mortgages, or loans extending over decades. Prices of long-term bonds, once issued in the marketplace, move opposite the general level of long-term interest rates: when long-term interest rates fall, prices of still-outstanding long-term bonds previously issued rise, since, unless their price increases, investors would prefer those older bonds bearing higher interest to the newer ones. Thus, changes in the outlook for future interest rates can cause booms or crashes in the long-term bond market.

For over a century, central banks (in the United States, the Federal Reserve) have exerted control over short-term rates. It is well known that these rates are easily set, at least approximately, by central banks. Long-term interest rates, however, are more speculative and more difficult to control, since, just as with the stock market, the public's demand for them depends on comparisons with the outlook for the distant future, which is dependent on things central banks cannot control today. Since the 2007–9 financial crisis, central banks have adopted important new policies to influence long-term interest rates, with names like "quantitative easing," "operation twist," and "forward guidance," but they still today do not really control this market.[1]

Discussions over the past century have sometimes used the phrase "bond bubble" to describe upswings in the bond market. Certainly, the bond market has something akin to bubbles in it from time to time, occurring when long rates are falling and so people are excited by the rise in bond prices, just as they are by stock prices in a stock market bubble. And bubbles in these two markets might sometimes be related to each other.

Interest Rates and CAPE

Interest rates are one of the most discussed terms relating to the level of the stock market. During the stock market boom of the 1990s, it was widely noted that long-term interest rates were falling. This can be seen from Figure 1.3 in the previous chapter, which includes, along with the CAPE, a plot of interest rates, long-term government bond yields. The idea that the decline in interest rates can explain the rise in the stock market was widely expressed during the 1990s.

The Monetary Policy Report that was submitted in conjunction with Alan Greenspan's testimony before Congress in July 1997[2] showed evidence of a noticeable negative correlation between the ten-year bond yield and the price-earnings ratio since 1982. Indeed, there did appear to be a relation between interest rates and the price-earnings ratio at that time. In fact, between the mid-1960s and the early 1980s, interest rates were rising and the price-earnings ratio was declining. Between the early 1980s and the late 1990s, when Greenspan spoke, interest rates were falling and stock prices were rising. This relation between the stock market and the ten-year interest rate came to be known as the "Fed Model." In the late 1990s and the early 2000s, it became fashionable to use the Fed Model to justify the level of the market. Indeed, with declining interest rates, one might well think that stock prices should be rising relative to earnings, since the prospective long-term return on a competing asset, bonds, was declining, making stocks look more attractive in comparison. In the late 1990s, it sometimes seemed that one heard reference to the Fed Model almost ad nauseam on the television business shows.

However, the evidence for the Fed Model is rather weak.[3] Over the whole period shown in Figure 1.3, no strong relation is seen between interest rates and the price-earnings ratio. In the Great Depression, interest rates were unusually low, which, by the Fed Model, would imply that the stock market should have been very high relative to earnings; that was not the case.

Interest rates continued to decrease after the peak in the market after 2000, and then we saw the opposite of the predictions of the Fed Model: both the price-earnings ratio and the interest rates were declining. Since this happened, one has heard a lot less about the Fed Model.

Although interest rates must have some effect on the market, stock prices do not show any simple or consistent relation with interest rates. Still, investors looking at a very high CAPE when long-term government bond yields are very low, as they have been especially since the financial crisis of 2008, will not be as discouraged from investing in stocks because of the poor alternative.

The CAPE has come under some criticism since the second edition of this book. Bill Gross, founder of PIMCO and now at Janus Capital, complained that discussions of the ratio often do not take into account the very low interest rates since the crisis. Indeed, the ten-year U.S. Treasury yield to maturity in July 2012 fell to a historical low of 1.43% per year, and while higher today, remains very low by historical standards. In such circumstances, perhaps investors will not want to switch from stocks to bonds even if the CAPE is high. Moreover, the U.S. bond market, showing such low yields, looks as if it may have been going through something of a bubble, too, and may collapse further eventually, especially given the imminent withdrawal of the support of quantitative easing from the Federal Reserve and a likely increase in inflation. Gross, with his "new normal" or "new neutral" pessimistic view of the economy, gives lower probability to such a collapse than I would, but he is right that the apparent overpricing of the stock market—whenever it occurs— has to be compared with the possible overpricing of other markets as well.[4]

Inflation and Interest Rates

Figure 2.1 shows a plot of U.S. government long-term interest rates (the ten-year Treasury rate since 1953) and inflation rates since 1881. Two inflation rates are shown. One is the annual rate of increase of a price index (Consumer Price Index since 1913) for the preceding ten years. The other is the annual rate of increase of the same price index for the succeeding ten years. The two inflation rate curves are the same, but one is shifted relative to the other by ten years. Both are plotted here to make a point. It is easy to see a positive contemporaneous relation between interest rates and *preceding* long-term inflation rates for much of the time—especially the most recent half century—but there appears to be practically no relation between long-term interest rates and *future* long-term inflation. It is the *future* inflation that ought to matter more if investors successfully priced long-term bonds to protect their real returns from inflation over the future life of the bond they are investing in, just the opposite of what we see. Jeremy Siegel and I documented this in 1977, and linked this observation to descriptions of earlier observers A. H. Gibson in 1923 and John Maynard Keynes in 1930.[5]

The relation between long-term interest rates and long-term inflation that can be seen in Figure 2.1 for the last half century is not the kind that a simple assumption of human rationality would lead one to expect. If investors are

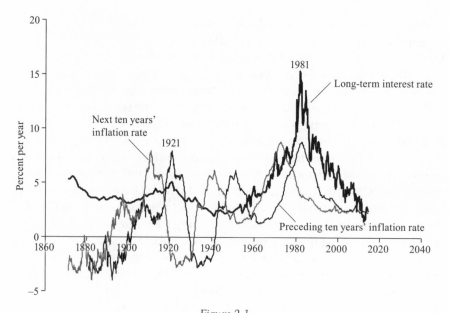

Figure 2.1
U.S. Long-Term Rates and Inflation, 1871–2014
U.S. government long-term interest rate (thick dark solid line), average inflation rate over preceding ten years (thin solid line), and average inflation rate over the succeeding ten years (thin gray line). *Source:* Author's calculations from same data used in Figure 1.3.

rational (have rational expectations), they should be employing past data on inflation in such a way as to adjust nominal bond yields to successful predictions of the future. We see that they did seem to respond to past data, but in a way that was very unsuccessful in predicting the future.

The fluctuations in yields that we do see in the long-term bond market cannot be well described as resulting from information about future inflation, nor are they well described as resulting from information about future short-term interest rates. They have a speculative component that is hard to pin down in terms of objectively rational behavior.[6]

Real Interest Rates

Over most of the period shown in Figure 2.1, many investors perhaps had no idea about what the relation between nominal interest rates and inflation rates should be. It was not until 1895 that Columbia University economics professor John Bates Clark introduced to the world the concept of *real* interest rates.[7] He wrote about this then-new concept, because he discerned widespread public

confusion about interest rates at the time of the national debate on the proposed bimetallic standard. The real interest rate on any debt instrument, he
said, is the interest rate minus the inflation rate over the life until maturity of
the instrument. If the inflation rate is greater than the interest rate, the bond
would be producing less than nothing in real terms for the investor, since the
buying power of money would be reduced by more than the increase in the
money the instrument provides to its investor. A search on Google Ngrams
shows that the phrase "real interest rate" was never used before 1895, began
to appear incrementally from that time, and did not really become common
until after 1960—after a very long gestation period for Clark's idea.

One might think, if investors have good information, are rational, and are
interested in the real interest that they will receive, that market-determined
bond yields would stay just a steady amount above the subsequent inflation
rate. One can see from Figure 2.1 that this has never been true for the United
States, although, since around 1960, it became somewhat true for *backward-
looking* rather than *forward-looking* inflation.

The significance of movements in long-term interest rates over time, as
seen for the United States since 1871 in Figure 2.1, is not clear. Clearly, people
were not pricing bonds as if they were just reacting to rational expectations
about future inflation rates. Theorists often say that ratios like the price-
earnings ratio in the stock market ought to be more closely related to expected
real (inflation-corrected) long-term interest rates, which have been largely
unknown, than to nominal rates. But that is based on the assumption that
investors routinely see through nominal rates to real rates.

Inflation-indexed bond markets, which directly reveal real interest rates,
did not exist in any major country in the early 1980s, but since then they have
begun to appear. These bonds promise to pay a constant real return. Figure
2.2 shows the behavior over time of inflation-indexed long-term government
bond yields for four countries that have had these markets for a long time.

All these countries show a long-term downtrend in real interest rates—
down to amazingly low levels by 2012. As can be seen in Figure 2.2, in some
of the most recent data, in both the United States and the United Kingdom the
real bond yields have reached negative values. It is quite striking that in 2012
in the United States, people were willing to tie up their money for thirty years
at an essentially guaranteed negative real return.[8] This fact would certainly
seem to have implications for the stock market, impelling it toward higher
valuation. Financial theorists, such as John Campbell and Luis Viceira, have
spoken of the long-term indexed bond yield as the true riskless rate, against
which all risky asset returns should be compared, and which should figure
into every long-term investor's most fundamental calculations.[9]

But most investors just do not seem to see the centrality of the indexed bond
yield that theorists often seem to attribute to it. They often do not even seem

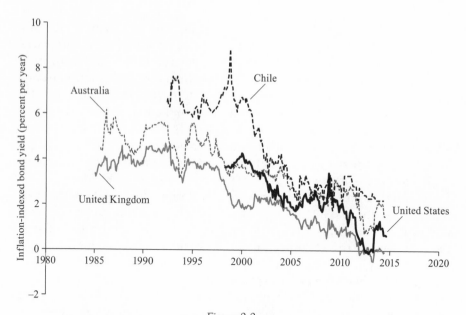

Figure 2.2
Inflation-Indexed Bond Yields for Four Countries, 1985–2014
United Kingdom: twenty-year inflation-indexed bond yield January 1985–
June 2014; Australia: ten-year inflation-indexed bond yield July 1985–July 2014;
Chile: ten-year inflation-indexed bond yield, April 1992–May 2014; United States:
thirty-year inflation-indexed bond yield, April 1998–August 2014. *Source:* Global
Financial Data (https://www.globalfinancialdata.com/index.html).

to understand that inflation indexation protects them from price-level risks,
and sometimes seem to think that indexation *introduces* a risk, the risk that
their nominal values will be lower. The path downward does not reflect the
ups and downs of the stock market any more than does the downward path
of nominal interest rates over this interval.

Unfortunately, even with these data, especially in the earlier years of
inflation-indexed bonds, it has not been completely clear what the broad
investing public likely thought over these years about expected real returns
on safe assets. When each of these countries in Figure 2.2 introduced their
inflation-indexed bond markets, they did so in the face of widespread public
indifference. The market for inflation-indexed bonds has grown somewhat
over the decades but is only gradually becoming important enough compared
to the market for nonindexed conventional bonds to pervade public thinking
as some theorists assume.[10] And so a few government officials in charge of
the auctions could in principle, by adjusting the amount offered, influence
the prices of inflation-indexed bonds.[11] It is one of the puzzles of behavioral

economics that people mostly just ignore inflation-indexed markets—that they have so much trouble appreciating the importance of inflation indexation.[12]

Still, it is clear that prices in both the market for nominal bonds and the market for inflation-indexed bonds have reached very high levels, and that this fact ought to be part of our thinking about the stock market. It remains unclear what this situation implies for the future. Some observers refer to a "bond market bubble" at the time of this writing in 2014 that might burst, though it seems that this is not a classic bubble as defined in this book, since expectations for long-term return are apparently very low—not high, as one would expect during a bubble. But these trends in the bond market might in some sense be bubble-like.

Jeremy Stein of Harvard University, in one of the last speeches he gave as Governor of the Federal Reserve System, in 2014, discussed concerns about a bond market bubble, though he did not adopt that term. He spoke of "overheating" in the credit markets and warned of economic consequences if the bond yields were to suddenly correct upward (bond prices correct downward); he worried about the economic consequences of such a correction.[13]

There must be some hard-to-pin-down cultural factors driving people to invest in bonds at a time when their yield is very low or negative and the stock market has been soaring. Some of the same precipitating factors for the stock market and housing market booms discussed in Chapter 4 might apply somewhat to the bond market. Also, falling bond yields have produced capital gains for bond investors over the decades, making bonds look successful even if they are guaranteed not to do well in real terms over their time to maturity.[14] The extreme low or negative yields after the financial crisis of 2007–9 might also have something to do with a kind of a flight response, at times of financial turmoil, that does not fit our usual theoretical paradigms. Where that response goes in future years remains to be seen. There is indeed reason to be concerned about the possible widespread economic effects of an end to this decades-long downtrend in real long-term interest rates, and of a corresponding drop in long-term bond prices.

We turn now to the third of our three major asset classes, the real estate market, and will see once again the importance of human speculative behavior in determining market prices.

Three

The Real Estate Market
in Historical Perspective

The same forces of human psychology that have driven the stock market and the bond market over the years have the potential to affect other markets. The market for real estate, particularly individual homes, would seem likely to display speculative booms from time to time, since the psychological salience of the price of the places we see every day and the homes we live in must be strong, and because home prices are such a popular topic of conversation. Yet the market for real estate is different from the stock and bond markets in important ways.

Home prices increased sharply in the first five years of the twenty-first century in cities in Australia, Canada, China, France, Hong Kong, Ireland, Italy, New Zealand, Norway, Russia, South Africa, Spain, the United Kingdom, and the United States.[1] There has been a breathtaking real estate construction boom in China.[2] These real estate booms have not taken place everywhere, but they have occurred in a variety of places. Many of these booms were followed by crashes. These crashes gave impetus to the financial crisis whose intensity peaked in 2009, and from which the world is still damaged as of this writing in 2014.

Real estate booms seem just as mysterious and hard to understand as stock market booms. When they happen, there are always popular explanations for them—explanations that are not necessarily correct.

A number of glib explanations have been offered for the run-up in prices in many places since the late 1990s. One such explanation is that population pressures have built up to the point that we have run out of land, and that home prices have shot up as a result. But we didn't just run out of land since the late 1990s: population growth has been steady and gradual. Another theory is that the things that go into houses—the labor, the lumber, the concrete, the steel—are in such heavy demand that they have become very expensive. But construction costs are not out of line with long-term trends. Another glib explanation is that the boom was due to the interest rate cuts implemented in many countries in an effort to deal with a weak global economy. But while low interest rates are certainly a contributing factor, central banks have cut interest rates *many* times in history, and such actions never produced such concerted booms.

So what did cause this real estate boom and crash to occur in so many parts of the world? It is important to understand this phenomenon. Many people are worrying that the boom in home prices in these places will end as badly as the dramatic 1980s boom in urban land prices in Japan, with prices declining in real terms for well over a decade after the peak. But understanding any such price movements, and what they might portend, is a difficult problem—a problem to which solutions will be offered in various parts of this book.

For starters I want to try to put these recent events into a longer historical perspective. Is the current situation new, or do we have scads of examples of such events? Is there really a strong and steady long-run uptrend in home prices as so many people with a boom mentality say, or are they just imagining this? What does history tell us about the genesis of real estate booms? An important conclusion of this chapter is that home price speculation is more entrenched on a national or international scale than ever before.

The Long History of Home Prices

I constructed an index of U.S. home prices all the way back to 1890 by linking together various available series that were designed to provide estimates of the price of a standard, unchanging, house, and by creating another index that my research assistants completed under my direction, to close the gap from 1934 to 1953. Figure 3.1 shows the home price index along with building costs, the population of the United States, and the long-term interest rate, all since 1890.[3]

The home price index we constructed, plotted in the figure, is imperfect, and I hope to improve it someday, but for now it appears to be the best that can be found for this long time period. Oddly, when this chart was first published in 2005, no such long series of home prices for any country had ever been released. At the time, no real estate professional I spoke with could refer me to one. So the unusually rapid appreciation of home prices up to the time of publication of the second edition of this book in 2005 attracted notice.

The reader must notice the striking recent behavior of home prices since the late 1990s. Home prices took off sharply between the late 1990s and 2006. There

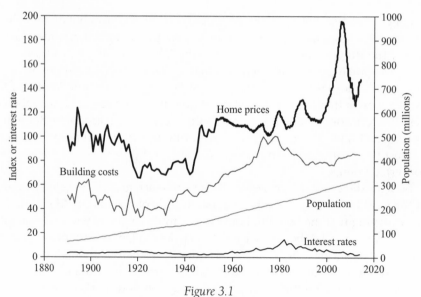

Figure 3.1

U.S. Home Prices, Building Costs, Population,
and Interest Rates, 1890–2014

Heavy solid line (left scale): real (inflation-corrected) home price index, 1890 = 100, for the United States, constructed by the author from various existing indices and raw data on home prices; top thin line (left scale): real (inflation-corrected) building cost index, 1979 = 100, constructed by the author from two published construction cost indices; middle thin line (right scale): U.S. population in millions, from the U.S. Census; lowest thin line (left scale): long-term interest rate constructed by the author from two sources. See note 3.

was a "rocket taking off" here, just as in the stock market in the Millennium Boom. As with the stock market, this rocket eventually crashed after 2006, and the disaster brought down the government-sponsored enterprises Fannie Mae and Freddie Mac; mortgage lending giants Countrywide Financial and Washington Mutual; and financial firms Bear Stearns, Merrill Lynch, and Lehman Brothers. And by 2008 it had caused the most severe financial crisis since the Great Depression of the 1930s.

The upswing in home prices during 1998–2006 (along with the stock market Ownership-Society Boom) that preceded the financial crisis may be regarded as its ultimate cause. Real home prices for the United States as a whole increased 85% between 1997 and 2006. The increase was higher in some areas of the United States and lower in others, but the fact that it was an 85% increase overall is remarkable. This is nothing like the tripling of the stock market between 1995 and 2000, but, when viewed in comparison with long-run historical patterns in home prices, it is still striking. We could not appreciate this pattern of home prices by looking at recent years alone; one could not appreciate how anomalous the early 2000s home boom was. There was only one other period of similarly large price increases in U.S. history: the period after World War II. The subsequent decline in the most recent boom, however, was substantially more precipitous.

The ascent in home prices after 1998 was much faster than the increase in incomes, and this raised concerns about the long-run stability of home prices, especially in the most volatile states. According to Standard & Poor's and the S&P/Case-Shiller Home Price Indices, the cost of buying a house relative to renting doubled in the United States from 1997 to 2006 and then fell almost all the way back down from 2006 to 2013.[4]

Looking at the figure before the 2006 peak, however, one got the impression that the end was not near and that the ascent of home prices since 1997 had been so robust and steady that one would expect it to continue for years. The steadiness of the path, up for each year between 1997 and 2006, and up at an increasing rate for almost each successive year, suggested that home prices could be forecasted to continue to rise.

How can prices be so forecastable? Isn't it supposed to be very hard to forecast speculative prices, and aren't such prices supposed to at least approximate a random walk? Actually, home prices *are* somewhat forecastable, as statistical analysis confirms.[5] Their forecastability is not well exploited by "smart money" as it would be in the stock market. The forays into the single-family house market made by The Blackstone Group and other investment funds are still, as of this writing, only a tiny part of the market. So no forces operate to prevent forecastability. The profit opportunities for buying at the right time are just not available to the smart money that operates in the stock market because of the costs of getting in and out of the housing market. It is not easy for most people to time the purchase of their homes to take advantage of trends.

But let us not exaggerate the forecastability of home prices either. Our statistical studies of forecasting models for home prices show that roughly half of the variability of home prices can be predicted one year ahead. Half of the variability may seem like a lot, but it still leaves much to be explained. Looking back at the figure, one would have to say, if one took a pencil to extrapolate judgmentally the recent trend in U.S. home prices, that there is still substantial uncertainty about where the price level will be in a year's time. It is difficult to judge whether the trend is building up or slowing down, and when it might eventually stop completely and then reverse itself. Moreover, if one extends a forecast to five or ten years out, one is likely to have virtually no idea where prices will be. And it is these longer-horizon forecasts that are most relevant to homebuyers who will expect to live in their home for many years.

Ultimately, we learn how to forecast by looking at past episodes. Unfortunately, there are not really any past episodes of national home price booms in the United States to look at, except for the period just after World War II, and that episode appears to have been fundamentally different from the recent home price boom. We have only one observation of the spectacular crash of U.S. home prices after 2006, so it is hard to know how to generalize from this experience. This presents a dilemma for statisticians who want a scientific basis for their forecasts.

Obviously, there is no hope of explaining home prices in the United States solely in terms of building costs, population, or interest rates, all shown in Figure 3.1. The pattern of change from year to year in home prices bears no consistent relation with any of these factors. None of these can explain the "rocket-taking-off" effect starting around 1998. Building costs have been mostly level or declining all the way back to 1980, with no major break in the trend.[6] Population growth has been very steady. While interest rates have been declining, the decline in long rates has been fairly steady, all the way back to the early 1980s.[7]

It is equally obvious, from comparing the home price path shown in Figure 3.1 with the stock price path shown in Figure 1.1, that in the United States, the booms in the stock market bear virtually no relation to booms in the housing market. A possible exception is the most recent boom in the housing market, which began around 1998, a few years after the sharp stock market takeoff that began around 1995. There may well be at least *some* tendency for home prices to respond to the stock market: a recent Bank of International Settlements study of house prices in thirteen industrialized countries concluded that peaks in the housing market tend to follow peaks in the stock market with an average lag of about two years.[8]

To understand how different the recent home price behavior has been, it is important to compare the recent behavior with that of long ago. Figure 3.1 shows that real home prices were generally declining from 1890 to 1940. The chart shows a number of wiggles in home prices before World War I, but our efforts to find confirming evidence of such sharp price movements in old newspapers for those dates turned up nothing significant. We suspect that some of the wiggles in the earliest years plotted in Figure 3.1 are just the result of sampling error and so do not reflect actual home price changes. I will return in Chapter 7 to the stories of some price movements from that era that we can begin to understand. But for now, we should note the downtrend in real prices and the absence of any major real estate boom before 1940.

The late nineteenth century and early twentieth century saw many *local* bubbles surrounding the building of highways, canals, and railroads, bubbles that do not show up in the national numbers on our chart. Obviously, it is plausible that the land surrounding such construction projects would suddenly become valuable. Even in days gone by, when land was so abundant that one could buy it, in some places, for a dollar an acre, there could be real estate booms. If land prices were to go up to two dollars an acre near a new rail line, an investment could double in value, and this prospect could be quite exciting to investors. *Regional* real estate booms are nothing new.

The sharp fall in home prices after World War I probably had something to do with the great influenza pandemic of 1918–19, which infected 28% of Americans and killed 675,000 of them. This epidemic caused people to stay at home and not look for new homes. It must have damaged the economy and also distracted attention and conversation away from the housing market. There was also an unusually severe recession in 1920–21.[9]

It is notable that there was no boom in home prices to accompany the sharply rising stock market of the Roaring Twenties. The famous Florida land bubble of the 1920s was not big enough to show up in these national numbers. Home prices were not carried along by the stock market and did not overshoot, nor did they drop when the stock market crashed starting in 1929. There was, however, a drop in nominal home prices after 1929; that is, home prices fell at just about the same rate as the Consumer Price Index fell. The drop in nominal home prices, when mortgage debt was not indexed to inflation, gave many homeowners negative equity in their homes and an incentive to default on their mortgages. In addition, the high unemployment rates during the Great Depression meant that many could not renew their short-term mortgages and so were forced to default on them and thus lost their homes. But we should not mistake the housing crisis of the early 1930s for a decline in real home prices. Real home prices showed remarkable stability over the whole boom-and-bust cycle of the stock market surrounding 1929.

This brings us to the most significant episode in the national home market until recent times: the sharp home price increases associated with the end of World War II. It is clear that there were large real home price increases at least in the big cities at this time, although the exact magnitude of the increases may not have been well measured.[10]

This does not appear to have been a runaway speculative boom. Home prices did not overshoot their new postwar equilibrium, and they did not have to come crashing back down. Newspaper accounts of the housing market did not use the term *housing bubble,* nor did they feature stories of crazy homebuyers buying just about anything to stay ahead of the curve, like those we were reading about in the early 2000s. The story that one gleans from the newspapers just after World War II is quite different.

Government restrictions had severely limited the supply of new homes during World War II. After the war, returning soldiers wanted to start families; they were about to launch the Baby Boom. Prices of existing homes actually started increasing after 1942, before the war was over, probably because people anticipated the shortage of housing that was to follow. But, even though demand soared after the war, there was no real buying panic, as the conventional wisdom of the time was that construction would soon greatly increase the stock of available homes.

The Servicemen's Readjustment Act of 1944, also called the GI Bill of Rights, immediately introduced the subsidization of home purchase for seventeen million people. This major government subsidy did not go away, and it helped lead to permanently higher home prices. But it did so in the context of the solidarity of the American people, and it never ignited a speculative atmosphere. President Franklin Roosevelt said that the GI Bill of Rights gave "emphatic notice to the men and women of our Armed Forces that the American people do not intend to let them down."[11] The people who bought at the high prices right after the war were those who felt that they could not wait to get settled in their new homes, not people who were speculating that prices would go up even higher. Other people simply found a temporary place to live and waited for the expected decline in home prices (which never came) or for their savings to increase to the point that they could afford housing. The fact that, after World War I, real home prices had gone through a protracted period of decline must also have served to diffuse any speculative worries. People must have remembered that episode in the aftermath of World War II. A widespread worry then that the Great Depression of the 1930s would reappear after the stimulus of the war ended further deflected any worries that home prices would soar.

It appears that people were for the most part not afraid of being priced out of the market, and that they did not fully anticipate the home price increases to come. They counted on new construction to prevent any severe price rise— and indeed, construction of new homes rose from 142,000 homes built in the United States in 1944 to 1,952,000 homes built in 1950. Even though this massive increase in supply did not stop price increases, the popular understanding seems to have been that it would.

It has been different in this century. We are increasingly feeling worried and vulnerable, and the market volatility that flares up from time to time, in both the stock market and the housing market, reflects this. Before the post-1997 boom, there were a couple of false starts (failed launches, so to speak), one in the late 1970s and one in the late 1980s. These were actually regional booms that did not extend so much to the nation as a whole. The 1970s boom was mostly confined to California, and the 1980s boom occurred on both the west coast and the east coast.

Figure 3.2 shows the path of real home prices for four U.S. cities. Prices in Boston and Los Angeles have gone through two dramatic swings, and at the end of the sample period shown, prices were soaring. But, in sharp contrast,

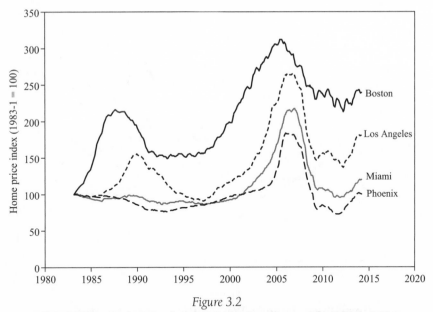

Figure 3.2
Home Prices in a Sample of U.S. Cities, Quarterly, 1983–2014
Source: Fiserv/S&P/Case-Shiller Home Price Indices Inc., deflated by the U.S. Consumer Price Index, U.S. Bureau of Labor Statistics, and rescaled to 1983 = 100.

prices in Miami and Phoenix completely missed the first of these two booms. Boston held much of its value increase—in 2014, remaining over twice its 1983 real value—but Miami and Phoenix hardly changed at all in real value between 1983 and 2014.

It is commonly said that there is no national home market in the United States, only regional markets. There is something to that statement, but it is not completely true and appears to be getting less true. While many markets in the United States had been highly stable and trendy, there were enough markets that were moving rapidly by the mid-2000s that the national series began to show signs of life, and it continues to be lively.

The period of home price increase starting in 1998 in the United States was concentrated in some states and metropolitan areas, and where it was concentrated, there were many stories about the psychological correlates of the boom. Stories abounded in the U.S. during the bubble years 2000–2006 of aggressive, even desperate, bidding on homes, of homes selling the first day on the market for well above the asking price, of people buying homes in a rush to beat the market—homes that they had sometimes hardly even had a chance to look at. People were afraid that the price of housing would soon rise beyond their means and that they might never be able to afford a house,

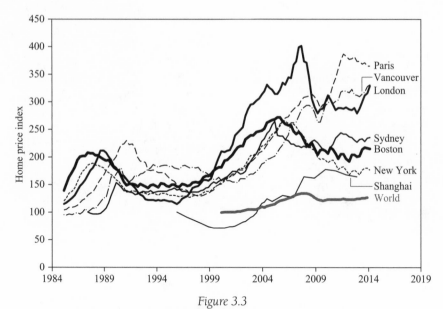

Figure 3.3

**Home Prices in Some World Cities and for the World,
Quarterly, 1985–2014**

Source: Boston (1983-1 = 100, heavy line) and New York (1983-1 = 100, dashed line):
S&P/Case-Shiller (Fiserv, CoreLogic); London (1983-1 = 100, heavy line): Halifax;
Paris (1983-1 = 100, dashed line) price per square meter of existing apartments in
Paris: Indice Notaire INSEE since 1991, before 1991 Chambre des Notaires de Paris,
data courtesy Philippe Trainar, Fédération Française des Sociétés d'Assurances;
Shanghai (1995-1 = 100, solid thin line): China Real Estate Index System through
2003 linked to eHomeday second-hand home price index starting 2003; Sydney
(1986-2 = 100, solid line): Australian Bureau of Statistics; Vancouver (1983-1 = 100,
dot-dash line): index through 2004 courtesy of Tsur Somerville, University of
British Columbia, linked to Teranet series starting 2004; Equally-Weighted Global
House Price Index (2000-2 = 100, gray line) from the International Monetary Fund
(52 countries). Each home price index is deflated by a Consumer Price Index of the
respective country. Each index was multiplied by a constant to be 100 in 1983-1
where possible.

and so they rushed to bid on homes. But, in other cities, where there was not
a history of home price volatility, there were few such stories, and investors
were relatively less reactive to home price changes.

It is in the big glamorous cities (and associated regions) of the world that
these bubbles tend to happen. Taken together, these regions can experience
a massive boom. It appears that for these cities, there is indeed more than a
national market for real estate. There is an international market, as Figure
3.3 illustrates.

This figure shows real home prices up to 2014 in Boston, London, New York, Paris, Shanghai, Sydney, and Vancouver, all of them glamorous international cities, and for the entire world. The similarity among the price paths for these cities is striking (really stunning price increases both in the late 1980s and after the late 1990s, with stagnant or falling prices in between), as is the similarity of popular stories of exaggerated excitement about and speculation in homes. And these were not the only prominent cities undergoing spectacular housing booms in the early 2000s. Others include Bombay, Copenhagen, Dublin, Hangzhou, Istanbul, Las Vegas, Madrid, Melbourne, Rome, San Diego, Tianjin, and Washington, D.C. Whatever it was that drove this excitement, it could cross vast oceans. This notable trend was part of what prompted my warning in 2005 that we were in the midst of a housing bubble of unprecedented proportions.

Since 2005, the picture has become more mixed. Some cities continued their upward trend, with only small retrenchments. Others fell from their lofty heights and have yet to return. Many have seen a leveling-off in price increases.

The cities shown in the figure were selected for this plot based on their newsworthiness and volatility in price movements. The Global House Price Index, produced by the International Monetary Fund for 52 countries around the world, shows much less volatility, and indeed, some other world cities showed a very different pattern. For example, real residential urban land prices in Tokyo more than doubled between 1985 and 1990, at the same time as the 1980s boom in the cities shown in the figure, but then embarked on a steady downtrend, showing no signs of the boom after 2000, and falling by nearly half by 2004.[12] Prime residential property in central Delhi doubled in real terms in the period from 1991 to 1995, when prices in the cities shown in Figure 3.2 were falling, and then fell by half by 2003, when prices in the cities shown in Figure 3.2 were rising.[13] Still, it is a puzzle that home prices in so many cities, such as those shown in Figure 3.3, among the most glamorous cities of the world, are so strikingly similar. We will try to understand this similarity later in this book.

The Absence of a Substantial Long-Run Uptrend in Real Home Prices

The reader may find it striking, in looking over the series of home prices since 1890 in Figure 3.1, that there appears to be no overall continuing uptrend in real home prices. It is true that for the United States as a whole, real home prices were almost twice as high in 2006 as in 1890, but all of that increase occurred in two brief periods: the time right after World War II (with the first increases occurring in the early 1940s, just before the war ended) and a period that appears to reflect a lagged response to the 1990s stock market boom (or a response to its boom and crash), with the first signs of increase occurring in

1998. Other than those two periods, real home prices overall have been mostly flat or declining. Moreover, the overall increase (with real prices up 48% in the 124 years from 1890 to 2014, or 0.3% a year) was not impressive.

Why then do so many people have the impression that home prices have done so well? I think that, since homes are relatively infrequent purchases, people still remember the prior purchase price of a home from long ago and are surprised at the difference between then (when prices, including consumer prices in general, were lower) and now. The same thing does not happen with stocks, since companies periodically authorize splits to keep the price of the stock, in the United States, around the conventional $30-a-share level. Thus, people do not have long-run comparisons thrust upon them for stocks as they do for houses.

For example, in closing out the estate of an elderly couple in the early 2000s, one may have been surprised to see that they purchased a house in 1948 for only $16,000 and that the estate sold that same house in 2004 for $190,000. The appearance is that the investment in the house did extremely well. But, in fact, the Consumer Price Index rose eightfold between 1948 and 2004, and so in fact the real increase in value was only 48%, an increase of less than 1% a year. Moreover, part of the increase should be attributed to a sequence of investments in the house or the neighborhood that improved its quality. Even if the house sold in 2004 for twice as much as the median then, $360,000, it still does not imply great returns on the investment, for that price would imply only a tripling of real value in over fifty years, a real annual rate of increase of a little less than 2% a year. About the only time that our attention is called to such long-term changes in asset value is when we hear stories about houses, and we may be over-impressed; most of us are not good at evaluating such stories.

To try to check further whether these data, showing so little real appreciation of homes, might be in error, I asked economists I know to direct me to other very long-term home price indices that might provide some independent evidence about the long-term behavior of such prices. I was able to locate a few other long-term home price indices, and, even though they are not for the full time period or for an entire country, they may provide some more clues about long-term trends.

The U.S. Census has asked, in its decennial censuses since 1940, for home-owners' estimates of the value of their homes. Their median reported value in real (inflation-corrected) terms increased by 2.0% a year from 1940 to 2000, considerably more than the 0.7% real increase over the same interval revealed by the home price index shown in Figure 3.1. A growth rate of 2.0% cumulated over 60 years implies twice the total appreciation in home value that the 0.7% growth rate implies. However, the Census data take no account of the increased quality and size of homes as does the index shown in Figure 3.1. There have been big changes in homes since 1940. Note, for example, that in 1940, according to the U.S. census, 31% of U.S. dwelling units did not have running water, and 38% did not have a bathtub or shower. The standard of living has improved massively since then, and surely homes are a lot better now. With the U.S. population doubling and real per capita income quadrupling since 1940, a great many more substantial homes have been built. The smaller and lower quality homes of 1940 have largely been torn down over the years, and so we are likely to have a mistaken impression from the older homes we observe today that homes of long ago were comparable to homes of today. Much of the Census' reported 2.0% per year increase in value must really reflect this, not the appreciation of individual unchanged homes.

There is a remarkable high-quality index from 1628 to 1973 of prices of houses along the Herengracht, one of the old canals of Amsterdam. According to Professor Piet Eichholtz of the University of Amsterdam, this area is a good place to construct a home price index, since the houses there have remained remarkably unchanged over the centuries and since home price sale data have been meticulously recorded and preserved. The index shows quite a number of ups and downs in home prices over this period—as one might expect from the city that gave us the tulip mania, the remarkable boom in the price of tulips in the early 1600s. According to Eichholtz's data, Herengracht home prices doubled between 1628–29 and 1632–33, just before the peak of the tulip mania, and home prices fell almost back to their 1628–29 level before tulips peaked in 1637. The market for these homes was certainly volatile. But when this index is corrected for inflation over this whole period, we see that there was not much overall home price increase. From 1628 to 1973 the Herengracht annual real price increase was only 0.2%. Real home prices did roughly double, but took nearly 350 years to do so.[14]

My colleague Karl Case produced a long historical index of land values in the Boston area by searching the Norfolk County Registry of Deeds for sales of property described in words such as "a certain parcel of pure land" or "a certain tract of land" and with no mention of buildings or improvements. This way he was able to purge the price index of the effects of quality change. He found that, from 1900 to 1997, the real increase in the price per square foot of land was 3.9% per year. This is a much higher rate of price increase than is suggested by the price index shown in the plot, exceeding the growth rate of real GDP.[15]

There is a famous study of land prices in Chicago by economist Homer Hoyt, *One Hundred Years of Land Values in Chicago*, published in 1933. Hoyt too found dramatic increases in land prices. For example, his data show that prices of lots per front foot on State Street and Michigan Avenue (major downtown addresses) rose 5.9% a year in real (inflation-corrected) terms from 1877 to 1931, for a twenty-two-fold increase overall.[16]

But, of course, these figures for Boston and Chicago are hardly reliable estimates of the increase in prices of real estate in the United States overall. Boston and Chicago are not typical of U.S. real estate, any more than Microsoft was typical of start-up companies. The success of these cities was a local surprise that people could not have predicted with confidence. Hoyt himself was quite clear about the surprising growth of Chicago, for he noted, "The growth of Chicago in the nineteenth century has been paralleled by no other city of a million population or over in either ancient or modern times. . . . It compressed within a single century the population growth of Paris for twenty centuries."[17]

Moreover, land prices are not a good proxy for home prices, which involve a structure as well as land. Land values long ago accounted for only a tiny fraction of a home's value, and so land prices could appreciate at a relatively high rate in successful cities without making home prices climb rapidly.

Reflections from casual observation ought to convince us that homes have not appreciated significantly over the decades. People are living in larger homes than they were decades ago and are spread out over more properties; more people are living in a house by themselves over the decades, if not during the slow years just after the 2007–9 financial crisis; more children have been moving out and starting their own homes rather than living with their parents until marriage.[18] How could they afford this if home prices were rising steeply? This suggests that in the United States, real home price growth must have been less than real per capita disposable income growth, which was 2.0% a year from 1929 to 2013.

The bottom line appears to be that, while there is some uncertainty about the actual path of home prices, most of the evidence points to disappointingly low average rates of real appreciation of most homes.

Why Has There Not Been a Strong Uptrend in Real Home Prices?

The reader may be puzzled that these data show so little evidence of an increase in real home prices in the United States over so long a period. The popular notion that real estate prices always go up is very strong, so strong that in Japan, Korea, and China there is a name for this notion: "the real estate myth." Isn't land scarce, and isn't its price going to go up steadily as population increases and as the level of prosperity increases?

Actually, the theoretical argument that home prices can be expected to appreciate faster than consumer prices in general is not strong. Technological progress in the increasingly mechanized construction industry may proceed faster than technological progress in other sectors, such as the important service sector. Barbers and teachers and lawyers and counselors are doing things more or less as they always have, but new materials, new construction equipment, and prefabrication, as well as new technology for building high-rise apartment buildings, help make housing cheaper. If new homes can be built more cheaply, then the price of homes should tend to fall relative to other prices to reflect that.

Public attention seems to focus most on congested big cities that have little land available for building, and where land prices can get very high. But most cities have abundant land. Developers who eye these abundant-land cities for prospective sites do sometimes complain about the shortage of land there, and about barriers erected by conservationists and neighborhood associations, but what they are really talking about is a shortage of lots in the prime areas where they would most like to build.

These abundant-land cities show long-run price paths that never deviate too far from building costs. This should come as no surprise. If ever home prices were to far exceed the cost of construction, there would be an incentive for builders to supply more houses, and a steady increase in supply would continue until the extra supply depressed price back down to cost.

The situation in these stable cities ought to be considered typical of much of the United States. The land on which homes are built is of course limited: except for a few projects to reclaim land from the sea, they are not making any more land. But almost all of the country's land is still in agriculture, forestry, or other non-intensive uses; this is land whose price is very low per buildable lot, and so there is still plenty of room to spread out. According to the 2010 census, urban land area was only 3.1% of total land area in the United States.

However, there is little empty land available to build on in Los Angeles or Boston or, for that matter, in London or Sydney. And yet the same safety valve ought to operate there to prevent home prices from rising too far, at least if people were rational and far-seeing. When home prices rise to the point that mortgage payments take up a large share of family income, there is a powerful incentive to move to a lower-cost area. This safety valve tends, in the long term, to prevent the price of homes from rising too much in real (inflation-corrected) terms and to burst bubbles that have inflated too far. The safety valve is more effective in cities where buildable land is abundant nearby, but it is also effective in cities far from buildable land, because people and businesses will, if home prices rise high enough, move far away, even leaving an area completely.

The problem is that people in glamorous regions often tend to believe that land prices, already a significant component of home value there, will keep going up and up. Surely, they think, there is some advantage to living in those areas. People do enjoy the prestige of living in an area where celebrities live, and they also benefit from the business opportunities there. It is easy for residents there to imagine that more and more people are thinking similarly, and that they will continue to bid up real estate prices in their city. This is irrational exuberance in the context of real estate.

But, in reality, if home prices get sufficiently high in a city relative to the income of the people who live there, and thus make it difficult to afford a decent home, people start taking a hard look at these assumptions. The fact is that the prestige one derives from simply living in a glamorous city is not very significant. And although individual cities may have reputations tied up with specific businesses, with a little imagination one sees that other centers in the same businesses are constantly being set up, like the North Carolina Research Triangle set up in former tobacco fields. These centers eventually cause corporate relocators to draw population away from older centers to these new centers, thereby relieving upward pressure on real estate prices in the older centers.

Beyond this, very high home prices create political pressures for the easing of land-use restrictions. Eventually there is an increase in supply of homes (as for example in high-rise apartments) in the glamorous cities themselves.

Thus, in glamorous speculative cities, there has been a tendency for home prices to rise and to crash, but to show little long-term trend. Prices rise while people are optimistic, but forces are set in motion for them to crash when they get too high. It is striking to note from Figure 3.2 that the increase in real home prices over the three decades from 1983 to 2013 in Miami and Phoenix was just about zero overall, though they had both doubled along the way. Based on these trends, owner-occupied housing is looking like a bad long-term investment relative to the stock market: despite the occasional volatility of real estate, nationally it has offered practically no capital gains for long-term investors. But one must remember the implicit dividends that one receives from living in a home, that is, the value of the shelter and other services provided by a home. These dividends are untaxed. It is often said (correctly) that there is a tax advantage to owning rather than renting. If one swapped houses with one's neighbor living in an identical house and each paid rent to the other (so that the rent received would cancel out the rent paid), the transaction would be virtually meaningless from an economic standpoint, but it would incur taxes, since the rent received would be taxable, while the rent paid would not be deductible. For this reason, most people are well advised to buy rather than rent the homes they live in.

Another reason to buy rather than rent is that the rental contract carries with it intrinsic moral hazard problems: the renter cannot be given proper incentives to maintain the property as would a homeowner. The moral hazard problem is reflected both in higher rents and in restrictions on the homeowner's rights to engage in certain activities or to remodel the property to taste.

There is no accurate measure of the tax-free implicit dividends in the form of housing benefits that housing provides to compare with the (usually taxable) dividends paid on stocks, nor of the costs of maintenance that must be offset against the dividends homes provide. There actually can be no accurate measure of the implicit dividends on homes, since there is no way to put a dollar value on the psychic benefit one gets by owning and living in one's own home, as against the psychic costs one incurs by having to take care of it. This psychic benefit is not the same as the rent one can charge on a home, since renters are people in substantially different circumstances. Homeowners can change their minds from one day to the next about these psychic benefits. Moreover, these psychic dividends are not directly proportional to the amount one invested in the home, as are the dividends on stocks; if one buys more house than one needs, one may realize a negative psychic dividend from maintaining too much property.

Thus, there is really no way that one can say authoritatively which has been the better investment historically, homes or stocks. The answer differs across individuals, and is ultimately a matter of taste and circumstance. But individual homeowners have no clarity on this point and can change their opinions from time to time about the advantages of investing in housing. We will see evidence of such changes later in this book.

Irrational Exuberance Then and Now

My research assistants and I have seen some clues to the changing nature of public thinking regarding real estate speculation over the years. Our reading of contemporary English-language newspaper and magazine accounts of real estate markets since the late nineteenth century has confirmed such changes. We have found relatively little talk about anything that could be considered national bubbles in home prices until the last decades of the twentieth century. There seemed to be only occasional mentions of "irrational exuberance." The word *boom* was frequently used to describe situations in the housing market throughout the twentieth century, but in earlier years it tended to refer to a boom in the construction industry (as measured by the number of new homes built). Accounts by economists of the situation in the national housing market did not often mention bubbles or speculation. Instead there was a tendency to stress that building costs were the ultimate determinant of home prices. Articles often tended to talk about shortages of homes for sale rather than price increases.

Before the last decades of the twentieth century, it is striking that there was relatively little public discussion of home prices. As evidence for this, or as part of the reason for this, note that there was no regularly published and regularly cited price index for existing homes in the United States until 1968, when the National Association of Real Estate Boards median price of existing homes first began to be cited in major newspapers.[19] There was no *high-quality* existing home price index until Karl Case and I developed the weighted repeat sales method, used it to estimate price indices for major U.S. cities, and published these in a couple of articles in the late 1980s. The method was later adopted by Fannie Mae and Freddie Mac and by the U.S. Office of Housing Enterprise Oversight and its successor (after it was shut down in 2009 after the failures of Fannie Mae and Freddie Mac) the Federal Housing Finance Agency and others. Data on the price-rental ratio (akin to the price-earnings ratio that is used by investors to test for over- or underpricing in the stock market) did not begin to be stressed in the news media until the *Economist* began publishing them for various countries after 2000.

Therefore, good public information about prices, information that might help generate irrational exuberance, was not really available until the close of the twentieth century. Before then, newspaper accounts would sometimes talk of price changes, but they usually cited either anecdotal evidence or the opinions of real estate brokers about what was happening. Even those stories were infrequent, apparently reflecting lack of public interest in national home price trends.[20]

Before 1960 general public attention to the housing market often tended to take the form of outrage at the exorbitant rents that landlords were able to extract from their tenants, rather than concern about the course of prices of single-family homes. People were living in a less avowedly capitalist economy, and they were not primed to believe that their well-being depended in large measure on their property.

Prior to the last decades of the twentieth century, public attention focused instead on rent control and on a housing cooperative movement, whereby groups of people would buy interest in an apartment building that they controlled as a group. From these conspicuous examples of government and collective intervention in markets, people might plausibly have imagined that something would be done by authorities to prevent home prices from getting out of control.

While rent control and housing cooperatives still exist, the idealistic ideology that created them is mostly gone. In recent decades, our increasing public commitment to market solutions to economic problems, rather than interventions and controls, has led people to worry more about the possible instability in home prices and hence to make them more prone to the kind of feedback that generates bubbles.

A Proquest search since 1740 and a Lexis-Nexis search since the 1970s for the term *housing bubble* or *home price bubble* in English-language newspapers around the world shows that these terms were hardly used at all until just after the 1987 stock market crash (a time when people were already talking about bubbles, and many countries were showing very rapid price increases), but those terms died out soon after 1987. The terms reappeared in the late 1990s, and their use took off dramatically after 2000.

Appearance in newspapers does not necessarily imply penetration into public awareness. On paper questionnaires that Karl Case and I have been distributing to recent U.S. homebuyers annually since 2003, we have a number of open-ended questions that asked for written sentence answers about interpretations of recent market phenomena. The printed questionnaires do not mention bubbles, nor do they ask directly about them. In 2003 and 2004 there was virtually no respondent who brought up the words "housing bubble." The respondents' use of the words surged in 2005, stayed high for several years surrounding the market peak, and then fell. News stories referring to a housing bubble were especially frequent then. This then suggests that the concept is not a natural one for most people, but that the idea had been planted in their minds by circumstances, media attention, and public talk, for a while.

Life was simpler once; one saved and then bought a home when the time was right. One expected to buy a home as part of normal living and didn't think to worry about what would happen to the price of homes. The increasingly large role of speculative markets for homes, as well as of other markets, has fundamentally changed our lives. The price activity that was once very local and confined to such events as the building of highways, canals, and railroads has become national and even international, and it is now connected to popular stories of new economic eras. The changing behavior of home prices is a sign of changing public impressions of the value of property, a heightening of attention to speculative price movements.

The Role of Lending Institutions in Housing Bubbles

During a bubble, attentional anomalies tend to affect lenders as well as buyers. They, too, focus their attention on the same investing opportunities. They, too, are not attentive to—are complacent about—the risk of a collapse in the market.

The effects of the housing bubble in the early 2000s on lenders in the United States are aptly described by Vermont Law School professor Jennifer Taub in her 2014 book *Other People's Houses: How Decades of Bailouts, Captive Regulators, and Toxic Bankers Made Home Mortgages a Thrilling Business*.[21] She describes the atmosphere at major mortgage lenders during the housing boom just before its peak around 2006 as one of excitement at their apparent new successes, in an atmosphere of flagrant disregard of the risks they were creating.

One of these lenders was Washington Mutual, Inc. (WaMu), a savings bank holding company whose origins go back to the Washington National Building and Loan Investment Association in 1889, which was renamed in the early twentieth century as the Washington Mutual Savings Bank. It was a mutual (a sort of cooperative, not for profit), but dropped its mutual status in 1983 during the Reagan years of deregulation and became for-profit. It was unfortunately allowed to keep the word "mutual" in its name anyway, as if the word "mutual" was a mere historical anachronism that no longer had meaning for the public. It lost its ideological roots and became a go-go success story by ignoring risks. It became the biggest savings and loan in the United States by aggressively pursuing borrowers. In fact, under WaMu's aggressive CEO

Kerry Killinger, it adopted and publicized the motto "The Power of Yes" to trumpet to potential borrowers with poor credit histories that their mortgage applications would not be turned down. After the crisis, it became the biggest bank failure in U.S. history. But during the boom years, the mood in the firm was that of tantalizing success and inattention to the possibility of a housing crisis that had not happened since the Great Depression.

Countrywide Financial, under Angelo Mozilo, another mortgage lender whose boom and collapse figured largely in the financial crisis, had a similar corporate culture. They had the motto "Price Any Loan."

Atif Mian of Princeton University and Amir Sufi of the University of Chicago have shown that in regions where lending standards were more relaxed, home prices rose more before the bubble and fell more after it burst.[22] Part of this phenomenon is regulatory complacency, allowing the "success-oriented" lenders to do their thing with little constraint.

Many people have complained to me after the post-2006 collapse: "why aren't more of these mortgage lenders in jail?" But it is hard to place such punishment on them, because it is not easy to demonstrate to everyone's satisfaction that they have broken any laws. Kerry Killinger was in fact sued by the Federal Deposit Insurance Corporation in 2011 for "reckless lending," but the suit ended with merely a financial settlement.[23] Angelo Mozilo was charged in 2009 by the Securities and Exchange Commission for insider trading and securities fraud, but again, this ended merely in a settlement, and all criminal investigations were stopped in 2010 without any admission of wrongdoing by Mozilo.[24]

Whatever the details of their actions, and whatever their culpability in a court of law, from the standpoint of our trying to understand bubbles, we should view their actions here as essentially a consequence of the same broader sense of excitement about investing opportunities and complacency about risks that infected the broader public.

The Path from Here

In the next part of the book, I develop carefully a theory of bubbles, a theory that applies both to the stock market and to the housing market, and in fact to any speculative market. The theory acknowledges multiple causes for these phenomena; they have no simple, one-liner explanations. And yet the theory also has a basic theoretical model, a model of feedback that is simple and indispensable for understanding how prices move. In later parts of this book I turn over and reexamine the theory of bubbles from a number of directions.

Part One

Structural Factors

Four

Precipitating Factors: The Internet, the Capitalist Explosion, and Other Events

What ultimately caused the values of the stock markets in so many countries to rise dramatically from 1982 to the remarkable peak around 2000? Why, after two major corrections, are the values of these markets returning again at the time of this writing to those elevated levels? What accounts for the long downtrend in real long-term interest rates in many countries over the past couple of decades? What ultimately caused the boom in real estate markets in so many cities around the world to follow the stock market boom? To answer these questions, and questions like them that will surely be generated in the future, it is not enough to say that the markets in general are vulnerable to bouts of *irrational exuberance.* We must specify what precipitating factors from outside the markets themselves caused the markets to behave so dramatically.

Most historical events, from wars to revolutions, do not have simple causes. When these events move in extreme directions, it is usually because of a confluence of factors, none of which is by itself large enough to explain these events.

Rome wasn't built in a day, nor was it destroyed by one sudden bolt of bad fortune. More likely, it owed its fall to a plurality of factors—some large and some small, some remote and some immediate—that conspired together. This ambiguity is unsatisfying to those of us seeking scientific certitude, especially given that it is so hard to identify and isolate the precipitating factors to begin with. But that is the nature of history, and such ambiguity justifies the constant search for new and better information to expose at least the overall contours of causation.

In Chapter 1, we saw some factors that have seemed, at certain times, to "explain" movements in the stock market, notably, long-term interest rates; these might help explain home prices as well. But one of the first lessons of economics should be that there are *many* factors that seem sometimes to "explain" speculative prices, too many for us to analyze them comfortably. We have to resist the temptation to oversimplify by singling out only one. Anyway, long-term interest rates are not really exogenous factors. They are market phenomena determined by many of the same supply and demand factors that determine the level of prices in the stock market, and their behavior is part of the same market psychology that drives the stock market. We have to try to understand the origins of market psychology itself.

Understanding the factors that precipitate market moves is doubly difficult because the timing of the major market events tends not to be lined up well with the timing of the precipitating factors. The precipitating factors often tend to be medium-term trends that catch the public's attention only after they have been in place for a long time. The timing of specific market events is, as we shall discuss in the next chapter, directly determined by people's reactions to the market and to one another, which impart to the market complex internal dynamics. But we must look at the precipitating factors if we are to understand why the market moves.

Those who predict avalanches look at snowfall patterns and temperature patterns over long periods of time before an actual avalanche event, even though they know that there may be no sudden change in these patterns at the time of an avalanche. It may never be possible to say why an actual avalanche occurred at the precise moment that it did. It is the same with the dramatic movements of stock markets and other speculative markets.

Recognizing these limitations, let us look at a list of factors that might be offered to help explain the increase in the value over the past twenty years of worldwide stock prices—and in some cases, of bond and real estate prices as well—as an exercise to help us understand what the future may hold.

These factors make up the *skin* of the bubble, if you will. I concentrate here mostly on *factors that have had an effect on the markets not warranted by rational analysis of economic fundamentals.* The list omits consideration of all the small variations in fundamental factors (for example, the growth in earnings, the change in real interest rates) that *should* rationally have an impact on financial markets. In more normal times or in markets for individual stocks, such rational factors would assume relatively greater prominence in any discussion of changes in prices. Indeed it is thanks to a market's ability to respond appropriately to such factors, for a variety of investments, that well-functioning financial markets generally promote, rather than hinder, economic efficiency.[1] The list of factors here was constructed specifically to help us understand the extraordinary situations that have occurred recently (and, arguably, are ongoing) in the stock markets and the housing markets, and so it concentrates on less rational influences.

In detailing these factors, I describe the reaction of the general public, not just of professional investment managers. Some observers believe that professional investment managers are more sensible and work to offset the *irrational exuberance* of the nonprofessional investing public. Therefore, these observers might argue that a sharp distinction should be drawn between the behavior of the professionals and that of the nonprofessionals.[2] Professional investors, however, are not immune to the effects of the popular investing culture that we observe in individual investors, and many of the factors described here no doubt influence their thinking as well. There is in fact no clear distinction between professional institutional investors and individual investors, since the professionals routinely give advice to the individual investors.

Some of these factors exist in the background of the market, including the advance of capitalism, the increased emphasis on business success, the revolution in information technology, the demographics of the Baby Boom, the decline of inflation and the economics of money illusion, and the rise of gambling and pleasure in risk taking in general. Others operate in the foreground and shape the changing culture of investment. These include greatly increased media coverage of business, the aggressively optimistic forecasts of stock analysts, the rise of 401(k) plans, the mutual funds explosion, and the expanding volume of trade in the stock market.

Twelve Precipitating Factors That Propelled the Late Stages of the Millennium Boom, 1982–2000

In the first edition of this book, published in 2000—just before the stock market peak of that year—I listed twelve precipitating factors for the build-up of bullish psychology and of stock prices to enormous levels by the beginning of the year. Here is the list as it was presented then, from the point of view of the zeitgeist of that time; some of these factors are still operative today, others less so.

The Arrival of the Internet at a Time of Solid Earnings Growth

The Internet and the World Wide Web invaded our homes during the second half of the 1990s, making us intimately conscious of the pace of technological change. The World Wide Web first appeared in the news in November 1993. The Mosaic web browser first became available to the public in February 1994. These dates mark the very beginning of the general public's exposure to the Internet, when only a few people had access to it. Significantly large numbers of users did not discover the web until 1997 and later, marking the very years when the NASDAQ stock price index (which was then even more heavily weighted toward startup high-tech stocks than it is today) soared, tripling to the end of 1999, and the price-earnings ratios took off into unprecedented territory.

Internet technology is unusual in that it is a source of entertainment and preoccupation for us all, indeed for the whole family. In this sense, it is comparable in importance to the personal computer or, before that, to television. In fact, the impression it conveys of a changed future is even more vivid than that produced when televisions or personal computers entered the home. Using the Internet gives people a sense of mastery of the world. They can electronically roam the world and accomplish tasks that would have been impossible before. They can even put up a website and become a factor in the world economy themselves. In contrast, the advent of television made them passive receivers of entertainment, and personal computers were used by most people before the Internet mainly as typewriters and high-tech pinball machines.

Because of the vivid and immediate personal impression the Internet makes, people find it plausible to assume that it also has great economic importance. It is much easier to imagine the consequences of advances in this technology than the consequences of, say, improved shipbuilding technology or new developments in materials science. Most of us simply do not hear much about research in those areas.

Spectacular U.S. corporate earnings growth in 1994, up 36% in real terms as measured by the S&P Composite real earnings, followed by real earnings growth of 8% in 1995 and 10% in 1996, coincided roughly with the Internet's birth but in fact had little to do with the Internet. Instead the earnings growth was attributed by analysts to a continuation of the slow recovery from the 1990–91 recession, coupled with a weak dollar and strong foreign demand for U.S. capital and technology exports, as well as with cost-cutting initiatives by U.S. companies. It could not have been the Internet that caused the growth in profits: the fledgling Internet companies were not making much of a profit yet. But the occurrence of profit growth coincident with the appearance of a new technology as dramatic as the Internet created an impression among the general public that the two events were somehow connected. Publicity linking these twin factors, the Internet boom and the profit growth, was especially strong because of the advent of the year 2000 and the new millennium, a time of much optimistic discussion of the future.

The Internet is, of course, an important technological advance in its own right, and it, as well as other developments in computer technology and robotics, does promise to have an unpredictable and powerful impact on our future. But one should question what impact the Internet and the computer revolution should have on the valuation of existing U.S. corporations. New technology will always affect the market, but should it really raise the value of existing companies, given that those existing companies do not have a monopoly on the new technology?[3] Should the advent of the Internet have raised the valuation of the Dow—which at the time contained no Internet stocks?[4]

The notion that existing companies would benefit from the Internet revolution was belied by the stories of E*Trade.com, Amazon.com, and other upstarts, which did not even exist just a few years before 2000. People might well have thought that still more new companies would appear in the future, in the United States and abroad, and these would compete with the companies in which they invested in the late 1990s. Simply put, the effect of new technology on existing companies can go either way: it can boost or depress their profits.

What matters for a stock market boom is not, however, the reality of the Internet revolution, which is hard to quantify, but rather the *public impressions* that the revolution has created. Public reaction is influenced by the intuitive plausibility of Internet lore, and this plausibility is ultimately influenced by the ease with which examples or arguments come to mind. If we are regularly spending time on the Internet, then these examples will come to mind very easily.

Triumphalism and the Decline of Foreign Economic Rivals

In the late 1990s, before the 2000 peak in the stock markets, most other countries seemed to be imitating the Western economic system. Communist China has been embracing market forces since the late 1970s. Increasing tolerance of free markets in the Soviet Union culminated with the breakup of that nation in 1991 into smaller, market-oriented states. The world seemed to be swinging our way, and therefore it started to seem only natural that the U.S. stock market should be most highly valued in the world.

These political events unfolded gradually after the bull market began in 1982. And the years after the start of the bull market witnessed the decline in the Japanese market after 1989, the prolonged economic slump in Japan, and the Asian financial crisis of 1997–98, which coincided roughly with the dramatic burst of the U.S. stock market into uncharted territory at the beginning of the new millennium. These foreign events might have been viewed as bad for the U.S. stock market—as the harbinger of bad things to come here—but instead they were seen by many as the weakening of major rivals. The relation between the United States and its economic rivals was often described in the media as a competition in which there can only be one winner, as in a sports event. The weakening of a rival was thus viewed simplistically as good news.

Cultural and Political Changes Favoring Business Success

The soaring of the stock market during 1982–2000 was accompanied by a significant rise in materialistic values. A Roper-Starch questionnaire given to survey participants in both 1975 and 1994 asked, "When you think of the good life—the life you'd like to have, which of the things on this list, if any, are part of that good life, as far as you personally are concerned?" In 1975, 38% picked the option "a lot of money," whereas in 1994, fully 63% picked that option.[5]

Such feelings transformed our culture into one that reveres the successful businessperson as much as or even more than the accomplished scientist, artist, or revolutionary. The idea that investing in stocks is a road to quick riches developed a certain appeal to born-again materialists.

Stay-at-home mothers, who devote their lives to their families, become less admired, and this is part of the reason women joined the work force in increasing numbers. This then also increased the availability of credit and home financing—starting around the 1970s, mortgage lenders began to count the spouse's income in qualifying a mortgage, expanding available mortgage credit. This helped propel home prices.

A decline in crime rates also, on the flip side, encouraged materialistic values by making people feel more secure, less worried that they would be robbed or physically harmed. In the United States, the rate of property crimes per 1,000 people fell 49% between 1993 and 2003, and the rate of violent crimes per 1,000 people fell 55%.[6] One could then more comfortably flaunt wealth, and so wealth became more attractive. Living in an ostentatious home was now more appealing. Fear of terrorism increased, but terrorists did not seem to strike wealthy people preferentially, and generally not in their homes. The declining crime rates in the U.S. made a capitalist lifestyle seem a better model for the entire world.

Note that materialistic values do not by themselves have any logical bearing on the level of the stock market. Whether or not people are materialistic, it is still reasonable to expect them to save for the future and to seek out the best vehicles for their savings. But it is plausible that such feelings would influence their demand for stocks, which have long held out at least the possibility of amassing substantial riches quickly. Moreover, such feelings have an unmistakable political impact, which in turn affects the success of corporate investments.

A Republican Congress and Capital Gains Tax Cuts

When Ronald Reagan was elected in 1980, so too was a Republican Senate, the first since 1948. In 1994, both houses became Republican (though with a Democratic president, just as happened again in 2014). Sensing the changed public attitudes that had elected them, these lawmakers were much more pro-business than their Democratic predecessors had been. This change in Congress boosted public confidence in the stock market because of a variety of controls that the legislature can exert over corporate profits and investor returns.

Consider taxation. No sooner had the Republican Congress been seated in 1995 than proposals to cut the capital gains tax became prominent. In 1997, the top capital gains tax rate was cut from 28% to 20%. As soon as this cut was enacted, Congress talked of cutting rates further. A 1999 tax bill would have cut capital gains taxes still further, but President Clinton vetoed it.

Anticipation of possible future capital gains tax cuts can have a favorable impact on the stock market, even when tax rates actually remain unchanged. From 1994 to 1997, investors were widely advised to hold on to their long-term capital gains, not to realize them, until after the capital gains tax cut. This had a strengthening effect on the market. At the time of the 1997 capital gains tax cut, there was fear that investors who had been waiting to sell would do so and bring the market down, as had apparently happened after capital gains tax cuts in 1978 and 1980. But this did not happen in 1997. Of course, many investors must have thought there could be an even more favorable capital gains tax rate in their future, and if so, there would have been no reason to sell right after the 1997 cut took effect.

It is likely that the general atmosphere of public talk of future capital gains tax cuts, of possible indexing of capital gains taxes to inflation, and of analogous tax cuts (for example, estate tax cuts) had created among investors a reluctance to sell their appreciated stocks. If capital gains tax rates may be cut sharply in the future, why sell when the rates are as high as 20%? Having been advised by experts to wait and see about capital gains tax cuts, many investors could be expected to defer sales of appreciated assets until they were more clearly at a historic low in capital gains tax rates. Such an atmosphere of holding, not folding, naturally placed upward pressure on stock prices.

The Baby Boom and Its Perceived Effects on the Markets

Following World War II, a substantial increase in the birth rate took place in the United States. Peacetime prosperity encouraged those who had postponed families because of the depression and the war to have children. There were also postwar birth rate increases in the United Kingdom, France, and Japan, but they were not as protracted or strong as that in the United States, no doubt at least in part because the economies of those nations were in such disarray after the war. Then, around 1966, the growth of U.S. and world population showed a dramatic decline, one that continues to this day. This decline was unusual, if not unique, by historical standards: it did not occur because of famine or war, but rather because of an endogenous decline in the fertility rate.[7]

Advances in birth control technology (the pill was invented in 1959 and became widely available by the mid-1960s in the United States and many other countries) and social changes that accepted the legality of contraception and abortion were instrumental in lowering the rate of population growth, as were growing urbanization and advances in education and economic aspiration levels. The Baby Boom and the subsequent Baby Bust have created a looming social security crisis in many countries of the world: they understood then that when the Boomers grew old and finally retired, the number of young working people available to support the elderly population would decline worldwide (as today we see it has indeed begun to do).[8]

The Baby Boom in the United States was marked by very high birth rates during the years 1946–66, and so there were, at the peak of the market in 2000, an unusually large number of people between the ages of 35 and 55. Two theories suggested then that the presence of so many middle-aged people ought to boost the stock market. One theory justified the high price-earnings ratios we saw in the Millennium Boom as the result of those Boomers competing against one another to buy stocks to save for their eventual retirement and bidding share prices up relative to the earnings they generate. According to the other theory, spending on current goods and services boosts stock prices, through a generalized positive effect on the economy: high expenditures mean high profits for companies.

These simple Baby Boom stories were just a bit too simple. For one thing, they neglected to consider *when* the Baby Boom should affect the stock market. Maybe the effect of the Baby Boom was already factored into stock prices by investors even before 1982. They also neglected such factors as the emergence of new capitalist economies worldwide and their demand, in another twenty years, for U.S. stocks. The theory that the Baby Boom drove the market up owing to Boomers' demand for goods would seem to imply that the market was high because earnings were high; it would not explain the high price-earnings ratios that were reached at the peak of the market.

If life-cycle savings patterns (the first effect) alone were to be the dominant force in the markets for savings vehicles, there would tend to be strong correlations in price behavior across alternative asset classes, and strong correlations over time between asset prices and demographics. When the most numerous generation feels they need to save, they would tend to bid up *all* savings vehicles: stocks, bonds, and real estate. When the most numerous generation feels they need to draw down their savings, their selling would tend to force down the prices of *all* these vehicles. But when one looks at long-term data on stocks, bonds, and real estate, one finds that there has in fact been relatively little relation between their real values.[9]

Another theory that was popular in the 1990s as to why Boomers may have had a positive impact on the market is that the Boomers, who have no memory of the Great Depression of the 1930s or of World War II, have less anxiety about the market and the world. There is indeed some evidence that shared experiences in formative years leave a mark forever on a generation's attitudes.[10] Over the course of the bull market since 1982, Boomers have gradually replaced as prime investors those who were teens or young adults during the depression and the war.

Although there is no doubt at least some truth to these theories of the Baby Boom's effects on the stock market, it may be public *perceptions* of the Baby Boom and its presumed effects that were most responsible for the surge in the market. The impact of the Baby Boom was one of the most talked-about issues relating to both the stock market and the housing market, and all this talk in and of itself had the potential to affect stock market value. People believed that the Baby Boom represented an important source of strength for the markets, and they did not see this strength faltering any time soon. These public perceptions contributed to a feeling that there was a good reason for the market to be high and a confidence that it would stay that way for some time. Congratulating themselves on their cleverness in understanding and betting on these population trends in their stock market investments, many investors failed to appreciate just how common their thinking really was. Their perceptions fueled continuing upward spirals in market valuations.

The most prominent exponent of the Baby Boom theory of the stock market and the housing market was Harry S. Dent. He began with a 1992 book titled *The Great Boom Ahead: Your Comprehensive Guide to Personal and Business Profit in the New Era of Prosperity,* which was so successful that he wrote several sequels. His 1998 book, *The Roaring 2000s: Building the Wealth & Lifestyle You Desire in the Greatest Boom in History,* was on the *New York Times* best-seller list for four weeks in 1998. His 1999 book, *The Roaring 2000s Investor: Strategies for the Life You Want,* was ranked in 1999 within the top 100 in sales among all books, according to Amazon.com. This book predicted that the stock market would continue to boom until 2009, when the number of people who are 46 will start to decline, and then the market would drop.

Dent's success with the Baby Boom theme during the bull market predictably spawned a number of imitators—all extolling the wonderful opportunities to get rich from the Baby Boom's effects on investments—with titles like *Boomernomics: The Future of Your Money in the Upcoming Generational Warfare* by William Sterling and Stephen Waite (1998) and *Boom, Bust & Echo: How to Profit from the Coming Demographic Shift* by David K. Foot and Daniel Stoffman (1996). Discussions of the Baby Boom and its effects on the markets were everywhere, and their general tone was that the Boom was good for the stock market and would continue to be for years to come.

An Expansion in Media Reporting of Business News

The first all-news television network, the Cable News Network (CNN), appeared in 1980 and gradually grew, with viewership boosted by such events as the Gulf War in 1991 and the O. J. Simpson trial in 1995—stories that fueled great demand for uninterrupted coverage. The public acquired the habit of watching the news on television throughout the day (and night), not simply at the dinner hour. CNN was followed by the business networks. The Financial News Network, founded in 1983, was later absorbed into CNBC. Then CNNfn and Bloomberg Television appeared. Together, these networks produced an uninterrupted stream of financial news, much of it devoted to the stock market. So pervasive was their influence that traditional brokerage firms found it necessary to keep CNBC running in the lower corners of their brokers' computer screens. So many clients would call to ask about something they had just heard on the networks that brokers (who were supposed to be too busy working to watch television!) began to seem behind the curve.

Not merely the scope, but also the nature, of business reporting changed in those years. According to a study by Richard Parker, a senior fellow at Harvard University's Shorenstein Center, newspapers in the last two decades of the twentieth century gradually transformed their formerly staid business sections into enhanced "Money" sections, which dispensed useful tips about personal investing. Articles about individual corporations that used to be written as if they would be of interest only to those involved in the industry or the corporations themselves were then written with a slant toward profit opportunities for individual investors; these articles regularly included analysts' opinions of the implications of the news for investors.[11]

According to a 2004 study by James Hamilton there had been a gradual decline over the preceding several decades in the "hard news" content of the U.S. television evening news in favor of news that is either of story quality or of immediate use to the viewer. Hamilton attributed this change to the increasing competitiveness of the news media business, and competitive advantage increasingly depends on maintaining marginal customers who are less interested in depth of understanding.[12] News about investing tips naturally prospers in such an environment.

Enhanced reporting of investing options led to increased demand for stocks, just as advertisements for a consumer product make people more familiar with the product, remind them of the option to buy, and ultimately motivate them to buy. Most advertising is really not the presentation of important facts about a product but merely a reminder of the product and its image. Given the heightened media coverage of investments, a stock market boom should come as no greater surprise than increased sales of the latest sports utility vehicle after a major ad campaign.

As further evidence that the media growth was boosting the stock market, we now know that after the peak in the market in 2000, business reporting took a major hit in reaction to declining public interest. Hip business magazines like *Red Herring*, the *Industry Standard*, and others went out of business.

Viewership of major business television networks also took a hit. Sales of business books fell sharply after 2000.

Attention to the stock market by surviving newspapers also declined after 2000. According to a Lexis-Nexis search, the number of articles mentioning the stock market in major U.S. newspapers more than tripled from 1990 to 1998, buoyed for a while by news about various financial scandals. But by 2004, the number had fallen by more than 50% from the peak.

Analysts' Increasingly Optimistic Forecasts

According to data from Zacks Investment Research about analysts' recommendations on some 6,000 companies, only 1.0% of recommendations were "sells" in late 1999 (while 69.5% were "buys" and 29.9% were "holds"). This situation stood in striking contrast to that indicated by previous data. Ten years earlier, the percentage of sells, at 9.1%, was nine times higher.[13]

Analysts were especially reluctant to make sell recommendations near the peak of the stock market for a couple of reasons. One reason often given for this reluctance is that a sell recommendation might have incurred the wrath of the company involved, and companies could retaliate by refusing to talk with analysts whom they viewed as submitting negative reports, excluding them from information sessions, and not offering them access to key executives as they prepared earnings forecasts. This situation, occurring in the lead-up to the peak of the market, represented a fundamental change in the culture of the investment industry and in the tacit understanding that recommendations are as objective as the analyst can make them.

Another reason that many analysts were reluctant to issue sell recommendations was that an increasing number of them were employed by firms that underwrote securities, and these firms did not want their analysts to do anything that might jeopardize this lucrative side of the business. Analysts affiliated with investment banks gave significantly more favorable recommendations on firms for which their employer was the co- or lead underwriter than did unaffiliated analysts, even though their earnings forecasts usually were not stronger.[14]

Those who knew the ropes realized that hold recommendations were more like the sell recommendations of earlier years. In 1999 James Grant, a well-known market commentator, wrote, "Honesty was never a profit center on Wall Street, but the brokers used to keep up appearances. Now they have stopped pretending. More than ever, securities research, as it is called, is a branch of sales. Investor, beware."[15]

Analysts' recommendations were transformed by something analogous to grade inflation in our schools: C used to be an average grade, yet now it is considered as bordering on failure. Many of us know that such inflation happens, and we try to correct for it when interpreting our children's grades. Similarly, in the stock market we factor inflation into analysts' recommendations. But not everyone was able to make adequate corrections for analysts' newly hyperbolic language, and so the general effect of their changed standards was to encourage the higher valuation of stocks.

Moreover, it was not just a change in the units of measurement that infected analysts' reports. Even their quantitative forecasts of earnings growth showed an upward bias. According to a study by Steven Sharpe of the Federal Reserve Board, analysts' expectations of growth in the S&P 500 earnings per share exceeded actual growth in nineteen of the twenty-one years between 1979 and 1999. The average difference between the projected and actual growth rate of earnings was 9 percentage points. The analysts breezed through both the steep recession of 1980–81 and the recession of 1990–91, making forecasts of earnings growth in the 10% range.[16] Since Sharpe's study, analysts failed to predict the magnitude of the sharp drop in earnings around 2001.

This bias in analysts' forecasts was a characteristic of their one-year forecasts; they were usually more sober in predicting the next earnings announcement just before it was released. Analysts tended to comply with firms' wishes to see positive earnings surprises each quarter, by issuing estimates that fell slightly short of the actual number. Then firms, just before making earnings announcements, talked with analysts whose forecasts were on the high side, urging them down, while neglecting to talk with analysts whose forecasts were on the low side, thereby creating a downward bias in the average earnings forecast without being blatantly untruthful.[17] Casual evaluation of analysts' forecasts by clients would most naturally take the form of comparing the latest earnings announcement with the latest forecast, and therefore analysts did not sharply overestimate earnings just before they were announced, which would have been an obvious embarrassment to them.

Analysts' upward bias came to the fore when predicting the vague, undifferentiated future, not immediate quarterly or yearly outcomes. And it was expectations for the vague, undifferentiated future, even far beyond one-year forecasts, that lay behind the high market valuations we saw at the peak of the millennium stock market. According to another study by Steven Sharpe, a 1 percentage point difference in analysts' industry-forecasted earnings growth caused a 5–8% boost in the industry's price-earnings ratio. Thus, Sharpe concluded that the rise in analysts' long-term growth expectations would "appear to have been a key factor driving equity market valuations skyward during the latter half of the 1990s."[18]

Analysts had few worries about being uniformly optimistic regarding the distant future; they apparently concluded that such generalized optimism was simply good for business. Certainly they perceived that their fellow analysts were demonstrating such long-run optimism, and there was, after all, safety in numbers. Glibly and routinely offering "great-outlook-for-the-U.S." patter to the investing public, they perhaps gave little thought to its accuracy.

The problems afflicting analysts' recommendations were reduced somewhat after the stock market had peaked. Some firms voluntarily instituted new rules requiring that their analysts really make sell recommendations. Because of Regulation FD, imposed by the U.S. Securities and Exchange Commission in October 2000, analysts who had been critical of a company could no longer be excluded from information meetings, which now had to be open to the general public. The Sarbanes-Oxley Act of 2002 mandated, among other things, that research reports by analysts not be subjected to prepublication clearance by persons involved with investment banking, that there not be any retaliation against analysts whose research reports conflicted with an investment banking business, and that firms set up informational partitions between their investment banking and securities analysis divisions. In 2003, the Securities and Exchange Commission announced a $1.4 billion Global Analyst Research Settlement for ten of the top investment firms in the United States, which were accused of offering their customers deliberately biased analysis with the aim of promoting their investment banking business. Of this sum, $80 million was earmarked for an investor education program. Analyst reports also started to disclose the percentage of sell-neutral-buy recommendations to provide context for investors reading the reports. This settlement appears to have reduced the optimistic bias in earnings forecasts that existed during the Millennium Boom, not only in the United States, but also, because of legal spillovers, in many countries.[19]

The Expansion of Defined Contribution Pension Plans

Changes over time in the nature of employee pension plans during the Millennium Boom encouraged people to learn about, and eventually accept, stocks as investments. Although these changes did not inherently favor stocks over other investments for retirement, they did—by forcing people to make explicit choices among their retirement investments, choices that previously were made for them—work in the direction of encouraging investment in stocks. Making such choices taught people about stocks and increased their level of familiarity with them.

The most revolutionary change in these institutions in the United States was the expansion of defined contribution pension plans at the expense of defined benefit plans. An important milestone came in 1981, when the first 401(k) plan was created; it was soon ratified by a landmark ruling by the Internal Revenue Service.[20] Prior to that date, employer pension plans had usually been of the defined benefit type, in which the employer merely promised a fixed pension to its employees when they retired. Reserves to pay the defined benefit were managed by the employer. With 401(k) plans (as well as such analogues as 403(b) plans), employees are offered the opportunity to have contributions to a tax-deferred retirement account deducted from their paychecks. They then own the investments in their 401(k) accounts and must allocate them among stocks, bonds, and money market accounts. The tax law began to encourage employers to make matching contributions to their employees' 401(k) accounts, so there came to be a powerful incentive for employees to participate.

Various factors also encouraged the growth of defined contribution pension plans since the bottom of the U.S. market in 1982. Labor unions traditionally sought defined benefit plans for their members as a way of ensuring their welfare in retirement, and the decline of unions meant diminishing support for these plans. The importance of the manufacturing sector, long a stronghold of labor unions and defined benefit pensions, was shrinking. Defined benefit plans became less popular with management, because so-called overfunded plans sometimes make companies vulnerable to takeovers. On the flip side, defined benefit plans could leave companies on the hook for growing and uncertain obligations as workers live longer. Defined contribution plans came to be seen as less costly to administer than defined benefit plans. Moreover, defined contribution plans became more popular with those employees who liked to monitor their investments, and therefore companies began to offer the plans to all employees.

Through these tax incentives for participation in plans offering choices between stocks and bonds, the government forced working people to learn about the advantages of stocks versus bonds or money market investments. Any incentive to learn about an investment vehicle is likely to boost demand for it. In 1954, when the New York Stock Exchange carried out a marketing study to understand how to promote public interest in the stock market, it concluded that most people did not know very much about stocks: only 23% of the public even knew enough to define what a share is. Moreover, the survey revealed a vague public distrust of the stock market.[21] So the exchange held a series of public information seminars to try to remedy this lack of knowledge and this prejudice against stocks as an investment. But no set of seminars that the exchange could ever afford could compare with the learning-by-doing effects of the defined contribution plan in encouraging public knowledge about and interest in stocks.

If one's attention to the stock market is filtered through the lens of a pension plan, it may encourage longer-term thinking. The stated purpose of a 401(k) plan is to prepare for retirement, which is, for most workers, many years away. A 401(k) plan sponsor does not call participants with tips about short-run investment opportunities, and statements about portfolio value are mailed out only infrequently. The participant cannot check his or her portfolio value every day in the newspaper. This longer-term thinking may boost stock market valuations by diverting investors from preoccupation with short-term fluctuations.

Encouraging longer-term thinking among investors is probably, all in all, a good thing. But an additional effect of 401(k) plans as they came, in the Millennium Boom, to be structured may have been to boost demand for stocks further through another psychological mechanism. By offering multiple stock market investment *categories* for employees to choose among, employers can create demand for stocks. An effect of categories on ultimate investment choices was demonstrated by economists Shlomo Benartzi and Richard Thaler. They found, using both experimental data and data on actual pension fund allocations, that people tend to spread their allocations evenly over the available options, without regard to the *contents* of the options. For example, if a 401(k) plan offers a choice of a stock fund and a bond fund, many people will put 50% of their contributions into each. If the plan instead offers a choice between a stock fund and a balanced fund (with, say, 50% stocks and 50% bonds in it), people will still tend to put 50% into each, even though they are now really putting 75% of their portfolio into stocks.[22]

The options offered as part of 401(k) plans tended to be heavily weighted in favor of stocks. In contrast, most 401(k) plans did not have any real estate options. In this way the growth of 401(k) plans encouraged the growth of public interest in the stock market relative to the real estate market. Indeed the typical 401(k) plan in the 1990s offered choices among a stock fund, a balanced fund (typically 60% stocks and 40% bonds), company stock (investments in the employer itself), possibly a specialized stock fund (for example, a growth fund), a bond fund, and a money market fund, as well as fixed-income guaranteed investment contracts. It is not surprising, from the findings of the Benartzi and Thaler study, that people put proportionately more into the stock funds, given that so many stock-related choices were laid out before them. Moreover, since there were more interesting "flavors" of stocks—just as, in the corner liquor store, there are more varieties of wine than of vodka—more attention is likely to be drawn to them.

It is in such subtle ways that the *interest value* or *curiosity value* of stocks, not any kind of rational decision-making process, encouraged investors during the Millennium Boom to want to buy more of them than they otherwise would. And this seemingly unconscious interest has helped bid up the price of the stock market.

The Growth of Mutual Funds

The Millennium Boom also coincided with a peculiar growth spurt in the mutual fund industry and a proliferation of advertising for mutual funds. In 1982, at the beginning of the recent long-term bull market, there were only

340 equity mutual funds in the United States. By 1998, there were 3,513—more equity mutual funds than stocks listed on the New York Stock Exchange. In 1984, there were 8.9 million domestic equity mutual fund shareholder accounts in the United States, about one for every ten U.S. households. By 2007, there were 145 million such shareholder accounts, or well over one account per household.[23] After the 2007 peak in the stock market, the growth in the number of accounts stalled, and by 2013 the number had fallen to 121.6 million accounts, well below the number at the 2007 peak.

Mutual funds are a relatively new name for a very old idea. Investment companies arose in the United States as early as the 1820s, though these were not then called mutual funds.[24] The Massachusetts Investors Trust, generally regarded as the first mutual fund, was created in 1924. It was different from the other investment trusts in that it published its portfolio, promised prudent investment policies, and was self-liquidating when investors demanded cash for their investments. But this first mutual fund got off to a slow start: investors were not quick to appreciate its advantages. The 1920s bull market instead saw the proliferation of many other investment trusts: investment companies without the safeguards we associate with mutual funds today, many of them dishonest operations, and some of them even, effectively, Ponzi schemes (see Chapter 5).

After the stock market crash of 1929, many of these became even more worthless than the market as a whole, and the public soured on investment trusts. In particular, they felt betrayed by the managers of the trusts, who were often pursuing their own interests in flagrant conflict with those of their investors. The Investment Company Act of 1940, which established regulations for investment companies, helped restore a measure of public confidence. But people needed more than just government regulations; they needed a new name, one that did not carry the unsavory associations of investment trusts. The term *mutual fund*, with its similarity to the mutual savings bank and the mutual insurance company—venerable institutions that had survived the stock market crash largely untouched by scandal—was much more reassuring and attractive to investors.[25]

The mutual fund industry was given new impetus by the Employee Retirement Income Security Act of 1974, which created Individual Retirement Accounts. But the industry really took off after the bull market began in 1982.

Part of the reason that equity mutual funds proliferated so rapidly after that date is that they are used as part of 401(k) pension plans. As people invest their plan balances directly in mutual funds, they develop greater familiarity with the concept; they are thus more inclined to invest their non-401(k) savings in mutual funds as well.

Another reason for the funds' explosive growth is that they have paid for a great deal of advertising. During the Millennium Boom, television shows, magazines, and newspapers frequently carried advertisements for them, and active investors received unsolicited ads in the mail. Mutual funds encouraged more naive investors to participate in the market by leading them to think that the experts managing the funds would steer them away from pitfalls.

The proliferation of equity mutual funds therefore focused public attention on the market, with the effect of encouraging speculative price movements in stock market aggregates rather than in individual stocks.[26] The emerging popular concept that mutual fund investing is sound, convenient, and safe has encouraged many investors who were once afraid of the market to want to enter it, thereby contributing to an upward thrust in the market. (See Chapter 12 for a further discussion of public attitudes toward mutual funds.)

The Decline of Inflation and the Effects of Money Illusion

The outlook for U.S. inflation, as measured by the percentage change in the Consumer Price Index, gradually improved over the course of the Millennium Boom. In 1982, even though U.S. inflation was then around 4% a year, there was still considerable uncertainty as to whether it would return to the high level (nearly 15% for the year) experienced in 1980. The most dramatic stock price increases of this bull market occurred once the inflation rate had settled down into the 2–3% range in the mid-1990s, and then it dropped below 2%.

The general public paid a lot of attention then to inflation, as late 1990s interview studies of public attitudes toward it revealed.[27] People widely believed that the inflation rate was a barometer of the economic and social health of a nation. High inflation was perceived to signify economic disarray, loss of basic values, and national disgrace before foreigners. Low inflation was viewed as a sign of economic prosperity, social justice, and good government. Many of these attitudes are still with us today, though probably not as strongly after twenty years of less-worrisome inflation. It is not surprising, therefore, that a falling inflation rate over the span of the Millennium Boom boosted public confidence and hence stock market valuation.

But from a purely rational standpoint, this stock market reaction to inflation is inappropriate. In 1979 economists Franco Modigliani and Richard Cohn published an article arguing that the stock market reacts inappropriately to inflation because people do not fully understand the effect of inflation on interest rates.[28] When inflation is high—as it was when they wrote, near the bottom of the stock market in 1982—nominal interest rates (the usual interest rates we see quoted every day) are high, because they must compensate investors for the inflation that is eroding the value of their dollars. Yet expected real long-term interest rates (interest rates as corrected for the expected effects of future long-term inflation) did not appear to be high then, and therefore there should not have been any stock market reaction to the high nominal rates.

Modigliani and Cohn suggested that the market tends to be depressed when nominal rates are high even when real rates are not high because of a sort of "money illusion," or public confusion about the effects of a changing monetary standard. When there is inflation, we are changing the value of the dollar, and therefore changing the yardstick by which we measure values. Faced with a changing yardstick, it is not surprising that many people become confused.[29]

Public misunderstanding about inflation near the climax of the Millennium Boom may have encouraged high expectations for real (inflation-corrected) returns. Most data on past long-run stock market returns is reported in the media in nominal terms, without correction for inflation, and people might naturally be encouraged to expect that such nominal returns would continue in the future. The (lagged ten-year average) inflation rate at the end of 1982 was over 8%; by the end of the Millennium Boom it was down to less than 3%. Therefore, expecting the same nominal returns in the late stages of that boom was the equivalent of expecting a lot more in real terms.

Plots of historical stock price indices in the media are almost invariably shown in nominal terms, not the real (inflation-corrected) terms shown in the figures in this book. By 2000, U.S. consumer prices had almost doubled since 1982. This inflation imparted a strong upward trend to long-run historical plots of stock price indices. Thus, the extraordinary behavior of the real stock market at the turn of the millennium, the spike up in stock prices that was visible in Figure 1.1, does not stand out in the long historical plots we see in the media. In fact, viewing these plots encourages us to think that nothing at all unusual was going on during the Millennium Boom in the stock market.

The reason news writers generally do not make corrections for inflation is probably that they think such adjustments are esoteric and would not be widely appreciated by their readers. And they are probably right. The general public has not by and large taken Economics 101, and those who did sit through it have probably forgotten much of what they learned. Thus, they have not assimilated the basic lesson that there is nothing natural about measuring prices in dollars when the quantity, and value, of those dollars has been highly unstable. The public at large does not fully appreciate that the more meaningful measure of the stock market level is in terms of some broad basket of goods, as it is when corrected for consumer price inflation.[30]

Expansion of the Volume of Trade: Discount Brokers, Day Traders, and Twenty-Four-Hour Trading

The turnover rate (the total shares sold in a year divided by the total number of shares) for New York Stock Exchange stocks nearly doubled between 1982 and 1999, from 42% to 78%.[31] The NASDAQ market, which emphasizes high-tech stocks, showed an even greater turnover rate increase, from 88% in

1990 to 221% in 1999.[32] The higher turnover rate may have been symptomatic of increased interest in the market as a result of other factors mentioned here. But another reason for the rise in turnover rate in the stock market was the declining cost of making a trade. After competitive brokerage commissions were mandated by the Securities and Exchange Commission (SEC) in 1975, there was an immediate drop in commission rates, and discount brokers came into being. Technological and organizational changes were also set in motion. Such innovations as the Small Order Execution System, introduced by NASDAQ in 1985, and new order-handling rules issued by the SEC in 1997 have resulted in ever lower trading costs. SEC regulations encouraging equal access to the markets spawned a growing number of amateur investors who can "day trade," that is, try to make profits by rapidly trading stocks using the same order execution systems used by professionals.

The significant growth of online trading services coincides roughly with the most spectacular increases in the stock market between 1997 and 2001. According to a study by the SEC, there were 3.7 million online accounts in the United States in 1997; by 1999 there were 9.7 million such accounts.[33] The growth of online trading, as well as the associated Internet-based information and communication services, may well have encouraged minute-by-minute attention to the market. After-hours trading on the exchanges also had the potential to increase the level of attention paid to the market, as investors could track changing prices in their living rooms during their leisure time.

Speculative prices seem to get a volatility nudge whenever markets are open. The magnitude of price changes tends to be lower over two-day intervals that include a day when markets are closed (as, for example, during a time when the New York Stock Exchange closed on Wednesdays).[34] It is therefore plausible to expect that the expansion of online trading and the opening of markets for longer hours raised their volatility. Whether it should have raised or lowered the level of prices is somewhat less certain.

There is, however, some evidence suggesting that more frequent exposure to price quotes might in fact diminish demand for stocks. Economists Shlomo Benartzi and Richard Thaler have shown that the time pattern of attention to market prices can have important effects on the demand for stocks. In experimental situations, if people are shown daily data on stock prices, they express much less interest in investing in stocks than if they are shown only longer-run returns.[35] Witnessing the day-to-day noise in stock prices apparently encourages more fear about the inherent risk of investing in stocks. Thus, institutional innovations that encourage viewing the market price more frequently might tend to depress the price level of the market.

In contrast, the increased frequency of reporting of stock prices caused by recent institutional and technological changes may have just the opposite effect to that observed in the experimental situation crafted by Benartzi and

Thaler. In a non-experimental setting, where people's focus of attention is not controlled by an experimenter, the increased frequency of price observations may tend to increase the demand for stocks by attracting attention to them. And changing public attention is a critical factor in the valuation of investments, a point that will be elaborated in Chapter 10.

The Rise of Gambling Opportunities

The prevalence of commercial and government-supported gambling was rising around the world during the Millennium Boom.[36] This increasing prevalence parallels an increasing respect for markets and private property, as well as an increasing admiration for "winners" and contempt for "losers."

In the United States, commercial gambling, both legal and illegal, experienced about a sixty-fold increase in real (inflation-corrected) terms between 1962 and 2000.[37] According to a 2000 telephone survey, 82% of adults in the United States gambled in the preceding year, up from 61% in a 1975 study.[38] The amount lost on gambling by people in the United States in 2000 was more than they spent on movie tickets, recorded music, theme parks, spectator sports, and video games combined.[39]

Most forms of gambling and lotteries were outlawed by the states of this country in the 1870s after a scandal in the Louisiana lottery, and the Louisiana national lottery itself was effectively shut down by an 1890 act of Congress prohibiting the sale of lottery tickets by mail. From then until 1970, opportunities to gamble legally were confined largely to racetracks, a form of gambling that has limited public appeal and which, at the time, required travel to a racetrack. But by 1975, there were thirteen state lotteries, and by 1999, there were thirty-seven, offering very convenient and easy means of wagering. Until 1990, legalized casinos operated only in Nevada and Atlantic City. By 1999, there were nearly 100 riverboat and dockside casinos and 260 casinos on Indian reservations. During the same interval, betting at racetracks also expanded dramatically, with the development of off-track betting relying on satellite broadcasts of the races. Cable and Internet wagering on races was possible from home. There was also a proliferation of electronic gambling devices, including slot machines, video poker, video keno, and other stand-alone devices. In some states, these could even be found at truck stops, convenience stores, and lottery outlets. The ubiquity and convenience of gambling opportunities, and the strength of the marketing campaign undertaken to promote gambling, were unprecedented in history.

The rise of gambling institutions, and the increased frequency of actual gambling, had potentially important effects on our culture and on changed attitudes toward risk taking in other areas, such as investing in the stock market. The legalization of gambling in the form of state lotteries has sometimes been observed to help the illegal numbers business, rather than replace it,[40] and thus it might also have promoted other capricious risk-taking activities. Gambling suppresses natural inhibitions against taking risks, and some of the gambling contracts, in particular the lotteries, superficially resemble financial markets: one deals with a computer, one receives a certificate (the lottery ticket), and, in the case of the so-called mega-lottos, one participates in a much-talked-about national phenomenon. Having established a habit of participating in such gambling, it would be natural to graduate to its more upscale form, speculation in securities.

The highest U.S. stock market volatility occurred between 1929 and 1933—when it was more than twice as high as had ever been previously recorded. This period of volatility occurred during a "gambling craze" that was brought on not by legalization, but by the organized crime that was inadvertently created by the prohibition of alcoholic beverages from 1920 to 1933.[41] The criminal gangs that grew after 1920 to satisfy the nation's thirst for alcohol found it natural to branch out into numbers games or speakeasy versions of craps and roulette. Organized crime developed a modern and efficient distribution, marketing, and retail system to supply the nation at large with liquor, going far beyond its traditional neighborhood strongholds, and this same infrastructure served to facilitate illegal gambling activities on a much larger scale. Certainly the widespread disrespect for the law fostered by Prohibition helped legitimize gambling.

A spillover from gambling to financial volatility may come about because gambling, and the institutions that promote it, yield an inflated estimate of one's own ultimate potential for good luck, a heightened interest in how one performs compared with others, and a new way to stimulate oneself out of a feeling of boredom or monotony. At the end of the 1990s, people were constantly subjected to highly professional advertisements that tried to foster such attitudes, even radio and television advertisements that depict typical gamblers' self-justifications as expressed by professional actors. These marketing efforts, and the experience of gambling or seeing others gamble, may well have the effect of encouraging frivolous risk-taking behavior in the stock market as well. Such ads were sometimes startlingly explicit. In 1999, near the peak of the stock market, a Connecticut billboard advertising off-track betting touted it, in big letters, as being "Like the Stock Market, Only Faster."

Precipitating Factors That Propelled the Ownership-Society Boom, 2003–7

When the second edition of this book came out in 2005, five years after I compiled the above list, I felt that some of the twelve precipitating factors whose psychological impacts were driving the market had gone away or had diminished. The Internet boom was still going strong, but the most optimistic inferences had become discredited by the bursting of the dot-com bubble. The Republican majority in both chambers in Congress, with its highly pro-business predilections, was gone. The 2006 election created a Democratic majority in both chambers. The triumph of capitalism in the former Soviet Union and China was now no longer news. But many of the precipitating factors were still operative. These factors need not have changed for the market to have turned down between 2000 and 2003—as we shall see in the next chapter, on amplification mechanisms—and these precipitating factors may still have been around to help with the upturn from 2003 to 2007.

Other boosts to the market, other precipitating factors, also appeared after 2003, as described in the second edition of this book. These additional factors also revved up both the stock market and the housing market.

The Ownership Society

The capitalist ideal at the beginning of the twenty-first century seemed to be evolving into an even more extreme ideal, one in which the value of our private property has a bigger influence on our lives. We had witnessed the demise of traditional communism and socialism, the decline in labor unions, and the end of the cooperative movement and other communal social movements. But now we witnessed such capitalist innovations as online auctions and brokerages.

President George W. Bush named this new society the "ownership society" and featured this phrase prominently in his successful 2004 presidential reelection campaign: "And there is a source of upward mobility in America that comes with ownership. When a woman owns her own business she's upwardly mobile. When a Latino or an African American starts his or her own business they become upwardly mobile. Ownership is a powerful part of the American Dream."[42]

Bush wanted to see homeownership extended to a larger portion of our society, and he tried (and failed) to alter the structure of Social Security to encourage people to invest in the stock market through individual retirement savings accounts. This model saw private property extending far beyond its traditional realm, into health savings accounts and school vouchers. Economists have extolled the virtues of private property in aligning incentives and creating committed citizens, and these ideas shaped public policy then.[43]

This political philosophy did not emphasize the importance of government monitoring of mortgage lending practices. Regulators in the years leading up to the financial crisis of 2007–9 left the rapidly growing subprime lenders in the United States to their own ambitious devices, allowing them to take great risks to make it possible for more people to own homes, by giving mortgages to borrowers having poor credit ratings or poorly documented mortgage applications.

Feeling that they had increasingly to rely on their own resources, people felt themselves less secure. They felt increasingly thrust into a rapidly changing world job market that might make them rich—or might suddenly dump them. In a survey of homebuyers in 2004, Karl Case and I asked: "Do you worry that your (or your household's) ability to earn as much income in future years as you expect might be in danger because of changes in the economy (someone in China competing for your job, a computer replacing your job, etc.)?" Nearly half of our 442 respondents (48%) said they were worried. Some of them said that one motivation for buying their house was the sense of security that homeownership provides in the face of the other insecurities.[44]

Paradoxically, the fears that drove people to look to investments for security in an increasingly capitalist economy may actually have lowered the personal savings rate, since the demand-induced increase in the price of their investments may have given them an illusion that they were saving through the appreciation of their assets. The increases in home values in the early 2000s far exceeded the amounts people were saving from their paychecks. The appreciation in households' real estate holdings from 2001 to 2003 increased U.S. household wealth on average ten times as much as personal savings did in that period.[45] For homeowners, actually saving from one's paycheck for the future seemed almost irrelevant in view of the increase in asset values that came from doing nothing more than just buying and holding.

Supportive Monetary Policy

Alan Greenspan continued to be Chair of the Federal Reserve until 2006, thus guiding the economy for most of the 2003–7 expansion. His reputation for believing in free markets thus remained as one of the reasons for thinking that the stock market, or the housing boom, would not be stifled by the Fed, even as the price-earnings ratio grew alarmingly high. His reputation increasingly encouraged optimism for the markets.

During the boom years of the late 1990s, Alan Greenspan and his Federal Open Market Committee (FOMC) had done nothing to stop the growth of the stock market until the very end, watching the dramatic bull market charge for over four years without any effort to rein it in. On the contrary, it appeared to many people during the Ownership-Society Boom that the Fed would act only to prevent a drop in the market, because of the fears Greenspan had mentioned that such a drop would impair the real economy.

Greenspan talked repeatedly of the "flexibility" of the U.S. economy. "The more flexible an economy," he said in a 2005 speech, "the greater its ability to self-correct after inevitable, often unanticipated disturbances."[46] The implication was that he would do nothing as Fed Chair to stop the Ownership-Society Boom.

Many thought that Greenspan was so supportive of the stock market that his presence as Fed chair was as good as having a put on the stock market to protect us from stock market declines. The rationale behind this talk of the Greenspan put was that Greenspan had used his power to prevent a stock market debacle: in 1987, after the stock market crash; in 1998, after the Russian debt crisis and the collapse of Long Term Capital Management, the flagship hedge fund; and on the eve of the millennium, when he took steps to prevent the "Y2K crisis." It was thought that he had proven through his actions that he would never let the market fall sharply.

Later, of course, some people would also credit him for cutting interest rates very aggressively on January 3, 2001, when the evidence of a recession on the horizon was only rather weak. In fact, the rate cut came two months before the beginning of the recession of 2001. The stock market was indeed significantly buoyed by the news that the Fed would cut rates so aggressively, and the NASDAQ index experienced its largest one-day increase ever: 14%. Ultimately, the Fed cut interest rates as the stock market fell, to a low of 1% by 2003. This aggressive rate cut, which put real (inflation-corrected) interest rates well into negative territory, was probably a significant contributing factor to the housing boom after 2001.

Expansionary monetary policy has not been a consistent factor in asset price booms. A 2003 study by Adam Posen of the Institute for International Economics concluded that of twenty-four stock market booms around the world since 1970, only six were accompanied by monetary easing, and of eighteen property price booms, again only six.[47] But his conclusion in no way contradicts my conclusion that the generally supportive stance of Alan Greenspan and other central bankers was a contributing factor both to the Millennium Boom and to the Ownership-Society Boom that came on its heels.

Precipitating Factors That Propelled the New-Normal Boom

After the 2007–9 stock market crash, stock markets around the world began another dizzy climb upward. The puzzle in understanding this is that the climb upward occurred while the world economy was still depressed from the financial crisis, and nations were increasingly troubled by political impasses and, after the Arab Spring revolts in 2011, roiled by heightened tensions internationally. The new precipitating factors this time had to do particularly with the decline in fears of an acute financial crisis and with the government policies to try to cure it, as well as with some new impressions of the technological revolution and the insecurity of our jobs. The new precipitating factors seem

less starry-eyed-everything-is-wonderful than was the case for the events leading up to the 2000 peak.

From Depression Scare to New Normal

At the height of the 2007–9 financial crisis, national leaders across the world
talked of the risk of a repeat of the Great Depression of the 1930s. They did so
because they needed to get support for their controversial economic stimulus
policies and efforts to bail out failing financial institutions. But by 2009, this
talk had quite a serious effect on public confidence, and there was genuine
anxiety that, despite the governments' efforts, there would indeed be another
Great Depression and another 1929-style stock market crash.

In 2009, the University of Michigan Consumer Sentiment survey found a
sharp increase in the percentage of Americans who worried about a repeat
of the Great Depression. Their question was: "Looking ahead, which would
you say is more likely—that in the country as a whole we'll have continuous
good times during the next five years or so, or that we will have periods of
widespread unemployment or recession, or what?"[48] The confidence index that
the Michigan survey administrators derive from answers to this question fell
in 2009 to its lowest value since the recession of 1990–91 and then followed an
irregular trend upward for the next five years.

Under the auspices of the International Center for Finance at the Yale School
of Management, I have constructed a number of indices of high-income investor
confidence from our questionnaire surveys. We regularly survey both high-
income individual and institutional investors in the United States. One of the
indices is a "crash confidence" index, which is based on the question: "What do
you think is the probability of a catastrophic stock market crash in the U.S., like
that of October 28, 1929 or October 19, 1987, in the next six months, including
the case that a crash occurs in the other countries and spreads to the U.S.?"[49]

In 2009, crash confidence set a record low (the surveys began in 1989), both
for individual and institutional investors, and then started an irregular trend
upward for the next five years. The market may have been low in 2009, but
people were temporarily really worried then in the heat of the most extreme
moments of the financial crisis that it could fall much lower.

The U.S. Federal Reserve launched a series of "stress tests" of financial
institutions, starting with the Supervisory Capital Assessment Program in
2009. Miraculously, these tests concluded that many bank holding companies had adequate capital to survive even an adverse economic scenario, and
others were given an estimated amount of capital to raise so that they, too,
could survive. The stress tests reassured markets.

U.S. corporate earnings, which had almost hit zero for the S&P 500 in
2009, rebounded quickly as companies instituted policies of cost cutting to
restore earnings and investor confidence. Massive layoffs of their employees

helped restore profits but led to high unemployment and a loss of consumer confidence. The cost cutting may also have lowered profits in the longer run, if the companies lost the help of these employees in preserving long-term value, but only time will tell if this has happened. However, the cost cutting did restore accounting earnings quickly, which was interpreted as a favorable sign by many investors who were looking for signs of hope at a fearful time.

In 2009 Bill Gross, founder of the investment management firm PIMCO, now at Janus Capital, summed up this weak optimism, which he called the "new normal": "it's time to recognize that things have changed and that they will continue to change for the next—yes, the next 10 years and maybe even the next 20 years. We are heading into what we call the New Normal, which is a period of time in which economies grow very slowly as opposed to growing like weeds, the way children do."[50]

The same moderately optimistic situation did not prevail in Europe, where the sovereign debt crisis intervened in 2010, leading to great worries of long-term stagnation there. Hence, the rebound in the stock markets after 2009 was not uniform around the world, and European stock markets still tend to be less highly priced as of this writing.

Extremely Loose Monetary Policy and Quantitative Easing

Short-term interest rates were driven to virtually zero in the New Normal by the Federal Reserve and other central banks through open market policy in response to the 2007–9 financial crisis. Long-term interest rates began to follow them down. In 2008, the Fed announced the first of its three quantitative easing programs, which had the Fed buying mortgage securities and treasury securities. Ultimately, through such purchases, the Fed increased its assets from less than one trillion dollars to over four trillion dollars, a radical departure from past practice.

In 2008, the Fed began a policy of "forward guidance," of preannouncing that it would not raise interest rates for some time to come, thereby encouraging long-term interest rates to fall more than they otherwise would. Ten-year Treasury yields fell to an all-time record low of 1.43% in July 2012, from over 5% before the crisis in 2007–9. The result was a situation in which most investors felt very disappointed with their return on bond investments, leading to a "reach for yield" attitude after the crisis. Even though the stock market was still perceived as risky, many thought that at least it had some real upside potential, encouraging them to buy stocks at higher and higher earnings multiples.

The very fact that U.S. long-term home mortgage rates in the fall of 2012 were at all-time record lows created an unprecedented demand for housing, despite a still-weak economy, since prospective homebuyers did not want to lose out on an opportunity that was perceived as once-in-a-lifetime.

End-of-Career Anxieties

The 2007–9 financial crisis spawned a massive decline in the labor force participation rate in the United States, from 66.4% in January 2007 to 62.8% in June 2014, according to the U.S. Bureau of Labor Statistics. The anxieties of being out of the labor force (or suspecting that one might soon be) may help further propel the "reaching for yield" in investing that low interest rates have already encouraged: people may take greater risks with their investments to keep alive a hope of living comfortably for years into the future without employment. The meaning of the term "reaching for yield" seems to have shifted somewhat around the time of the New-Normal Boom. It was most often used to describe investing in high-interest-rate bonds or mortgages with diminished regard for their risk. Now, with real interest rates near zero, it is more often used to describe aggressive investing in risky stocks or complicated new investment products.

Part of this decline in the percentage of the population working is due to the long-expected retirement of Baby Boomers. But there is another, more worrisome component. Those laid off during or after the 2007–9 financial crisis may have viewed the experience as the end of an era, because many layoffs have been described as long-term cost cutting—the corporation becoming leaner and meaner—not as jobs that are likely to come back when the crisis recedes. Those losing jobs may have felt that in the current economy it would be pointless to start retraining for a different job. They may have retired earlier than they planned, sometimes much earlier, perhaps by claiming disabilities. The U.S. Social Security Administration has documented a significant increase in disability benefit applications since the financial crisis.

Even for young people, there are vivid, psychologically salient, new career risks that are apparently increasing a desire to save, and a wishful-thinking bias toward speculative investments like stocks. New job-replacing technology has been highly visible. Particularly noticeable is the rapid expansion of mobile connections to computers and the Internet, with tablet computers, smart phones, and soon even Google Glass. These are vivid new images in our minds, because everywhere one goes in 2014 one sees people fiddling with these devices, which were not so prominent before 2009. One now even hears people talking to their devices. Apple introduced their automated assistant "Siri" for the iPhone in 2011. I now can talk to my mobile phone in my pocket and ask, "OK: what is the traffic to work like right now?" and a voice comes out from my pocket, providing the estimated driving time to work (it already knows where I am and where I work and the best route to work). One naturally wonders: where is all this technology going, and what jobs will it replace?

Other technological talk since the Ownership-Society Boom has raised further existential angst about employment. Testing of driverless cars on public streets began in 2011. The Massachusetts Institute of Technology's Computer

Science and Artificial Intelligence Laboratory has more recently unveiled a BakeBot robot that can bake a cake in a conventional kitchen, and the lab is working on a robot that will change a baby's diapers.[51]

Most people have some new worries about their jobs since the New-Normal Boom began in 2009, and that increased worry probably should be on the list of precipitating factors for the stock market boom (as well as being considered as a source of weakness for the aggregate economy).

Many people are accustomed to thinking that bad news about projected future employment income, or bad news about its uncertainty, should tend to push stock prices down rather than up, but economic theory (as explicated by Robert E. Lucas, for example) suggests just the opposite.[52] One might call this a "life preservers on the Titanic theory." When passengers on a ship think the vessel is in danger of sinking, a life preserver, a table, or anything that floats may suddenly become extremely valuable, and not because these assets have changed their physical attributes. Similarly, at a time when people are worried about the sustainability of their labor income, and there are not enough really good investment opportunities, they may tend to bid up prices of all manner of existing long-term assets in their efforts to save for the dangerous lean years seen ahead. They may not manage to save more in real terms. They may hold such assets even if they now believe the assets are overpriced and in danger of losing value in the future.

The actual effects of changes in perceived risk further depend on psychological and sociological factors. The perceived increase in risks in the employment market—the perceptions of rapid technological and industrial change—have broad cultural effects that are sometimes blamed for other problems as well, such as the rise of nationalism around the world and a tendency to aggression between nations, as exemplified by the 2014 conflict in Ukraine and tensions in many other places.[53]

Rising Inequality

Quite apart from the effect of the general fear people have of losing out in the economy of the future, there is a related effect of the rising inequality that may be directly connected to rising asset prices. The current trend, which started in the United States and other countries around the time of the Ronald Reagan presidency in 1981 and of the beginning of the Millennium Bubble in 1982, is that of a steady increase in labor income inequality. As shown by Thomas Piketty in his 2014 book *Capital in the Twenty-First Century*, there was a clear turning point upward at that time in the earnings of the top 1% of incomes in the United States, and the trend was closely related to an uptrend in the share of the top wage percentile in the total wage bill.[54] According to Piketty's data, the last time such an increase occurred in the share of income going to the top 1% was in the 1920s, which corresponded roughly to the bull market of the Roaring Twenties, and inequality of total income and of labor income peaked around the peak of the market in 1929.

There are a number of mechanisms by which a rise in the share of income going to the top 1% could give an upward impulse to asset prices. Higher income people tend to save more, as Piketty emphasized, and if there are not enough available opportunities for new investments, then as time goes on and there are more and more such people, they could bid up the value of the existing capital stock. The advent of a new rich class could change the politics—or the perceived politics—of the future, to incent regulators to favor business, making the outlook for after-tax profit higher. The higher inequality may be related to lower business moral standards and greater willingness of businesses to play games with their earnings statements. The perceptions of inequality may favor people with modest incomes "reaching for yield" with a wishful-thinking bias in their investments.

But the effect of income inequality on asset prices is not entirely clear. Public awareness of rising inequality increased dramatically during the New-Normal Boom after 2009. Notably, the Occupy Wall Street movement of 2011–13, in the United States and other countries, with its slogan "We are the ninety-nine percent," may mark the beginning of a time when the repugnance toward inequality is more important in politics, and when government policy will be less favorable to investors. The prospect of government policy hurting asset values in the future may adversely affect their prices today. On the other hand—surprisingly to some—the capture of both houses of the U.S. Congress by Republicans seems to suggest a shift in public policy against redistributive policies and toward a policy of protecting wealth and thus supporting asset prices.

The Rise of Nationalism and War Stirrings

A final precipitating factor for the New-Normal Boom should also be mentioned, though it too has ambiguous effects on the pricing of asset markets. To the alarm of many people, we see now, in a number of countries, the rise of nationalistic and xenophobic political parties. In some cases exaggerated stories of abuses of nationals in foreign countries is a new source of anger and conflict, and in other cases weakly controlled immigration is increasingly resented.

This change may be indirectly caused by the effects on popular psychology of some of the precipitating factors listed above: the 2007–9 financial crisis with the economic crisis that has continued after it, the end-of-career fears associated with globalization and advancing technology, and the rising inequality.

As Benjamin Friedman documented in his 2005 book *The Moral Consequences of Economic Growth*, prolonged periods of disappointing economic growth seem to be periods of public anger and increasing intolerance toward minority groups or other countries. These periods can then descend into unrest, terrorism, or war. Rising inequality associated with rapid economic growth may be bearable, he argues, but may become unbearable as growth slows.

At the time of this writing we have now recently seen an outbreak of wars in Gaza, Iraq, Israel, Syria, and Ukraine, the establishment of a terrorist Islamic State, and an associated rise in terrorist threats around the world. We can only hope that we do not see more of these events in the future.

Such events have already created anxieties that may have propelled asset prices up even further, as people have tried to find a safety net for themselves, bidding prices of existing assets up rather than successfully saving. But it is also possible that this sense of unrest may have had the net effect of encouraging people to hold their assets in more liquid form. Some may even have feared confiscation or wartime taxation, and long-term asset prices might have been adversely affected.

The stock markets of the world collapsed in the summer of 1914, when World War I broke out in Europe. In contrast, some of the world stock markets soared on the day when World War II officially began.[55] On Sunday, September 3, 1939, Great Britain, France, India (which included today's Bangladesh and Pakistan), Australia, and New Zealand declared war on Germany, which was defying demands to evacuate its forces from Poland. When U.S. markets opened after Labor Day, on Tuesday, September 5, the S&P Composite Stock Price Index rose 9.63%, one of its biggest one-trading-day increases in history.

We can only hope that nothing as dramatic as those events is in store for us. But we will have just to wait and see how evolving conflicts develop and play out in public imagination and then later, through amplification mechanisms, have their effects on markets.

Summing Up

Looking back at the list of potential precipitating factors for the three recent booms, in the stock market, bond market, and real estate, one may be struck by the sheer multiplicity of factors that appear to have been at work. It is worth remembering that there is no air-tight science of speculative market pricing. We have certainly made progress in understanding these markets, but the complexity of real life continues to prevail.

Many of the factors that led to these booms had a self-fulfilling aspect to them, and they are thus difficult, if not impossible, to capture in predictive scientific explanations. Yet many of them also have indisputable markers. The Internet boom, the rise of online trading, the Republican Congress, and the proposed capital gains tax cuts occurred just as the stock market started its most breathtaking ascent in the 1990s. Other factors—including the rise of

Figure 5.1
Stocks as Best Investment, 1996–2014

Percentage of U.S. high-income individuals who said they agreed with the state-ment, "The stock market is the best investment for long-term holders, who can just buy and hold through the ups and downs of the market," along with the real S&P 500 Stock Price Index. *Source:* Author's calculations using surveys conducted at Yale International Center for Finance, Standard & Poor's, U.S. Bureau of Labor Statistics.

investors' thinking: the notion that stocks are the "best investment" and inves-tors cannot go wrong with them over the long run. This idea appears in sharp contrast to the notion that seemed to prevail in the late 1970s, after the stock market crash of 1973–74, when most people appear to have thought that real estate was the "best investment." But I was not doing questionnaire surveys then, so I do not have evidence of what they thought then.

Starting in 1996, after concluding that the belief that stocks are the best investment and cannot fail had become a real staple of popular culture, it occurred to me that I ought to tabulate how belief in this simple notion has changed through time. I added a question to my high-income individual investor questionnaire, asking whether the respondent agreed with the state-ment, "The stock market is the best investment for long-term holders, who can just buy and hold through the ups and downs of the market." The data I collected, and that are now being updated by the Yale School of Management, are shown in Figure 5.1.

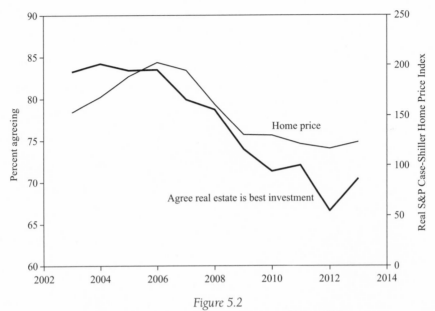

Figure 5.2
Real Estate as Best Investment, 2003–2013
Percentage of recent U.S. homebuyers who said they agreed with the statement, "Real estate is the best investment for long-term holders, who can just buy and hold through the ups and downs of the market," along with the real Case-Shiller/S&P Home Price Indices. *Source:* Author's calculations using surveys conducted at Yale International Center for Finance, Standard & Poor's, U.S. Bureau of Labor Statistics.

Agreement that stocks are the best investment during the boom years leading to 2000 was obviously very strong. Fully 97% of the respondents agreed in the peak year of the market, 2000. A 97% level of agreement with just about any statement put forth in a survey question is remarkable, and it is all the more so when the statement is about something as personal as investing strategy.[2] After the market started to sag, the strength of agreement with this statement also started to sag. The percentage of respondents who agreed fell from 97% in 2000 to 72% in 2011. Belief in the stock market is still strong (I would conclude that irrational exuberance is still here), though it is eroding. But the point here that stock price changes feed back into corresponding changes in long-term optimism is well supported by this evidence.

During the recent housing boom, my colleague Karl Case and I asked essentially the same question about real estate as we had about stocks as a part of a survey of a random sample of recent homebuyers in each of four cities—Boston, Los Angeles, Milwaukee, and San Francisco.

Figure 5.3
Opinion of Aftermath of a Stock Market Crash, 1996–2014
Percentage of high-income U.S. investors who agree "If there is another crash like October 19, 1987, the market will surely be back up to its former levels in a couple years or so," along with the real S&P 500 Stock Price Index. *Source:* Author's calculations using surveys conducted at Yale International Center for Finance, Standard & Poor's, U.S. Bureau of Labor Statistics.

As shown in Figure 5.2, we find the same striking correlation between prices and opinions about best investment: generally when home prices are going up, the percentage who think real estate is the best investment also goes up. When home prices are going down, the percentage who think real estate is the best investment goes down too. This is feedback.[3]

Associated with these "best investment" views is a feeling that prices always go up in the longer run, if not immediately, and this belief varies through time and across markets. As part of our survey of high-income investors, we asked the following question: "How much do you agree with this statement? 'If there is another crash like October 19, 1987, the market will surely be back up to its former levels in a couple years or so.'" Figure 5.3 shows the responses.

The agreement with this statement roughly tracks the market. When the market was near its peak in 1999, near the end of the Millennium Boom, 88% agreed with this statement. After 2000, when the stock market started sliding, the percentage who agreed also started sliding, to 69%, by 2004. When the stock market rose with the Ownership-Society Boom, the percentage who agreed started increasing as well, to 76% in 2007. When the market corrected down after 2007, so did the percentage agreeing, though it was not until 2012 that agreement fell to its lowest point of 56%. Eventually, with the New-Normal Boom, the percentage agreement recovered to 68% in 2014. A rising market seems indeed to foster a sort of complacency: there may be drops in the market, but there is an increase in the blithe assurance that any such downturns do not matter in the longer run. Falling markets seem to damage this complacency, even though the falling markets themselves do not add observations about how the market will behave after a major crash.

It is curious that people do not seem to believe the converse of the premise stated in our question: they do not believe that the market will surely go back down in a couple of years if it goes up dramatically.[4] Their belief in the resilience of the market seems to stem from a generalized feeling of optimism and assurance, rather than a belief in the long-run stability of prices.

There is some evidence suggesting that in 1929—the peak of the bull stock market of the 1920s—many people felt as certain about the long-run success of the stock market as did people in the late 1990s. Although we do not have survey data from the time, we do have contemporary accounts of investor confidence. In his 1931 history of the 1920s, *Only Yesterday*, Frederick Lewis Allen wrote:

> As people in the summer of 1929 looked back for precedents, they were comforted by the recollection that every crash of the past few years had ultimately brought prices to a new high point. Two steps up, one step down, two steps up again—that was how the market went. If you sold, you had only to wait for the next crash (they came every few months) and buy in again. And there was really no reason to sell at all: you were bound to win in the end if your stock was sound. The really wise man, it appeared, was he who "bought and held on."[5]

Some Reflections on Investor Confidence

It is important to consider the nature, and likely sources, of the changes we have observed in investor confidence, not only to understand the present situation but also to lead us into a discussion, later in this chapter, of feedback loops. We will see that the feedback that reinforces investor confidence occurs in the context of a complex social and psychological environment.

Where did people get the idea that, if there is ever a stock market crash, the market is sure to rise to past levels within a couple of years or so? History certainly does not suggest this. There are many examples of markets that have done poorly over long intervals of time. To pick just one from recent memory, the Nikkei index in Japan is still selling at less than half its peak value in 1989. Other examples are the periods after the 1929 and 1966 stock market peaks discussed in Chapter 1. However, during a booming market, these examples of persistent bad performance in the stock market are not prominent in the public mind.

One reason that the recent domestic market performance is more prominent in investors' minds is simply that they have *experienced* these domestic stock prices every day. During the bull stock market of the 1990s, they watched and reacted to a U.S. market that had been rising since 1982. U.S. investors of the 1990s did not have the same experience with Japanese stocks, or with the U.S. market of decades past. Many people fixed their attention on plots of rising stock prices in newspapers every day, and they seemed to come away with an intuitive feeling that every decline is reversed, to be followed swiftly by new highs. The same human pattern-recognition faculty that we used when we learned to ride a bike or to drive a car, giving us an intuitive sense of what to expect next, shapes our expectations for the market. For investors in the middle years of their lives in the 1990s, this upward trend characterized most of the years they had been observing or investing in the market.

The subjective experience over the years of seeing stock market declines consistently reverse themselves has a psychological impact on our thinking that is hard to appreciate, or reconstruct, after the fact. Those who thought the market would go down and stay down became sensitized to their bad feelings from being repeatedly wrong, year after year. Those who consistently predicted a decline became painfully aware of a loss of reputation from being so wrong so often. Since our satisfaction with our views of the world is part of our self-esteem and personal identity, it is natural for the formerly pessimistic to want to settle on a different view, or at least to present themselves to the public with a different theme. Thus, the changed emotional environment will have an impact on their views—or certainly the expression of them—that is independent of any objective evidence supporting or refuting those views.

Even if they had not personally paid attention to the stock market since 1982, the investors of the booming stock market of the 1990s were living in a time and place where recitations of the feelings of others who had experienced the market were heard regularly. To appreciate this sense, it is helpful to quote one person's argument against market timing, from the 1999 book *Dow 40,000* by David Elias:

> An example of what can happen when an individual waits for the Dow to indicate "the perfect time" to invest is the saga of Joe, a friend of mine. Joe started calling me in 1982 when the Dow was just over 1000, looking for the right time to get into equities. Over the years, he continued to seek a pullback that would be his perfect moment. Today, at age 62, Joe still has his money parked in bank CDs. He has missed the entire bull market and all its thousand-point milestones. Even now, Joe does not realize that there never is a perfect time. When the market recovers from a pullback, it generally goes to new highs.[6]

There is something superficially convincing about this passage, especially when it is combined, as in the next paragraph in Elias's book, with illustrations of the power of compound interest when returns are high (as they had recently been in the stock market when that book was written), suggesting that the stock market is your chance to become really and truly rich. The tale has emotional immediacy, as would a story about a driving mistake that led to a serious accident or a story about the advantages of asking the boss for a raise.

A related reason why an argument built around such a story has such appeal is that by presenting successful investing as a process of mastering one's own internal impulses rather than taking account of our present situation in history, it invites the reader to forget what is special about the present time in terms of the level of the market. Normal people think a lot about controlling their own impulses—for example, about disciplining themselves to perform good work rather than wasting time, about staying slim rather than getting fat—and so arguments that appeal to such self-control have more resonance than articles about the history of price-earnings ratios. The appeal of Elias's argument is also that it calls to mind the pain of regret, the emotional reasons we have for investing *now*, a point to which I will return later in this chapter. When arguments become so detached from an analysis of historical data, the only impact on people's thinking made by actual data is a vague sense, from casual inspection of very recent data, that the market has always reversed declines.

Many media accounts routinely tell stories about the satisfaction felt by those who have invested in stocks in years past, with the clear suggestion to the reader that "you can do it too." To cite only one among numerous examples, a 1999 article in *USA Weekend*, a national Sunday magazine insert for newspapers, carried an article titled "How to (Really) Get Rich in America." The article gave examples of investor successes and offered the hypothetical story of a twenty-two-year-old college graduate earning $30,000 a year with annual real income raises of 1%. "If she saved only 10% of her income and invested the savings in an S&P index fund she'd have a net worth of $1.4 million on retirement at age 67, in today's dollars."[7] These calculations assume that the S&P index fund earns a risk-free 8% real (inflation-corrected) return. There is no mention of the possibility that the return might not be so high over time, and that the investor might *not* end up a millionaire. An article with a very similar title, "Everybody Ought to Be Rich," appeared in the *Ladies' Home Journal* in 1929.[8] It performed comparable calculations, yet similarly omitted to describe the possibility that anything could go wrong in the long term. The article became notorious after the 1929 crash.

These seemingly convincing discussions of potential increases in the stock market are rarely offered in the abstract, but instead in the context of stories about successful or unsuccessful investors, and often with an undertone suggesting the moral superiority of those who invested well. A strong public admiration for those who make money patiently and slowly, unfazed by market fluctuations, has evolved. It is a theme developed in many popular books. Notable among these is *The Millionaire Next Door: The Surprising Secrets of America's Wealthy* by Thomas Stanley and William Danko, which was on the *New York Times* hardcover best-seller list for eighty-eight weeks after its publication in 1996 and continued on the *Times* paperback best-seller list until May 2001, that is, until after the peak of the stock market. The book, which extolled the virtues of patience and frugality, sold over a million copies in its heyday.[9]

Indeed, such stories of patient investing transcended U.S. borders. In Germany, the 1999 best-seller *The Road to Financial Freedom: A Millionaire in Seven Years* by Bodo Schäfer set a seven-year horizon for investors and gave as the first of ten "golden rules" the dictum that any stock market decline must soon be reversed. A new edition of this book was issued in 2003, but this time without the subtitle, *A Millionaire in Seven Years,* apparently because four years had gone by and readers were generally a lot less close to becoming millionaires. Another German book from 1999, *No Fear of the Next Crash: Why Stocks Are Unbeatable as Long-Term Investments* by Bernd Niquet, devoted itself entirely to the theme that patient investing in stocks always wins.[10]

In viewing the popular expressions of confidence in the market, whether from the 1990s or the 1920s, and in trying to understand how people felt about them at the time, it is important to bear in mind that in most cases the statements of confidence in the stock market that we see are not the focal point of attention in the contexts in which they appear. Thus, for example, Suze Orman has built a remarkable reputation for herself by stressing the emotional and spiritual steps one should take to acquire a fortune. Since the 1990s, Orman has been a highly successful investment adviser and a best-selling author, with books like *The 9 Steps to Financial Freedom* (1997) and *The Courage to Be Rich: Creating a Life of Material and Spiritual Abundance* (1999) and, after 2002, following the peak of the stock market, with her own cable TV show, *The Suze Orman Show.* Her concrete advice is to get out of debt and into stocks, and her example of the power of compound interest with a rate of return of 10% is never the focus of attention. Most of her audience is apparently interested in her spiritual message, and her confronting their difficulty with saving is on target and attention-grabbing for them. Her assumption that the market will surely produce a return of 10% a year is mere background information that her viewers and readers do not have the time or the inclination to examine. The repetition that she and others like her give to this assumption nonetheless promotes it to the status of conventional wisdom.

Survey Evidence about Expectations

In my surveys of U.S. high-income individuals and institutional investors, we have found some evidence of changes in expectations for the stock market.

We ask investors, in open-ended questions, about their expectations for the Dow for various horizons. We do not ask them to select from categories or ranges of price increase; they have to come up with a number on their own, without our suggesting anything. In the 1989 survey of individual investors, the average expected one-year-ahead change in the Dow was 0.0%. In 1996, it was 4.1%, in 2000 it was 6.7%, and in 2001 it was 8.4%. Thus, average expectations for stock market appreciation rose quite substantially from 1989 to just after the peak of the stock market in 2000. After that, the individual one-year-ahead expectations fell somewhat—to 6.4% in 2004. Institutional investors did not show this pattern of changing expectations, perhaps because their greater professionalism inclines them to rely on authoritative analysis for the expectations they report to others.

Some might be surprised at how modest the average reported expectations among individuals were, no expectation of an increase at all in 1989, and only 8.4% even just after the peak of the market. This does not fit the usual assumptions about irrational exuberance. But, looking at the individual answers, it seems obvious why the averages were so low. In 1989, 34% of the individuals said they thought the market would go *down* in the next year, and many of them predicted major declines. The individuals who thought it would not fall reported average expectations for an increase of 10.0%. The large number of pessimists brought the average expectation for *all* respondents down to zero.

In 1996, the percentage of individuals who said they thought that the market would decline fell somewhat, to 29%. But, among those who said they thought that the market would not fall, the average one-year expectation was about the same as in 1989, 9.3%. Fewer pessimists meant that the average expectation for all respondents rose from 1989.

By 2001, the percentage of individuals who thought that the market would decline fell much further, to 7.4%. Among those who said they thought that the market would not fall, the average expectation was still about the same: 10.1%. The sharply reduced number of pessimists caused the average expectation to increase to 8.4%.

By 2004, the percentage of individuals who thought that the market would decline was even lower than in 2001, at 7.1%. Now, the average expectation was brought down from its 2001 level by a decline in expectations of those who thought that the market would not fall, to 7.3%.

It seems that most of the expectations for an increase have stayed roughly the same, near what experts would say is the historical average return, but that there has been a major change in the percentage of respondents reporting that they expect declines. What this survey demonstrates is that growing irrational exuberance until the peak of the market in 2000 just took the form of declining fears of market drops.

It is not surprising that few people answered that they expected the market to go up 20% or 30% in the following year. At a gut level, near the peak of the market some of them no doubt anticipated such increases. But that was just not a respectable answer, not something one would expect to see validated in media accounts of what experts think. The respectable thing to say was that the market would continue to post the same impressive returns it had on average over the previous thirty years or more. It was equally respectable to venture that there could be a correction—one hears that in the media, too—hence the predictions of a decline by some respondents. Did people in fact believe the answers they wrote on the questionnaire? Probably most of them did not know what to believe, and probably they considered their own answers as good as anything else to believe, but harbored other suspicions or hopes that are not captured on the surveys.

The UBS Index of Investor Optimism (formerly called the PaineWebber/Gallup index, before UBS took over PaineWebber in 2000 and then after 2007 replaced the index with the Wells Fargo/Gallup Investor and Retirement Income Optimism Index) reported much more optimistic average expectations among individual investors around the peak of the stock market. Their July 1999 surveys showed that these investors expected on average a 15.0% return on the stock market over the next twelve months. This sounds like quite an optimistic expectation, much higher than that in our surveys. The difference in results may have to do with subtle differences in wording. Their question was: "Thinking about the stock market more generally, what overall rate of return do you think the stock market will provide investors during the coming twelve months?" Ours was: "How much of a change in percentage terms do you expect in the following (use a + before your number to indicate an expected increase, a − to indicate an expected decrease; leave blanks where you do not know)," and the questionnaire then provided spaces to give answers for the Dow for one month, three months, six months, one year, and ten years. Note the different *tone* of the two questions. UBS/Gallup asked respondents for a percentage return. We asked for a percentage change in price. The significant difference between the two questions is probably more than just that return includes dividend while price change does not. Asking respondents what return the market will provide suggests a positive number for an answer. Our question mentioned the possibility that the answer could be negative.

Answers to survey questions can be sensitive to the wording of the questions. But if the wording is kept unchanged over time on the questionnaires, the changes in the answers over time should still be indicative of the direction of changes in expectations. The UBS Index of Investor Optimism confirms the conclusion from our survey that people were getting more optimistic about the stock market until its peak, then less optimistic.

Some Reflections on Investor Expectations and Emotions

Economists usually like to model people as calculating optimally their investment decisions based on expectations of future price changes and estimates of the risk in alternative investments. However, in fact, the typical investor's actual decision about how much to allocate to the stock market overall and to other asset classes, such as bonds, real estate, or other investments, tends not to be based on careful calculations. Investors are not often assembling forecasts for the returns on these different asset classes and weighting these with estimated probabilities.

Part of the reason they are not is that investors more often feel that experts have little or no idea what to expect of future price changes for these asset classes, or how much risk there is in each. After all, experts disagree all the time, and one might easily conclude that there is no great loss in ignoring what they are currently saying about the outlook for any given asset class. Investors must therefore base their judgments on basic principles on which most experts seem always to agree.

The evidence used by experts to predict the relative returns on broad asset classes has little immediacy for most people. Experts talk about the potential actions of the Federal Reserve Board in Washington, about shifts in the Phillips curve, or about distortions on aggregate earnings caused by inflation and conventional accounting procedures. Most individuals have little interest in such esoterica.

And yet investors must make some decisions. What factors might then enter into one's mind when making a decision about how much to put into the stock market? The feeling that the stock market is "the only game in town," in some emotional sense, might play a pivotal role at this point in the decision making.

One knows that the stock market *could* repeat the performance of recent years. That possibility seems quite real, just as real as the possibility of a major correction in the market. But how does one feel about the decision at this point? How does one feel, for example, when one knows, late at night, that it is time to fill out the 401(k) allocation form, and one is tired and annoyed by the necessity to make such an important decision based on so little solid information?

How one feels certainly depends on one's recent experience in investing. If one has been out of the market and has not participated in the profits that others have recently enjoyed, one may be feeling a sharp pain of regret. And regret is an emotion that, psychologists have found, provides considerable motivation.[11]

Envy of others who may have made more in the stock market than one earned at work in the past year is a related painful feeling, especially so in that it diminishes one's own ego. If these people who made so much in the market were really smarter and knew better, then one really feels like a laggard. Even if they were not smarter, just lucky—smiled on by God—it may not feel much better. One can always seek emotional refuge in the thought that it was just luck that made others more successful, and bad luck that accounts for one's own lack of success. But, as Nassim Taleb argued so eloquently in his book *Fooled by Randomness,* our emotions make it difficult for us to benefit from such rationalizations of our failure, and the envy of others' successes just continues to haunt us.[12]

One may feel that if one can participate in just one more year of an advancing stock market—assuming it advances for another year—that will help assuage the pain. Of course, one also thinks that the market may well go down. But how does one weigh the potential emotional expense of such a possible loss at the time that one is making the asset allocation decision?

Perhaps one feels that the potential loss will not be much more damaging to one's ego than the failure to participate has already been. Of course, one likely realizes that one takes the risk of entering the market just as it begins a downward turn. But the psychological cost of such a potential future loss may not be so much greater than the very real regret at having been out of the market in the past. Therefore, although there are many other ways to deal with the thought that one is a "loser," such as rediscovering the importance of being a good friend, spouse, or parent, or pursuing the simple things in life, it may well end up that the only truly emotionally satisfying decision to make now is to get into the stock market.

Of course if one has been in the stock market and is deciding after a boom has gone on for a while whether to stay in the market, one has a very different emotional frame of mind. One feels satisfaction and probably some pride in one's past successes, and one certainly feels wealthier. One may feel as gamblers do after they have raked in winnings: that one is "playing with the house money" and therefore has nothing to lose emotionally by wagering again.[13]

The emotional state of investors when they decide on their investments is no doubt one of the most important factors behind the bull market. Although their emotional state may be in part a consequence of the factors described in the previous chapter, such as the rise of materialistic sentiment and individualism, it is also amplified by the psychological impact of the increasingly strong uptrend observed in the market.

Public Attention to the Market

The level of public interest in and attention to the market changes significantly over time, just as the public's interest jumps from one newsworthy topic to another. Attention shifts from news stories about Jacqueline Kennedy to stories about Princess Diana to stories about Kim Kardashian. Interest in the stock market goes through fads in just the same way, depending on the story quality of the precipitating events.

Some writers have indicated that 1929 was a time of dramatically height-ened investor attention to the stock market. John Kenneth Galbraith, in his 1961 book *The Great Crash: 1929,* wrote:

> By the summer of 1929 the market not only dominated the news. It also dominated the culture. That *recherché* minority which at other times has acknowledged its interest in Saint Thomas Aquinas, Proust, psychoanalysis and psychosomatic medicine then spoke of United Corporation, United Founders and Steel. Only the most aggressive of the eccentrics maintained their detachment from the market and their interest in autosuggestion or communism. Main Street had always had one citizen who could speak knowingly about buying or selling stocks. Now he became an oracle.[14]

That public attention was focused on the stock market in the late 1920s is supported by many other such commentaries. One should bear in mind that Galbraith's 1961 argument contains some journalistic overstatement that he no doubt could not have gotten away with had he been writing in the 1920s. But Galbraith was on the right track in terms of the direction of change over the 1920s.

If one looks at the *Reader's Guide to Periodical Literature* year by year throughout the 1920s, one sees that only a tiny percentage of the articles in periodicals, always less than 0.1%, were about the stock market in any given year. People were thinking about plenty of other things besides the market. However, the percentage of articles concerning the stock market grew markedly over the course of the decade. There were 29 articles about the stock market in 1922–24, or 0.025% of all articles listed; 67 articles in 1925–28, or 0.035% of all articles listed; and 182 articles in 1929–32, or 0.093% of all articles listed. Thus, over the 1920s the percentage of articles about the stock market almost quadrupled.

We see a similar pattern of changed interest in the stock market from an iden-tical study of the *Reader's Guide* in the Millennium Boom market, although the percentage of articles that were about the stock market was higher throughout this period than in the 1920s. In 1982, at the bottom of the stock market, there were 242 articles about the stock market, or 0.194% of all articles. In 1987, the year of the crash, there were 592 articles, or 0.364% of all articles, almost twice as many. After the crash, interest waned again, and there were only 255 articles, or 0.171% of all articles, in 1990. Over the 1990s, the number of articles rose again, somewhat irregularly. There were 451 articles in 2000, or 0.254% of all articles. After 2000, the peak of the market, the number of articles fell. In 2003, there were only 327 articles, or 0.175% of all articles, close to the percentage in 1990.

Another source of evidence on investor attention to the market is the num-ber of investment clubs, as reported by the National Association of Investors Corporation (NAIC), now BetterInvesting. Investment clubs are small social groups, typically meeting at members' homes in the evening, that together invest small sums of money for fun and for the purpose of learning about investments. The NAIC was founded in 1951 by four investor clubs at the beginning of the 1950s bull market; the number of clubs grew to 953 by 1954, reached a peak of 14,102 in 1970 (near the top of the market), and fell with the market to 3,642 in 1980 (near the bottom of the market), a drop of 74%. By 1999, the number of clubs rose up well beyond its prior peak, to 37,129.[15] But by 2004, the number of clubs fell to 23,360, a drop of 37%. The crude conformity of the number of investment clubs to the performance of the market is noteworthy, confirming that investors' attention is indeed attracted by bull markets and deflected by bear markets. The drop in the number of clubs after 2000 was smaller than between 1970 and 1980, suggesting that as of 2004 investor interest in the market had not yet fallen as far yet, and this fact might be considered consistent with the smaller decline since 2000 in the price-earnings ratio as well.

Investment clubs did not recover after the Millennium Bubble. Membership in these clubs have fallen every year since 1998, despite major upswings in the market in 2003–7 and 2009–14. As of 2013, memberships are down over 90% from the peak in 1998. This decline suggests that the resurgences of the stock market in 2003–7 and 2009–14 are fundamentally different, less entertaining or social, from the Millennium Bubble, just as the real estate boom of 2012–14 appears less so when compared with the huge boom in 1997–2006.[16]

When people first experience success in any area, there is of course a natural tendency for them to take new initiatives and develop their skills in hopes of achieving more such success. In a study of investors who switched from phone to online trading, comparing them with investors who continued to use telephones to make their trades, economists Brad Barber and Terrance Odean found that the switchers on average had been beating the market by over 2% a year. After they went on line, these switchers traded more speculatively and actively, and then proceeded to lag the market by more than 3% annually.[17] This finding may be interpreted as showing that overconfidence from past success encourages people to expend the fixed cost of learning about online trading. Having acquired these capabilities and interests, they are likely to pay greater attention to the market for a sustained period, measured in years, in order to see that their skills in investment "pay off."

Near the peak of the market, around 1999, it seemed that conversations about the stock market were everywhere. I used to play a game then with my wife: when we went out to a restaurant to eat, I would predict that someone at an adjacent table would be talking about the stock market. I did not listen to others' conversations, but I developed an ability to hear the word "stock market." Usually I was able to catch it. Bringing up the stock market was seen then as an accepted, even mildly exciting, conversational gambit. The market was an agreeable topic. Five years later, bringing up the stock market at a social occasion no longer seemed so appealing; it might have seemed like an intrusion, a faux pas, a poorly judged attempt to mix business with pleasure. By 2004, one was more likely to hear about the housing market. The difference between 1999 and 2004 is subtle, but nevertheless revelatory of the fundamental change in investor enthusiasm for the market.

Feedback Theories of Bubbles

In feedback loop theory, initial price increases (caused, for example, by the kinds of precipitating factors described in the previous chapter) lead to more price increases as the effects of the initial price increases feed back into yet higher prices through increased investor demand. This second round of price increases feeds back again into a third round, and then into a fourth, and so on. Thus, the initial impact of the precipitating factors is amplified, resulting in much larger price increases than the factors themselves would have suggested. Such feedback loops may be a factor not only in the historic bull and bear markets for the aggregate stock market but also, with some differences in details, in the ups and downs of the housing market and of individual investments as well.

Feedback is a familiar term for engineers, who are aware of the many occurrences and effects of feedback. A familiar example of feedback occurs when one brings a microphone (which receives sound and sends the electronically encoded sound) close to a loudspeaker (which translates the electronically encoded sound into actual sound). The result can be an eerie whistle, which varies through time. The whistle occurs because the sound feeds back from microphone to speaker to microphone to speaker, and on and on in a long sequence of loops. The variations in the whistle are the natural consequence of feedback systems, which have inherently complicated dynamics. This feedback operates in the same way as feedback that produces stock market bubbles, though of course the loudspeaker-microphone feedback is much faster, occurring in milliseconds, than that in the stock market, which occurs in days, months, and years.

To better understand feedback, one can try an experiment. If one brings a microphone before a speaker in total silence, there is no whistle. If there is no sound to begin with, there is nothing to feed back. But if one claps one's hands once, the whistling sound begins, and takes its own course through time after that. The whistling sound may build up for a while and then die out. Obviously, all this sound has been the result of the handclap, and yet the actual sound may have lasted for a substantial time after the handclap. The ups and downs of the sound were ultimately caused by the precipitating factor, the handclap, but the timing of these ups and downs was caused by the feedback mechanism itself, not the original sound.

When we observe the variations in feedback output from a loudspeaker in a normal room setting, with various small noises disturbing equilibrium, we are likely to be puzzled about their source. The precipitating sounds do not occur at the same time as the feedback variation, and so their causal role is easy to miss. It is the same in speculative markets, but here the feedback lasts for years. The disturbances that have begun the feedback may be so remote in time that it seems hardly possible that they could have been the cause of the price movements.

The theory of feedback is, as I have noted, widely known, but most people do not use the term *feedback loop* to describe it. The phrase is a scientist's term for what might popularly be called a vicious circle, a self-fulfilling prophecy, a bandwagon effect. Although the term *speculative bubble* has more than one meaning in common discourse, it usually appears to refer to such feedback.

In the most popular version of the feedback theory, one that relies on *adaptive expectations,* feedback takes place because past price increases generate expectations of further price increases.[18] In another version of the feedback theory, feedback takes place because of increased *investor confidence* in response to past price increases. Usually such feedback is thought to occur in response not so much to a sudden price increase as to a pattern of consistency in price increases.

The evidence discussed earlier in this chapter is consistent with both adaptive expectation and investor confidence feedback playing a role in the current stock market situation. The feedback can also occur for emotional reasons, reasons unconnected with either expectations or confidence. The effect of "playing with the house money," as discussed previously, can result in a sort of feedback: this frame of mind may reduce investors' inclination to sell after a price increase, thus amplifying the effects of the precipitating factors on price.[19] The past behavior of prices can have a wide range of emotional impacts, depending on their contexts.

Ultimately, there are a number of different kinds of feedback. Price-to-price feedback is the most basic: price increases, via investor enthusiasm, feed back directly into further price increases. Price-to-GDP-to-price feedback is another form: as the value of the stock market or the housing market increases, the resulting wealth and optimism encourages expenditures: consumption and investment in such things as new houses, factories, and equipment. The reaction to higher investment values is called the "wealth effect"; the wealth effect has been shown to operate both from the stock market and from the housing market.[20] When these higher expenditures have their impact on GDP, the appearance of economic success encourages people to bid up the markets more. The higher GDP is interpreted by the public as evidence of a healthier and stronger economy rather than of a bubble, which is its ultimate cause. Price–to–corporate earnings–to–price feedback is yet another form. When stock market prices increase, people spend more, and this boosts corporate profits, which is interpreted as fundamental good news about the corporations themselves, encouraging people to have higher expectations for the stock market and therefore to bid up prices even more.

Underlying this feedback is a widespread public misperception about the importance of speculative thinking in our economy. People are accustomed to thinking that there is a basic state of "health" of the economy, and that when the stock market goes up, or when GDP goes up, or when corporate profits go up, it means that the economy is healthier, no more and no less. It seems as if people often think that the economy is struck by some exogenous maladies, akin to earthquakes or meteor impacts, or exogenous breakthroughs, such as sudden advances in technology, and that the movements in the stock market, in GDP or in profits, are just a reflection of such shocks. It is true that the economy is sometimes struck by such shocks. But people do not seem to perceive how often it is that their own psychology, as part of a complex pattern of feedback, is driving the economy.

Regardless of which feedback theory applies, the speculative bubble cannot grow forever. Investors' demand for speculative assets cannot grow forever, and when it stops growing, price increases will stop. According to the popular version of the expectation feedback theory, at that point we would expect a drop in the market, a bursting of the bubble, since investors no longer think prices will continue to rise and therefore no longer see a good reason to hold the stock. However, other versions of the feedback theory do not suggest a *sudden* bursting of the bubble, since they are not predicated on continually increasing prices.

Indeed, even according to the most popular versions of the feedback theory, there is actually no reason to think that there should be *sudden* bursts of bubbles. There must be some noise in investor demand, some unpredictability of response to past price changes, some lack of synchrony across investors. Moreover, the enticement to enter or exit the market that past price changes creates is not likely to be determined only by the most recent change in price. It is plausible that investors will look back over many days, weeks, or months of price changes in deciding whether they find recent market performance enticing. Thus, the simple feedback theory is consistent with a price pattern that shows many interruptions and jiggles.[21]

With any of these feedback theories, we can also expect that *negative* bubbles should occur, in which feedback occurs in a downward direction, as initial price declines discourage some investors, causing further price declines, and so on.[22] (The term *negative bubble* always reminds me of watching a sealed plastic soda bottle filled with warm air gradually implode as it cools, and seeing it pop back into shape when the cap is loosened—though this metaphor is really no more apt than the soap bubble metaphor for positive speculative events.) Price continues to decline until further price decreases begin to seem unlikely, at which point there is no reason for people to want to stay away from the stock and the negative bubble fills back up—even though, as with positive bubbles, the burst will probably not be sudden.

Feedback loop dynamics can generate complex and even apparently random behavior. The so-called random number generators in some types of computer software are really just simple nonlinear feedback loops, and even some quite simple feedback loops have been demonstrated to yield behavior that looks so complicated as to suggest randomness. If we suppose that there are many kinds of feedback loops operating in the economy and many kinds of precipitating factors, then we may conclude that the apparent randomness of the stock market, the tendency it has to create sudden moves for no apparent reason, might not be so inexplicable after all. The branch of mathematics that studies nonlinear feedback loops, called *chaos theory*, may be applicable to understanding the complexity of stock market behavior.[23]

Perceptions of Feedback and Bubbles among Investors

The feedback theory of speculative bubbles is so widely known as to be considered part of our popular culture. It is natural to wonder, therefore, whether public perceptions of a bubble might play a role in a bubble. Conceivably, a bubble might exist only because people *think* that there is a temporary bubble and want to ride with it for a while.

A *Barron's* Big Money Poll of professional money managers in April 1999, less than a year before the 2000 peak of the market, asked, "Is the stock market in a speculative bubble?" Seventy-two percent of the respondents said yes, only 28% said no.[24] That is pretty solid evidence that some people thought they were in a bubble.

One of the indices we compute at the International Center for Finance at Yale, which we call a "valuation confidence" index, indicates the percentage of respondents who think that the stock market is not overvalued. The question that we pose to our respondents is this: "Stock prices in the United States, when compared with measures of true fundamental value or sensible investment value, are: (1) Too low, (2) Too high, (3) About right, (4) Do not know."

The valuation confidence index indicates the number of respondents who choose 1 (Too low) or 3 (About right) as a percentage of those who choose 1, 2, or 3. I have been asking this question, unchanged, and as the very first question on the questionnaire, since 1989. A plot of the valuation confidence index for both individual and institutional investors since 1989 is shown in Figure 5.4.[25]

Valuation confidence declined throughout the 1990s for both individual and institutional investors and hit bottom just before the peak in the stock market in 2000. Valuation confidence soared right back, almost to its 1989 levels, as the stock market declined after 2000. This behavior of valuation confidence is further evidence that the stock market went through a bubble around 2000.

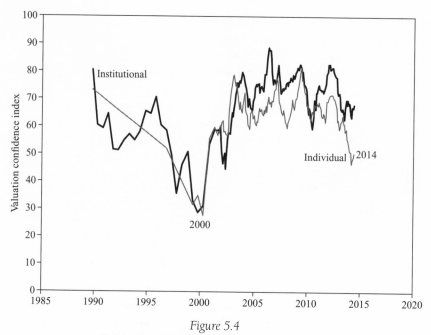

Figure 5.4
Valuation Confidence Index, 1989–2014
Percentage of respondents who think that the stock market is not overvalued,
1989–2014: Institutional investors (heavy line), high-income individual investors
(light line). *Source:* Author's surveys through 2000, Yale International Center for
Finance surveys thereafter.

Notably, people just did not believe in the market in 2000. As of this writing, in
2014, individual investors have been rapidly losing confidence again, though
we are not back to 1999 levels in this measure.

That said, it would still be inaccurate to think that most people have firmly
in mind that a feedback process is under way, operating through investor
psychology, and that they are knowingly participating in the bubble but hop-
ing to get out before it collapses. The investment professionals that *Barron's*
surveyed are, by their training, likely to be a little more savvy about these
things than are the general public. The general public is likely to think that
the market *might* be overvalued, and *might* be unstable, but does not have a
clear picture of the dynamics of a bubble.

In our questionnaire surveys of homebuyers in boom cities, we gave people
ample space to write in what they thought was going on in the real estate
market in which they had just participated. Some did indeed say that they
thought market psychology was driving events, and some even used the word

bubble. But in our 2004 survey, the word *bubble* was volunteered in reference to the real estate boom by only 1% of our respondents. Five times as many volunteered the term *supply and demand,* and much of what respondents in boom cities offered was about the shortage of houses on the market and the high demand. The overwhelming impression that one gets in reading their answers is that they believed there was good reason for the real estate boom to happen and to continue.

As part of our homebuyer surveys in 2003 and 2004, when the housing boom was going at its fastest pace, we asked:

> Which of the following better describes your theory about recent trends in [name of city] home prices?
> 1. It is a theory about the psychology of homebuyers and sellers
> 2. It is a theory about economic or demographic conditions such as population changes, changes in interest rates or employment growth (or decline)

Only 13% (of 771 respondents) chose 1 (psychology); 87% chose 2 (economic or demographic conditions).

As these answers reflect, the idea that some kind of psychological feedback drives market prices is not a natural one that informs a lot of thinking among the general public. Indeed, the very enthusiasm that one senses during a bubble seems inconsistent with a widespread awareness of the presence of a bubble. If one thought that the price increases were just another instance of herd behavior that was going to come to an abrupt end at some unpredictable date, it would be hard to imagine being so excited.

Ponzi Schemes as Models of Feedback and Speculative Bubbles

It is hard to prove that a simple mechanical price feedback model, producing heightened investor attention and enthusiasm, is actually a factor in financial markets. We may have a casual impression that investors are showing enthusiasm for investments in response to past price increases, but we do not see any concrete evidence that such feedback actually affects their decisions.

To provide evidence that such feedback mechanisms do play a role in financial markets, it is helpful to look at the example of Ponzi schemes, or pyramid schemes, by means of which hoaxers create positive feedback from putative current investment returns to future investment returns. These schemes have been perpetrated so many times that governments have had to outlaw them, yet they still keep popping up. They are particularly interesting since they are, in a way, controlled experiments (controlled by the hoaxer!) that demonstrate characteristics of the feedback that cannot be seen so plainly either in normal markets or in the experimental psychologist's laboratory.

In a Ponzi scheme, the manager of the scheme promises to make large profits for investors by investing their money. But little or no investment of contributors' funds in any real assets is actually made. Instead, the manager pays off the initial investors with the proceeds of a sale to a second round of investors, and the second round with the proceeds from a sale to a third, and so on. The name of the scheme derives from a particularly famous (though certainly not the first) example, perpetrated by one Charles Ponzi in the United States in 1920. A Ponzi scheme entices initial investors, after they have made a lot of money, to tell their success stories to another round of investors, who then invest even more in the scheme, allowing the hoaxer to pay off the second round of investors, whose success story entices an even larger round of investors, and so on. This scheme must end eventually, since the supply of investors cannot increase forever, and the perpetrator of the scheme no doubt knows this. The perpetrator may hope to exit, not having paid off the last and largest round of investors, and then hide from the law. (Or, possibly, he or she may imagine that with luck, fantastic investment opportunities will be found later, thereby saving the scheme.)

We know that Ponzi schemes have been successful in making their perpetrators rich, at least until they were apprehended. Charles Ponzi attracted 30,000 investors in 1920 and issued notes totaling $15 million, all within seven months.[26] The recent Bernie Madoff Ponzi scheme, carried on from the 1970s until its collapse in 2008, is considered to be the largest financial fraud in U.S. history, estimated at almost $65 billion. Neither experience nor sophistication seems to effectively immunize investors against falling victim to this type of fraud.

Bubbles can appear in the unlikeliest of places and can entrap even small rural investors. In a recent celebrated story, a former housewife, Raejean Bonham, set up an enormous Ponzi scheme on her own in the tiny town of Fox in rural Alaska. She promised to pay 50% returns in two months and enticed 1,200 investors in forty-two states to pay her a total of between $10 and $15 million between 1989 and 1995.[27]

A particularly dramatic story emerged in Albania in 1996 and 1997 when a number of Ponzi schemes promising fantastic rates of return enticed a good share of the people of that country. Seven Ponzi schemes accumulated some $2 billion, or 30% of Albania's annual GDP.[28] Enthusiasm for the schemes was so intense that in the 1996 local elections, members of the ruling government party included symbols of the Ponzi scheme funds on their campaign posters, apparently wanting to gain some credit for the new wealth sources. When the schemes failed in 1997, enraged protesters looted banks and burned buildings, and the government was forced to call out the army to restore peace; a number of rioters were killed. The collapse of the schemes forced the resignations of Prime Minister Aleksander Meksi and his cabinet.[29]

As part of their strategy, successful Ponzi schemes present to investors a plausible story about how great profits can be made. Charles Ponzi told investors that he was able to make money for them by exploiting an arbitrage profit opportunity involving international postage reply coupons. These coupons were sold by postal services so that the purchaser could enclose the coupon in a letter to another country and thereby prepay a reply. There were apparently some genuine potential profit opportunities in buying postage reply coupons in Europe and selling them in the United States, because the currency exchange rate did not correspond exactly to the rate implicit in the coupons. Ponzi's story of profit opportunities from trading the coupons, eventually published in newspapers during the scheme, sounded plausible to some influential people. But the actual profit opportunities were not realizable since there was no easy way to sell the coupons, and the hoax began to unravel when the New York postmaster declared that the world's supply of international postage reply coupons was not enough to make the fortune Ponzi claimed to have made.

Raejean Bonham in Alaska claimed she was buying unused frequent-flier miles from large companies, repackaging them as discount tickets, and then selling them at a large profit. The Albanian investment company VEFA was supposedly making a number of conventional investments in a reviving economy. (There was also a rumor in Albania at the time that VEFA was a front for money-laundering, an activity that also sounded like a plausible source of big money to many investors.)[30]

A critical observation to be made about these examples of Ponzi schemes is that initial investors were reportedly very skeptical about the schemes and would invest only small amounts. A story about an arbitrage profit opportunity in postage reply coupons, if merely told directly, without the evidence that it had made others a lot of money, would not sound credible enough to entice many investors. Investors do not become truly confident in the scheme until they see others achieving large returns.

The possibility that the so-called investment payoffs are in fact coming only from new money is typically raised repeatedly and publicly well before the collapse of these schemes, and the hoaxers must of course deny the claim publicly. This was the case both for the original Ponzi scheme and for the Albanian example. The fact that many people continue to believe in the scheme afterward seems puzzling, and to outside observers the believers in the scheme may seem quite foolish.[31] But this only shows the powerful effect on people's thinking of seeing others having made substantial sums of money. That others have made a lot of money appears to many people as the most persuasive evidence in support of the investment story associated with the Ponzi scheme—evidence that outweighs even the most carefully reasoned argument against the story.

Fraud, Manipulation, and White Lies

The process that generates a speculative boom is in some dimensions analogous to these Ponzi schemes. Also part of a boom is activity expressly designed to deceive people, deliberate attempts by many people to exploit thinking errors among general investors. Doing this effectively often requires breaking the law. But, given the slowness of our justice process, the perpetrators of such schemes may be able to get away with deception for many years. This, too, is part of the process of a speculative bubble.

My erstwhile professor at the Massachusetts Institute of Technology, Charles Kindleberger, was a great influence on my thinking. He lived to be 92 years old, and I corresponded with him last just before he died in 2003. In his 1989 book *Manias, Panics and Crashes,* he wrote: "We believe that swindling is demand determined. . . . In a boom, fortunes are made, individuals wax greedy, and swindlers come forward to exploit the demand."[32]

The value of most investments depends on expectations for the near to distant future, something that cannot be seen clearly today, and so a public focusing of attention on investments creates an opportunity for deception and misrepresentation. During a boom, opportunists try to find some ways of profiting from the public's speculative attention by pretending to be the epitome of capitalistic success, and also pretending, one way or the other, to be the advance guard of the great new economy.

One of the reasons we are so deceived by bubbles is the same reason that we are deceived by professional magicians. When clever persons become *professionals* at deceiving people and devote years to perfecting an act, they can put seemingly impossible feats before our eyes and fool us, at least for a while. They only need to fool us for long enough to collect our money and leave the scene. A public preoccupation with investments generates an immense incentive for such professionals to advance their careers in the realms of finance and management. When we have the equivalent of professional magicians running some of our companies or acting as some of our real estate brokers, we have to expect that what we see is not reality.

The extreme cases are those of outright criminal behavior, like that of the Enrons and the Parmalats. In the aftermath of a boom, the political environment changes, the public who lost money is outraged, offenders are prosecuted, and regulation is tightened. We saw that happen again in the United States and other countries after the market peaked in 2000. We saw another round of prosecutions after the runaway securitization that led to the 2008 crash. It is an important job that the regulators and prosecutors do, and the aftermath of a speculative boom is a sort of cleansing of our financial markets that makes it possible for them to function even more effectively in the aftermath of the bubble.

More common than the examples of criminal behavior, however, are examples of people who stayed entirely within the law and exploited a boom, building businesses that they did not themselves believe in. These are cases of disingenuity rather than fraud.

Some of these people have already taken their money and gone home. Since 2000, many top managers of tech companies that were built promoting a fundamentally flawed business concept have made their initial public offerings and have retired to their estates, and they hardly care that the price of their stocks has dropped so far. Some business magazines that prospered not so much because readers demanded them, but because companies wanted to advertise in them as part of their act, have shut down their operations. But more such ventures are still appearing, if at a lower rate, and the story is by no means over.

I remember vividly an experience I had in 1998 when I became involved in an attempt to sell a small firm. The small firm made a presentation to some investment bankers to help them decide whether they could market the firm privately to potential corporate buyers. The scene lingers in my memory. The president of the small firm was describing a sound business model to these bankers, I thought. The investment bankers seemed a little sleepy. At one point in his presentation, the president mentioned that the firm sells its product over the Internet, and so one *could* say it was an Internet firm. At this point one of the investment bankers sprang to life. He said that the market was hungry for Internet firms, and if they could present the small firm as one of these, his bank could raise serious millions of dollars for the sale. But, he said, the firm would have to come up with a story of a grand future trajectory for the firm, a plausible story that might conceivably lead to hundreds of millions of revenue in a few years, and the management would have to start living that story, taking business initiatives that signaled belief in the story. Later, the president of the small firm told me he toyed with the idea of changing the firm's name to something ending in .com. But, on further reflection, he said that the story was not real: "I just couldn't do it," he concluded.

Others could and did do that sort of thing. In fact, there was a trend over the 1990s toward installing showmen and media-savvy personalities as heads of corporations, to lure investors and boost stock prices. In his 2002 book *Searching for a Corporate Savior*, Rakesh Khurana documented a pattern of hiring expensive celebrities from the outside to run companies with an eye on the stock market. Those who had a genuine and deep knowledge of the business, who felt a loyalty to the others who worked there, and who were willing to take the steps that would ensure long-term success, were often pushed aside.[33]

Speculative Bubbles as Naturally Occurring Ponzi Processes

It would appear, by extrapolation from examples like those given earlier, that speculative feedback loops that are in effect naturally occurring Ponzi schemes do arise from time to time without the contrivance of a fraudulent manager. Even if there is no manipulator fabricating false stories and deliberately deceiving investors in the aggregate stock market, tales about the market are everywhere. When prices go up a number of times, investors are rewarded sequentially by price movements in these markets, just as they are in Ponzi schemes. There are still many people (indeed, the stock brokerage and mutual fund industries as a whole) who benefit from telling stories that suggest that the market will go up further. There is no reason for these stories to be fraudulent; they need only emphasize the positive news and give less emphasis to the negative. The path of a naturally occurring Ponzi scheme—if we may call speculative bubbles that—will be more irregular and less dramatic, since there is no direct manipulation, but the path may sometimes resemble that of a Ponzi scheme when it is supported by naturally occurring stories. The extension from Ponzi schemes to naturally occurring speculative bubbles appears so natural that one must conclude, if there is to be debate about speculative bubbles, that the burden of proof is on skeptics to provide evidence as to why Ponzi-like speculative bubbles *cannot* occur.

Recently, many of the major finance textbooks, which have promoted a view of financial markets as working rationally and efficiently, have not provided arguments as to why feedback loops supporting speculative bubbles cannot occur. In fact, at least until recently they may not even *mention* bubbles or Ponzi schemes.[34] These books convey a sense of orderly progression in financial markets, of markets that work with mathematical precision. If the phenomena are not mentioned at all, then students are not given any way to judge for themselves whether they are in fact influencing the market.

Feedback and Cross Feedback between the Stock Market and the Housing Market

We noted in previous chapters that in the United States, there has been very little relation historically between price changes in the stock market and price changes in the housing market, but that the housing market boom that began in 1998 appeared several years after the beginning of the sharpest ascent of the stock market starting in 1995. We also noted that, internationally, home price booms show some tendency to peak a couple years after stock market booms. This raises the possibility that there is sometimes cross feedback, that is, feedback from one market to another, between the stock market and the housing market. While the housing market grows more speculative as our society changes, it is also possible that the feedback will intensify in the future.

It does not seem surprising that a home price boom would begin a few years after a stock market boom. The stock market boom produces perceived wealth, and the greater wealth ought to encourage people to spend more on their homes and thus bid up the price of homes. This effect could easily operate with a lag of years, since it takes people years to make decisions to change their housing arrangements. But it is challenging to envision a feedback model that has home prices rising rapidly even after stock prices are sharply falling. It may seem unlikely that we will ever understand such a phenomenon.

It could be that the home price boom, which began in the United States and other countries before the peak of the market, started in 1998 in response to the stock market boom and just fed on itself through its own internal feedback after the stock market fizzled. It could also be that the home price boom was a sort of long-lagged response to stock market increases that had built up since 1982, because the decline in the market after 2000 only brought the market partway back down and left people feeling a lot wealthier even after the post-2000 stock market drop than they had felt in 1982. Or perhaps the stock market boom produced some cultural changes that continued on their own after the corporate earnings drop that is so closely tied to the stock market drop, an earnings drop that did not directly affect housing.

But we should add to these possibilities another that would help explain rapidly increasing home prices concurrent with the post-2000 stock market drops: that the drops in the stock market after 2000 had the perverse effect of further intensifying the demand for housing by transferring investor enthusiasm from the stock market to the housing market. This may seem like a theory contrived to fit the facts, but we have evidence for it. In our questionnaire surveys of recent homebuyers in 2003 and 2004, Karl Case and I asked homeowners directly about possible feedback from the stock market to the housing market. We asked the following question, with the results indicated:

The experience with the stock market in the past few years
[Please circle one number]
1. Much encouraged me to buy my house   12%
2. Somewhat encouraged me to buy my house   14%
3. Had no effect on my decision to buy my house   72%
4. Somewhat discouraged me from buying my house   2%
5. Much discouraged me from buying my house   1%

$$[n = 1{,}146]$$

At the time of these surveys, respondents' experiences with the stock market in the past few years would of course usually have been very bad, since the aggregate market had fallen so sharply after 2000. The great majority of respondents said the stock market had no effect on their decision to buy a house. This is actually not at all surprising, since most people have a multitude of personal reasons to buy a house that must figure more prominently in their minds. But the interesting thing about these answers is that, of those who replied that the experience did affect their decision to buy a house, an overwhelming percentage said that it *encouraged* them. In fact (taking account of the rounding error in the percentages given), more than ten times as many said that the stock market encouraged them than said it discouraged them.

Right after this question on the questionnaire, we had a follow-up question: "Please explain your thinking here." The respondents wrote some substantial answers explaining their answers to the previous question, and it is in reading so many of these answers that one gets a real sense of the cross feedback from stock prices to home prices. Here is a sampling of some of these answers from people who said the stock market encouraged them to buy a house:

> I watched my IRAs & 401Ks decline. I decided I would invest in real estate instead.
>
> Housing does not lose as much as stocks.
>
> Stock market shares are too volatile in values, making the risk higher. Buying a house & land retain better investment value because land will not be depleted over times.
>
> Diminishing returns & huge losses. Looked for alternative use of capital.
>
> Home ownership is the number one investment for personal financial security. Everything else is second.
>
> Housing is inherently safer investment. You can always just live in it.
>
> We lost a high percentage of 401K & Roth IRA funds during 2000/2002. We've never lost money on real estate.
>
> Real estate is safer. At least you own the property. With stocks, if you lose, you have nothing.

After we read many such answers, some clear patterns seem to emerge. The drops in the stock market in 2000–2003 had just gotten people increasingly fed up with the stock market and ready to transfer their affections to another market, one that they increasingly believed was the best investment for them. It is as simple as that; what they wrote seems plain and easily understood. There *was* a sort of cross feedback from the stock market to the housing market, and that must account for a good part of the housing boom that we saw.[35] This cross feedback also helps account for the international nature of the housing boom, as the stock market collapse was experienced in all of the advanced countries that had seen booming markets since the late 1990s.

This seeming evidence of cross feedback from the stock market to the housing market may seem fragile, since such feedback does not always occur, but one must remember that we are dealing with social science, not theoretical physics. We do not fully understand why feedback between markets has the form it does and why it changes through time, but we have learned something about it.

Irrational Exuberance and Feedback Loops: The Argument So Far

There are many precipitating factors ultimately causing irrational exuberance, as detailed in the previous chapter, and the effects of these causes can be amplified by a feedback loop, a speculative bubble, as we have seen in this chapter. As prices continue to rise, the level of exuberance is enhanced by the price rise itself.

In this chapter, we have only begun to describe the process of feedback. We have seen that feedback does not merely come about as individuals look at past price increases and make arithmetical calculations to adjust for individual levels of confidence and expectations. The changes in thought patterns infect the entire culture, and they operate not only directly from past price increases but also from auxiliary cultural changes that the past price increases helped generate. For a better understanding of how precipitating factors exert their effects and how they are amplified, we turn, in the next part, to a discussion of the cultural changes that have accompanied the recent stock market and other speculative booms.

Part Two

Cultural Factors

Six

The News Media

The history of speculative bubbles begins roughly with the advent of newspapers.[1] One can assume that, although the record of these early newspapers is mostly lost, they, or their pamphlet analogues, reported on the first bubble of any consequence: the Dutch tulip mania of the 1630s.[2]

Although the news media—newspapers, magazines, and broadcast media, along with their new outlets on the Internet—present themselves as detached observers of market events, they are themselves an integral part of these events. Significant market events generally occur only if there is similar thinking among large groups of people, and the news media are essential vehicles for the spread of ideas.

In this chapter, I consider the complexity of the media's impact on market events. As we shall see, news stories rarely have a simple, predictable effect on the market. Indeed, in some respects, they have less impact than is commonly believed. However, a careful analysis reveals that the news media do play an important role both in setting the stage for market moves and in instigating the moves themselves.

The Role of the Media in Setting the Stage for Market Moves

The news media are in constant competition to capture the public attention they need to survive. Survival for them requires finding and defining interesting news, focusing attention on news that has word-of-mouth potential (so as to broaden their audience), and, whenever possible, defining an ongoing story that encourages their audience to remain steady customers.

The competition is by no means haphazard. Those charged with disseminating the news cultivate a creative process, learning from one anothers' successes and failures, that aims to provide emotional color to news, to invest news stories with human interest appeal, and to create familiar figures in the news. Years of experience in a competitive environment has made the media professions quite skillful at claiming public attention.

The news media are naturally attracted to financial markets, because, at the very least, the markets provide constant news in the form of daily price changes. Nothing beats the stock market for sheer frequency of potentially interesting news items.

The stock market has star quality. The public considers it the Big Casino, the market for major players, and believes that on any given day it serves as a barometer of the status of the nation—impressions that the media can foster and benefit from. Financial news may have great human interest potential to the extent that it deals with the making or breaking of fortunes. And the financial media can present their perennial lead, the market's performance, as an ongoing story—one that brings in the most loyal repeat customers. The only other regular generator of news on a comparable scale is sporting events. It is no accident that financial news and sports news together account for roughly half of the editorial content of many newspapers today.

Housing has also been a source of endless fascination for the general public, because we live in houses, we work on them every day, and our sense of our individual social position is tied to the kind of houses we live in. The fascination increased for a while with the housing bubble. Newspapers launched whole sections devoted to homes or real estate, and in the United States, the housing boom led to the creation of an entire TV channel devoted to housing: HGTV. In the United Kingdom, the reality TV show *Property Ladder,* launched in 2001, was initially a great success, with spinoffs in the Netherlands and the United States. The show depicted the adventures of property flippers who buy homes, fix them up, and quickly sell them with hope of an impressive profit. After the housing crash, the U.K. version relaunched as *Property Snakes and Ladders,* reflecting the increased awareness of the potential for both ups and downs in the housing market, and refocusing on making your own house nice rather than fixing it for resale.[3] The U.S. TV show *Flip that House,* launched in the time of the housing bubble, 2005, was shut down in 2008 after the bubble burst.

Media Cultivation of Debate

In an attempt to attract audiences, the news media try to present debate about issues on the public mind. This may mean creating a debate on topics that experts would not otherwise consider deserving of such discussion. The resulting media event may convey the impression that there are experts on all sides of the issue, thereby suggesting a lack of expert agreement on the very issues that people are most confused about.

Over the years, I have been called by news people asking me whether I would be willing to make a statement in support of some extreme view. When I declined, the next request would sometimes be to recommend another expert who *would* go on record in support of the position.

Five days before the 1987 stock market crash, the *MacNeil/Lehrer NewsHour* featured Ravi Batra, author of *The Great Depression of 1990: Why It's Got to Happen, How to Protect Yourself.* This book took as its basic premise a theory that history tends to repeat itself in exact detail, so that the 1929 crash and the subsequent depression had to repeat themselves. Despite Batra's significant scholarly reputation, this particular book of his is not one that would be viewed with any seriousness by most reputable scholars of the market. But it had been on the *New York Times* best-seller list for fifteen weeks by the time of the crash. On the *NewsHour*, Batra confidently predicted a stock market crash in 1989 that would "spread to the whole world"; after it, he declared, "there will be a depression."[4] Batra's statements, made as they were on a highly respected show, may—even though they predicted a crash two years thence—have contributed in some small measure to an atmosphere of vulnerability that brought us the crash of 1987. Although Batra's appearance on the *NewsHour* just before the crash might be considered a coincidence, one must keep in mind that predictions of stock market crashes are actually quite rare on national news shows. The proximity of his appearance to the actual crash is at the very least highly suggestive.

Should the media be faulted for presenting debates on topics of little merit? One can argue that they ought to focus on a variety of topics of interest to general audiences, so that the public can refine their views. Yet in doing so, the media seem often to disseminate and reinforce ideas that are not supported by real evidence. If news directors followed only their highest intellectual interests in judging which views to present, the public might indeed find its consciousness constructively broadened. But that is apparently not how the media see their mission—nor do competitive pressures encourage them to rethink the matter.

Reporting on the Market Outlook

There is no shortage of media accounts that try to answer our questions about the market today, but there *is* a shortage in these accounts of relevant facts or considered interpretations of them. Many news stories in fact seem to have been written under a deadline to produce something—*anything*—to go along with the numbers from the market. The typical such story, after noting the remarkable bull market, focuses on very short-run statistics. It generally states which groups of stocks have risen more than others in recent months. Although these stocks are described as leaders, there is no good reason to think that their performance has caused the bull market. The news story may talk about the "usual" factors behind economic growth, such as the Internet boom, in glowing terms and with at least a hint of patriotic congratulation to our powerful economic engine. The article then finishes with quotes from a few well-chosen "celebrity" sources, offering their outlook for the future. Sometimes the article is so completely devoid of genuine thought about the reasons for the bull market and the context for considering its outlook that it is hard to believe that the writer was other than cynical in his or her approach.

What are the celebrity sources quoted as saying in these articles? They typically give numerical forecasts for the Dow in the near future, tell stories or jokes, and dispense their personal opinions. For example, when Abby Joseph Cohen of Goldman Sachs & Co. coined a quotable phrase—as with her warnings against "FUDD" (fear, uncertainty, doubt, and despair) or her phrase "Silly Putty Economy"—it was disseminated widely. Beyond that, the media quote her opinions but pay no critical attention to her analysis. In fact, although she no doubt has access to a formidable research department and performs extensive data analysis before forming her opinions, they are ultimately reported as just that—her opinions. Of course, she should not be faulted for this, for it is the nature of the sound-bite-driven media that super-ficial opinions are preferred to in-depth analyses.

Record Overload

The media often seem to thrive on superlatives, and we, their audience, are confused as to whether the price increases we have recently seen in the stock market are all that unusual. Data suggesting that we are setting some new record (or are at least close to doing so) are regularly stressed in the media, and if reporters look at the data in enough different ways, they will often find *something* that is close to setting a record on any given day. In covering the stock market, many writers mention "record one-day price changes"—measured in points on the Dow rather than percentage terms, so that records are much more likely. Although the media have become increasingly enlightened about reporting in terms of points on the Dow in recent years, the practice still persists among some writers.

This *record overload*—the impression that new and significant records are constantly being set—only adds to the confusion people have about the economy. It makes it hard for people to recognize when something truly and importantly new really *is* happening. It also, with its deluge of different indicators, encourages an avoidance of individual assessment of quantitative data—a preference for seeing the data interpreted for us by celebrity sources.

Do Big Stock Price Changes Really Follow Big News Days?

Many people seem to think that it is the reporting of specific news events, the serious content of news, that affects financial markets. But research offers far less support for this view than one would imagine.

Victor Niederhoffer, while he was still an assistant professor at Berkeley in 1971 (before he became a legendary hedge fund manager), published an article that sought to establish whether days with news of significant world events corresponded to days that saw big stock price movements. He tabulated all very large headlines in the *New York Times* (large type size being taken as a crude indicator of relative importance) from 1950 to 1966; there were 432 such headlines. Did these significant-world-event days correspond to big movements in stock prices? As the standard of comparison, Niederhoffer noted that the S&P Composite Index over this period showed substantial one-day increases (of more than 0.78%) on only 10% of the trading days, and substantial one-day decreases (of more than 0.71%) on only another 10% of the trading days. Of the 432 significant-world-event days, 78 (or 18%) showed big price increases, and 56 (or 13%) showed big decreases. Thus such days were only slightly more likely to show large price movements than other days.[5]

Niederhoffer claimed that, on reading the stories under these headlines, he thought it unlikely that many of the world events reported would have had much impact on the fundamental value represented by the stock market. Perhaps what the media *thought* was big national news was not what was really important to the stock market. He speculated that news events that represented crises were more likely to influence the stock market.

Defining a crisis as a time when five or more large headlines occurred within a seven-day period, Niederhoffer found eleven crises in the sample interval. These were the beginning of the Korean war in 1950, the capture of Seoul by the Communists in 1951, the Democratic National Convention of 1952, Russian troops' threatening Hungary and Poland in 1956, the Suez crisis of 1956, Charles de Gaulle's taking office as French premier in 1958, the entry of U.S. marines into Lebanon in 1958, Russian premier Nikita Khrushchev's appearance at the United Nations in 1959, Cuban tensions in 1960, the Cuban arms blockade in 1962, and President John Kennedy's assassination in 1963. During these crises, so defined, 42% of the daily price changes were "big" changes, compared with 20% for other, "normal," time periods. Thus, the crisis periods were somewhat, but not dramatically, more likely to be accompanied by big stock price changes.

Note that there were only eleven such weeks of "crisis" in the whole seventeen years of Niederhoffer's sample. Very few of the aggregate price movements in the stock market show any meaningful association with headlines.

Tag-Along News

News stories occurring on days of big price swings that are cited as the causes of the changes often cannot, one suspects, plausibly account for the changes—or at least not for their full magnitude. On Friday, October 13, 1989, there was a stock market crash that was clearly identified by the media as a reaction to a news story. A leveraged buyout deal for UAL Corporation, the parent company of United Airlines, had fallen through. The crash, which resulted in a 6.91% drop in the Dow for the day, had begun just minutes after this announcement, and so it at first seemed highly likely that it was the cause of the crash.

The first problem with this interpretation is that UAL is just one firm, accounting for but a fraction of 1% of the stock market's total value. Why should the collapse of the UAL buyout have such an impact on the entire market? One interpretation at the time was that the deal's failure was viewed by the market as a watershed event, portending that many other similar pending buyouts would also fail. But no concrete arguments were given in support of this view; rather, dubbing it a watershed seemed to have been nothing more than an effort to make sense after the fact of the market's move in response to the news.

To try to discover the reasons for the October 13, 1989, crash, survey researcher William Feltus and I carried out a telephone survey of 101 market professionals on the Monday and Tuesday following the crash. We asked: "Did you hear about the UAL news before you heard about the market drop on Friday afternoon, or did you hear about the UAL news later as an explanation for the drop in the stock market?" Only 36% said they had heard about the news before the crash; 53% said they had heard about it afterward as an explanation for the drop; the rest were unsure when they had heard about it. Thus it appears that the news story may have *tagged along* after the crash, rather than directly caused it, and therefore, it was not as prominent as the media accounts suggested.

We also asked the market professionals to interpret the news story. We queried:

Which of the following two statements better represents the view you held last Friday:

1. The UAL news of Friday afternoon will reduce future takeovers, and so the UAL news is a sensible reason for the sudden drop in stock prices.
2. The UAL news of Friday afternoon should be viewed as a focal point or attention grabber, which prompted investors to express their doubts about the market.

Of the respondents, 30% chose 1 and 50% chose 2; the rest were unsure. Thus, they were mostly reacting to the news as an *interpretation of the behavior of investors*.[6] It may be correct to say that the news event was *fundamental* to this stock market crash, in that it represented a "story" that enhanced the feedback from stock price drops to further stock price drops, thereby preserving the feedback effect for a longer period than would otherwise have been the case. Yet it was unlikely to have been its cause.

The Absence of News on Days of Big Price Changes

We can also look at days of unusually large price movements and ask whether there were exceptionally important items of news on those days. Following up on Niederhoffer's work, in 1989, David Cutler, James Poterba, and Lawrence Summers compiled a list of the fifty largest U.S. stock market movements, as measured by the S&P Index, since World War II, and for each, they tabulated the explanations offered in the news media. Most of the so-called explanations do not correspond to any unusual news, and some of them could not possibly be considered serious news. For example, the reasons given for large price movements included such relatively innocuous statements as: "Eisenhower urges confidence in the economy," "further reaction to Truman victory over Dewey," and "replacement buying after earlier fall."[7]

Some would argue that perhaps we should not expect to see prominent news on days of big price changes, even if markets are working perfectly. Price changes in a so-called efficient market occur, so the argument goes, as soon as the information becomes public; they do not wait until the information is reported in the media. (This is a topic to which I return in Chapter 11.) Thus, it is not surprising, according to this line of reasoning, that we often do not find new information in the newspaper on the day of a price change: earlier information, appearing to the casual observer as tangential or irrelevant, has already been interpreted by perceptive investors as significant to the fundamentals that should determine share prices.

Another argument advanced to explain why days of unusually large stock price movements have often not been found to coincide with important news is that a confluence of factors may cause a significant market change, even if the individual factors themselves are not particularly newsworthy. For example, suppose certain investors are informally using a particular statistical model that forecasts fundamental value using a number of economic indicators. If all or most of these particular indicators point the same way on a given day, even if no single one of them is of any substantive importance by itself, their combined effect will be noteworthy.

Both of these interpretations of the tenuous relationship between news and market movements assume that the public is paying continuous attention to the news—reacting sensitively to the slightest clues about market fundamentals, constantly and carefully adding up all the disparate pieces of evidence. But that is just not the way public attention works. Our attention is much more quixotic and capricious. Instead, news functions more often as an *initiator* of a chain of events that fundamentally change the public's thinking about the market.

News as the Precipitator of Attention Cascades

The role of news events in affecting the market seems often to be delayed, and to have the effect of setting in motion a *sequence of public attentions*. These attentions may be to images or stories, or to facts that may already have been well known. The facts may previously have been ignored or judged inconsequential, but they can attain newfound prominence in the wake of breaking news. These sequences of attention may be called *cascades* as one focus of attention leads to attention to another, and then another.

At 5:46 A.M. on Tuesday, January 17, 1995, an earthquake measuring 7.2 on the Richter scale struck Kobe, Japan; it was the worst earthquake to hit urban Japan since 1923. The reaction of the stock markets of the world to this event provides an interesting case study, since in this case we know without doubt that the precipitating event, the earthquake, was truly exogenous and not itself generated by human activity or business conditions—not a response to a subtle hint of economic change nor the result of a confluence of unusual values of conventional economic indicators. In the Cutler-Poterba-Summers list of media explanations for the fifty largest postwar movements in the S&P Index in the United States, discussed earlier, not a single one of the explanations referred to any substantial cause that was definitely exogenous to the economy.[8]

The earthquake took 6,425 lives. According to estimates by the Center for Industrial Renovation of Kansai, the total damage caused by the earthquake was about $100 billion. The reaction in financial markets was strong, but delayed. The Tokyo stock market fell only slightly that day, and prices of construction-related companies generally rose, reflecting the expected increased demand for their products and services. Analysts reported at that time that the probable effects of the earthquake on corporate value were as yet ambiguous, since the wave of rebuilding after the quake might stimulate the Japanese economy.

The biggest reaction to the earthquake did not come until a week later. On January 23, the Japanese Nikkei index fell 5.6% on no apparent news except the gradual unfolding of numerous news accounts of earthquake damage. Over the ten days following the earthquake, the Nikkei lost over 8% of its value. If viewed as the direct result of the earthquake damage alone, the loss of value would be an overreaction.

What was going on in investors' minds over the ten days following the earthquake? Of course, there is no rigorous way to find out. We know only that during this period, the Kobe earthquake dominated the news, created new and different images of Japan, and may have led to very different impressions about the Japanese economy. Moreover, the quake sparked discussions about the risk of an earthquake centered in Tokyo. Despite the fact that geological evidence suggesting that Tokyo is at risk for a major earthquake was already known, greater attention was now focused on this potential problem. The damage that an earthquake of the severity of the 1923 quake could cause to modern-day Tokyo was put at $1.25 trillion by Tokai Research and Consulting, Inc.[9]

Even more puzzling than the direct effect of the Kobe earthquake on the domestic Japanese markets was its effect on foreign stock markets. On the day that the Nikkei fell 5.6%, the FTSE 100 index in London fell 1.4%, the CAC-40 in Paris fell 2.2%, and the DAX in Germany fell 1.4%. The Brazilian and Argentine stock markets both fell about 3%. These diverse countries around the world suffered no earthquake damage on this occasion.

The best interpretation of the effects of the Kobe earthquake on the stock markets of the world is that news coverage of the earthquake, and of the accompanying stock market declines, engaged the attention of investors, prompting a cascade of attentions that brought to the fore some more pessimistic factors.

Another market reaction to news illustrates how media attention may, through a cascade of attentions, lead many investors to eventually take seriously news that would normally be considered nonsense and irrelevant. A sequence of news stories about Joseph Granville, a flamboyant market forecaster, appears to have caused a couple of major market moves. The only substantive content of these media stories was that Granville was telling his clients to buy or sell, and that Granville himself was influential.

Granville's behavior easily attracted public attention. His investment seminars were bizarre extravaganzas, sometimes featuring a trained chimpanzee playing Granville's theme song, "The Bagholder's Blues," on a piano. He once showed up at an investment seminar dressed as Moses, wearing a crown and carrying tablets. Granville made extravagant claims for his forecasting ability. He said he could forecast earthquakes and once claimed to have predicted six of the past seven major world quakes. He was quoted by *Time* magazine as saying, "I don't think that I will ever make a serious mistake in the stock market for the rest of my life," and he predicted that he would win the Nobel Prize in economics.[10]

The first Granville episode took place on Tuesday, April 22, 1980. With the news that he had changed his recommendation from short to long, the Dow rose 30.72 points, or 4.05%. This was the biggest increase in the Dow since November 1, 1978, a year and a half earlier. The second episode occurred on January 6, 1981, after Granville's investor service changed from a long recommendation to a short recommendation. The Dow took its biggest dive since October 9, 1979, over a year earlier. There was no other news on either of these occasions that might appear responsible for the market change, and on the second occasion, both the *Wall Street Journal* and *Barron's* squarely attributed the drop to Granville's recommendation.

Can we be sure that media reporting of Granville and his supposed powers of prognostication caused these changes? Many people wondered whether the Granville effect was not just a coincidence that the news media exaggerated. We *can* be sure that a sequence of news stories about Granville's pronouncements, with their substantial word-of-mouth potential, had a cumulative effect on national attention, and that public reactions to his pronouncements and to market declines at the time of his announcements were fundamentally altered by this cascade.[11]

News during the Crash of 1929

The role of the news media in causing the stock market crash of 1929 has been debated almost since the crash itself. In fact, the puzzle facing historians and economists has been, by some interpretations, that just before the crash there was no significant news at all. Ever since, however, people have wondered how this record stock market crash could get under way with no news. What common concerns were on the minds of sellers that caused so many of them to try to sell at the same time?

The Monday, October 28, 1929, stock market crash was the biggest single-day drop (measured between the closing price the previous trading day and the closing price on the day) in the Dow until the October 19, 1987, crash. On October 28, 1929, the Dow fell 12.8% in one day (13.01% measured from the high to the low on that day). The second-biggest drop in history (until 1987) occurred the following day, when the Dow dropped 11.7% (15.9% measured from the high to the low on that day). The combined close-to-close drop in those two days in 1929 was 23.1%. What news had arisen that might rationally account for such a sizable stock market decline?

On reading the major newspapers over that weekend and on the morning of Tuesday, October 29, one is easily led to conclude that nothing of any consequence for the fundamentals of the market was happening. Indeed, that was the conclusion reported in the newspapers themselves. On the morning of October 29, newspapers around the country carried an Associated Press story that said in part, "In the absence of any adverse news developments over the week-end, and in the face of the optimistic comments on business forthcoming from President Hoover and leading industrial and banking executives, Wall Street's only explanation of today's decline was that a careful checking up of accounts over the week-end disclosed numerous weak spots, which had been overlooked in the hectic sessions of last week." The *New York Times* attributed the drop only to a "general loss of confidence." The *Wall Street Journal* reported that "business in general shows no signs of disintegration" and that the decline was due to "necessitous liquidation of impaired accounts."[12]

What else was in the news on those days? As of Monday morning, there was news that the Interstate Commerce Commission would proceed with its plan to recapture some excess railroad income. There was a favorable report on the earnings of U.S. Steel. New information was reported on charges that the Connecticut Manufacturer's Association had succeeded in introducing into a tariff bill provisions favoring Connecticut. Mussolini had made a speech saying that the "men and institutions of fascism can face any crisis, even if it is sudden." A new aspirant to the French premiership, Edouard Daladier, had announced the foreign minister of his prospective cabinet. A British airliner was lost at sea with seven aboard. The *Graf Zeppelin* planned a trip to explore the Arctic. Richard Byrd's party was making progress toward the South Pole.

After Black Monday, early on Tuesday morning, the second day of the crash, it was reported that prominent financiers had asserted that heavy banking support would come into the market that day, in search of bargains. If this was significant news at all, one would think it was good news. Other news on Tuesday morning was that two senators had called on President Hoover to declare his position on duties on agricultural and industrial products, that Senator Hiram Bingham had complained that the Lobby Inquiry had treated him unfairly, that a Hungarian count and countess had been given the right to enter the country, and that another airliner had been lost with five aboard.

All of these stories sound very typical. If there really was a good reason for the drop in the market, then certainly there must have been *something* happening at the time that people knew about. And one would think that such concerns would have made it into the news in some form. Perhaps one must read the papers more carefully. One author, Jude Wanniski, indeed claimed that there was a story in the *New York Times* on the morning of Monday, October 28, 1929, that might conceivably account for such a decline. This front-page story was an optimistic report on the likelihood of passage of the Smoot-Hawley tariff, then still in committee. The story was picked up by the Associated Press and United News the following day and given front-page treatment around the country on Tuesday, October 29.[13]

It has been argued by some that the Smoot-Hawley tariff might have been expected to hurt the outlook for U.S. corporate profits. This may seem surprising: one might have thought that it would generally benefit corporations, since so many of them actively sought the tariff. But it has been argued by historians of the 1929 crash that the tariff might have been expected to have the opposite effect, given the retaliation from other countries that it would engender. Allan Meltzer in fact argued that the tariff could be the reason "why the 1929 recession did not follow the path of previous monetary contractions but became the Great Depression."[14] However, other economists, including Rudiger Dornbusch and Stanley Fischer, pointed out that exports were only 7% of the gross national product (GNP) in 1929 and that between 1929 and 1931 they fell by only 1.5% of 1929 GNP. This hardly seems like the cause of the Great Depression. Moreover, they pointed out that it is not clear that the Smoot-Hawley tariff was responsible for the decline in exports. The depression itself might be held responsible for part of the decline. Dornbusch and Fischer showed that the 1922 Fordney-McCumber tariff increased tariff rates as much as the Smoot-Hawley tariff, and the Fordney-McCumber tariff was of course followed by no such recession.[15]

Even if we were to allow that the possibility of passage of the Smoot-Hawley tariff was important enough to account for a decline in share values of this magnitude, one must still ask whether there was any news over the weekend that would substantially alter one's estimation of the likelihood that the tariff would be passed. Just what was the content of the story in the *New York Times?* On Saturday, October 26, Senator David Reed declared that the Smoot-Hawley tariff bill was "dead" in committee. This provoked denials by Senators Reed Smoot and William Borah. The *Times* quoted Senator Smoot as saying, "If that is Senator Reed's opinion, I suppose he has a right to express it. But it isn't the view of the Finance Committee." Senator Borah said, "My opinion is that the tariff bill is not going to die." The next morning, October 29, the *Times* reported that Senator Reed had reiterated his conviction that the bill was dead and went on to cite other opinions on both sides of the issue. Although the original *Times* story had sounded optimistic for the bill, the United News version of the story published on October 29 was pessimistic. The *Atlanta Constitution,* when it ran the story on October 29, carried the headline "Senate Gives Up Hope of Enacting New Tariff Bill."

Nonetheless, it is hard to see that this interchange among senators, so typical of political wrangling, amounts to important news. The same sort of news accounts had been coming out all along with regard to the tariff bill. A week earlier, on October 21, the *Times* had quoted Senator James Watson, Republican leader of the Senate, offering his view that the Senate would pass the bill within another month. On October 13, Senator Smoot was reported as telling President Hoover that there was a chance the bill would pass by November 20. Alternately optimistic and pessimistic news on the tariff bill had been coming in since Hoover's election.

Far more significant than news about fundamentals among the newspaper stories on Monday, October 28, 1929, are clues to the importance attached in people's minds to the events of just a few days earlier, when the stock exchange had seen a record decline in share prices. That was the so-called Black Thursday, October 24, 1929, when the Dow had fallen 12.9% within the day but recovered substantially before the end of trading, so that the closing average was down only 2.1% from the preceding close. This event was no longer news, but the memory of the emotions it had generated was very much part of the ambience on Monday. The *New York Times* noted in its Monday morning edition that Wall Street, "normally deserted and quiet on Sunday as a country graveyard, hummed with activity as bankers and brokers strove to put their houses in order after the most strenuous week in history. . . . When the bell clangs at 10 o'clock this morning for the resumption of trading, most houses will be abreast of their work and ready for what may come." The atmosphere of that Sunday on Wall Street was described: "Sightseers strolled from street to street, gazing curiously at the Stock Exchange Building and the Morgan banking offices across the way, centers of last week's dramatic financial happenings. Here and there a sightseer picked up from the street a vagrant slip of ticker tape, as visitors seize upon spent bullets on a battlefield as souvenirs. Sightseeing buses made special trips through the district."[16]

Indeed, on that Monday morning of the crash, the *Wall Street Journal* saw fit to run a front-page editorial stating that "everybody in responsible positions says that business conditions are sound."[17] The editorial staff of the *Journal* must have had reasons to suspect that reassurance was needed if the market was to remain stable. Presumably they had heard snippets of popular conversation, or could at least guess how people might react following the weekend, given the huge debacle on Thursday.

So perhaps what happened on Monday, October 28, 1929, was just an echo, albeit a very exaggerated one, of what had happened the previous week. What had the media said about this? Again, the newspapers seemed to think that there was no important news. The *Chicago Tribune* wrote, on Sunday, October 27, 1929, "It has been the collapse of a vastly inflated bubble of speculation, with little or no cause in the country's general situation. A top-heavy structure has collapsed of its own weight—there has been no earthquake." The *New York Times* said, "The market smash has been caused by technical rather than fundamental considerations." The *Guaranty Survey,* published by the Guaranty Trust Company, remarked that "to suppose that the selling wave of the last few weeks was due to adverse developments of corresponding importance in the general business situation would be a fundamental error."[18]

Let us go back in time and look at the news on the morning of Black Thursday, October 24, 1929. Once again, the news does not seem to have been very significant. President Hoover had announced a plan to develop inland waterways. Atlantic Refinings' earnings for the year were reported to be its highest ever. The president of a sugar company had told a Senate committee investigating lobbying that $75,000 had been spent by the sugar lobby since December in a campaign to reduce duties on sugar. Negotiators had reported a setback in efforts to establish the Bank for International Settlements. A

Carnegie Fund report decried the subsidization of college athletes. The America's Cup committee had announced the rules for the next running of the yacht race. An amateur pilot attempting a solo flight across the Atlantic was reported lost. President Hoover had taken a trip on a picturesque river boat down the Ohio River.

Nothing here seems remotely to suggest anything fundamental about the outlook for the stock market. But let us look back yet another day. There was news on the Wednesday before Black Thursday of a major drop in the market (the Dow closed on Wednesday down 6.3% from Tuesday's close) and that total transactions had had their second highest day in history. Should we then look for the cause in the news of October 23, 1929? Again there was no national news of any apparent significance, but again there were references to past market moves. The most significant concrete news stories in the newspapers seem consistently to have been about previous moves of the market itself. The most prominent content in the news appears to have been interpretations of the reasons for these previous moves, often in terms of investor psychology.

There is no way that the events of the stock market crash of 1929 can be considered a response to any real news stories. We see instead a *negative bubble,* operating through feedback effects of price changes, and an *attention cascade,* with a series of heightened public fixations on the market. This sequence of events appears to be fundamentally no different from those of other market debacles—including the notorious crash of 1987, to which we now turn.

News during the Crash of 1987

When the stock market crashed on October 19, 1987—setting a new record one-day decline that nearly doubled that of either October 28 or October 29, 1929 (to this day it is the all-time record one-day price drop)—I considered it a unique opportunity to inquire directly of investors what they considered to be the significant news on that day. It was no longer necessary, as it had been for those who studied the 1929 crash, to rely on media interpretations suggesting what was the important news on investors' minds. As far as I have been able to determine, no one else took advantage of this opportunity. The results of my questionnaire survey, sent out to a sample of institutional investors and a sample of individual investors the week of the crash, were the only published findings of a survey asking investors what they were thinking on the day of the crash.[19]

In my 1987 survey, I listed all the news stories published in the few days preceding the crash that seemed at all relevant to the changing opinions of the market, ending with news that had appeared in the papers on the morning of the crash. I asked the investors:

> Please tell us how important each of the following news items was to you
> personally on October 19, 1987, in your evaluation of stock market prospects.
> Please rate them on a one-to-seven scale, with 1 indicating that the news item
> was completely unimportant, 4 indicating that it was of moderate importance,
> 7 indicating that it was very important. Please tell how important *you* then felt
> these were, and not how others thought about them.

I included ten news stories, and, in the eleventh position, a space marked
"Other" where respondents could write in their own choices.

The results were broadly similar between institutional and individual
investors, and between those who had actually bought or sold on October 19.
Respondents rated everything as relevant. They thought that most of the news
stories rated at least a 4, that is, they were of moderate importance. The only
news story that merited an average score less than 3 was the sell signal that
investment guru Robert Prechter was reported to have given on October 14,
and even that received a score of around 2. Even the news that the United States
had attacked an Iranian oil station, a minor skirmish reported on October
19, received a rating of over 3. Respondents were not very forthcoming with
other news stories in the "Other" category. They tended to mention concerns,
rather than news stories that broke at the time of the crash. The most common write-in answer was a concern about too much indebtedness, referring
variously to the federal deficit, the national debt, or taxes. Such a response
was offered by a third of the individual investors who wrote in answers and
a fifth of the institutional investors.

But the striking result was that the most highly rated news stories among
those I listed were those about *past price declines themselves*. The most important
news story, according to the respondents, was the 200-point drop in the Dow
on the morning of October 19, a news story that yielded an average score of 6.54
among individual sellers on October 19 and of 6.05 among institutional sellers
on October 19. The preceding week's news of the record (in terms of points
lost) stock market declines was considered the second most important story.

One of the questions asked respondents to give their recollections of
the interpretations they had attached to the price declines on the day of the
crash: "Can you remember any specific theory you had about the causes
for the price declines October 14–19, 1987?" Respondents were given space
to write answers in their own words, which I read and categorized. The
most common theme in the 1987 answers to this open-ended question was
that the market had been overpriced before the crash. Overpricing was
mentioned by 33.9% of the individual investors and 32.6% of the institutional investors. Although this response accounts for fewer than half the
answers, it is noteworthy that so many thought to mention this in answer
to an open-ended question. (I also asked them directly elsewhere on the
questionnaire whether they thought, just before the crash, that the market

was overpriced, and 71.7% of the individual investors [91.0% of those who had sold on October 19] and 84.3% of the institutional investors [88.5% of those who had sold on October 19] said yes.)[20] Another important theme in answer to the open-ended question was one of institutional stop-loss, identified by the presence of the words *institutional selling, program trading, stop-loss,* or *computer trading:* 22.8% of the individuals and 33.1% of the institutional investors mentioned such a theme. There was also an investor irrationality theme, identified by statements to the effect that investors were crazy or that the fall was due to investor panic or capricious changes in opinion: 25.4% of the individuals and 24.4% of the institutional investors touched on this theme. None of these major themes had anything to do with breaking news events other than the crash itself.

Immediately after this question, I asked on the questionnaire, "Which of the following better describes your theory about the declines: a theory about investor psychology [or] a theory about fundamentals such as profits or interest rates?" Most—67.5% of the institutional investors and 64.0% of the individual investors—picked a theory about investor psychology.

Thus, it appears that the stock market crash had substantially to do with a *psychological feedback loop* among the general investing public from price declines to selling and thus to further price declines, along the lines of a negative bubble, as discussed in Chapter 5. The crash apparently had nothing in particular to do with any news story other than that of the crash itself, but rather with theories about other investors' reasons for selling and about their psychology.

President Ronald Reagan, reacting to the crash, set up a study commission headed by former Treasury Secretary Nicholas Brady. He asked the Brady Commission to tell him what had caused the crash and what should be done about it. Investment professionals are generally uncomfortable going on record to explain the causes of such events, and many reports about the crash tended to focus the inquiry away from its ultimate causes. But the members of the Brady Commission were under orders from the president of the United States to face the matter head on. As a result, we have in their report the only major effort to collect all the relevant facts and explain the crash of 1987. They wrote in their summary the following explanation for the crash:

> The precipitous market decline of mid-October was "triggered" by specific events: an unexpectedly high merchandise trade deficit which pushed interest rates to new high levels, and proposed tax legislation which led to the collapse of the stocks of a number of takeover candidates. This initial decline ignited mechanical, price-insensitive selling by a number of institutions employing portfolio insurance strategies and a small number of mutual fund groups reacting to redemptions. The selling by these investors, and the prospect of further selling by them, encouraged a number of aggressive trading-oriented

institutions to sell in anticipation of further market declines. These institutions included, in addition to hedge funds, a small number of pension and
endowment funds, money management firms and investment banking houses.
This selling, in turn, stimulated further reactive selling by portfolio insurers
and mutual funds.[21]

This conclusion by the Brady Commission sounds in some ways very
much like the one I drew from my own survey-based study of the crash. By
"price-insensitive selling" they mean selling that comes in response to a price
drop but is insensitive to how low the price goes before the sale is concluded—
selling at any price. The commission was saying here, most prominently, that
the crash was caused by what I have called a feedback loop, with initial price
declines influencing more investors to exit the market, thereby creating further
price declines. The Brady Commission was saying, in effect, that the crash of
1987 was a negative bubble.

A strength of the Brady Commission's study of the crash relative to my
own was their unparalleled access to major investing institutions. Their study
complements my own in reaching the conclusion that a feedback loop was at
work in the crash. However, their conclusion sounds a bit different from mine
in that it gives prominence to the substantive content of news stories. In addition, theirs suggests that much of the selling was "mechanical" or "reactive,"
rather than psychological or herd-like.

Based on the results of my study, the news stories that the Brady Commission
mentions about the merchandise trade deficit and about new highs in interest rates cannot be considered central to investors' thinking. In my survey,
I included these in my list of news stories and got a lukewarm response from
respondents (mostly 4s). Moreover, if one looks at long-term plots of both
the trade deficit and interest rates, it is very clear that there was no sudden
break in either of these series that could possibly be seen as standing out in a
historical perspective. Virtually nothing happened to either the trade deficit
or interest rates.

The proposed tax legislation that the Brady Commission mentions had
completely escaped my notice as an important news story to include on my
list. The news had broken on October 14, five days before the crash, and it
had not seemed to me to be the subject of significant public comment in the
days leading up to the crash. Representative Dan Rostenkowski's House Ways
and Means Committee was considering tax changes that would have had the
effect of discouraging corporate takeovers. Changing capital gains tax provisions struck many would-be interpreters of the crash after the fact as having
fundamental importance for stock prices in an efficient market.

When I learned of the potential importance of this news story, I went back
over the questionnaires I had received to see how many respondents had
mentioned it in their answers under "Other." I found no mention at all among

the 605 individual responses, and only three mentions among the 284 institutional responses. Clearly, this news story does not deserve to be singled out as a major cause of the crash.[22]

The Brady Commission put quite a bit of stress on a tool of institutional investors called "portfolio insurance." Portfolio insurance is a strategy for limiting losses that was invented by Professors Hayne Leland and Mark Rubinstein at the University of California at Berkeley and was successfully marketed by them to many institutional investors in the 1980s. Portfolio insurance is really a misnomer; the strategy is merely a plan for selling stocks. It involves impressive mathematical models, but in fact it is nothing more than a formalized procedure for getting out of the market by selling stocks when they start to go down. Leland himself, in his classic 1980 article on portfolio insurance, admits as much: "Some 'rules of thumb' such as 'run with your winners, cut your losses' and 'sell at a new high, buy at a new low,' will be shown to approximate the optimal dynamic trading strategies for certain types of investors."[23] So, by using portfolio insurance, investors are merely doing what has always come naturally, only with a little more mathematical precision and careful planning. But with the fancy new name "portfolio insurance," which suggests that the strategy is prudent and sensible, and with its high-tech image, the advent of this strategy quite likely made many investors more reactive to past price changes.

The adoption of portfolio insurance by many institutional investors was a sort of fad—a sophisticated fad, but a fad nonetheless. Since it has a distinctive name (the term *portfolio insurance* had essentially not been used before 1980), it is possible to trace the course of this investor fad by means of word counts in the press. I performed such a count on ABI/INFORM, a database of business periodicals, and found no more than one reference to portfolio insurance in each of the years 1980–83, four in 1984, six in 1985, forty-one in 1986, and seventy-five in 1987. References to portfolio insurance were growing along the type of steady growth path that characterizes simple word-of-mouth epidemic models, which will be discussed in Chapter 10.[24]

So the development of portfolio insurance changed the way some investors reacted to past price changes just before the crash of 1987. There were probably other changes in the nature of the feedback loop that, because they were not so concretely programmed as portfolio insurance, we could not observe directly. But the important point is that *it was the changed nature of the feedback loop, not the news stories that broke around the time of the crash*, that was the essential cause of the crash.

Feedback can be modified by many factors, and the news media themselves can certainly have an impact on it. The *Wall Street Journal*, on the morning of the 1987 crash, ran a plot showing the Dow in the 1980s and, just below it, a plot showing the Dow in the 1920s up to and for a month after the crash of

1929.[25] The two plots were aligned so that the current date lined up with the date of the 1929 crash, and so the plot suggested that the crash of 1929 might be about to repeat itself. Investors had the opportunity to see this plot at breakfast a matter of minutes before the crash of 1987 actually started. The *Journal* was openly suggesting the possibility of a crash starting that day. True, this was not a front-page story, and no one story by itself is decisive in causing a crash. But this little story and the accompanying plot, appearing as they did on the morning of the crash, probably did help prime investors to be more alert to suggestions of a crash.

When the big price declines on the morning of October 19, 1987, began, the archetype that was the 1929 crash encouraged many people to question whether "it" was happening again—the "it" being the Great Crash as illustrated in the *Journal,* not the crash of 1907, nor the up-crash of 1932, nor any of the numerous other historical stock market events that by then had been almost completely forgotten. The mental image of the biggest crash in history possibly happening on that very day had the potential to enhance the feedback from initial price declines to later price declines. The image also provided a suggestion of how far the market would decline before it rebounded, a crucial factor in determining how far the market actually did fall. In fact, in the crash of October 19, 1987, the Dow actually fell in one day almost the same amount as it did on October 28–29, 1929—22.6% in 1987 versus 23.1% in 1929. That it fell roughly the same amount on both occasions might be regarded as just a coincidence, especially since the 1987 crash took two days rather than one, and few investors in 1987 even knew exactly how far the market fell in 1929. However, many did have a rough impression of the extent of the 1929 plunge, and there was little other concrete information available to investors on October 19, 1987, to suggest when the market should stop falling.

The changed feedback that occurred at the time of the 1987 crash should be thought of as just one example of continually changing price-to-price feedback, as investors' theories and methods change over time. It would be a mistake to describe the changed feedback as the result solely of the technological innovation represented by portfolio insurance. Despite the use of computers in executing portfolio insurance strategies, it is still people who decide to deploy the tool and who decide how quickly it will take effect in a declining market. And there are of course many other people who, aware that portfolio insurance is being used, adjust their own informal responses to past price changes depending on their perceptions of other investors' use of the strategy. Portfolio insurance is of interest to us in this context only because it shows us concretely how people's thinking can change in ways that alter the manner in which feedback from stock price changes affects further stock price changes, thereby creating possible price instabilities.

A Global Media Culture

We noted in Chapter 1 that there is a striking similarity in the behavior of stock markets over many countries, and in Chapter 3 that there is also a striking similarity in the behavior of the markets for homes in many cities around the world. This similarity stands as a sort of puzzle, since the usual economic variables do not suggest strong reasons for such similarity. It would not seem plausible that the similarity occurs directly as a result of cross feedback from the prices in one country to the prices in another. Most people rarely, if ever, look directly at data from another country. One of the reasons for this similarity must be the presence of the news media as a supporter of a global culture, and as a supporter of a speculative global culture worried that certain prices will soar or crash.

People in Paris do not watch British television and rarely read British newspapers, and people in London do not watch French television and rarely read French newspapers. And yet the people who write for these media outlets certainly do keep an eye on each others' stories. That is one of the tricks that they learn as professionals. Of course, reporters of the news, especially the serious news, feel an obligation to read the news from other countries, so as not to miss an important piece of news. But, beyond this, reporters learn from experience that an excellent way to produce good copy is to piggyback on others' successes. A sequence of stories in foreign news media is a sign of a successful story, and such a success can probably easily be replicated at home if the story is copied with only a few tweaks and adjustments for local tastes and associations.

Economists rarely talk of the news media as a force of similarity across countries; the public's expectations of economists is that they should be calculating the effects of such things as interest rates and exchange rates, not that they should be interpreting the stories that appear in newspapers around the world. We have noted that the general public does not generally think that culture and psychology are important influences on the markets, and so economists, particularly business economists who largely have to present their case to the broad public rather than to other professional economists, naturally find it to their advantage to try to live up to the public's expectations of them. The economists' behavior then only reinforces the public's impressions about the sources of market fluctuations.

One of the reasons the U.S. stock market appears to have a disproportionate effect on markets of other countries is that the United States uses the English language, which has emerged as a world language. It is much easier for foreign reporters, who invariably know English, to respond to stories from the United States or the United Kingdom than to stories from Germany or Brazil. Producing news stories is a business with tight deadlines, and it requires fast action. A lot of reporters have the ability to pick up a story from another country in English and turn it into a local story in a pinch. It's a sure-fire strategy. Even though the original story was in English, practically no viewers or readers will ever know that the reporters took the story from abroad. But trying this in a less commonly studied language would entail a significant challenge for most reporters.

One of the reasons that a housing boom in Boston in the mid-1980s moved to London and then to Paris and then to Sydney (as Figure 3.3 shows) is that the story that appeared in the earlier booms was market tested in the first countries to experience a boom and was just copied in the other countries. The story did not spread to Berlin, or to Tokyo, perhaps because the story did not have the same credibility in those countries, which have been undergoing some soul searching about the weakness of their economies. The story associated with the housing booms was one of spectacular economic success, and that kind of story just does not fly everywhere. Media professionals know instinctively when a story is ripe for copying in their country and when it is not.

Stories of foreign provenance may be especially resonant in media outlets (such as intellectual newspapers) favored by people who live in glamorous international cities. The sociologist Robert K. Merton argued that there are really two kinds of people in the world: cosmopolitans (who orient themselves to the whole world) and locals (who orient themselves to their village or town).[26] The cosmopolitans have a culture shared over the whole world. The people who inhabit the glamorous international cities of the world may, aided by the news media, become culturally closer to others in such distant cities (despite language barriers) than to rural people in their own country. It is not so surprising then that the home prices in these cities often move together.

The Role of News Media in Propagating Speculative Bubbles

The role of the news media in the stock market is not, as commonly believed, simply as a convenient tool for investors who are reacting directly to the economically significant news itself. The media actively shape public attention and categories of thought, and they create the environment in which the speculative market events we see are played out.

The examples given in this chapter illustrate that the news media are fundamental propagators of speculative price movements through their efforts to make news interesting to their audience. They sometimes strive to enhance such interest by attaching news stories to price movements that the public has already observed, thereby enhancing the salience of these movements and focusing greater attention on them. Or they may remind the public of past market episodes, or of the likely trading strategies of others. Thus, the media can sometimes foster stronger feedback from past price changes to further price changes, and they can also foster another sequence of events, referred to here as an attention cascade. This is not to say that the news media are a monolithic force pushing ideas onto a purely passive audience. The media represent a channel for mass communication and the interpretation of popular culture, but popular culture has an inherent logic and process of its own. We turn next to a study of some of the basic ideas in our culture, whose transformation over time bears a relation to the changing speculative situation in speculative markets.

Seven

New Era Economic Thinking

Speculative market expansions have often been associated with popular perceptions that the future is brighter or less uncertain than it was in the past. The term *new era* has periodically been used to describe these times.

Of course, there is some obvious validity to the new era notion. The general trend over the past century was a rise in the standard of living and a decline in the impact of economic risks on individuals. By many measures the world has indeed been gradually growing into a new and better era. But the most salient characteristic of popular new era thinking is that it is not continuously in evidence; rather, it occurs in pulses.

In contrast to the irregular references to a new era in popular culture, economists or other influential commentators who have proclaimed a new era at various times in history have usually been quite cautious in their choice of words. Often, they merely seem to be betting on the continuation of long-term trends.

Sometimes the economists may be missing things by focusing too much on the data and not on what is uniquely new about the latest changes in technology or institutions many people see as heralding a new era. But, more often, it is the general public that is missing something by overreacting to the new era stories that become suddenly popular—missing the basic similarity between the latest stories and similar stories that appeared many times in the past.

For example, the arrival of the Internet in the mid-1990s was interpreted by many casual observers as a fundamental change that would boost the productivity of the economy, since the Internet is a communications and distribution system of fundamental importance. But, if we wish to consider whether the Internet is a communications and distribution system that will produce *faster* economic growth than in the past, we have to compare it with similar systems of the past, such as those represented by postal services, railroads, telegraph, telephones, automobiles, aircraft, radio, and express highways. All of these networks had profound effects on the economies of their days, helping transform their economies from a much more primitive state. It is difficult to argue that the Internet is more important to the growth of our economy today than these were to the growth of economies of the past, and so there is no reason to expect faster growth than in the past. But the general public is not usually thinking of these past historical episodes for the purpose of comparison.

Impressions that the public is affected in different ways at different times by new era thinking—or, for that matter, by any other popular economic theory—are hard to pin down. For example, it is difficult to trace the evolution of ideas through questionnaire survey work, because one only knows to question the public about specific ideas *after* those ideas have attracted a good deal of attention.

We can do word counts of publications using computerized databases, and thereby get some idea of the changing frequency with which certain economic terms are used, but such searches are crude and miss the often subtle ways in which the use of the terms changes over time. When I tried to establish how often the phrase *new era* was used in the years leading up to the 2000 peak in the stock market, I found that the term was used in so many different contexts that a search on this phrase alone is not meaningful for our purposes. In contrast, I have established from the Lexis-Nexis database that in the English language the term *new era economy* did not have any currency until a *Business Week* cover story in July 1997 attributed this term to Alan Greenspan, marking an alleged turning point in his thinking since the "irrational exuberance" speech some months earlier.[1] The term *new era economy* remained in regular use on the way to the peak of the stock market in 2000. (The association of this term with one powerful figure provides yet another striking example of how individual actors or media events can change public thinking.)

The use of the term *new era* in this context actually preceded the *Business Week* article; in June 1997 the *Boston Globe* published a pair of articles that used the terms *new era thesis, new era theorists,* and *new era school* and identified Ralph Acampora, technical research director at Prudential Securities, as a member of the so-called school. In August 1997, a much-talked-about article by Paul Krugman in the *Harvard Business Review* attacked the newly prominent new era theory, and this of course gave the term even greater currency.[2] In the decade before 1997, the Nexis search reveals that the term *new era* was used only rarely to denote optimistic economic outlooks; in those years, the term apparently had little currency.

It is a curious fact that the development of the "new era" stories around 1997 corresponds to the approximate date when the real estate boom began in the United States and other countries. The beginning of this boom (visible in Figure 3.3) started quite sharply around 1997 in Boston, Los Angeles, Paris, and Sydney; it appears that London's increases had begun more than a year earlier.

The popularity of the term *new era* to describe the economy took hold after the 1990s stock market had advanced far enough that it was beginning to amaze people, and all the new era stories featured the stock market.[3] It was not as if some economists proclaimed a new era after looking at national income data or other data relevant to the real economic outlook. The new era theory emerged principally as an after-the-fact interpretation of a stock market boom. This is surely no surprise. A stock market boom is a dramatic event that calls for an equally dramatic interpretation. In contrast, an increase in the growth rate of the gross domestic product—from, say, 2% to 3%—although perhaps exciting to economists, does not make the same impression on the general public. It is insubstantial, esoteric, and simply cannot hold its own against the flashier news offerings bombarding the public.

Whenever the market reaches a new high, public speakers, writers, and other prominent people suddenly appear, armed with explanations for the apparent optimism seen in the market. Reporters may not always get the timing right, and they may suggest that it was the words spoken by these great men and women that caused the market shifts. Although prominent people can certainly move markets, often their wisdom merely tags along with market moves. Nevertheless, the new era thinking they promote is part of the process by which a boom may be sustained and amplified—part of the feedback mechanism that, as we have seen, can create speculative bubbles.

A defender of markets' rationality might point out that even if discussions of a new era really are the cause of the boom, it does not follow that news accounts of these discussions must precede the boom. Technically, of course, it is possible—in spite of the fact that most media discussions of new era theories seem to coincide with or come after stock market booms—that the *word-of-mouth* discussions did in fact precede and cause the booms. The news media might have been late to recognize the discussions.

But that defense of markets' rationality is not very plausible if we consider the nature of the thought patterns observed among the general investing public. There is such a lack of interest among the public in reasoned arguments about the future course of the corporate sector that it is highly unlikely that the public could have been harboring secret thoughts of a new era in corporate profits unrelated to past stock price increases.

It appears that most people are not interested in long-run economic growth forecasts for the aggregate economy. Economic theory would suggest that they should be interested, if they are behaving rationally. But in fact the topic is too abstract, boring, or technical. The public is interested in expansive descriptions of future technology—for example, in what amazing new capabilities computers will soon have—not in gauging the level of U.S. corporate earnings in coming years. In fact, it is doubtful that more than a small percentage of the populace today could give an estimate of aggregate U.S. corporate earnings accurate to within an order of magnitude. They are hardly likely to be interested in predicting changes in those same earnings.

History does show that there are at times strong unseen forces acting on public opinion that are not revealed in the media or in public discussions until some key event brings them out of the woodwork. But such currents in public opinion typically relate to naive theories based on personal observations or ill-founded prejudices against minority groups or foreign countries. The public simply does not harbor secret opinions about the economic growth rate.[4]

Conventional wisdom interprets the stock market as reacting to new era theories. In fact, it appears that the stock market often *creates* new era theories, as reporters scramble to justify stock market price moves. The situation reminds one of the Ouija board, where players are encouraged to interpret the meaning of movements in their trembling hands and to distill forecasts from them. Or the stock market is seen as an oracle, issuing mysterious and meaningless pronouncements, which we then ask our leaders to interpret, mistakenly investing their interpretations with authority.

In this chapter, I analyze the "new era" thinking that accompanied previous stock market and real estate market booms in the United States. I also offer some indications of the public's thinking in the times when the "new eras" had run their course. I make liberal use of contemporary quotations, since these provide the most direct evidence of people's thoughts and concerns.

The 1901 Optimism: The Twentieth-Century Peak

As noted in Chapter 1, the first of the three major peaks in the price-earnings ratio since 1881 occurred in June 1901, right at the dawn of the twentieth century. Prices had achieved spectacular increases over the preceding twelve months, and in mid-1901, observers reported real speculative fervor: "The outburst of speculation during April, 1901, was something rarely paralleled in the history of speculative manias. . . . The newspapers were full of stories of hotel waiters, clerks in business offices, even doorkeepers and dressmakers, who had won considerable fortunes in their speculations. The effect on the public mind may be imagined."[5]

With the beginning of the century in January 1901, there was much talk of the future and of technological progress to come: "trains [will be] running at 150 miles per hour, . . . newspaper publishers will press the buttons and automotive machinery will do the rest, . . . phonographs as salesmen will sell goods in the big stores while automatic hands will make change."[6] Guglielmo Marconi made the first transatlantic radio transmission in 1901, and there were predictions that we would soon be in radio communication with the planet Mars.

The Pan-American Exposition in Buffalo, New York, from May 1 to November 1, 1901, emphasized high technology. It had as its centerpiece the 375-foot Electric Tower, illuminated by 44,000 light bulbs powered by faraway generators at Niagara Falls. The tower was "indescribably brilliant" and held visitors "spellbound."[7] The exposition's Electricity Building featured exhibits about the wonders of electricity. There was an electrograph, a machine that transmitted pictures by wire (forerunner of the fax machine), and a tel-autograph, a machine that enabled one to transmit one's signature over long distances (forerunner of credit card signature-verification devices). The exposition even offered a simulated trip to the moon on the airship *Luna:* the visitor could take a stroll through the streets and shops of the moon before returning to earth.

In a sense, the high-tech age, the computer age, and the space age seemed just around the corner in 1901, though the concepts were expressed in different words than we would use today. People were upbeat, and in later years the first decade of the twentieth century came to be called the Age of Optimism, the Age of Confidence, or the Cocksure Era. The mood was perhaps similar to that of a century later, just past the dawn of the twenty-first century. Given the modern media's exploitation of anniversary or threshold events, and the human tendency to consider such events as symbolic new beginnings, investing them with exaggerated hopes and expectations, the transitions to new centuries may tend to be optimistic times. The 1901 example suggests that today our new-century optimism might in fact extend for years into the new millennium, at least in some forms and assuming it is not too impacted by unfavorable world events. Whether the events of 9/11, the global financial crisis of 2008, wars and revolutions in the Middle East, and political tensions elsewhere in the world will be enough to shake our confidence in a lasting way remains to be seen.

But there was another reason people in 1901 thought that the stock market ought to be highly valued. The most prominent business news in the papers in recent years had been about the formation of numerous combinations, trusts, and mergers in a wide variety of businesses, stories such as the formation of U.S. Steel out of a number of smaller steel companies. Many stock market forecasters in 1901 saw these developments as momentous, and the term *community of interest* was commonly used to describe the new economy dominated by them. An April 1901 editorial in the *New York Daily Tribune* explained:

But a new era has come, the era of "community of interest," whereby it is hoped to avoid ruinous price cutting and to avert the destruction which has in the past, when business depression occurred, overtaken so many of the competing concerns in every branch of industry. In the great iron and steel industry, for example, which, as Andrew Carnegie has said, has been the prince and the pauper of the industrial world, now highly prosperous again and again deeply depressed, consolidations of scores of scattered concerns into a dozen larger ones within the last two years have now been followed by the combination of the latter into the most gigantic combination the world has ever known, a combination which, if the expectations of its projectors are fulfilled, will result in the avoiding of much economic waste through eliminating the possibility of the erection of unnecessary plants for competitive reasons, in the effecting of many economies through the abolishing of duplicate official positions and establishment of a uniform price list, and in the enlargement of export trade by reason of the lower prices which can be fixed in consequence of the various economies coincident to consolidation.

In the railroad field, too, combination is the ruling idea, and for the same reasons. Competing roads are being consolidated or leased, with resulting economy of operation and permanent cessation of rate cutting, and representatives of powerful roads are going into the boards of heretofore incorrigible rate cutting lines, in which bodies they have an influence potent, if not controlling.[8]

These reasons for optimism for the stock market are certainly plausible. It is easily believable that elimination of competition might create monopoly profits for corporations, thus boosting their share prices.

But the editorial does not mention the potential for antitrust law to end the "community of interest" era. In September 1901, the pro-business president William McKinley was assassinated while visiting the Pan-American Exposition; he was succeeded by his "cowboy" vice-president, Teddy Roosevelt. It was only six months later, in March 1902, that Roosevelt dusted off the almost-forgotten Sherman Antitrust Act of 1890 and used it against the Northern Securities Company. Over the next seven years, he embarked on a vigorous antitrust policy. When the defects of the Sherman Act became apparent, the Clayton Antitrust Act of 1914 furthered the government's assault on corporate combinations.

The premise of the "community of interest" theory of stock prices turned out to be wrong; those who expressed high optimism for stocks on this basis were not thinking of all that could go wrong. People were not considering the possibility that society would not tolerate this shift of wealth toward stockholders. Presumably they did not consider this because there had not yet been any concrete antitrust activity. Yet in thinking about the level of the stock market, one must of course consider the long-run earnings, spread over future decades, that the market represents, and the potential for society to make adjustments, positive or negative, to control this earnings stream.

Rarely do discussions of the level of the stock market consider the possibility of government reaction to the level of profits, even though government policy toward corporations has changed substantially and dramatically over time. The U.S. Federal statutory corporate profits tax alone has been adjusted many times, from 0% in 1901, to 1% in 1911, to 10% in 1921, to 14% in 1931, to 31% in 1941, to 50.75% with a 30% excess-profits tax in 1951, to 35% today. Despite the fact that the U.S. government's past actions raised the corporate profits tax from 0% to 50.75%, effectively nationalizing something on the order of half the stock market (to the extent that they actually enforced and sustained the tax), potential future adjustments in this tax are rarely mentioned in discussing the outlook for the market.

The 1901 example illustrates one way in which new era thinking can go wrong: such thinking concentrates attention on the effects of events currently prominent in the news. Little attention is paid to "what-ifs," even if they have substantial probability.

There was another important theme in 1901—that stocks were now being held in "strong hands": "The ownership of stocks has changed hands. The public speculators do not now own them. They are owned by people who are capable of protecting them under any circumstances, such as the Standard Oil, Morgan, Kuhn Loeb, Gould and Harriman Interests. These people who are the foremost financiers of the country evidently know when they go into a proposition what ultimate results may be expected."[9] This theory, like theories expressed at other market peaks, finds it inconceivable that there could be a selling panic. In the shortest run, perhaps this theory was right. But those strong hands did not stop the stock market crash of 1907 or the dramatic slide of stock values between 1907 and 1920.

The 1920s Optimism

The bull market of the 1920s was apparently a time of relatively great public enthusiasm for and interest in the stock market, and the enthusiasm seemed to peak in 1929 with the market. In his 1931 book *Only Yesterday*, Frederick Lewis Allen wrote of 1929:

> The rich man's chauffeur drove with his ears laid back to catch the news of an impending move in Bethlehem Steel; he held 50 shares himself on a twenty-point margin. The window cleaner at the broker's office paused to watch the ticker, for he was thinking of converting his laboriously accumulated savings into a few shares of Simmons. Edwin Lefevre (an articulate reporter on the market at this time who could claim a considerable personal experience) told of a broker's valet who made nearly a quarter of a million in the market; of a trained nurse who cleaned up thirty thousand following the tips given her by grateful patients; of a Wyoming cattleman, thirty miles from the nearest railroad, who bought or sold a thousand shares a day.[10]

Although this account may create an exaggerated impression of the level of public attention to the stock market, there is no question that attention was much keener in the 1920s than at other times, and that enthusiastic investors were not hard to find.

The 1920s were a time of rapid economic growth and, in particular, of the widespread dissemination of some technological innovations that had formerly been available only to the wealthy. The automobile came into common use at roughly this time. In 1914, only 1.7 million automobiles were registered in the United States, but by 1920 there were 8.1 million, and by 1929, there were 23.1 million. The automobile brought with it a new sense of freedom and possibility and a widespread awareness that these personal values could be attained by new technology.

The 1920s were also the time when the electrification of the country was extended beyond the major cities, which had already been electrified. By 1929, twenty million U.S. homes were wired. Kerosene lamps were out; electric light bulbs were in. By 1929, nearly half of all wired homes had vacuum cleaners, and a third had washing machines. Moreover, the 1920s saw the expansion of radio broadcasting and the development of radio as a mature national entertainment medium. In 1920, there were only three radio stations in the entire United States; by 1923, there were over five hundred. Nationally known radio stars like Rudy Vallee and nationally popular shows like *Amos 'n' Andy* appeared in the 1920s. The National Broadcasting Company formed the first national network in 1926, and regular shows created a sense of national culture previously unknown. Sound also invaded our movies. Lee De Forest invented the sound-on-film system in 1923, and talkies had completely displaced silent movies by the end of the decade. Because these innovations had such an impact on everyday lives, affecting people in their homes and in their hours of leisure, the 1920s were a time when massive technological progress was unusually apparent to even the most casual observer.

There were, at the time of the 1920s stock market boom, many clear statements proclaiming a new era for the economy. For example, as early as 1925 we hear, "There is nothing now to be foreseen which can prevent the United States from enjoying an era of business prosperity which is entirely without equal in the pages of trade history."[11]

John Moody, head of Moody's Investors Service, a rating agency, said in an article about the stock market in 1928, "In fact, a new age is taking form throughout the entire civilized world; civilization is taking on new aspects. We are only now beginning to realize, perhaps, that this modern, mechanistic civilization in which we live is now in the process of perfecting itself."[12]

Given the public enthusiasm for stocks and the enormous run-up in the market, there was a corresponding demand for books that interpreted and justified the market boom. In 1929, Charles Amos Dice, in *New Levels in the*

Stock Market, gave a number of reasons to expect the increase to continue. He preferred the term *new world* to *new era,* but the idea was the same. He wrote of a "new world of industry," referring to techniques of mass production, large research departments, the beginning of the electrical age, the industrialization of the South, the emergence of large-scale production, and the mechanization of agriculture. Furthermore, Dice wrote of a "new world of distribution," predicting the proliferation of installment credit, the chain-store movement, new techniques of advertising that would stimulate demand, and new market research techniques. He also spoke of a "new world of finance," referring to the expansion of investment banking to provide new sources of funds for corporations, the rise of the holding company as a tool to make financing more flexible, and advances in the Federal Reserve System's understanding of how to stabilize business. Dice described the Federal Reserve as analogous to the governor on a steam engine, regulating the speed of the economy.[13]

The Dice book, curiously, was printed in August 1929, a month before the peak of the market prior to the onset of the Great Depression. The timing of the book's appearance seems even more remarkable when one finds attached at page 69 a small slip of paper titled "Errata." The slip, apparently added after the text was printed but before the book was bound, notes that the Dow Jones Industrial Average rose on September 3, 1929, to over 20 points above the level indicated in the book. The slip of paper instructs the reader to adjust upward the projections for the Dow given in the printed book by 15 to 20 points. Thus Dice managed to time his book for the exact peak of the market, and thus managed to make the most catastrophic error possible in forecasting the market.

Professor Irving Fisher at Yale, who has been described as one of America's most eminent economists of his day, argued that the U.S. stock market was not at all overvalued. He was quoted as saying just before the peak in 1929 that "stock prices have reached what looks like a permanently high plateau." He wrote a book titled *The Stock Market Crash—and After,* with a preface dated less than two months after Black Thursday. Fisher must have been working on this book at the same time as Dice was writing his, but his timing was not so bad. The 1929 crash came while he was still at work on the book. Yet Fisher was still able to be optimistic after the crash, especially since the market had gone down only a fraction of the distance it ultimately would by 1932, and the crash did not yet seem to signal anything like the end of an era.

Fisher argued in his book that the outlook was for rapidly increasing earnings for a number of reasons, some of them parallel to those cited by Dice. First, he pointed out that the merger movement of the 1920s allowed economies of large-scale production. He noted that "the economies from mergers take time to develop, while the effect on the stock market of their formation is instant." Scientific research and invention were proceeding at a faster pace than before. The advantages of the automobile were only just beginning to be exploited, with the development of a rapidly widening network of surfaced highways. Much was being learned about the efficient use of waste products. In agriculture, recent inventions included subsoil plowing, better fertilizers, enhanced breeds of farm animals, and new and improved crops. As all of these inventions gradually came to be applied, further earnings increases could be anticipated from them. Fisher also maintained that the management of American corporations was improving, thanks to the application of "scientific" methods, improved layouts of manufacturing facilities, and more sophisticated management techniques. Businesses were able to plan better for the future, he claimed, partly because of his own invention of "master-charting," a pencil-and-paper method of priority planning for executives. Fisher also was encouraged by his perception that labor unions were now accepting joint responsibility for the solution of industrial problems.[14]

Others argued that the market valuations of the 1920s were sound because we were in a more sober time—and not just figuratively. The prohibition of alcoholic beverages was thought to be a sign of greater steadiness and intelligence: "Many different things contributed to this happy result. . . . [including] the elimination from our national life of the saloon and its destructive elements, and consequent comparative sobriety among the population as a whole. Most of the money formerly spent in the saloon has since gone into continually higher standards of living, investments and savings banks."[15]

Of course, optimistic sentiments for the market were not the only sentiments expressed at the time. The high price of the market relative to rough measures of fundamental value did not go unnoticed in 1929. The *New York Times* and the *Commercial and Financial Chronicle* consistently pointed out what they interpreted as speculative excess. Paul M. Warburg of the International Acceptance Bank decried the "unrestrained speculation."[16] Yet we know, from the level of the stock market itself, that the weight of public sentiment was overwhelmingly positive in the 1920s.

New Era Thinking of the 1950s and 1960s

New era thinking also seemed, judging from media accounts, to undergo a sudden surge in the mid-1950s, when the market increased 94.3% in real (inflation-corrected) terms between September 1953 and December 1955. The market had been stalled during most of the early 1950s, amid lingering fears that the economy might sink back into a depression now that the stimulus of increased World War II production was absent. But the sudden near-doubling in the stock market, supported by a solid growth in earnings, apparently caused the investing public to forget such fears and to indulge in genuine new era thinking. In May 1955, *U.S. News and World Report* wrote:

Once again the feel of a "new era" is in the air. Confidence is high, optimism almost universal, worry largely absent.

War is receding as a threat. Peace is a growing prospect. Jobs are quite plentiful. Pay never was so good. The promise is that taxes will be cut. Everywhere things are in a rising trend.

Three times in 10 years a depression scare has come and gone without amounting to much. The first scare came in 1946, right after World War II. Military spending was cut drastically with scarcely a ripple. The second scare came in 1949. The public went right on buying, oblivious to the worries of businessmen, and this scare faded. The third scare began in mid-1953. It now is little more than a memory.[17]

The sense that investors were terribly optimistic and confident of the market was in and of itself part of the new era thinking. *Newsweek* wrote in December 1955 that "basic to the upsurge [in the stock market] was an investor faith in the overwhelming strength of the economy—and the fact that corporations were cashing in on this prosperity."[18]

In a development strongly paralleling the evolution of radio in the 1920s as the vehicle for a mass national culture, the early 1950s had seen the widespread introduction of television. In 1948, only 3% of U.S. families owned television sets; by 1955, 76% did. Like the Internet, television was a vivid technological innovation that captured the imagination of almost everyone. It was evidence for technological progress that could not be overlooked; within a few short years the majority of Americans began regularly spending hours watching an electronic device.

Inflation was very low at the time, and people credited this to newly enlightened Fed policy. Treasury Secretary George Humphrey boasted in 1955:

In the past 2¾ years, the value of the dollar has changed only one-half of one cent. We have kept inflation's hand out of your savings almost entirely.

We regard inflation as a public enemy of the worst type. But we have not hesitated, either, to ease or restrict the basis of credit when need was indicated. The full force of monetary policy has been made effective more promptly than ever before to respond to natural demands. This has been done by the timely use of monetary policy and credit; by the return to the public of purchasing power through the biggest tax cut in the history of the nation; by cutting unjustified Government spending; by timely encouragement to construction, home building and needed improvements.[19]

Something analogous to the "strong hands" theme seen in the 1900s—the idea that the demand for stocks was stable enough to prevent any downturn—was present in the 1950s as well. *Newsweek* wrote in 1955:

Many financial men like to think that the nation has developed a "new capitalism" with an ever-broadening base. Some 7.5 million people hold stock in publicly owned corporations, compared with 6.5 million three years ago. Assets of mutual funds, which give the small investor a chance to spread his risk, have soared from $1.3 billion in 1946 to $7.2 billion. Thousands of workers have become owners of the firms they work for via employee stock-purchase plans.

All this may not add up to an absolute guarantee against another '29, but most experts are confident that it goes a long way.[20]

The idea that Irving Fisher had presented in the 1920s as a reason for optimism, that businesses were able to plan better for the future, was floated again as a new idea in the 1950s: "There is a new attitude of business itself that promises to avoid deep depressions in the future. Business firms today make long-term plans and appear to be less influenced than in the past by short-term fluctuations in activity."[21]

The Baby Boom was seen as another important factor driving prosperity and the market, because people needed to spend money on their babies (just as the grown-up babies themselves, despite having fewer children, are now perceived as bidding up stock prices as they save for their retirement): "It is this boom in babies that is being counted on now to make the latest 'new era' different from the last one. Families are growing bigger. Good roads and fine automobiles are opening the countryside. The urge is toward suburban living and for houses with three or four bedrooms instead of one or two."[22]

The increase in the use of consumer credit was also cited, as it had been in the 1920s, as a reason to expect prosperity: "This willingness to lay out cash amounted, in the opinion of one influential Washington individual, to a 'consumer spending revolution.' . . . In spending his money, the average individual's wants have gradually been upgraded."[23]

With the election of John Kennedy as president in 1960, and given his advocacy of economic stimulus measures, it was generally thought that the economy ought to do especially well. Kennedy inspired confidence beginning with his initial State of the Union message in 1961. He was perceived as showing vision and optimism, and he hit upon a dramatic symbol for that vision by promising, in a special message to Congress in May 1961, that the United States would land men on the moon before 1970. Americans expected that such an achievement would be remembered for centuries, marking as it would humankind's first escape from its planet of origin. Kennedy was viewed as the incarnation of the national optimism and of the strength of the stock market: "Wall Street has a simple description for the phenomenal strength of stock prices, 'The Kennedy Market.'" The confidence inspired by the Kennedy economic program led some to conclude that the country was entering a "new economy" in which "businessmen can enjoy reasonably continuous prosperity indefinitely" and that there was "more justification for confidence" in monetary policy than in times past.[24] The Kennedy initiatives were expanded by the "Great Society" program of his successor, Lyndon Johnson, beginning in

1964; Johnson's program set as its primary goals nothing less than an end to poverty and urban decay.

In the 1960s, the theory that the stock market is the "best investment" was prominent: "Investors feel that stocks are the best investment medium—as a hedge against possible inflation, as a means of participating in the future growth of business." "Investors seem to be betting that inflation will accompany recovery—and that common stocks, even at present prices, represent the only real hedge."[25] At that time, investors believed that if inflation broke out, the stock market would go up, rather than down, as is now commonly thought; therefore, the prospect of inflation was a reason to own stocks. There was concern in the early 1960s that, even though there was virtually no inflation, the Kennedy-Johnson economic programs could become inflationary.

A possibly significant factor behind the 1960s market peak was the Dow's approach to 1,000. That the approach of a new milestone such as a four-digit Dow would have an impact on the public imagination may seem silly, but, given the lack of any other solid basis for the market's valuation, talk of such an arbitrary level provided a solid anchor for people's expectations.

Even before the Dow got close to 1,000, the press was counting the milestones. A 1965 *Business Week* article noted, "Like the four-minute mile, psychological barriers are made to be cracked. It's no less so in Wall Street, where the 900 'magic' mark on the Dow-Jones industrial average (as the 600, 700, and 800 marks before it) will probably crumble sooner or later." *Newsweek* wrote that the 900 barrier had reached "almost mystical significance in the minds of many observers." In 1966, when the 1,000 level loomed, *Time* wrote, "At week's end the average had reached 986.13, less than 14 points from the 1000 mark that the Street considers a mystical number. Even though that number may be more mystical than meaningful, the date of the breakthrough will appear in history books of decades, or perhaps even centuries, to come—and the date is not far off."[26] The market appears to have raced to just under 1,000, but it would not pass the magic number for a long time. Although the Dow was not then computed on a minute-by-minute basis, it finally rose above 1,000 (if computed using the highs for the day) in January 1966. It was not until 1972, the eve of the stock market crash, that the Dow closed above 1,000, and even then, it stayed above 1,000 only briefly.

The Dow did not rise solidly above 1,000 until 1982, and, if one computes a real stock price, it did not rise above the 1966 high in real terms—and stay above it—until January 1992, twenty-six years later.[27] The period from January 1966 to January 1992 was one of low returns, confined as it was (with no capital gain) to income from dividends; the average annual real stock market return was only 4.1% per year.[28] These are signs consistent with a notion that the market was in some sense "reaching" toward 1,000 in 1966, and that it became relatively overpriced.

New Era Thinking during the Bull Market of the 1990s

I have already described some of the new era thinking that characterized the 1990s in Chapter 4. Here I make just a few additional observations and then contrast the new era thinking of the more recent Millennium Boom and the Ownership-Society Boom with that during the new eras described in this chapter.

As with all major stock market booms, there were writers during the 1990s who offered new era theories to justify the market. Michael Mandel, writing in *Business Week* in 1996 in an article titled "The Triumph of the New Economy," listed five reasons for his belief that the market was not crazy: increased globalization, the boom in high-tech industries, moderating inflation, falling interest rates, and surging profits.[29]

A prominent theory during this boom was that low inflation makes for a strong market outlook. In the 1990s, theories about inflation dominated discussion of the market outlook just as they did in the 1960s, but now the prevalent theory had been reversed. In the 1990s, it was thought that if inflation were to break out, the market would go down rather than up. The idea that the stock market is a good investment because it is a hedge against inflation (that is, it will go up if there is an outbreak of inflation) was dead.

Why did people in the 1990s think that inflation would push the market down, whereas in the 1960s they thought it would push it up? In the 1990s, investors may have been reacting to literature published by economists showing that economies do more poorly during sudden outbursts of very high inflation. In fact, these studies do not show much of a relation between moderate or long-run inflation and real economic performance; over the relevant range, they would suggest that the 1960s-era theory was right—that the real value of the stock market should be relatively immune to news of inflation, and that the stock market should move with consumer prices, not against them.[30] More likely, people in the 1990s were reacting to the fact that the stock market had in recent years moved against inflation, rather than with it.

Many of the same themes that appeared in the 1920s, 1950s, and 1960s after stock market booms were repeated in the 1990s.

Roger Bootle, in his 1998 book *The Death of Inflation*, argued that the "inflationary era," during which "managed capitalism" and strong labor unions had induced an inflationary spiral, was drawing to a close. In "managed capitalism," "prices were decided, not determined by the interplay of interpersonal supply and demand." Now, Bootle declared, we were entering the "zero era," brought on by global capitalism, privatization, and the decline of labor unions, all of which made it impossible for prices to be decided by committee.[31]

Steven Weber, with his 1997 article "The End of the Business Cycle" in the public policy journal *Foreign Affairs*, argued that macroeconomic risks were lower now: "Changes in technology, ideology, employment and finance, along with the globalization of production and consumption, have reduced the volatility of economic activity in the industrialized world. For both empirical and theoretical reasons in advanced industrial economies the waves of the business cycle may be becoming more like ripples." Weber presented a number of reasonable-sounding arguments. For instance, he noted that the economy has come to be dominated by the service sector in a way that it was not thirty years ago, and he pointed out that service employment has always been more stable than industrial production.[32]

Downsizing and restructuring—terms describing so-called managerial revolutions in the 1980s—were thought then to be important reasons for the growth of profits since 1982. The thought that they are still sources of profit growth lingers in some people's minds today. Yet there has also been substantial skepticism about these managerial revolutions, as exemplified by the comic strip *Dilbert*, which dwells on petty labor-management conflicts in the new era economy.

The statistics on the growth of labor productivity made some impressive gains in the United States in the late 1990s. This helped confirm, in many people's minds, the advantages that the Internet and other new forms of high technology were offering to the economy, and was seen as justifying the appreciation in the stock market. And yet the high productivity growth in the late 1990s was partly a data error: the U.S. Bureau of Labor Statistics revised the 1998–2000 growth figures substantially downward in 2001, well after the stock market boom.[33] Moreover, even to the extent that the productivity growth numbers were good, people read far too much into them. The numbers became a justification for admiring the Internet, when in fact the growth of productivity then had nothing to do with the fledgling new Internet, which was not yet a significant factor in the overall economy. Even beyond this, people didn't realize how tenuous the historical relation between productivity growth and stock market gains really is.[34] Productivity growth hasn't been a reason to expect the stock market to do well. But the story in the 1990s that the reported productivity growth justified and explained the spectacular stock market appreciation was too good for stock market boosters and the news media to pass up.

It should be noted that not all stories in the media in the 1990s were slanted toward new era thinking compared with stories during earlier episodes of high pricing. I could not find 1990s accounts that were as expansively and breathlessly optimistic as some in 1901 or 1929, and although there was much optimism in the media in the 1990s, it was usually a matter of background presumption rather than bold assertion. There appears to have been a media attitude change, and optimistic hyperbole was out in the 1990s, just as it is still out of fashion today in the second decade of the twenty-first century.

If anything, many writers in the 1990s seemed rather more influenced by concerns about market overpricing and speculative mania. In fact, many media accounts in the mid- to late 1990s focused on what they considered the craziness of investors. For example, a *Fortune* story in April 1996 told of reporters stopping random people on the street and asking them for stock tips. They stopped a policeman, a Starbucks barista, a carpenter on a billboard crew, and an ID checker at a fitness club, and all of them offered expansive stock recommendations. They could not find a shoeshine boy, but otherwise their experience mirrored that of Bernard Baruch before the crash of 1929, who remarked that he had received stock tips from the shoeshine boy and interpreted that as a sign of market excess.[35] Articles with titles like "Gamblers High: Is This a Market Where Yesterday's Yardsticks Don't Apply?" or "It's Tulip Time on Wall Street" or "Say Goodbye to the Last Bear" abounded. The possibility that the stock market boom was a speculative bubble was certainly thrust before the minds of readers in the 1990s. But the evidence in the markets is that the public in the 1990s found these possibilities at best mildly amusing; they were far more swept up in the new era thinking symbolized for them by the coming of the new millennium.

Some New Era Thinking in Real Estate Booms

Real estate booms are driven by new era thinking just as much as are stock market booms. Price-to-price feedback may be in a sense the primary driver of a real estate boom, but a new era story contributes as well, or may appear as part of the feedback. As we have noted, national booms in large countries appear to be a new thing, but there are plenty of examples from long ago of *regional* real estate booms, and these have their *regional* new era stories.

A real estate boom covering a substantial area of California occurred in the 1880s, peaking in 1887. The boom was primarily in Los Angeles, San Diego, and Santa Barbara, sparsely populated then and so of little significance to the United States as a whole. This boom appears to have been connected with the rapid development at the time of railroads, which were just making much of this land more accessible. The boom was apparently precipitated by a rate war between the Santa Fe and the Union Pacific railroads, which made it suddenly very cheap to travel to and from Southern California. The railroads also, with hopes of recouping their investment in trackage, financed a legion of promoters who attracted people to migrate to the region by extolling the wonderful climate and brilliant future of southern California. They were a success: "Los Angeles was a crowded, seething city of promoters, amateur and professional; hotels bulged with occupants, prices soared to astronomic levels, and everywhere—on the streets, in print, in homes and clubs—the incessant topic was land, the land of southern California."[36] The boom was followed by a collapse in prices in 1888–89: "Persons who had been talking 'land and climate' for two years now regretted intensely the lack of a stable industrial basis for southern California's economy. Worried citizens looked back upon their frenzied existence during 1887 and began to realize that 'never, perhaps, did a community more completely lose its sense of values and proportion.'"[37] The story of the boom of the 1880s serves to remind us that people were capable of worrying that available land was getting scarce even more than 100 years ago. The difference then was only that the story didn't spread nationally. California already had circumstances then that set it apart, and apparently no one thought the boom would spread nationwide.

In the early twentieth century, another remarkable regional home price bubble occurred in Florida, especially in the Miami area, peaking in 1925. It seemed to be driven by a new era story that after World War I people with the new wealth and automobiles of the Roaring Twenties were just discovering the possibility of commuting to Florida for the winter, and the land was selling fast. People who believed this story might feel some urgency to buy. Another precipitating factor for this bubble was the 1924 Florida constitutional amendment prohibiting income and inheritance taxes, a factor encouraging wealthy retirees to relocate to Florida, as well as an extensive advertising campaign by the Miami Chamber of Commerce. There was also the story, for fun-loving people, of the "Florida lifestyle" with so many speakeasies and gambling casinos. The fact that many celebrities were making the area their home, including even gangster Al Capone, gave this story some newsworthiness, as well as credibility. This bubble is famous for the "binder boys" who persuaded would-be homebuyers all over the country to pay a binder fee to buy Florida land, and who then were able to sell the binders. The bubble ended abruptly after a 1926 hurricane reminded people of some Florida dangers, and when newspapers around the country turned on the bubble and recounted stories of gullible people who had been persuaded to buy land they had not even seen that later turned out to be unusable, even under water.[38]

Like the 1880s land boom in southern California, the 1925 Florida boom was intrinsically regional. There were stories that genuinely excited people, but they did not, could not, extend to the country as a whole.

In the closing decades of the twentieth century, we began to see rather strong regional real estate booms in the United States, as well as other countries, and these covered a large enough part of their respective countries that they began to affect the national home price indices. The causes of these movements are harder to see. In the last decades of the twentieth century, the booms appear to have been broader in geographical scope and tied up with broader sentiment, political issues, or issues about the economic base of the area.

In the United States, there were two major regional home price booms that were big enough that they had an effect on the national home price index that was plotted in Figure 3.1, a boom in California in 1975–80 and a boom in the northeastern United States in 1984–88, which eventually carried over into California in 1986–89.

Real (inflation-corrected) home prices in the entire state of California rose 60% between 1975 and 1980, before falling in the mid-1980s.[39] A factor driving this boom was a relatively sudden appearance of a political movement advancing environmental interests in California, which created more stringent zoning laws and building restrictions. California had grown with relatively few zoning restrictions, but, starting around in the 1960s, Californians decided collectively to do something about this. The effect was to make California, around the 1970s, one of the most difficult places in the country to build new houses.[40]

This political change limited the supply of new homes, so that the safety valve that had prevented price increases from taking place was no longer so effective. It was viewed by some critics as a victory for the haves versus the have-nots, the people who already owned homes versus those who did not. This victory was widely appreciated and served to boost the value of existing homes.

Another factor driving this bubble was Proposition 13, a voter referendum in June 1978 that produced a change in the California constitution that had the immediate effect of cutting property taxes by more than half and guaranteed that property taxes would remain lower. This was another political move that was viewed as increasing the value of property by cutting taxes on it. The fact that voters had put Proposition 13 in place despite dire warnings about the consequences of lower tax revenues from established political figures was viewed as the harbinger of a new economic era.

Both the enhanced zoning standards and Proposition 13 were signals of a new era when existing individual property rights would be more respected, and when one might imagine that one's real estate investments would become more valuable. It was one of the beginnings of the ownership society—one that, along with the election of Margaret Thatcher in the United Kingdom, boosted the career of California governor Ronald Reagan, soon to become president of the United States based on his new message, and would later spread to much of the world.

One wonders, though, how the California boom of the 1970s could have happened then, given that mortgage rates were setting new record highs, reaching over 10% in the same year as the fastest home price increase: 1978. Such high mortgage rates would certainly seem to have the effect of putting a damper on a bubble, because they would mean that homebuyers would have to make very large mortgage payments if they bought an expensive house. In 1978, with such high interest rates, purchasing a house worth four years' income would result in interest payments alone amounting to over 40% of one's income, very difficult for most families to budget. But this boom should dispel any notions that real estate booms are always stopped by high interest rates.

One of the explanations of how this could have happened in the 1970s is that homeowners, upset with the high interest rates, used the political process to challenge due-on-sale clauses in mortgages with lower interest rates and thereby avoid paying the higher interest rates.[41] During the 1970s boom, and for a couple of years thereafter, assumable mortgages shielded the housing market from the effects of high interest rates. Also, during the late 1970s, a new institution called "creative financing" appeared and flourished.[42]

This resulted in the first U.S. regional real estate boom large enough to have a real impact on the national home price numbers. It was interrupted by the severe recessions of the early 1980s.

Another home price boom appeared in the northeastern United States in the mid-1980s, with its epicenter in Boston. In 1985 alone, home prices in the Boston metropolitan area went up 38%.

It is hard to identify any local factor that explains the Boston real estate boom. In a 1986 study, Karl Case reviewed all of the fundamental factors that might be driving a boom in Boston home prices and concluded that nothing had changed very much in Boston in recent years: "While the economy is healthy and income is growing, market 'fundamentals' do not seem to offer an adequate explanation for the very rapid increase in home prices in the Boston area since 1983."[43]

Low interest rates were often cited by the media as responsible for producing the boom. Indeed, interest rates were lower in the late 1980s than they had been in the early 1980s. But lower interest rates cannot directly account for the boom in Boston, since the boom was regional, not national, and the interest rates were lower everywhere. The best one can say about lower interest rates as a factor leading to the Boston boom is that they were permissive, reducing the barriers to a bubble that was precipitated by something else. By the way, mortgage rates were even lower in the mid-1990s, when Boston prices were falling, than they were during the boom of the 1980s.

The remarkable home price boom in Boston in the mid-1980s had a new era story connected with it as well, but again not a suddenly new story. It is true that in the 1980s, Boston was emerging as a high-tech powerhouse, but it had apparently been doing that for decades. It appears, though, that a *story* of Boston as a high-tech center was emerging that had word-of-mouth potential that was contagious. The personal computer revolution that was just then putting a computer on everyone's desk would increase the contagion of any stories relating to computers. Wang Laboratories, Digital Equipment Company, Data General Corporation, and Lotus Corporation made Boston a world center for computers.[44]

What matters most for the contagion is how the story looked to people who lived in Boston, who bought the property. Local people saw the construction in 1985 of the massive new Lotus Corporation headquarters in East Cambridge and a boom in construction along Route 128. A story developed that Boston was a rival to Silicon Valley in California. Boston would even beat Silicon Valley. One Boston observer remarked in 1985: "In Boston, there's a great deal of history and variety of cultural roots that shape people's view of the world. There was nothing in Silicon Valley before Silicon Valley except for orchards."[45] The story mixed local pride with some facts about the new industry in the area to tell a new era story. The economic success came to be called the "Massachusetts Miracle," and the story had sufficient resonance that Michael Dukakis, the governor of Massachusetts who tried to claim credit for this boom, was nominated by the Democratic Party in 1988 to run for president of the United States.

The story has substantial plausibility to it, for indeed the trend for the last decades of the twentieth century had been for cities with highly skilled or educated populations to grow somewhat faster.[46] The precipitating factor for the Boston boom of the 1980s indeed did substantially affect fundamental value in that city, although the feedback generated by this boom apparently overshot fundamental value, resulting in a fallback in home prices in the 1990s.

The 1980s boom in Boston was not confined to Boston, but to some extent covered the entire northeastern United States. In fact, it went far beyond the United States, for a similar boom was happening across the Atlantic from Boston, in London, and in other cities around the world. It is plausible that the same kind of new era story that drove Boston, tied as it is to the emerging idea that a city with a highly educated and sophisticated populace has a unique future in today's world, may be transposed to other glamor cities as well.

We have already covered, in Chapter 4, a number of precipitating factors that have contributed to the home price boom since the late 1990s, and some of these could be classified as "new era" theories. It should also be noted that there is a sort of new era theory that is becoming attached specifically to vacation or second-home properties, which may account for the rapid price increases for these properties in many places around the world since 2000.

It is widely thought that the advent of the Internet, the cell phone, and the mobile office has made it easy for working people to travel to some rather remote sanctuaries and continue to do their work. There has been a presumption that once Baby Boomers started retiring around 2008, they would want to move out of the city to beautiful places. It is sometimes also said that, as standards of living continue to rise, the increasingly large number of newly wealthy people will want to buy second homes in scenic places, such as ocean fronts or mountain tops, which are inherently scarce, because the supply of such properties cannot be increased. Flaunting one's wealth by building bigger and bigger first homes perhaps has become increasingly passé. Because so many people were doing this during the housing boom that crashed after 2006, it may have started to seem pointless—uniquely beautiful rather than big may seem better in the future.

There appears to be an element of truth to such new era stories about second homes. But such stories, reminiscent of the stories that fed the Florida land bubble in the 1920s, may have increased acceptance during real estate bubbles, because the feedback that is driving home prices increases the contagion of such stories. There are some disquieting similarities between new era stories around 2003 or 2004 about vacation and second homes and those of the 1920s Florida bubble. For example, in Florida in 1925, the boom was supposed to be driven by the advent of the automobile; more recently, the second home boom is supposed to be driven by the advent of the Internet. In both cases, a rush of retirees was supposed to drive the market. The housing crash once again particularly affected those markets, like Florida, driven by speculative and unreliable new era stories.

The Ends of New Eras

Despite the suggestion inherent in the phrase *speculative bubble* that there may be a dramatic burst—a stock market crash—speculative bubbles and their associated new era thinking do not end definitively with a sudden, final crash. On reflection, this is not surprising, given that speculative prices are essentially formed in the minds of the millions of investors who buy and sell, and it is unlikely that so many people would simultaneously arrive at sudden and enduring changes in their long-run perceptions.

People today remember the stock market crash of 1929 as occurring in one or two days. In fact, after that crash, the market recovered almost all of its lost ground by early 1930. The significance of 1929 is not the one-day drops in October, but the fact that the year marked the beginning of the end: the beginning of the three-year period that reversed much of the stock market gains of the 1920s. The same is true of other stock market drops. One-day events do not figure prominently, except as symbols of the malaise in the markets.

I noted in Chapter 1 that the high pricing of the market in 1901 was not followed by any immediate or dramatic price decline, but rather that prices ceased to increase and that eventually, after some twenty years had elapsed, the market had lost most of the real value it had had in 1901. The change took so long to work itself out that it is rather more generational in character, and therefore it is hard to find comment about it in the media.

If we look at 1920–21, when the real stock market was at its lowest since 1901, discussions of the stock market centered on what had gone wrong; the glowing descriptions of future prosperity seen in 1901 were no longer to be found. The biggest factor in most commentary of the period centers on the 1920–21 recession, which was unusually severe. Coverage focused on recent losses by businessmen and on paper fortunes that had disappeared. In place of the "community of interest" keeping prices up, there was instead discussion of hostility from farmers and shippers toward railroads, of customers demanding reductions in rates. The cancellation of government contracts following the world war was thought to have revealed weakness in existing businesses. Strained political conditions abroad following the war were also viewed as a negative factor for the U.S. economy. The actions of "conscienceless" short sellers or bear raiders were considered negative influences on the market, as were the effects of tax-loss selling for income tax purposes.

There is some evidence that investors in 1921 had learned not to be influenced by exaggerated claims and inflated schemes. A 1921 article in the *Saturday Evening Post* by Albert Atwood describes highly speculative prices as a thing of the past and quotes a stockbroker as saying that "the promotions of the last few years have been neither as wild nor as fantastic as those of the boom period of 1900 and 1901."

Another theme running through accounts of the period is that market psychology somehow mysteriously changes, and that it had, at that time, become inexplicably negative. Atwood quotes a banker in 1921: "All the world got together to drive down prices, and when the whole world makes up its mind, when everyone thinks alike and is determined that prices shall go lower, nothing can resist the movement."[47]

The end of the 1929 new era thinking was more dramatic and was directly tied to the Great Depression that followed; by 1932, it was already plain that the United States was into the deepest depression it had ever experienced, and there seemed to be prima facie evidence that the new era was over. The optimists who had been extolling a bright future for the economy were silenced by events that deviated so markedly from their forecasts that it seemed they could not be explained by any convenient adjustments in theories. Economic forecasters demonstrated extreme uncertainty about the future, and observers of consumer behavior claimed that consumer uncertainty had stalled demand.[48]

The depression of the 1930s was a time of widespread concern that our economic system was failing. Oscar Lange, a University of Chicago professor of economics, wrote in the *American Economic Review* in 1939 that "the view is widely held that the American economy has lost its momentum of expansion and reached a stage of more or less permanent stagnation."[49]

The perceived failure of capitalism ushered in the heyday of communism in the United States. Communism seemed to many to be the wave of the future, even inevitable. Many of the best writers of the era became openly sympathetic to communism in the 1930s, including Kenneth Burke, Erskine

Caldwell, Robert Cantwell, Jack Conroy, Edward Dahlberg, John Dos Passos, James Farrell, Langston Hughes, and William Saroyan.[50]

Further evidence of the loss of hope for the uncontrolled capitalist economy can be seen in the ascendance of radical political movements abroad. The rise of Nazism in Germany is itself a telling symptom of the widespread despair that took hold of many people's thinking after 1929. The change in mindset of the German public within the space of a few years seems astonishing, and it is a useful reminder of how changeable any public mood may be.

The end of 1965 new era thinking was associated with suddenly magnified fears of the consequences of world population growth, exhaustion of natural resources, and the appearance of high inflation. These fears inhibited further stock price growth, and promoted commodity price growth.

The great population scare began quite abruptly in the early 1960s. A Proquest search of historical databases of the *Los Angeles Times*, *New York Times*, and *Washington Post* for articles containing the word "population explosion" found no articles during 1945–49, one article during 1950–54, 169 articles during 1955–59, and 1,319 articles during 1960–64. Paul Ehrlich's 1968 book *The Population Bomb*, which predicted devastating economic problems to come within a decade, was a symptom of the public discourse generated by this great public fear. The number of articles with the words "population explosion" fell steadily after its early 1960s peak, down to only 177 in 1985–86.

Over the course of the 1960s, inflation fears began to reignite. The Kennedy administration's claim that it could lower unemployment through high-pressure economics without kindling inflation was found to be false; in fact we entered a period of "stagflation," with both high unemployment and high inflation. In 1974, Arthur Okun, who had been a staff member of the Council of Economic Advisors under President Kennedy and later was its chairman, called the attempt at high-pressure economics "one of the greatest failures of economic analysis in modern times." Inflation began to be seen as a significant brake on the economic outlook. Arthur Burns, the Chair of the Federal Reserve Board, said, "No country that I know of has been able to maintain widespread economic prosperity once inflation got out of hand."[51] Even though this fact is unsupported by economic analysis, there was a general perception that it was true.[52]

By the early 1980s, there was a widespread feeling that the United States was losing its preeminence to Japan. In a *USA Today* article titled "How Japan Is Taking Over Our Markets," an expert is quoted as saying, "The only problem is that no targeted industry in history—not autos, not steel, ball bearings, televisions, motorcycles—has been able to cope with the onslaught from the Japanese." Japan was seen then as especially strong in the high-tech fields, in which our past successes had always been integral to our national self-esteem and identity.

The California real estate boom of the 1970s was interrupted, due at least in part to the most severe economic recessions since the Great Depression of the 1930s: a pair of back-to-back recessions in 1980 and 1981–82. These recessions produced small declines in real California home prices and a quiescent period in the markets until the late 1980s, when the boom resumed. Here is an example of a speculative boom that took a breather and then resumed in even greater force a few years later. The twin recessions and the real price declines in the early 1980s did nothing to hamper the stories that had propelled the first bubble. Indeed, in the 1980s, the free-market tax-cutting former California governor Ronald Reagan was president of the United States, and many Californians no doubt continued to believe that their economy was in the vanguard of the world.

Another economic recession occurred in 1990–91, and this helped bring the real estate booms of the 1980s to an end. This time, price declines were severe. In Los Angeles, after peaking at the end of 1989, real home prices declined 41% by 1997. However, it is not clear that the recession caused the ends of the booms. The price declines in Boston began in 1988, two years before the recession. The price declines in Los Angeles began in 1990, before the recession, and did not end until long after the recession. The recession lasted much longer in California, as measured by employment numbers, but it is hard to say whether that was an exogenous cause of the price declines or was caused by them. Once again, the change in thinking that represented the end of the new era had no clear alignment with any precipitating factor, but had rather more to do with the feedback from price movements themselves.

Any interpretation of the end of the stock market bubble in 2000 has to confront what was different about the stock market when compared with the housing market, which continued to flourish for years after the stock market crashed.

The recession of 2001 was part of the reason for the sharp drop in corporate earnings in 2001, which of course affected the stock market, and not the housing market. In the United States, the only major metropolitan areas that suffered a drop in home prices between 2000 and 2001 were those near the technology center, Silicon Valley—San Jose and San Francisco.

As a matter of history, the first stocks to go after 2000 were the Internet or dot-com stocks. The downturn in these stocks from their peak in March 2000 was extremely sudden. The Dow had its all-time peak on March 9, 2000. In a little more than a month, by April 14, it had lost more than half its value.[53] What happened in that month-long interval? Except for the price declines themselves, there was nothing so dramatic, nothing that one could point to, that should have reduced the outlook for these stocks by half in such a short time.

In a *Financial Times* article dated April 29, 2000, the interpretation given was this: "People are beginning to recognize that the basic fundamentals are still true and just adding a dotcom (to the company name) is an indication of nothing."[54] That is what the article itself was: a public recognition, not a concrete news story. The fascination with the Internet stocks suddenly appeared to have been a silly, in fact embarrassing, fad. It was basically a change in perception.

Behind this change in public perception was a lot of talk. According to a count of news stories from Lexis-Nexis, the number of newspaper stories about Internet stocks had already started to pick up dramatically by late 1999, often reporting dramatic successes of initial public offerings, but often also expressing skepticism. By the beginning of 2000, the number of stories using the words *Internet* and *stock* had surpassed 1,000 a week; that number peaked the week of April 16, 2000, at over 1,400 stories. After this extended period of media attention, the number of stories with these two words began to decline gradually, with a half-life of about a year.

The stories right at the turning point in the stock market may have been especially significant. One, a March 14, 2000, article in the *Wall Street Journal* by Jeremy J. Siegel, "Big-Cap Tech Stocks Are a Sucker Bet," showed price-earnings ratios for large market capitalization stocks that were over 100. In this article, Siegel asserted that history shows "the failure of any large-cap stock ever to justify, by its subsequent record, a P/E ratio anywhere near 100." This statement was very quotable, and was often quoted.

Another article, in *Barron's*, "Burning Up" by Jack Willoughby, included a ranking of Internet companies that were losing money, by the number of months it took until they had burned through all their cash.[55] Willoughby's idea of ranking Internet companies this way made these companies' problems suddenly vivid and clear, and was eminently quotable. His article was a bombshell that led to the kind of skeptical talk that can in turn lead to the undoing of stocks.

Given the many thousands of newspaper articles and other media accounts about stocks that appeared at the peak of the market, there are many more that one could mention as influential. In this context, it might be noted that my own first edition of *Irrational Exuberance* saw a lot of coverage right at the peak of the market, between late February 2000 and the beginning of April 2000, by Paul Krugman in the *New York Times*, David Henry in *USA Today*, and John Cassidy in the *New Yorker*, as well as by *The Economist*, *Newsweek*, and *Business Week*. All these stories, occurring as they did in rapid succession at the very time that Internet stocks were collapsing, might have added to the effect of the other market skeptics who were suddenly proliferating.

But none of these publications seems to have been so influential by itself as to do something like break the upward stock market trajectory. Probably some of the more influential of them had some role in stimulating a public dialogue that led to the change in public opinion; probably they played a role much like that of the innocent child in Hans Christian Andersen's story "The Emperor's New Clothes," whose remark, "The emperor has no clothes," set everyone whispering to one another what the child had said, until, observing each other, they realized how much everyone else was harboring doubts as well.[56] Possibly, too, the attention these various stories got was just a symptom of the beginnings of public doubts that would have broken the bubble one way or another whether these stories had been written or not. In that sense, the public interest in these publications was mostly a symptom of a feedback mechanism's working its way out in the downside direction.

The subsequent massive decline in the entire market appears to have been related to the break in confidence about stocks in general that came about first for the Internet stocks. The decline in Internet stocks became a symbol of a malaise that gradually became diffused throughout the stock market. The stock market decline after 2000 did not extend to housing at the same time, perhaps in part because the analogy to Internet stocks did not seem to extend to housing.

The stock market decline was certainly related as well to the recession of 2001, and to the sharp decline in reported corporate earnings between 2000 and 2001. But these cannot be considered exogenous causes of the decline in the market, since they may be regarded as part of the same feedback mechanism that led to the decline in stock prices. Probably the whole decline in the market could be attributed to the natural process of feedback and correction, not to any events completely exogenous to the market.

We have already seen that, as the years went by after the peak in the market, public opinion became gradually less sanguine about the stock market and the economy. Consumer confidence had declined sharply from its peak in 2000 to levels fairly typical of prior decades, and, as we have seen, confidence in the stock market as an investment had fallen as well. By 2004, while the market still remained at high levels, the excitement of the late 1990s seemed very remote.

But the decline in confidence toward more normal levels after 2000 seemed actually to stimulate the demand for housing, and, in fact, to strengthen its upward momentum. Recall that in Chapter 4, we saw some evidence that uncertainty about jobs encouraged people to invest in real estate, and in Chapter 5, we saw that the decline in the stock market encouraged people to think that real estate was a better investment than stocks. Thus, with the help of feedback, we were able to have a real estate boom even in an economy that was less upbeat than it was a few years earlier. When the feedback that was causing the upward thrust in real estate came to an end, and the stock market took another tumble after the global financial crisis, we found ourselves in post-bubble situations in both the stock market and the housing market.

The end of the boom in the stock market of 2003–7 seems to roughly correspond with the end of the housing boom of 1997–2006. In our minds, we may imagine that both were ended by the financial crisis that followed. However, there is actually a considerable gap between these two endings, and between their end and the first real signs of the financial crisis. These events must surely have some relationship, but it is not an obvious one. Indeed, even after these two booms were well on their way to correction, economic forecasters still did not see the financial crisis coming. Hites Ahir and Prakash Loungani of the International Monetary Fund point out that in 2008–9, sixty-two countries had slipped into recession, but as of September of the year before, not a single one of these recessions had been predicted by prominent economic analysts polled by *Consensus Forecasts*.[57]

It was noted in Chapter 3 that around 2005, public attention to the concept of a housing bubble increased in the United States. Indeed, public thinking changed from glamorous new era thinking to "I was a fool to believe this" thinking. Magazines and newspapers gave prominent cover stories about housing bubbles in mid-2005. Google Trends, a website that produces counts through time of search queries on the Internet beginning in 2004, shows a huge spike in searches for the term "housing bubble" in 2005, and these searches gradually trailed off to almost nothing by 2014. It appears that people had to learn the meaning of, or get comfortable with, the idea of a housing bubble. The sudden new vocabulary and view that what we had experienced was not a new era but a bubble led to what was effectively a run on the shadow banking system that was making the most aggressive loans and a collapse of confidence in the whole financial sector.

Ends of new eras seem to be periods when the focus of debate can no longer be so upbeat. At such times, a public speaker may still think that it would be good business to extol a vision of a brilliant future for the economy, but it is simply not credible to do so. One can, at such times, present a case that the economy must recover, as it always has, and that the stock market should go up, as it historically has, but public speakers who make such a case cannot achieve the command of public attention they do after a major speculative market run-up and economic boom. There are times when an audience is highly receptive to optimistic statements and times when it is not.

Eight

New Eras and Bubbles around the World

L arge stock market moves like the U.S. examples I discussed in the previous chapter have also occurred in many other countries over the years, affording us numerous other observations. These suggest that speculative bubbles— periods of exaggerated but temporary investor enthusiasm, often associated with "new era" theories—are in fact commonplace.

In this chapter, I examine the largest stock market moves around the world that preceded the peak of the Millennium Bubble in 2000. For some of these, I rely on accounts by the news media. Of course, media accounts are not always reliable, and I cannot claim to have done exhaustive research on any of these examples. However, they illustrate the significance in these countries of factors I have identified in previous chapters as important in U.S. stock market moves. I show that prices in these countries have tended to reverse after making exceptionally large increases, as one would expect if bubbles were common among them.

The Largest Stock Market Events

Table 8.1 shows the twenty-five largest recent one-year real stock price index increases before 2000 for thirty-six selected countries, and Table 8.2 shows the twenty-five largest decreases for the same countries. Table 8.3 shows the twenty-five largest recent five-year real stock price increases, and Table 8.4 shows the twenty-five largest decreases. The tables are based on monthly

Table 8.1
Largest Recent One-Year Real Stock Price Index Increases

Country	Percentage increase	One-year period	Price change over subsequent one-year period (percent)
1. Philippines	683.4	Dec. 1985–Dec. 1986	28.4
2. Taiwan	400.1	Oct. 1986–Oct. 1987	65.7
3. Venezuela	384.6	Jan. 1990–Jan. 1991	33.1
4. Peru	360.9	Aug. 1992–Aug. 1993	15.8
5. Colombia	271.3	Jan. 1991–Jan. 1992	–19.9
6. Jamaica	224.5	Apr. 1992–Apr. 1993	–59.2
7. Chile	199.8	Jan. 1979–Jan. 1980	38.9
8. Italy	166.4	May 1985–May 1986	–15.7
9. Jamaica	163.4	Aug. 1985–Aug. 1986	8.7
10. Thailand	161.9	Oct. 1986–Oct. 1987	–2.6
11. India	155.5	Apr. 1991–Apr. 1992	–50.3
12. Italy	147.3	Apr. 1980–Apr. 1981	–32.1
13. Austria	145.4	Feb. 1989–Feb. 1990	–19.8
14. Finland	128.3	Sept. 1992–Sept. 1993	46.3
15. Denmark	122.9	Apr. 1971–Apr. 1972	–12.4
16. Spain	119.8	Dec. 1985–Dec. 1986	4.2
17. Luxembourg	113.4	Dec. 1992–Dec. 1993	–10.8
18. Sweden	111.5	Aug. 1982–Aug. 1983	–9.6
19. Portugal	103.8	Apr. 1997–Apr. 1998	–34.1
20. Luxembourg	103.6	Jan. 1985–Jan. 1986	2.6
21. Hong Kong	101.0	Jan. 1993–Jan. 1994	–38.5
22. Hong Kong	99.1	Feb. 1975–Feb. 1976	–3.4
23. Korea	98.8	Feb. 1975–Feb. 1976	31.9
24. Hong Kong	98.6	Nov. 1979–Nov. 1980	–22.4
25. Sweden	96.6	Aug. 1977–Aug. 1978	–50.8

data starting at varying dates for the different countries, but for over half the thirty-six countries, the data begin in or before 1960.[1]

It is clear that very large stock price movements are commonplace by world standards. Many are much larger, in the percentage terms shown, than those we have recently experienced in the United States. Indeed, no example from the United States even appears in any of the tables. (We should bear in mind that the U.S. market is the largest in the world, and there are a

Table 8.2
Largest Recent One-Year Real Stock Price Index Decreases

Country	Percentage decrease	One-year period	Price change over subsequent one-year period (percent)
1. Taiwan	−74.9	Oct. 1989–Oct. 1990	85.1
2. Jamaica	−73.8	Jan. 1993–Jan. 1994	69.6
3. Sweden	−63.6	Aug. 1976–Aug. 1977	96.6
4. United Kingdom	−63.3	Nov. 1973–Nov. 1974	72.7
5. Thailand	−62.8	Aug. 1997–Aug. 1998	71.9
6. South Africa	−62.1	July 1985–July 1986	48.9
7. Philippines	−61.9	Oct. 1973–Oct. 1974	−14.1
8. Korea	−61.9	June 1997–June 1998	167.0
9. Pakistan	−59.5	Oct. 1990–Oct. 1991	9.0
10. India	−58.4	Nov. 1963–Nov. 1964	−18.8
11. Denmark	−56.0	July 1969–July 1970	−15.3
12. Hong Kong	−55.5	Aug. 1997–Aug. 1998	90.0
13. Hong Kong	−55.1	Dec. 1981–Dec. 1982	7.7
14. Norway	−54.2	May 1967–May 1968	39.9
15. Spain	−54.1	Oct. 1976–Oct. 1977	−15.6
16. Norway	−53.6	Jan. 1974–Jan. 1975	−2.1
17. Australia	−53.0	Oct. 1973–Oct. 1974	33.6
18. France	−49.0	Sept. 1973–Sept. 1974	25.3
19. Indonesia	−48.1	Mar. 1997–Mar. 1998	−45.1
20. Canada	−47.9	June 1981–June 1982	69.4
21. Finland	−47.5	Feb. 1990–Feb. 1991	6.3
22. Colombia	−47.1	Jan. 1980–Jan. 1981	74.2
23. Italy	−46.1	Apr. 1974–Apr. 1975	−31.3
24. Norway	−46.1	Dec. 1989–Dec. 1990	68.6
25. Denmark	−45.8	Sept. 1973–Sept. 1974	14.7

few near misses even in percentage terms. For example, the 184.8% real U.S. stock market increase from April 1994 to April 1999 almost makes the list of the biggest five-year price increases. In addition, the U.S. stock market fell 44.1% in real terms from October 1973 to October 1974, which almost puts it on the list of biggest one-year drops. And the real 113.9% rise from June 1932 to June 1933 would qualify for the list of biggest one-year increases, except that this period, from the depths of the Great Depression to the beginnings

Table 8.3
Largest Recent Five-Year Real Stock Price Index Increases

Country	Percentage increase	Five-year period	Price change over subsequent five-year period (percent)
1. Philippines	1,253.2	Nov. 1984–Nov. 1989	43.5
2. Peru	743.1	Sept. 1991–Sept. 1996	—
3. Chile	689.7	Mar. 1985–Mar. 1990	104.2
4. Jamaica	573.9	Dec. 1980–Dec. 1985	38.7
5. Korea	518.3	Mar. 1984–Mar. 1989	−36.6
6. Mexico	501.7	Jan. 1989–Jan. 1994	−50.9
7. Taiwan	468.1	May 1986–May 1991	−12.7
8. Thailand	430.7	May 1986–May 1991	17.0
9. Colombia	390.7	Apr. 1989–Apr. 1994	−52.0
10. Spain	381.9	Oct. 1982–Oct. 1987	−33.7
11. India	346.1	Apr. 1987–Apr. 1992	58.4
12. Finland	336.3	Sept. 1992–Sept. 1997	—
13. Austria	331.3	Jan. 1985–Jan. 1990	−39.7
14. Portugal	329.1	Apr. 1993–Apr. 1998	—
15. Finland	291.0	Sept. 1982–Sept. 1987	−55.5
16. Jamaica	280.2	July 1984–July 1989	10.9
17. Japan	275.6	Aug. 1982–Aug. 1987	−48.5
18. France	262.6	Mar. 1982–Mar. 1987	10.2
19. Finland	262.5	Feb. 1968–Feb. 1973	−68.2
20. Hong Kong	261.6	Jan. 1975–Jan. 1980	−17.2
21. Netherlands	256.6	July 1993–July 1998	—
22. Norway	253.1	Sept. 1982–Sept. 1987	−18.9
23. Norway	248.4	Oct. 1992–Oct. 1997	—
24. Sweden	247.1	Aug. 1982–Aug. 1987	−36.9
25. Hong Kong	230.9	Oct. 1982–Oct. 1987	−14.6

of recovery, occurred much earlier than the sample period used to construct the tables.)

The rightmost column in each of the tables also shows, whenever possible, what happened during the twelve months or five years after each of these periods of dramatic price change.[2] As can be seen, there is considerable variability across these countries as to whether the market continued in the same direction over the subsequent interval or reversed itself. At the end of

Table 8.4
Largest Recent Five-Year Real Stock Price Index Decreases

Country	Percentage decrease	Five-year period	Price change over subsequent five-year period (percent)
1. Spain	−86.6	Dec. 1974–Dec. 1979	0.1
2. Jamaica	−85.5	July 1973–July 1978	185.2
3. Venezuela	−84.9	May 1977–May 1982	138.9
4. Thailand	−84.0	Jan. 1994–Jan. 1999	—
5. Philippines	−83.1	Feb. 1980–Feb. 1985	1,000.0
6. Italy	−80.7	June 1973–June 1978	72.6
7. Pakistan	−78.3	Feb. 1994–Feb. 1999	—
8. Norway	−77.1	July 1973–July 1978	74.1
9. Jamaica	−76.9	Jan. 1993–Jan. 1998	—
10. Philippines	−76.6	Sept. 1969–Sept. 1974	−40.7
11. India	−74.6	Aug. 1962–Aug. 1967	0.7
12. United Kingdom	−73.5	Dec. 1969–Dec. 1974	81.5
13. South Africa	−73.4	Apr. 1981–Apr. 1986	16.6
14. Colombia	−73.3	July 1971–July 1976	−24.8
15. Colombia	−72.7	July 1979–July 1984	36.9
16. Chile	−72.6	June 1980–June 1985	587.9
17. Philippines	−72.2	Apr. 1976–Apr. 1981	24.4
18. Finland	−71.3	Oct. 1973–Oct. 1978	99.0
19. Korea	−68.3	June 1993–June 1998	—
20. Portugal	−67.9	Jan. 1988–Jan. 1993	222.6
21. Jamaica	−64.2	Nov. 1969–Nov. 1974	−68.9
22. Korea	−63.6	Aug. 1978–Aug. 1983	375.0
23. Italy	−62.6	Jan. 1970–Jan. 1975	−46.1
24. France	−62.5	Jan. 1973–Jan. 1978	5.7
25. Italy	−62.3	Sept. 1960–Sept. 1965	−0.5

this chapter, I describe what we know about the sequelae of the large price changes tabulated here.

Stories Associated with the Largest Price Changes

It is easier to find stories associated with one-year price changes than with five-year price changes. Five years is such a long time that factors underlying the rise or decline in stock markets are often lost from public consciousness—seen as underlying trends rather than salient events. Fortunately for our purposes, fourteen of the twenty-five five-year intervals of real price increase shown in Table 8.3 contain twelve-month intervals, shown in Table 8.1, and eleven of the twenty-five five-year intervals of real price decline shown in Table 8.4 contain twelve-month intervals, shown in Table 8.2.

Some of the twelve-month price increases seem to be associated with good reasons for a rational price change. This is especially so for the very largest one-year changes: typically something very unusual was going on. But even in these cases, there often seems to be a suggestion of some market overreaction to events.

The biggest one-year real stock market increase of all, in the Philippines from December 1985 to December 1986, was an amazing 683.4%. The biggest five-year real price change, of 1,253%, also occurred in the Philippines. The five-year period, from November 1984 to November 1989, included the record one-year period.

During the twelve-month period from December 1985 to December 1986, the regime of Ferdinand Marcos collapsed, Marcos fled the country, and a new government led by Corazon Aquino took charge of the country. In the period just before the price increase, a communist insurgency had threatened to turn the country into another Vietnam. The Marcos government had assassinated Corazon Aquino's husband. With demonstrations in the streets, it was in general a time of enormous uncertainty about the future. Once the new government was in place, the country developed renewed hope: a "new era" certainly seemed at hand. Moreover, the price changes were not reversed during the subsequent one- or five-year intervals, as can be seen from the tables.

One might suspect that the very low values for the Philippine stock market in December 1985, at the beginning of the record twelve-month period, were the result of a sort of negative bubble. Indeed, three of the top twenty five-year price decreases shown in Table 8.4 occurred in the Philippines by 1985. The Philippine stock market had a truly dismal record prior to its spectacular increase. Newspaper accounts in 1985 and earlier puzzled over the unusually low price-earnings ratios, often around 4. When viewed from this perspective, the largest stock increase in our tables was but a reversal of a series of decreases.

The second biggest one-year increase (October 1986 to October 1987) and the biggest one-year decrease (October 1989 to October 1990) both occurred in Taiwan. Taiwan is also the home of the seventh-largest five-year increase, from May 1986 to May 1991, and to the twenty-seventh-largest five-year decrease, from October 1988 to October 1993.

During the year of the highest speculative increase in Taiwan, October 1986 to October 1987, there were some impressive "new era" reasons for optimism.

Booming exports had pushed economic growth rates into the double-digit range, and it was widely predicted that with this steep growth trajectory, the economy would soon be producing such high-tech items as computer chips. The new affluence was visible everywhere: expensive foreign cars cruised the streets of Taipei, and businessmen freely downed $100 bottles of wine at glamorous new restaurants. Even so, the savings rate was very high, and the country was investing heavily in its future.

In the fall of 1987, after a series of antigovernment street demonstrations, the government finally lifted the martial law that had been in force since 1949 and also allowed the formation of opposition parties for the first time. Later in that twelve-month period, September 1987, the government made two historic and highly visible announcements: permitting foreign investors to establish companies in Taiwan and allowing Taiwanese citizens to visit their relatives on the mainland for the first time since 1949.

Despite these good reasons to anticipate the dawning of a "new era" in the Taiwanese economy, many observers still believed there was an air of speculative excess to the Taiwan stock market of 1986–87. Volume of trade soared, increasing sevenfold from January to September 1987, to exceed the combined volume of all Asian markets excluding Japan.[3] Price-earnings ratios reached 45, compared with 16 at the beginning of the year.

Taiwan was in the grip of a gambling fever that expressed itself in other venues besides the stock market. An illegal numbers game, called Ta Chia Le or Happiness for All, unknown until 1986, suddenly became a national obsession. It was so popular that "on days when winning numbers are announced, peasants neglect their fields and workers fail to report to their factories."[4]

A Taiwanese student of mine at Yale later confided to me that, while he was still a teenager in Taiwan in 1987, his mother had forced him to go regularly to the stock exchange, observe the trading, and report back to her if something significant should happen. It was while carrying out these surveillance missions that he became convinced, he told me, of the utter madness of the speculative situation.

The Taiwan stock market increase was not reversed right away: following the year of most rapid price increase, there was yet another year of price increase. But starting a year later, we see the 74.9% decline in the Taiwan stock market, the biggest one-year decline on our list.

The third-largest one-year price increase, of 384.6%, occurred in Venezuela between January 1990 and January 1991. This price surge came on the heels of a severe economic slump that had produced an economic growth rate of –8%, an unemployment rate of 10%, and inflation of 85% in 1989.[5] Then the Iraqi occupation of Kuwait (from August 1990 to February 1991) resulted in an interruption of Persian Gulf oil supplies, a rapid rise in international oil prices, and increased demand for Venezuelan oil. The stage was set for a period of sudden prosperity in Venezuela. The Kuwaiti experience supposedly convinced investors of the importance of Venezuela as an alternate oil supplier outside the unstable Persian Gulf. But this seems unlikely as a rational explanation for the run-up in the Venezuelan stock market, because the potential for disruptions of Persian Gulf oil supplies was already known long before the invasion. President Carlos Andres Perez warned that "Venezuela is living with a totally artificial economy" supported only by the oil price increase; nevertheless, the stock market soared.[6] The price increase was not reversed in the subsequent year, but by January 1993, Venezuelan real stock prices had lost 60.3% of their January 1991 value, and by January 1999, they had lost 82.0% of that value.

The fourth-largest one-year price increase, at 360.9%, took place in Peru from August 1992 to August 1993. The increase occurred after a stock market plunge in April 1992, when Alberto Fujimori seized dictatorial powers, dissolving congress and suspending the constitution amid a protracted civil war with the Shining Path guerrillas. But in September 1992, the Shining Path leadership was captured, and by April 1993, democracy had been restored in Peru, ending fourteen years of guerrilla violence that had killed 27,000 people. Inflation had reached 7,000% and economic growth was negative in 1990, but by 1993 inflation was being brought under control and economic growth was positive. A wonderful sense of a "new era" was certainly in evidence—but a quadrupling of stock prices within a year left many wondering whether the increase was excessive. The market did go up a bit more the following year, and then it lost a little of its value. By January 1999, the real level of the market was lower, but only by 8%; it then crashed in 2000 and went through some wild gyrations.

The stock market increase in India from April 1991 to April 1992, eleventh on the list in Table 8.1, began just as the assassination of Rajiv Gandhi in May 1991 ended the thirty-eight-year Nehru family dynasty. Gandhi's successor immediately appointed as finance minister Manmohan Singh, then a former professor at the Delhi School of Economics (later, in 2004, he would become prime minister). The new government announced a deregulation plan that was viewed as a substantial turn away from socialism. Foreign investment was now invited. Singh presented a budget plan that exempted financial assets from the calculation of the wealth tax. Previously, managers had tried to keep their companies' share prices as low as possible to avoid taxation; now they took steps to encourage high prices. The budget plan also reduced regulations on the pricing and timing of new stock issues. These reforms were certainly plausible reasons for a stock market increase, but the actual increase was widely described as excessive, and authorities warned the nation of the potential for speculative excess. This was also a time of widespread attempts at stock price manipulation. The machinations of Harshad "Big Bull" Mehta, a Mumbai stockbroker, set off a national scandal in 1992, after the market peak had been reached. He was described as creating a "vortex effect" in individual stocks by buying in the market, selling at depressed prices to friendly institutions, and then buying again in the now-diminished pool of available shares, thereby pushing prices up.[7] The 1992 rise in Indian stock prices is now referred to as the "Mehta Peak." It was indeed a peak, since the market fell 50.3% during the following year.

In these examples, there was always some event, or series of events, outside the market itself that suggested the start of a genuine new era. Even if the market was *believed* to be overreacting to the event, it is hard to argue with any certainty that this was the case. In some of the other large price increases, in contrast, there are no such plausible explanations for the magnitude of the price changes, and media interpretations therefore center on reinterpretations of long-term processes or on market psychology.

For example, in the Italian stock market boom of May 1985 to May 1986, when the market rose 166.4% in real terms, it was noted that economic growth was solid, that inflation remained low, and that the government of Prime Minister Bettino Craxi was stable and well liked. But none of this was really news. One Italian newspaper quoted an analyst as saying, "There are no explanations. . . . Everyone has gone crazy and that's it. This is a collective madness; total. It is useless to try to understand, to stop or to guide."[8] The *Financial Times* of London said, "A fever has gripped Italy: hundreds of first-time small investors are pouring money into the stock market as though they were buying lottery tickets."[9] The real level of the Italian market fell by 15.7% the following year. By September 1992, the Italian market had lost 68.0% of its May 1986 real value.

In France at around the same time, investors' "love affair with the market"[10] surprised observers by its intensity and lack of good explanation, and the French stock market makes our list, increasing 262.6% in real terms from March 1982 to March 1987. The "new era" story that the French government under François Mitterrand was departing from its socialist rigidity seemed inadequate to explain the market surge. Rather, if there was a new era, it seemed to many observers to be only in terms of market psychology, with French investors embracing free markets with renewed ardor. This period of enthusiasm was followed by the worldwide stock market crash of 1987, which set the French stock market back as well, although it still managed to gain another 10.2% over the succeeding five years: March 1987 to March 1992. Curiously, the French market went upward from there, with the growth of French real stock prices between 1992 and the turn of the millennium almost as dramatic, and as mystifying, as that in the United States.[11]

Ends of New Eras and Financial Crises

The sequelae of the extraordinary price increases described in the previous section were highly variable. They were frequently followed by dramatic reversals, but this is by no means always the case. Do the increases carry the seeds of their own destruction, or are the interruptions due to other causes?

Often the ends of bull markets appear to be caused by concrete events unrelated to any irrational exuberance in the stock market. Notable among these are financial crises, such as banking or exchange rate crises. These other events then become the focus of analysis, since their causes appear more definite than those of the stock market crisis. According to such an analysis, the ends of the "new eras" have a narrow technical origin, rather than a psychological or social origin.

The 1994 Mexican crisis appears as the aftermath of the sixth most spectacular five-year stock price increase in Table 8.3. The anatomy of this crisis is a complicated one. Analysts stress an investor run on the peso, followed by investors' refusal to accept again the *tesobono*, the dollar-denominated short-term debt of the Mexican government. The investing public knew that the Mexican government did not have enough dollars in reserve to support the peso exchange rate if many people were to sell pesos, and although this knowledge alone need not have caused a currency devaluation, in combination with a belief that the devaluation of the peso was imminent, it in fact forced the devaluation. A devaluation of the peso, of course, is not itself a bad thing, and in fact it might have been the boost that the Mexican economy needed. But then investors were mistrustful and decided not to reinvest in the *tesobono* debt. Since the Mexican government could not sell new debt, as its old debt came due, it was unable to repay. Fortunately, the government was saved by an international loan that enabled it to make good on this debt after all, and an economic crisis was resolved.

However, note—despite having identified the source of the problem as related to the peso, despite the short duration of the Mexican economic crisis, and despite the international loans to Mexico to fix the problem—that the real Mexican stock market was still, as of 1999, 50% below its 1994 peak; it did not pass the 1994 peak in real (inflation-corrected) terms until ten years later. The period after 1994 saw a fundamental change in the public's attitude toward the Mexican stock market. Before the 1994 crisis, under the Salinas government, with the advent of the North American Free Trade Agreement and with Mexico's admission into the Organization for Economic Cooperation and Development, there seems to have been an exaggerated "new era" sense of invulnerability and of a great future ahead for Mexico, which faded after the crisis.

The Asian financial crisis of 1997–98 was also much more than a stock market crisis. It included exchange rate and banking crises, and again these tended to attract the attention of analysts. But, as can be seen from Table 8.3, the Asian crisis was preceded by a good number of the largest five-year price increases, and these came substantially before the exchange rate and banking crises. Japan had had a 275.6% five-year real stock price increase from August 1982 to August 1987; Hong Kong, a 230.9% stock price increase from October 1982 to October 1987; Korea, a 518.3% stock price increase from March 1984 to March 1989; Taiwan, a 468.1% stock price increase from May 1986 to May 1991; and Thailand, a 430.7% stock price increase over the same period. Most of these price increases came during 1982–87, as the world experienced a recovery from the Great Recession of 1981. In all of these countries, the stock market was already down from its peak by December 1996, before there was any hint of the Asian financial crisis. It appears that the collapse of a speculative bubble in these countries preceded the crisis and was part of the ambience that produced the crisis. Yet when the crisis finally came, the stock market stories, as well as stories of public confidence, appeared only vaguely in the background, as attention centered on changes in currency exchange rates, the sudden withdrawal of foreign investors, banking problems, inflation, and labor difficulties.

These financial crisis stories illustrate the complicated factors that sometimes capture the attention of economic and financial analysts. Each of them may seem to be "the" technical story that explains events. Discussions may focus on these factors and pull attention away from the large changes in public opinion that are reflected in speculative prices. Therefore, the underlying story of investors overreacting to news and of the feedback of price increases leading to further price increases often tends to get lost.

What Went Up (Down) Usually Came Back Down (Up)

It is impossible to *prove* the assertion that some speculative excesses were behind many of these events. One can always argue that the fundamental reasons offered by investors to justify them were valid in terms of the evidence that was available when the market was going up, and that "new era" stories are never completely without merit as theories of what *might* happen. But one can also ask whether these price movements have tended to be reversed. If the price increases are, on average, reversed, then we have some evidence that the fundamental reasons were not sound.

The data on which these tables are based confirm for countries the result first discovered by Werner De Bondt and Richard Thaler: that winner stocks—if winner status is measured over long intervals of time such as five years—tend to do poorly in subsequent intervals of the same length, and that loser stocks—if loser status is measured over equally long intervals—tend to do well in subsequent intervals of the same length.[12]

From the data used to produce the tables, we find that of the twenty-five winning countries shown in Table 8.3, seventeen (68%) experienced a decrease in real stock prices in the five-year periods after large five-year real price increases, and the average price change for the seventeen countries was a decrease of 14.7%.[13] Similarly, of the twenty-five losing countries shown in Table 8.4, twenty (80%) experienced an increase in real stock prices in the five-year periods after large five-year price decreases, and the average price change was an increase of 119.7%. We thus see quite a substantial, though imperfect, tendency for major five-year stock price movement to be reversed in another five years, both for up movements and down movements.

When we look at one-year real price changes in Tables 8.1 and 8.2, we find that the tendency toward reversals is less pronounced, as we would expect from past literature, on prices of individual stocks. We find that of the twenty-five winning countries shown in Table 8.1, fifteen (60%) experienced a decrease of real stock prices in the twelve-month period after large twelve-month price increases, so that the direction of change was more equally split between up and down, and the average change was a decrease of 4.2%. Of the twenty-five losing countries shown in Table 8.2, eighteen (72%) experienced an increase in real stock prices in the twelve-month periods after large twelve-month price decreases, and the average real price change was an increase of 36.3%. Twelve months does not appear to be long enough to begin to see as strong a tendency for extreme price movements to reverse themselves.

Quite possibly, the tendency for individual countries' stock market valuations to grow dramatically and then to be reversed will diminish in the future. With freer capital movements than were possible during the periods covered by the examples in the tables, and with more and more global investors seeking profit opportunities buying undervalued countries or shorting overvalued countries, markets may become more stable. Even so, it is unlikely that these forces will soon eliminate the potential for such movements, particularly infrequent and slow large-country events or worldwide events, for which the attendant profit opportunities are slow and hard to diversify. The possibility of major speculative bubbles, now and in the future, cannot be ignored.

In this part on cultural factors, we have explored the justifications people have given, at various points in history, for changing market valuations, and we have seen evidence of the transitory nature of these cultural factors. Ultimately, however, the conclusions we draw from such evidence depend on our view of human nature and the extent of human abilities to produce consistent and independent judgments. To consolidate our understanding of the argument, we turn, in the next part, to a study of fundamental psychological factors—human tendencies to act independently or to acquiesce, to believe others or to disbelieve them, to feel confidence or self-doubt, to be attentive or inattentive. These tendencies bear on the plausibility of our view of speculative bubbles.

Part Three

Psychological Factors

Nine

Psychological Anchors for the Market

We have seen that the market is not well anchored by fundamentals. People do not even know to any degree of accuracy what the "right" level of the market is: not many of them spend much time thinking about what its level should be or whether it is over- or underpriced today. So what is it that ties down the market's level on any given day? What anchors the market? What is it that determines whether the Dow is at 4,000 or 14,000? What ultimately limits the feedback from price changes to further price changes that amplifies speculative price movements? Why does the market stay within a certain region for days at a time, only to break out suddenly? We have already seen some partial answers to these questions, but to understand the true nature of the anchors at work here, we must also turn to psychology.

In considering lessons from psychology, it must be noted that many popular accounts of the psychology of investing are simply not credible. Investors are said to be euphoric or frenzied during booms or panic-stricken during market crashes. In both booms and crashes, investors are described as blindly following the herd like so many sheep, with no minds of their own. Belief in the rationality of markets starts to sound a lot better when the only alternatives are such pop-psychological theories.

We all know that most people are more sensible during such financial episodes than these accounts suggest. Financial booms and crashes are, for most of us, not emotion-laden events on a par with victories in battle or volcanic eruptions. In fact, during the most significant financial events, most people are preoccupied with other personal matters, not with the financial markets at all. So it is hard to imagine that the market as a whole reflects the emotions described by these psychological theories.

However, solid psychological research does show that there are patterns of human behavior that suggest anchors for the market that would not be expected if markets worked entirely rationally. These patterns of human behavior are not the result of extreme human ignorance, but rather of the character of human intelligence, reflecting its limitations as well as its strengths. Investors are striving to do the right thing, but they have limited abilities and certain natural modes of behavior that decide their actions when an unambiguous prescription for action is lacking.[1]

Two kinds of psychological anchors will be considered here: *quantitative anchors*, which themselves give indications for the appropriate levels of the market that some people use as indications of whether the market is over- or underpriced and whether it is a good time to buy, and *moral anchors*, which operate by determining the strength of the reason that compels people to buy stocks, a reason that they must weigh against their other uses for the wealth they already have (or could have) invested in the market. With quantitative anchors, people are weighing numbers against prices when they decide whether stocks (or other assets) are priced right. With moral anchors, people compare the intuitive or emotional strength of the argument for investing in the market against their wealth and their perceived need for money to spend now.

Quantitative Anchors for the Market

Designers of questionnaires have learned that the answers people give can be heavily influenced by suggestions that are given on the questionnaires themselves. For example, when people are asked to state within which of a number of ranges their income falls, their answers are influenced by the ranges given. The ranges serve as "anchors" to which they make their answers conform.

Psychologists have shown that people's decisions in ambiguous situations are influenced by whatever available anchor is at hand. When you must come up with an estimate, and you are unsure what to say, you take whatever number is before you. Psychologists Amos Tversky and Daniel Kahneman demonstrated this tendency clearly in an experiment involving a wheel of fortune: a large wheel with the numbers from 1 to 100 on it, similar to those used in television game shows, that is designed to stop at a random number when it is spun. Subjects were asked questions whose answers were numbers between 1 and 100, difficult questions such as the percentage of African nations in the United Nations. They were asked first to say whether the answer they would give was above or below the number just produced by the wheel of fortune. Then they were asked to give their answer. The experimenters found that the answer was quite substantially influenced by the random number on the wheel. For example, if the wheel stopped at 10, the median percentage of African nations according to their subjects was 25, whereas if the wheel stopped at 65, the median percentage was 45. This experiment was particularly interesting, because it was designed so that the subject clearly knew that the number produced by the wheel was purely random and, moreover, because the number produced by the wheel should have had no emotional significance for the subject.[2]

In making judgments about the level of stock prices, the most likely anchor is the most recently remembered price. The tendency of investors to use this anchor enforces the similarity of stock prices from one day to the next. Other possible anchors are remembered past prices, and the tendency of past prices to serve as anchors may be part of the reason for the observed tendency for trends in individual stock prices to be reversed. Another anchor may be the nearest milestone of a prominent index such as the Dow, the nearest round-number level, and investors' use of this anchor may help explain unusual market behavior surrounding such levels. Past price *changes* may also provide an anchor, if attention is suitably drawn to them. Recall from Chapter 6 that the drop in the market in the October 19, 1987, crash was nearly the same in percentage terms as that in the October 28–29, 1929, crash that was so much discussed at the time of the 1987 crash.

For individual stocks, price changes may tend to be anchored to the price changes of other stocks, and price-earnings ratios may be anchored to other firms' price-earnings levels. This kind of anchoring may help to explain why individual stock prices move together as much as they do, and thus, ultimately, why stock price indices are as volatile as they are—why the averaging across stocks that is inherent in the construction of the index doesn't more solidly dampen its volatility.[3] It may also explain why stocks of companies that are in different industries but are headquartered in the same country tend to have more similar price movements than stocks of companies that are in the same industry but are headquartered in different countries, contrary to one's expectation that the industry would define the fundamentals of the company better than the location of its headquarters.[4] And it may explain why real estate investment trusts traded on stock exchanges tend to behave more like stocks than like the appraised value of their underlying commercial real estate.[5] Indeed, all of these anomalies noted in financial markets have a simple explanation in terms of quantitative anchoring to convenient numbers.

Moral Anchors for the Market

With moral anchoring, the market is tied down by people's comparisons of the intuitive force of stories and reasons to hold their investments against their perceived need to consume the wealth that these investments represent. The market is not prevented from going up to arbitrarily high levels because people have any idea what its intrinsically "right" level is or what level would be too high. Rather, if the market were to get too high, the discrepancy between the wealth many people would then have in the market and their current living standards would, when compared with their reasons for holding stocks, encourage them to sell. One can appreciate the nature of this anchor with an extreme example. Suppose, counterfactually, that the psychology of the market caused the level of the stock market to rise so as to make most holders of stocks multimillionaires— on paper. Then, unless the reason these people have to continue holding every single share is perceived to be extremely strong, they would want to start *living* a little more like multimillionaires and sell some of their stocks to be able to spend the money. Such selling would obviously bring stock prices down, since there would be no buyers, and obviously there just isn't sufficient current national income available to sustain anything like this many multimillionaires. The stock market can reach fantastic levels only if people think that they have good reasons not to test it by trying to enjoy their newfound wealth.

Underlying this notion of moral anchors is the psychological principle that much of the human thinking that results in action is not quantitative, but instead takes the form of *storytelling* and *justification*. That is why, in the case of moral anchors, people are weighing a story, which has no quantitative dimension, against the observed quantity of financial wealth that they have available for consumption. Such reasoning is not well described by the usual kind of economic theory, but there is a large amount of evidence in support of the assertion that investor reasoning does take this form.

Psychologists Nancy Pennington and Reid Hastie have shown the importance of stories in decision making by studying how jurors reached decisions in difficult cases. They found that jurors' approach to reasoning through the complicated issues of the trial tended to take the form of constructing a story, filling out the details that were provided to them about the case into a coherent narrative of the chain of events. In describing their verdict, they tended not to speak of quantities or probabilities, or of summing up the weight of the evidence, but rather merely to tell a story of the case, typically a chronology of events, and to remark how well their story fit together and how internally consistent it was.[6]

By analogy, those who sell stocks to the general public often tend to tell a story about the stock, a vivid story describing the history of the company, the nature of the product, and how the public is using the product. The sales call does not as often engage in discussions of quantities or probabilities, or of whether the price is at the right level in terms of quantitative evidence about future dividends or earnings. These quantitative factors are not as congenial to the narrative-based decision making that comes naturally to people.

There is a basic human interest in gambling, seen in one form or another in all cultures,[7] an interest that also expresses itself in speculative markets. Some of the attraction to gambling, despite odds that are often openly stacked against gamblers, apparently has to do with narrative-based thinking. When gamblers are heard talking, they are usually telling stories, not evaluating probabilities, and the possibilities suggested by the stories often seem to have more substantive reality than any quantitative concepts. In these stories, gamblers use a different vocabulary than do probability theorists, preferring the words *luck* or *lucky day,* and rarely uttering the words *probability* or *likelihood.* There are stories of their winnings and losses, of the chains of events that preceded their best or worst luck, of the strength of their intuition that yielded good bets. These stories can convey a sense of meaning and significance to events that are in fact purely random.[8]

It has been noted that employees have a tendency to invest in company stock (that is, stock issued by the firm that employs them), even though it would appear to be more in their interest to diversify away from the source of their own livelihood. As of 2003, eleven million participants in U.S. 401(k) plans invested more than 20% of their assets in company stock, and in some companies, such as Coca-Cola, company stock has reached 90% of assets.[9] This tendency to invest in company stock can be interpreted as consistent with investors' being influenced by stories: they know many more stories about their own companies and so invest in those companies' stocks.

People also appear to want to construct simple reasons for their decisions, as if they feel the need to justify those decisions in simple terms—if not to others, then to themselves. The need to have a simple reason to explain a decision is similar to the need to have a story behind a decision; both the stories and the reasons are simple rationales that can be conveyed verbally to others.

Psychologists Eldar Shafir, Itamar Simonson, and Amos Tversky demonstrated experimentally an effect that appears to represent decision biases caused by people's search for simple reasons to justify decisions. They presented their subjects with a simple choice between two options: one option was "impoverished," with no striking positive or negative features. The other was "enriched," displaying both distinctly positive and distinctly negative features. In one of their experiments, subjects were asked to choose to which parent they would award sole custody of a child. Parent A, the impoverished option, was described with the words "average income, average health, average working hours, reasonable rapport with the child, and relatively stable social life." Parent B, the enriched option, was described with the words "above-average income, very close relationship with the child, extremely active social life, lots of work-related travel, minor health problems." The experimenters found that the subjects' choices depended on how they were asked about the two choices. When a group of subjects was asked to select the parent to whom they would award custody, 64% chose Parent B. When a second group was asked to pick the parent to whom they would *deny* custody, 55% again chose Parent B. The predominant answers given by the two groups are logically inconsistent, but they are consistent with a feeling that one must have a solid reason to justify a decision. The psychologists found that the same tendency occurs even for purely personal decisions that will never need to be explained to others.[10]

Reasons to hold stocks or other investments can take on ethical as well as practical dimensions. Our culture may supply reasons to hold stocks and other savings vehicles that are related to our sense of identity as responsible people, as good or levelheaded people. Recall the 1996 book *The Millionaire Next Door*, which was a best-seller throughout the stock market boom of the 1990s. It made the point that most millionaires in the United States are not exceptional income earners, but merely frugal savers: average folks who are not enticed by a new car every year, an extravagant house, or other such money pits.[11] This book was not only an interesting study of millionaires; it also projected a subtle message suggesting the moral superiority of those who hold and gradually accumulate wealth over a lifetime. It therefore provided an attractive reason to save and invest. The book offered no analyses of price-earnings ratios or anything remotely like specific investment advice, thus subtly reinforcing the impression that these are irrelevant. Instead, it offered lots of stories of successful, frugal people, many of whom prospered during the 1980s and 1990s bull market—stories with vivid details and great immediacy for readers. The book's enticing story about investing millionaires who do not test the market by trying to cash out and consume their wealth was just the kind of moral anchor needed to help sustain an unusual bull market.

Overconfidence and Intuitive Judgment

In judging the significance of these psychological anchors for the market, it is important to bear in mind that there appears to be a pervasive human tendency toward *overconfidence* in one's beliefs. People are ready to act on stories or reasons that one might think they should have little confidence in.

People think they know more than they do. They like to express opinions on matters they know little about, and they often act on these opinions. We have all observed at one time or another that there are a lot of know-it-alls out there. But psychologists have described the tendency toward overconfidence with some care and indications of its generality.

Psychologists Baruch Fischhof, Paul Slovic, and Sarah Lichtenstein showed that if people are asked simple factual questions (such as which of two popular magazines has the higher circulation or which of two common causes of death is the more frequent) and are then asked to give the probability that their answer is right, they tend to overestimate the probability that they are right. In fact, when people said they were certain they were right they were in fact right only about 80% of the time.[12]

This result has been the subject of controversy among psychologists, and the overconfidence phenomenon has not been found to be universal. It has been shown that people can sometimes be trained out of their overconfidence in the experimental setting.[13] Yet some basic tendency toward overconfidence appears to be a robust human character trait: the bias is definitely toward overconfidence rather than underconfidence. I find that overconfidence is apparent when I interview investors; they seem to express overly strong opinions and rush to summary judgments.

Psychologists have long wondered why it is that people seem to be overconfident. One theory has been that, in evaluating the soundness of their conclusions, people tend to evaluate the probability that they are right on only the last step of their reasoning, forgetting how many other elements of their reasoning could be wrong.[14] Another theory is that people make probability judgments by looking for similarities to other known observations, and they forget that there are many other possible observations with which they could compare.[15] The reason for overconfidence may also have to do with hindsight bias, a tendency to think that one would have known actual events were coming before they happened, had one been present then or had reason to pay attention.[16] Hindsight bias encourages a view of the world as more predictable than it really is.

Another factor in overconfidence as it relates to speculative markets is *magical thinking*. When we speak of people's intuition about the likelihood that investments will do well or poorly and their own decisions to invest, we are speaking of their innermost thoughts—thoughts that they do not have to explain or justify to others. Patterns of thought referred to as "magical thinking" or "quasi-magical thinking" by psychologists are likely to play a role. People have occasional feelings that certain actions will make them lucky even if they know logically that the actions cannot have an effect on their fortunes.

People will make serious decisions based on thinking that they would, if pressed, admit was illogical. It has been shown that people will place larger bets on a coin that has not yet been tossed than on a coin that has already been tossed (and for which the outcome has been concealed). And people will, if asked how much money they would demand to part with a lottery ticket they already hold, give a figure over four times greater if they themselves chose the lottery number on the ticket. Apparently, at some magical level people think that they can influence a coin that has not yet been tossed and influence the likelihood of winning the lottery by choosing the number.[17]

Based on such experimental results, it seems clear that people are capable of thinking, at least at some intuitive level, "If I buy a stock, then it will go up afterward" or "If I buy a stock, then others will probably want to buy the stock, too, because they are like me" or "I have a hot hand lately; my luck is with me." Such thinking is likely, in a subtle way, to contribute to the overconfidence that may help the propagation of speculative bubbles.

Another aspect of overconfidence is that people tend to make judgments in uncertain situations by looking for familiar patterns and assuming that future patterns will resemble past ones, often without sufficient consideration of the reasons for the pattern or the probability of the pattern repeating itself. This anomaly of human judgment, called the *representativeness heuristic*, was demonstrated in a number of experiments by behavioral economists Tversky and Kahneman.

For example, these researchers asked people to guess the occupation, from a list of occupations, of people with a given personality description. If the description given was that the person was artistic and sensitive, they tended to choose conductor or sculptress, rather than laborer or secretary, disregarding entirely the fact that the former occupations are extremely rare and thus that the answers are much less likely to be right.[18] It would be wiser, in answering such questions, almost never to guess the occupation conductor or sculptress, since the base rate probabilities are so low. But people look for the best-fit occupation, disregarding the base rate probabilities.[19]

Overconfidence, however generated, appears to be a fundamental factor promoting the high volume of trade we observe in speculative markets. Without such overconfidence, one would think that there would be little trading in financial markets. If people were completely rational, then, roughly speaking, half the investors should think that they are below average in their trading ability and should therefore be unwilling to do speculative trades with the other half, who they think will probably dominate them in trading. Thus, the above-average half would have no one to trade with, and there should ideally be no trading for speculative reasons.[20]

Overconfidence in judgments can at times influence people to believe that they know when a market move will take place, even if they generally believe as an intellectual matter that stock prices are not forecastable. In the survey that I conducted with investors right after the crash of October 19, 1987, I asked, "Did you think at any point on October 19, 1987, that you had a pretty good idea when a rebound was to occur?" Of individual investors who had bought on that day, 47.1% said yes; of institutional investors, 47.9% said yes. Thus, nearly half of those trading that day thought they knew what the market would do that day. I find this remarkable. Even among all individual investors, most of whom did not buy or sell at all on that day, 29.2% answered yes to this question; among all institutional investors, 28.0% answered yes.

Why would anyone think that they knew what the market would do on any given day, and especially on such a tumultuous day? The idea that one would know such things stands contrary to the most elementary observations about markets' forecastability, and contrary to the conventional wisdom that accurate market timing is very difficult. Quite a few people apparently do not consistently believe that the market is never very forecastable.

The next question on the questionnaire was, "If yes, what made you think you knew when a rebound would occur?" There was a striking absence of solid grounding for the answers. References were made to "intuition," "gut feeling," "historical evidence and common sense," or "market psychology." Mentions of concrete facts or references to explicit theories were rare, even among the institutional investors.

These intuitive feelings about the future course of the market were extremely important for the course of the stock market crash, for apparently it was these intuitive judgments that set the anchors that stopped the price decline. To understand speculative bubbles, positive or negative, we must appreciate that overconfidence in one's own intuitive judgments plays a fundamental role.

The Fragility of Anchors: Difficulty Thinking Ahead to Contingent Future Decisions

The anchors discussed here account for the stability of the market from day to day, but we must also account for the ability of these anchors to let loose occasionally—sometimes suddenly. Markets do make dramatic shifts. Part of the reason for the surprises the market hands us from time to time is that news events have an effect on people's reasons that even they could not have expected.

Psychologists Eldar Shafir and Amos Tversky have described a phenomenon they call *nonconsequentialist reasoning:* reasoning that is characterized by an inability to think through the elementary conclusions one would draw in the future if hypothetical events were to occur. According to Shafir and Tversky, people cannot decide until the events actually occur. When we learn to play games of logic (chess, for example), we must practice thinking ahead to the decisions we will make in the future in response to the other player's decisions. One learns to think, "If I move here, then she might move either here or there, and if she moves here I will be fine, but if she moves there I will be faced with a difficult situation. . . ." That is, one learns to think through the ramifications of all relevant branches of a decision tree. In everyday life, we to some extent practice the same modes of thinking that we learned in playing these games. But real-world decisions are clouded by emotions and a lack of clearly defined objectives, and people do not generally behave as if they have thought things through well in advance.

Shafir and Tversky give an example of students' decision making about whether to take a vacation in Hawaii after learning whether they had passed or failed an important exam. Faced with such a choice, they look into their own minds for their feelings about the choice. Some students who have passed the exam will think, "I should take the vacation as a celebration and a reward." Some students who have failed the exam will think, "I should take the vacation as a consolation, to improve my mood after having failed." Some students will decide to take a vacation whether or not they pass the exam. Those students who would take the vacation in either case should be able, if they were fully logical, to book the vacation well in advance of the exam, knowing that the information about the outcome of the exam is not really relevant to their decision. But these people sometimes have great difficulty making such a choice before they know the outcome of the exam. Before the exam, they cannot fully anticipate the emotional reason for taking the vacation, and so they cannot feel good about committing themselves to it.[21]

Although this example presents a situation in which the difficulty people face is in deciding how they themselves will feel in the future, rather than in deciding on questions of simple fact as in the game of chess, in reality decisions about investments are likely to have as much of an emotional component as decisions about whether to go on a vacation.

For this reason, the effects of news stories on the stock market sometimes have more to do with discovery of how we *feel* about the news than with any logical reaction to the news. We can make decisions then that would have been impossible before the news was known. It is partly for this reason that the breaking off of a psychological anchor can be so unpredictable: people discover things about themselves, about their own emotions and inclinations, only *after* price changes occur.

Psychological anchors for the market hook themselves on the strangest things along the muddy bottom of our consciousness. The anchor can skip and drag, only to snag again on some object whose strength would surprise us if we saw it at the surface. We have considered in this chapter some of the psychological factors that explain the nature of such anchors. But the anchors can have significance for the market as a whole only if the same thoughts enter the minds of many. In the next chapter, we turn to the social basis of thinking: the tendencies toward herd behavior and the contagion of ideas.

Ten

Herd Behavior and Epidemics

A fundamental observation about human society is that people who communicate regularly with one another think similarly. There is at any place and in any time a zeitgeist, a spirit of the times. It is important to understand the origins of this similar thinking, so that we can judge the plausibility of theories of speculative fluctuations that ascribe price changes to faulty thinking. If the millions of people who invest were all truly independent of one another, any faulty thinking would tend to average out, and such thinking would have no effect on prices. But if less-than-mechanistic or irrational thinking is in fact similar over large numbers of people, then such thinking can indeed be the source of stock market booms and busts.

Part of the reason people's judgments are similar at similar times is that they are reacting to the same information—the information that was publicly available at that time. But, as we shall see in this chapter, rational response to public information is not the only reason that people think similarly, nor is the use of that public information always appropriate or well reasoned.

Social Influence and Information

Acclaimed social psychologist Solomon Asch reported an experiment in 1952 that he interpreted—and that was widely interpreted by others—as showing the immense power of social pressure on individual judgment. His paper was published at a time of widespread public concern with the effects of communist propaganda, alarm at the apparently successful brainwashing

techniques of Chinese communists, and continuing puzzlement over the ability of the Nazis in Germany to obtain an obedient response when ordering
mass exterminations of Jews and other "undesirables." Asch's findings were
widely cited in the media as providing a scientific basis for claims that people
do not have fully independent judgment. His results are still cited today; those
who found serious flaws in his interpretation of those results are not nearly
as well remembered.

In his famous experiment, Asch placed the subject in a group of seven to
nine other people who were, unbeknownst to the subject, confederates who
had been coached by Asch. The entire group was asked to answer a sequence
of twelve questions about the lengths of line segments shown to them on cards,
and the subject would hear most of the others' answers before giving his own
answer before the group. The correct answers to the questions were obvious,
but the confederates deliberately gave wrong answers to seven of the twelve
questions. Faced with a group of people who were unanimously giving what
seemed to be obviously wrong answers to the questions, a third of the time
the subjects caved in and gave the same wrong answers as had been given by
the confederates. Furthermore, the subjects often showed signs of anxiety or
distress, suggesting that fear of being seen as different or foolish before the
group had swayed their judgment.[1]

Asch explained his results as due to social pressure. There is probably
some validity to this interpretation, but it turns out that the subjects' wrong
answers were not primarily due to such pressure. Three years after Asch
published his findings, psychologists Morton Deutsch and Harold Gerard
reported a variant of Asch's experiment in which the subjects were told that
they had been placed *anonymously* into a group of people, people that they
never saw and never would see, and whose answers they could observe only
indirectly through an electronic signal. (In fact there was really no group at
all.) Subjects could give their answers to the questions merely by pressing a
button, unobserved by others, so that there was no need to stand up to a group
face to face. Otherwise, the experiment proceeded as it had under Asch—and
the subjects gave nearly as many wrong answers as they had before.[2]

Deutsch and Gerard concluded that the wrong answers in the Asch experiment had been given in large part because people simply thought that all the
other people could not be wrong. They were reacting to the *information that a
large group of people had reached a judgment different from theirs*, rather than merely
the fear of expressing a contrary opinion in front of a group. This behavior
is a matter of rational calculation: in everyday living, we have learned that
when a large group of people is unanimous in its judgment on a question of
simple fact, the members of that group are almost certainly right. The anxiety
and distress that Asch's subjects expressed may have come partly from their
conclusion that their own senses were somehow not reliable.

Another widely cited series of experiments relevant to herd behavior is Stanley Milgram's investigations of the power of authority. In Milgram's experiments, the subject was asked to administer electric shocks to another person sitting close by, who was, again unbeknownst to the subject, a confederate. There really were no electric shocks, but the confederate pretended to be experiencing them, feigning pain and suffering. The confederate asserted that he was in great distress and asked that the experiment be stopped. But when the experimenter told the subjects to continue administering the shocks, insisting that the shocks would cause no permanent tissue damage, many did so.[3]

These results were widely interpreted as demonstrating the enormous power of authority over the human mind. Indeed, the results may be understood partly on those terms. But there is another interpretation: that people have learned that when experts tell them something is all right, it probably is, even if it does not seem so. (In fact, it is worth noting that in this case the experimenter was indeed correct: it *was* all right to continue giving the "shocks"—even though most of the subjects did not suspect the reason.) Thus, the results of Milgram's experiment can also be interpreted as springing from people's past learning about the reliability of authorities.[4]

Asch's and Milgram's studies are as interesting as ever when viewed from the standpoint of this information-based interpretation. The experiments demonstrate that people are ready to believe the majority view or to believe authorities even when they plainly contradict matter-of-fact judgment. And their behavior is in fact largely rational and intelligent. Most people have had many prior experiences of making errors when they contradicted the judgments of a larger group or of an authority figure, and they have learned from these experiences. Thus, the Asch and Milgram experiments give us a different perspective on the overconfidence phenomenon: people are respectful of authorities in formulating the opinions about which they will later be so overconfident, transferring their confidence in authorities to their own judgments based upon them.

Given the kind of behavior observed by Asch and Milgram, it is not at all surprising that many people are accepting of the perceived authority of others on such matters as stock market valuation. Most must certainly trust their own judgment in this area even less than the experimental subjects trusted the evidence of their own eyes about the lengths of lines on cards or the pain and suffering that a person sitting next to them was experiencing.

Economic Theories of Herd Behavior and Information Cascades

Even completely rational people can participate in herd behavior when they take into account the judgments of others, and even if they know that everyone else is behaving in a herd-like manner. The behavior, although individually rational, produces group behavior that is, in a well-defined sense, irrational. This herd-like behavior is said to arise from an *information cascade*.[5]

A simple story will illustrate how such an information cascade could get started. Suppose two restaurants open next door to each other. Each potential customer must choose between the two. Would-be customers may be able to make some judgments about the quality of each of the restaurants when viewing it through the front window, but such judgments will not be very accurate. The first customer who arrives must choose based only on viewing the two empty restaurants and makes a choice. However, the next potential customer can rely not only on his or her own information, based on the appearance of the restaurants, but also—by seeing the first customer eating in one or the other of the restaurants—on information about the choice made by the first customer. If the second customer chooses to go to the same restaurant as the first, the third customer will see two people eating in that restaurant. The end result may be that all customers wind up eating at the same restaurant—and it could well be the poorer restaurant, since there was no real consideration of the combined evidence inherent in all their observations about the two restaurants. If all of them had been able to pool their first impressions and discuss these as a group, they might have been able to deduce which restaurant was likely to be the better one. But in this scenario, they cannot make use of each other's information, since they do not reveal their own information to others when they merely follow them.

The restaurant story, and the economic theory that underlies it, is not in itself a theory of stock market bubbles. However, it has clear relevance to stock market behavior, and it can provide a foundation for a theory about how rational investors may be led astray.[6] According to such a theory, the popular notion that the level of market prices is the outcome of a sort of vote by all investors about the true value of the market is just plain wrong. Hardly anyone is really voting. Instead people are rationally choosing not to, as they see it, waste their time and effort in exercising their judgment about the market, and thus choosing not to exert any independent impact on the market. Ultimately, all such information cascade theories are theories of *the failure of information about true fundamental value to be disseminated and evaluated.*

It is important to emphasize that this failure to disseminate information to others can be modeled in economic theory in terms of purely rational behavior with no limitations of intelligence, only limitations of revealed information. But to achieve a better understanding of the issues relevant to financial market mispricing, one must also understand some parameters of human behavior, of limitations of human information processing, that are relevant to the transmission of information and the potential for speculative bubbles.

Human Information Processing and Word of Mouth

The human mind is the product of evolution almost entirely in the absence of the printed word, e-mail, the Internet, or any other artificial means of communication. Human society has been able to conquer almost all habitats of this planet primarily because of its own innate information processing ability. A fundamental component of this information processing ability is effective communication of important facts from one person to another.

This superior ability to communicate knowledge has been made possible over the past few million years by evolutionary changes in the human brain that have optimized the channels of communication and created an emotional drive to communicate effectively. It is because of this emotional drive that most people's favorite activity is conversation. Look around you. Everywhere you go, when two or more people are not working or playing or sleeping (and, in some cases, even when they are doing these things), they are talking. The incessant exchange of information is a fundamental characteristic of our species. The information that tends to flow most rapidly is the kind that would have helped society in centuries past in its everyday living: information about such things as food sources, dangers, or other members of society.

For this reason, in modern society there is likely to be rapidly spreading conversation about a buying opportunity for a hot stock, or about immediate threats to personal wealth, or about the story of the people who run a company. These topics resemble the kinds of things our ancestors have talked about since time immemorial. But conversation seems to flow less well about abstract topics, such as the mathematics of finance, or statistics about asset returns, or optimal levels of saving for retirement. Transmission of such knowledge is of course effortful, infrequent, and imperfect.

Face-to-Face Communications versus Media Communications

The conventional media—print media, television, and radio—have a profound capability for spreading ideas, but their ability to generate active behaviors is still limited. Interpersonal and interactive communications, particularly face-to-face or word-of-mouth communications, still have the most powerful impact on our behavior.

In a 1986 study of individual investors, John Pound and I sought to determine how their attention was first drawn to a stock. We mailed a questionnaire to a random sample of individual investors and asked them to consider the company whose stock they had purchased most recently. We asked, "What first drew your attention to the company?" Only 6% specified periodicals or newspapers. The majority of the answers named sources that would involve direct interpersonal communication.[7] Even if people read a lot, their attention and actions appear to be more stimulated by interpersonal communications.

The power of interpersonal, word-of-mouth communication about investments has been amply illustrated by the work of the market surveillance units at the exchanges and in the Securities and Exchange Commission. Their brief is to detect insider trading, and to that end they carefully follow the trail of communications among individual investors. Court documents reveal, for example, that a sequence of word-of-mouth communications was touched off in May 1995, when a secretary at IBM was asked to photocopy documents that included references to IBM's top-secret takeover of Lotus Development Corporation, a deal scheduled to be announced on June 5 of that year. She apparently told only her husband, a beeper salesman. On June 2, he told another person, a co-worker, who bought shares eighteen minutes later, and another friend, a computer technician, who initiated a sequence of phone calls. By the time of the June 5 announcement, twenty-five people connected to this core group had spent half a million dollars on the investment based on this tip. They included a pizza chef, an electrical engineer, a bank executive, a dairy wholesaler, a former schoolteacher, a gynecologist, an attorney, and four stockbrokers.[8] Clearly word-of-mouth communication can proceed with great speed and across disparate social groups.

Word-of-mouth transmission of ideas appears to be an important contributor to day-to-day or hour-to-hour stock market fluctuations, even though direct word-of-mouth transmission cannot proceed across the nation quite as fast as markets move. In the questionnaire survey of investors that I sent out during the week of the stock market crash of 1987 (described in detail in Chapter 6), I asked them about word-of-mouth communications. Of the individual investor respondents, 81.6% said that they had learned of the crash before 5 P.M. on the same day. Thus, they had learned of the crash from sources other than the next day's morning newspaper or that day's evening news. The average time of day that these investors heard of the crash was 1:56 P.M. Eastern Daylight Time (EDT). For institutional investors, the average time that they heard of the crash was 10:32 A.M. EDT. Individual investors reported talking on average to 7.4 other people about the market situation on the day of the crash; institutional investors reported talking on average to 19.7 other people.

The channels of human communication that we know today seem to favor the interpersonal face-to-face and word-of-mouth communication that developed over millions of years of evolution, during times when such communication was virtually the only form of interpersonal communication. The patterns of communication hard-wired into our brains rely on there being another person's voice, another person's facial expressions, another person's emotions, and an associated environment of trust, loyalty, and cooperation.

Because these elements are missing from the written or electronic word, people find it somewhat more difficult to react to these sources of information. They cannot give these other sources the same emotional weight, nor can they remember or use information from these other sources as well. This is an important reason why we still have teachers—why we cannot tell our children to simply sit down and read books or rely on computer-aided instruction.

It is also for this reason that television is such a powerful medium, in that it mimics much of the appearance of direct interpersonal conversation. Watching television simulates the very stimuli—the voices, faces, and emotions—that we experience in conversation. Indeed, television advertisers often recreate images of everyday conversation about their products. Television today has become more interactive, now that viewers will chat on social media while watching it, but the communication it offers is primarily one-way, and so it is still not as effective as direct person-to-person communication.

The telephone, invented well over a hundred years ago, may still be the most important artificial medium for interpersonal communication today, because it so closely simulates face-to-face communications, lacking only the visual stimuli. Studies by sociologists and communications researchers have found that telephone conversations come very close to face-to-face communications in information transmission and problem-solving functions, though they still fall somewhat short in conflict-resolution and person-perception functions.[9]

The impact of the telephone appears to have been a factor behind the volatile stock market of the 1920s. Although the telephone was invented in 1876, it was slow to be adopted. Clarence Day, in his book *Life with Father*, recalled why his family did not get a telephone in the 1890s: "Since almost nobody had them but brokers, there was no one to talk to . . . though people saw vaguely that a telephone might be a convenience if everyone had one, they decided to wait in a body until everyone did."[10] The telephone did not become widely used until a number of improvements brought the cost down and made the case for a telephone more compelling—improvements such as the invention in 1915 of vacuum tube amplification of longer-distance telephone calls. By the mid-1920s, the average person was making over two hundred telephone calls per year in the United States. The 1920s saw the spread of "boiler rooms" and "bucket shops" that actively sold stocks to the public using the telephone, employing questionable tactics that easily slipped past ineffective "blue-sky" legislation at the level of the states. The proliferation of telephones undoubtedly made it easier to sell stocks to the public, and the resulting impetus to fraud helped bring the country to the point of enacting the Securities Act of 1933 and the Securities Exchange Act of 1934, which created the Securities and Exchange Commission.[11]

During the 1990s stock market boom, we were witnessing another explosion of technological innovations that facilitate interpersonal communication, consisting of e-mail and chat rooms, and after 2000 these led to social media. Like the telephone, many people were slow to use these innovations at first, but as time went by, it became increasingly clear that it was inevitable that virtually everyone would be making them part of their daily lives.

These new and effective media for interactive (if not face-to-face) communication may have the effect of expanding yet again the interpersonal contagion of ideas. They may have allowed enthusiasm for the market to spread much more widely than it would otherwise have. Certainly we are still learning how to regulate the use of these new media in the public interest.

Although e-mail and other Internet platforms were significant changes in the technology of communications, it is not clear that their advent was more significant than that of the telephone many decades ago. Because the telephone allows communication of emotions as expressed vocally, it may yet be a better simulator of effective communication than those that rely on the written word, like e-mail, Twitter, or Weibo. However, the advances in video interaction, like Skype, Facetime, or Google Hangouts, may further enhance the potency of long-distance communication by more nearly mimicking human interaction.

Epidemic Models Applied to Word-of-Mouth Communication

The mathematical theory of the spread of disease has been used by epidemiologists to predict the course of infection and mortality.[12] These models can be used to better understand the transmission of attitudes and the nature of the feedback mechanism supporting speculative bubbles.

In the simplest epidemic model, it is assumed that the disease has a given *infection rate* (the rate at which the disease spreads from contagious people to susceptible people) and a given *removal rate* (the rate at which infected people become no longer contagious, through recovery or death).

If the removal rate is zero, the graphical plot of the number of infected people after the introduction of one contagious person follows a mathematical curve called the *logistic curve*.[13] With the logistic curve, the percentage of the population that is infected rises initially at the infection rate. Although the rate of increase is nearly constant at first, the absolute number of people recorded as contracting the disease rises faster and faster: as more and more people become contagious, more and more people become infected and are seen in doctors' offices complaining of the first symptoms of the disease. But the rate of increase starts to decline as the pool of yet-to-be-infected susceptibles begins to be depleted. Even though the intrinsic infection rate of the disease is unchanged, the rate at which new infected people are being produced declines, because those who are infected meet fewer people who have yet to become infected. Eventually the entire population is infected and the logistic curve becomes flat, at 100%; then of course there are no new cases.

If the removal rate is greater than zero but less than the infection rate, the model predicts instead that the course of the epidemic will be bell shaped: the number of infectives will at first rise from zero, peak, and then drop back to zero. The peak can occur before 100% of the population is ever infected.

If the removal rate is greater than the infection rate, then the epidemic will never get started and will never even be observed.

Epidemiologists use these models constructively to understand the pattern of disease outbreaks. Using such models they can infer, for example, that if the removal rate is just above the infection rate, then a nearly healthy population is in danger of an epidemic, for any small uptick in the infection rate or downtick in the removal rate can tip the balance toward a new epidemic. Thus, epidemiologists can infer that a change in weather patterns that will tend to keep people indoors together (where they are more likely to infect one another) may cause the infection rate to increase above the removal rate. The epidemic will then begin, but the absolute number of infectives will grow slowly at first. If, in this example, the weather changes fairly soon again in such a way that the infection rate is brought back down, so that the number of infectives never becomes very large, then the epidemic will fail to be noticed by the general public. But if the bad weather lingers long enough relative to the difference between the bad-weather-infection rate and the removal rate, then the epidemic will become large and noticeable in the population at large. Epidemiologists can use this model to predict, according to this example, how long a spell of bad weather is necessary to produce a serious epidemic.

The same type of epidemic models has been applied to other biological phenomena that may have relevance to financial markets. Economist Alan Kirman has used them to model the behavior of ants in exploiting food sources, and he notes that the models also seem relevant to stock market price changes.[14] It has been found experimentally that ants, when presented with two identical food sources near their nest, tend to exploit both sources, but one more intensively than another. Over time (and as the experimenter constantly replenishes the food sources so that they remain exactly equal), the primary attention of the ants may switch from one source to the other. Why should they not exploit the two equally, and what causes them to switch their attention? Kirman notes that ants *individually* recruit other ants to food sources; there is no central direction for the nest as a whole. Recruitment is done by contact and following (tandem recruitment) or by laying a chemical trail (pheromone recruitment). Both of these processes are the ant equivalent of word-of-mouth communication. Kirman shows that if there is randomness in the recruitment process, the experimentally observed phenomena can be explained in terms of a simple epidemic model.

Although disease spread and ant behavior are of theoretical interest in our consideration of stock market bubbles, of greatest practical relevance is the fact that epidemic models have been applied by sociologists to predict the course of word-of-mouth transmission of ideas.[15] Here, the infection rate is the rate of communication of ideas, and the removal rate is the rate of forgetting or of losing interest. The dynamics of such transmission may mimic that of disease. The formal mathematical theory of epidemics appears, however, to be less accurate for modeling social processes than for modeling disease spread or ant behavior, and it has yet to spawn an influential and successful literature by social scientists. This lack of success may be explained by the fact that the basic parameters of these models are not as constant in the social sciences as in biological applications.

One reason for the lack of success in applying epidemic models to the spread of ideas may be that the mutation rate, the rate of transmission errors, is much higher for ideas than for disease or other biological processes. Many of us recall the children's game of telephone, in which the first person selects a simple story and whispers it into the ear of the second person, who then whispers it into the ear of the third, and so on. When the story is finally told to the group by the last person in the chain, the distortion of the original story is often so dramatic as to provoke laughter. The person-to-person transmission of stories of any complexity is just not very reliable.

For this reason, pure word-of-mouth transmission of ideas, even if abetted by the telephone, is not likely to extend widely enough to infect an entire nation all by itself. The accuracy of transmission will falter long before that happens. In contrast, computer-to-computer transmission is unerring. Computer viruses can spread nationally and internationally with no alteration whatsoever. But viruses do not have the ability to change people's thinking; they do not get beyond the machine. The ability of users of e-mail to forward others' messages or to provide web links effectively permits word of mouth to spread unerringly. And new technology that makes it possible and natural to forward word-of-mouth messages from others as part of a telephone conversation or a video conference or the social media would again dramatically improve the accuracy and persistence of interpersonal communications.

Although the imprecision and variability of interpersonal communications as they currently occur prevent formal mathematics from predicting with any reliability how ideas spread, epidemic models are still helpful in understanding the kinds of things that can bring about changes in market prices.

For example, it is useful to consider that any change in the infection rate or removal rate will change the rate of spread of new ideas.

Thus, for example, a major national news story unrelated to speculative markets may lower the infection rate of ideas related to speculative markets by deflecting attention from them. This phenomenon may help explain why, as noted in Chapter 6, stock price movements are not notoriously volatile at times of national crisis despite the potential importance of such crises for the nation's businesses and why most large stock market movements occur when there is not much other news. In contrast, national news that ties in with or encourages discussion of the stock market may raise the infection rate. This may be part of the explanation for the Internet's apparently exaggerated effect on the stock market: attention being paid to the Net promotes conversation about technology stocks in general, thereby raising the infection rate for theories about these stocks.

The word-of-mouth transmission of ideas does not have to infect the entire nation to affect national prices in the stock market or the market for homes. Moreover, word of mouth may function to amplify public reaction to news events or to media accounts of such events. It is still necessary to consider the infection rate relative to the removal rate in order to understand the public impact of any new idea or concept, since most people's awareness of any of these is still socially mediated. Thus, the likelihood of any event affecting market prices is enhanced if there is a good, vivid, *tellable* story about the event.

The importance of a tellable story for keeping the infection rate of ideas high can be seen in many examples drawn from new-product marketing, such as the promotion of motion pictures. Marketers launch an ad campaign as the movie is first screened, to attract the attention of especially receptive people. Only a small fraction of the population responds directly to the initial advertisements. Yet the success of the movie ultimately depends on the reaction of these people to the film—and the opinions they pass on to others. It is well known that the advice of movie critics has less impact than the mass effect of such word of mouth. Producers have learned over the years the importance of including set pieces in movies. These are scenes that in and of themselves have story quality, scenes that, either during a screening or even as part of a trailer, pack word-of-mouth potential analogous to that of popular jokes or tall tales—or stories linked to high-flying companies on the nation's exchanges.

The effect of story quality on the contagion of ideas can have a real impact on market value. Why are certain paintings valued so highly among others? When I took my older son to the Louvre and we viewed the Mona Lisa, he expressed puzzlement that this painting should be considered so much more valuable than the others. He said it was undeniably good, but it did not stand out among all the other remarkable paintings. We then found ourselves betting that many people in the crowd viewing the painting were saying to each other—in whatever language—much the same thing.

To understand the exaggerated value of the Mona Lisa, we must consider the powerful word-of-mouth potential of a certain story about Mona Lisa's smile, apparently created by embellishment in word-of-mouth transmission from a story that first appears in Giorgio Vasari's biography of Leonardo written shortly after Leonardo's death. The story, which now appears in many forms, is that the artist had difficulty capturing her smile and worked four years on it but never felt he had fully succeeded. In his original biography, Vasari reported that Leonardo tried musicians, singers, and jesters to get the model to show the right expression. Vasari said that the smile in the painting "was a thing more divine than human, and it was held to be a marvel."[16] Vasari's description of the painting does not match the Mona Lisa that we see today, and so there may be some confusion; the story might actually be from a different painting. But no matter—the story is attached to that painting in the Louvre today.

That story has real currency; why it does is hard to pin down. The story seems to attach to many other thoughts. Mona Lisa's smile was used as a theme by poets and essayists over the centuries. Public attention could never have fixated on this painting without the story of Leonardo's long struggle to capture the smile, a story with powerful word-of-mouth potential.

The story of Mona Lisa's smile gained further impetus from two events that occurred in the year 1910. Both events enriched the story of her smile and provided immense publicity for it.

The first was the publication in 1910 of a provocative book by Sigmund Freud that undertook to examine Leonardo's subconscious and that dwelled on the Mona Lisa. Freud thought that for Leonardo, Mona Lisa's smile was a suppressed memory of his birth mother, from whom he was separated at age four, and who had expressed an unnatural affection for her son.

The second was the story of the theft of the Mona Lisa from the Louvre in 1910 and the continuing saga of the law authorities' attempts to recover it, then the story of the return of the painting and the trial of the thief. Of course the newspaper writers mentioned the smile: good writers covering the theft would not miss it. The theft story evolved over a period of years, a period long enough to reinforce the smile story firmly in the public consciousness. The smile story was ubiquitous in the press coverage. Even a 1914 story about the thief's final sentencing concluded with the ridiculous assertion, "He listened to his sentence with a facial expression somewhat akin to 'Mona Lisa's' enigmatic smile."[17] The reporter just *had* to get that smile story in.

According to a Proquest search of English language publications, the number of references to Mona Lisa during 1915–25 (after the theft story was completed) was twenty times greater than during 1899–1909, that is, before 1910. The legacy of the news coverage during 1910–14 is still with us today, since it amplified a media and word-of-mouth feedback about that smile, reinforced by continuing news mentions and parodies of the painting, that continue to this day. The 1910 events are forgotten in themselves by most people today, but the enhanced smile story is not, and the events are thus an important cause of the extraordinary value placed on the Mona Lisa today.

By analogy, news events that are more likely to be transmitted in informal conversations are in turn more likely to contribute to the contagion of ideas. The dry, analytical outlook an expert may offer for the nation's economy is very unlikely to be transmitted by word of mouth. In contrast, news that the stock market or the housing market has made a sudden move is vastly more likely to be communicated. To be sure, experts' opinions sometimes tag along with news stories about price movements, but they are seldom vivid enough to become the focus of word-of-mouth communications by themselves.

Word-of-mouth communications, either positive or negative, are an essential part of the propagation of speculative bubbles, and the word-of-mouth potential of any event must be weighed in judging the likelihood of that event to lead to a speculative bubble. Thus, for example, the predictions of widespread computer problems after the beginning of the new year in 2000 due to the so-called Y2K bug was a classic word-of-mouth story because of its association with both the world's fascination with computers and the new millennium. Thus—although fears ultimately proved groundless—it was likely to have an exaggerated impact on the markets compared with other, less vivid stories.

A Pool of Conflicting Ideas Coexisting in the Human Mind

One reason the contagion of ideas can sometimes happen rapidly, and public thinking can experience such abrupt turnarounds, is that the ideas in question are already in our minds. Even conflicting ideas can coexist at the same time in our minds, and a shift in supporting facts or public attentions may suddenly bring to the fore an apparent belief that contradicts formerly stated beliefs.

For example, people widely believe that the stock market is unforecastable and that market timing is futile. But they also believe (as we saw in Chapter 5) that if the stock market were to crash, it would surely come back up. Such views are clearly inconsistent.

One explanation for the fact that people are able to hold such conflicting views simultaneously is that they *think* they have heard both views endorsed by experts. The culture transmits a number of supposed facts, often attributed only to "them," as in: "They say that. . . ." When stories are casually accepted on some imagined authority, conflicts are likely.

Sometimes, stories achieve currency even though they can be traced to no competent authority whatsoever. One hears again and again, for example, that "they say" that only 10% of the human brain is actually used by most people—a myth that extends back to the nineteenth century, when neurological science was clearly incapable of either establishing or disproving such a fact. "They say" also that the birth rate in New York City jumped nine months after a 1965 power blackout left New Yorkers with nothing to do for a while: but there was no jump in the birth rate.[18] And, more apropos, "they say" that there were an unusually high number of suicides at the time of the crash of 1929, but there were not.[19] Stories that are useful in conversations, and in media presentations, have a currency often unrelated to the facts.

Given this tendency to attribute views to real or imagined experts, people do not worry much about apparent contradictions among the views they hold. There is a willingness to free-ride here—to suppose that the experts have thought through the apparent contradictions and therefore to assume that the experts know why they are not in fact contradictions at all. It is certainly true that sometimes theories that appear to be contradictory really are not. And from there it is but a short step to the supposition that the experts could explain away most apparent contradictions—if one asked.

People's thinking about the arcane field of investments is surely clouded with many half-thought-through ideas that may be mutually contradictory, or at least have not been put into any coherent analytical framework. It is a real challenge to try to infer what these ideas will mean for concrete investment decisions.

The significance of the fact that contradictory views are held simultaneously is that people may have no clear attachment to many of their views. Therefore, we cannot attach too much credence to investors' stated belief that the market will surely come back up after a crash, for the circumstances of the actual crash could bring to the forefront other, contradictory, views that were only dimly remembered before the crash. Investors would then react in ways that could not have been foreseen based on their previously expressed confidence.

Socially Based Variations in Attention

The human brain is structured to have essentially a single focus of conscious attention at a time and to move rapidly from one focus to another. The sensory experience that comes to us from our environment is vastly complicated, and the brain manages to filter out almost all of this complexity to produce a sense of the here and now—an interpretation of what is most important at present—and a sequence of thoughts that weave in this interpretation. Thus, for example, when one is sitting in an airport waiting to board one's plane, one's attention constantly returns to the theme "waiting to board" and organizes many thoughts and observations around it, as if it were the essence of current reality. One usually does not study the weave of the carpet or the smudges of dirt on the windows, or ponder the shape of the letters on the information screen, though in principle one could. These details are typically beyond our consciousness, even though we are receiving, and processing, sensory information about them.

The ability to focus attention on important things is one of the defining characteristics of intelligence, and no one really understands how the brain does it. Failure to focus attention on the proper things is also one of the most characteristic of human judgment errors. The mechanism for focusing attention that has evolved in the human brain, although remarkable, is still far from perfect.

If one looks back on some of the most significant errors one has made in life, one is likely to find that these often arose from a failure to pay attention to details. One would have responded instantly and changed one's actions had someone repeatedly demanded attention and pointed out certain key facts. Thus, in understanding errors that people have made in the past, it is important to consider what it was that they were *not* paying attention to.

One of the mechanisms that the brain has evolved to direct attention properly is a socially based selectivity. We pay attention to many of the same things that others around us are paying attention to. This social basis for attention allows individuals who recognize the importance of some information to bring it to the attention of other members of the community, and it creates a view of the world and an information set that are common to the community. Such a view and information set allow the community to act well in concert. At the same time, the social component of attention does not work perfectly, and it may cause errors to be made in common by the entire group, because the common focus of attention pushes aside attention to details that individuals might otherwise notice. As with individual attention, the phenomenon of social attention is one of the great creations of behavioral evolution and is critical for the functioning of human society, but it is also an imperfect creation.

The social attention mechanism generates a sudden focus of the attention of the entire community on matters that appear to be emergencies. Thus, to return to the epidemic model, the infection rate may suddenly and dramatically increase. A sudden major move in the stock market is one of those events that pushes aside all other conversation.

This social basis for attention, operating by word of mouth and facilitated by media transmission of ideas, can generate attention focuses that spread rapidly across much of the world. With a substantial fraction of the human minds on the planet suddenly grabbed by the market, it should not be at all surprising that markets on opposite sides of the globe move together, even if the fundamentals in different countries do not suggest any reason for such co-movement.

People Cannot Explain Changes in Their Attention

Furthermore, people often find it very difficult to explain what made them decide to take a certain course of action; the original attentional trigger may not be remembered. This is a principal reason why changes in speculative asset prices, which very quickly reflect changes in attention, often seem so inexplicable.

Price changes themselves may be an attention grabber, even among professional investors. In a study of institutional investors' choice of individual stocks, John Pound and I produced a list of stocks whose prices had increased rapidly within the preceding year and that also had high price-earnings ratios. We then obtained a list of institutional investors who had reported to the Securities and Exchange Commission that they had bought one of the stocks (the experimental group) and compared this with a list of institutional investors in a random sample of stocks (the control group). We asked respondents on both lists if they agreed with the following statement regarding their stock (the rapid-price-increase stock for the experimental group or the random stock for the control group): "My initial interest was the result of my, or someone else's, systematic search over a large number of stocks (using a computerized or similar search procedure) for a stock with certain characteristics."[20] Since these were investment professionals, it is perhaps not surprising that 67% of the random sample, the control group, said they agreed with this statement. But, among the experimental group, the investors in the rapid-price-increase stocks, only 25% agreed. Since attentional triggers are often poorly remembered, we cannot *expect* them to tell us that the price increase stimulated their interest, but our experimental design shows that the price increase, or associated events, did play a role in attracting their attention. The important point is that most of the investors in rapid-price-increase stocks themselves say that they were unsystematic in their decision making.

When variations in attention are important causes of changing behavior, we cannot expect people to tell us the reasons for their changed behavior. People usually cannot easily explain what drew their attention to something, and so they cannot explain their own behavior. A 1931 experiment by psychologist N.R.F. Maier will illustrate. Maier presented his subjects with the challenge of tying two cords together: cords that were suspended from the ceiling far enough apart that one could not reach them both at the same time unless they were somehow brought together. Subjects were given a number of tools with which to attempt this task and were asked to see how many different ways they could invent to tie the two cords together. One way to complete the task was to tie a weight to the end of one of the cords, set it swinging like a pendulum, grab the end of the other cord with one hand, and then catch the swinging cord with the other hand. When the experimenter himself set one of the cords swinging, many subjects quickly came up with this idea. But when asked how they had hit upon the idea, only a third of them mentioned having seen the swinging cord. The swinging cord merely changed the focus of their attention, and most subjects could not see the connection between their actions and the stimulus that had given them the idea.[21]

By analogy, a stock market boom can start for no better reason than that some factor, like the swinging cord, calls attention to the market. In the context of the present stock market situation, such events as spotting an ad for a mutual fund or the receipt of election forms for an employer's 401(k) plan may be the swinging cord. But we will never learn about the importance of these stimuli from most of our subjects by simply asking them. Even if people recall the stimuli, they will not be able to tell us *how* they affected them.

The Story So Far

This chapter concludes the essence of my argument that *irrational exuberance* is at work in producing the ups and downs of the stock and real estate markets. We began in Part One with lists of precipitating factors that gave rise to recent booms in the stock market, the bond market, and the market for homes. We saw that the effect of these factors is sometimes amplified via feedback loops and naturally occurring Ponzi schemes, aided by the lubricant of the news media as sometime promoter of market exuberance. We saw evidence of strangely high investor confidence and undiminished expectations for the market at the time of the Millennium Peak in the stock market in 2000, confidence that faded or only partly persisted despite the bursting of the Ownership-Society Bubble.

We then considered, in Part Two, the cultural components of exuberance, the varying degrees of social attention to new era theories, and the tendencies of these new era theories both to react to the market and to stimulate it temporarily. In Part Three, we have stepped back and examined some of the basic psychological factors that allowed the changes described in the earlier parts to exert their effects. Chapter 9 showed how trivial and barely visible psychological anchors may ultimately determine market levels, and how investor overconfidence can strengthen the pull of these anchors. The present chapter has attempted to resolve the essential puzzle of the current market situation: that we see newly high valuations but cannot detect a cause for those valuations that is associated with rational public thinking.

In the remainder of the book, I place the theory of irrational exuberance into a broader context. In the next part, I consider some influential arguments against the notion that anything irrational is going on. In the concluding chapter, I turn to the ultimate questions that this exuberance poses for policy: individual, institutional, and governmental.

Part Four

Attempts to Rationalize Exuberance

Eleven

Efficient Markets,
Random Walks, and Bubbles

The theory that financial markets are efficient forms the leading intellectual basis
for arguments against the idea that markets are vulnerable to excessive
exuberance or bubbles. Extensive academic research has been widely seen as
supporting this theory.

The *efficient markets theory* asserts that all financial prices accurately reflect
all public information at all times. In other words, financial assets are always
priced correctly, given what is publicly known, at all times. Price may *appear* to
be too high or too low at times, but, according to the efficient markets theory,
this appearance must be an illusion.

Stock prices, by this theory, approximately describe "random walks"
through time: the price changes are unpredictable, since they occur only
in response to genuinely new information, which by the very fact that it is
new is unpredictable. The efficient markets theory and the random walk
hypothesis have been subjected to many tests using data on stock markets, in studies published in scholarly journals of finance and economics.
Although the theory has been statistically rejected many times in these
publications, by some interpretations it may nevertheless be described as
approximately true. The literature on the evidence for this theory is well
developed and includes work of the highest quality. Therefore, whether or
not we ultimately agree with it, we must at least take the efficient markets
theory seriously.

Basic Arguments That Markets Are Efficient
and That Prices Are Random Walks

The idea of efficient markets is so natural that it has probably been with us for centuries. Although the term *efficient markets* apparently first became widely known through the work of University of Chicago professor Eugene Fama (who was jointly awarded the Nobel Prize in Economic Sciences with me in 2013, despite our different views on some basic issues) in the late 1960s, the theory itself preceded this name by many years.[1] It was clearly mentioned in 1889 in a book by George Gibson titled *The Stock Markets of London, Paris and New York*. Gibson wrote that when "shares become publicly known in an open market, the value which they acquire may be regarded as the judgment of the best intelligence concerning them."[2]

The efficient markets theory has been a fixture in university economics and finance departments ever since the 1970s. The theory has commonly been offered to justify what seem to be elevated market valuations, such as the 1929 stock market peak. Professor Joseph Lawrence of Princeton concluded in 1929 that "the consensus of judgment of the millions whose valuations function on that admirable market, the Stock Exchange, is that stocks are not at present over-valued. . . . Where is that group of men with all-embracing wisdom which will entitle them to veto the judgment of the intelligent multitude?"[3]

The most simple and direct argument for efficient markets theory comes from the observation that it seems to be difficult to make a lot of money by buying low and selling high in the stock market. Many seemingly capable people try but fail to do this with any consistent degree of success. Moreover, one observes that in order to make money one must compete against some of the smartest investors, the so-called "smart money," who trade in financial markets looking for the same opportunities. If one thinks that an asset is either under- or overpriced, one must then reflect on why it remains so despite the efforts of the smart money to make a profitable trade.

If the smart money were able to find ways to make profits by buying low and selling high, then the effect of such smart money would be, according to the efficient markets theory, to drive asset prices to their true values. They would be buying underpriced stocks and thereby tending to bid their prices up. They would be selling overpriced stocks and thereby tending to bid their prices down. Moreover, if there were substantial mispricing of securities, then their profits doing this trading would tend to make the smart money into rich people, thereby increasing their influence on the market and increasing their power to eliminate mispricing.

Unfortunately, this argument for the efficient markets hypothesis does not tell us that the stock market cannot go through periods of significant mispricing lasting years or even decades. The smart money could not make money rapidly by exploiting such a profit opportunity, and there would be considerable uncertainty about when the mispricing would end. If indeed one knew today that the market would do poorly over the next ten or twenty years, but did not know exactly *when* it would begin to do poorly and could not prove one's knowledge to a broad audience, then there would be no way to profit significantly from this knowledge. There is therefore no substantial reason to think that the smart money must necessarily eliminate such stock mispricing.

But this limitation of the efficient markets theory is often overlooked. The assumption is made that the same efficient markets theory that says that it is difficult to predict day-to-day changes implies that one cannot predict *any* changes.

Reflections on "Smart Money"

At its root, the efficient markets theory holds that differing abilities do not produce differing investment performance. The theory claims that the smartest people will not be able to do better than the least intelligent people in terms of investment performance. They can do no better, because their superior understanding is already completely incorporated into share prices.

If we accept the premise of efficient markets, not only is being smart no advantage, but it also follows immediately that being *not so smart* is *not a disadvantage* either. If not-so-smart people could lose money systematically in their trades, then this would suggest a profit opportunity for the smart money: just do the opposite of what the not-so-smart money does. Yet according to the efficient markets theory, there can be no such profit opportunity for the smart money.

Thus, according to this theory, effort and intelligence mean nothing in investing. In terms of expected investment returns, one might as well pick stocks at random—the common metaphor of throwing darts at the stock market listings to choose investments. It is ultimately for this reason that so many people have thought that they do not need to pay any attention at all to whether any given stock is or is not overpriced, and why they have felt they could ignore the unusual valuation of the market at the time of this writing, or at the height of the stock market boom in 2000.

But why should the very smartest people set all prices, as efficient markets theory implies? Many apparently less-intelligent or less well-informed people are buying and selling—why should they not have an impact on prices?

One notion, referred to previously, is that the smartest money has already mostly taken over the market through its profitable trading and has now set prices correctly; the less-intelligent investors are holding so little as to be insignificant forces in the market. This is an easy argument to dismiss.

First of all, if this is the reason the smart money dominates, then it must have been the case that there *were* profitable trades for them; otherwise, they could not have used their intelligence to take over the market. But if there *were* profitable trades, then there must *still be* profitable trades, since smart money investors retire from the business and must be replaced. One cannot argue that smart money took over the market 100 years ago and that ever since they have dominated the market, since those smart traders of yore are all dead now.

Another piece of evidence that has been offered in support of the efficient markets theory is that professional investors, institutional money managers, or securities analysts do not seem to have any reliable ability to outperform the market as a whole, and indeed they often seem to underperform the market once account is taken of transactions costs and management fees. This result may seem puzzling, since one would think that professional investors are more educated about investing and more systematic than individual investors. But perhaps the result is not as puzzling as it at first seems. Individual investors get advice from professional investors, and they can also observe (albeit with some time lag) what professional investors are doing. So there may be no significant difference between the success of professional investors and the market as a whole, even if their analysis is very valuable to others. Individual investors with substantial resources tend to be educated and intelligent people, too. Moreover, some studies have documented that professional analysts' advice is indeed worth something, if it is acted upon swiftly enough.[4]

Ultimately the reason that studies have not found stronger evidence that people who are smarter tend to make more money is that there is no good way to measure how smart investors are. Institutional investors as a group are not necessarily smarter than individual investors as a group. We do not have databases giving the IQ scores of investment managers to enable us to compare their performances with their scores, and even if we did, it is not clear that the available intelligence tests would measure the right abilities.

One study, by Judith Chevalier and Glenn Ellison, did come close to acquiring data about investment managers' intelligence, even though they did not have access to their individual test scores, by tabulating the average Scholastic Aptitude Test (SAT) scores of the colleges the investment managers attended. They did indeed find some evidence that firms whose managers attended higher-SAT colleges performed somewhat better, even after controlling for other factors.[5]

Another approach to testing whether smarter people can make money by trading stocks relies on persistence of investing success. If we have data on individual trades, and if some people are smarter than others at trading, then we should find that some people persistently lose money, while others persistently make money. In effect, we can measure a trader's investing intelligence by his or her own past successes, and then see how this compares with subsequent successes.

It has been found that mutual funds trading success is only moderately persistent through time.[6] But mutual funds are organizations, not individuals. The problem has been that, at least until recently, comprehensive databases of trades that identify individual traders through time have not been available.

One recent study, however, was able to use data on all day traders on the Taiwan Stock Exchange that consistently identified individuals for a five-year period. The study found substantial persistence of trading success.[7] It also found that most day traders did not make enough money from their trades to offset their trading costs, but a small number of them consistently did. Unsuccessful day traders tended to drop out through time; successful ones tended to trade very heavily.

These studies do not settle the issue of intelligence and investing success. Yet, from the available evidence, I see no reason to doubt the thesis that smarter and more hard-working people will, in the long run, tend to do better at investing.

Examples of "Obvious" Mispricing

Despite the general authority of the efficient markets theory in popular thinking, one often hears examples that seem to offer flagrant evidence against it. There are in fact many examples of financial prices that, it seems, cannot possibly be right. They are regularly reported in the media. In the 1990s stock market boom, many of these examples were Internet stocks; judging from their prices, the public appears to have held an exaggerated view of their potential.

For example, consider eToys, a firm established in 1997 to sell toys over the Internet. Shortly after its initial public offering in 1999, eToys' stock value was $8 billion, exceeding the $6 billion value of the long-established "brick and mortar" retailer Toys "R" Us. And yet, in fiscal 1998, eToys' sales were $30 million, while the sales of Toys "R" Us were $11.2 billion, almost 400 times larger. And eToys' profits were a negative $28.6 million, while the profits of Toys "R" Us were a positive $376 million.[8] In fact, Toys "R" Us, like other established toy retailers, had already created its own website. Despite some initial difficulties getting its site launched, Toys "R" Us was seen by many as having a longer-run advantage over eToys in that dissatisfied purchasers of toys on the Internet could go to one of its numerous retail outlets for returns or advice. In addition, customers who were already shopping at one of those outlets would naturally gravitate to the Toys "R" Us website when making online purchases. Despite these publicly aired doubts, investors loved eToys. But it didn't take long for the doubters to be proven right: eToys.com filed for bankruptcy and was delisted from NASDAQ in March 2001. The final step was the May 2001 sale of the eToys.com web address to KB Toys, which in turn filed for bankruptcy in January 2004.

The valuation the market placed on such stocks as eToys at the peak of the market in 1999 and 2000 appears absurd to many observers, and yet the influence of these observers on market prices does not seem to correct the mispricing. What could they do that would have the effect of correcting it? Those who doubt the value of these stocks could try to sell them short, and some do, but their willingness to do so is limited, partly since there is always a possibility that the stock will be bid up even further by enthusiastic investors. We will see other reasons later. Absurd prices sometimes last a long time.

It seems obvious that investors in these stocks are not thinking very clearly about long-run investment potential, and also that there are no forces in the market to prevent these investors from causing substantial overpricing. Doesn't such evidence clearly speak against market efficiency, at least for some stocks? And if some stocks can be overpriced, then does it not follow that the market as a whole can be overpriced, given that those stocks are part of the market?

Short-Sales Constraints and the
Persistence of Obvious Mispricing

There is reason to think that obvious mispricing really ought to occur, even in a world with huge quantities of smart money searching for mispriced assets. That reason: there are often obstacles to short sales, to borrowing the assets and selling them, thereby in effect holding negative quantities of the assets. Edward Miller, an eccentric professor at the University of New Orleans who has written provocative papers on a wide range of academic disciplines, first pointed this out in a 1977 article in the *Journal of Finance* that seemed to take efficient markets theorists by surprise.[9]

Miller's argument was actually very simple. Suppose a particular stock, or a particular tulip, or whatever, comes into great demand by a small group of zealots, who bid eagerly against one another to buy as much of this investment as they can. Efficient markets theory does not say that there are no zealots, which would be an absurd claim; it says only that somehow the smart money ultimately sets market prices. But if these zealots have really lost their sense, and if they buy so aggressively that they end up being the only people holding these assets, who is to say that these assets won't become wildly overpriced? The smart money, who are not crazy, would like to short the overpriced assets, to profit from the eventual fall in price, but if they cannot find any of the assets to borrow, the only way they can participate is by *buying*. As a result, they must just sit on the sidelines. The market with short-sales constraints can be wildly overpriced, and the smart money knows it, but there is no way for the smart money to use that knowledge.[10]

Short-sales constraints are very real. Some countries' governments do not allow short sales at all. Even in countries where short sales are allowed, the institutions supporting them may not work very well. Part of the reason is that even in these countries, there is a widespread antipathy to short sellers. Short sellers are blamed for all sorts of bad things. The New York Stock Exchange used to have an orderly market for the borrowing and lending of shares, the "loan crowd" on the floor of the exchange, but shut this market down some years after the stock market crash of 1929—a move that was widely blamed on short sellers.[11] Short sellers are commonly targeted as "boogeymen" for fluctuating or falling equity prices, a position echoed by regulators—short sales of financial stocks were temporarily banned in the United States and Europe after the market crash of 2008 in an attempt to stem market declines.

The difficulty of making short sales has played a real role in the mispricing of securities. A good example is the mispricing of the shares sold during the 3Com sale of Palm near the peak of the stock market in March 2000. In this initial public offering, 3Com sold 5% of its subsidiary Palm, a maker of personal digital assistants, to the general public, and announced at the same time that the rest of Palm would be sold later. This initial 5% of Palm went for such a high price in the market that, if one assumed that the other 95% of the Palm shares were worth as much, these shares exceeded the market value of their owner, 3Com. This is obvious mispricing if there ever was such a thing. But the interest cost of borrowing Palm shares grew to extraordinary levels, 35% per year by July 2000, high enough to make it impractical for smart money to profit from knowledge of this mispricing by shorting Palm and buying 3Com.[12]

The Palm example is extreme, but it illustrates the effects of restrictions on short sales. There are many barriers to short selling, not just the explicit interest cost; some of these barriers are bureaucratic, psychological, and social.

Statistical Evidence of Mispricings

It is difficult to make any solid judgments about market efficiency based on a few anecdotes about alleged extreme mispricing of assets. But, in fact, there is no shortage of systematic evidence that firms that are "overpriced" by conventional measures have indeed tended to do poorly afterward. Many articles in academic finance journals show this, not by colorful examples, but by systematic evaluation of large amounts of data on many firms.

Stocks that are difficult to short tend to do relatively poorly as investments, as was shown by Stephen Figlewski in 1981.[13] More generally, stocks that are just overpriced by various measures tend to do poorly relative to stocks that are underpriced. Sanjoy Basu found in 1977 that firms with high price-earnings ratios tend to underperform, and in 1992, Eugene Fama and

Kenneth French found the same for stocks with high price–to–book value.[14] Werner De Bondt and Richard Thaler reported in 1985 that firms whose price had risen a great deal over five years tend to go down in price in the next five years, and that firms whose price had declined a great deal over five years tend to go up in price in the succeeding five years.[15] (In Chapter 8 we saw that a similar tendency has held for national stock markets around the world.) Jay Ritter found in 1991 that initial public offerings tend to occur at the peak of industry-specific investor fads and then to show gradual but substantial price declines relative to the market over the subsequent three years.[16] Thus, there is a sort of regression to the mean (or to longer-run past values) for stock prices: what goes up a lot tends to come back down, and what goes down a lot tends to come back up.

These findings, and similar findings by many other researchers, have encouraged an approach to the market called *value investing,* that of picking portfolios of stocks that are underpriced by conventional measures, on the theory that they have been overlooked only temporarily by investors and will appreciate eventually. The other side of this strategy is to sell overpriced stocks short. One might think that the effect on the market of so many value investors would be to reduce, and even possibly eliminate for a time, the relation across stocks between value and subsequent returns. Value investors are after all buying the underpriced assets and bidding up their prices, and also diverting demand away from overpriced assets.

Sometimes value investing strategies will probably cease to work as investors flock to exploit them, yet it certainly does not follow that value investing as a whole will ever be out for good. Certainly avoiding investments that have become so overpriced that only the zealots own them is a sensible strategy. There are many different ways to define value, and the market as a whole is not going to find it easy to eliminate all such profit opportunities.

Moreover, even if the effect of value on return *across stocks* disappears, it does not follow that the effect of value on return *over time for the market as a whole* must also disappear. The characteristic strategy of value investors is to pull out of overvalued individual stocks but not to pull out of the market as a whole when it appears to be overvalued.

Earnings Changes and Price Changes

Another argument that markets are basically efficient, in the most global sense, is merely that stock prices roughly track earnings over time—that despite great fluctuations in earnings, price-earnings ratios have stayed within a comparatively narrow range.

Peter Lynch, an investment analyst who appeared frequently in the media during the bull market of the 1990s, was quoted in banner red letters in a 1999 advertisement for Fidelity Investments featuring a full-page photograph of him: "Despite 9 recessions since WWII, the stock market's up 63-fold because earnings are up 54-fold. Earnings drive the market." The ad, first seen just before the peak of the market, appeared to be designed to sell Fidelity's stock mutual funds by convincing readers that price growth is approximately justified by earnings growth. But in fact the numbers were deceptive. When such a long time interval is chosen for comparison, when no inflation correction is made, and since earnings were very low right after World War II, it is not surprising that Lynch could find such a correspondence. But if other examples are chosen, price changes may seem far less justified by earnings growth.[17] Lynch's statement was indicative of a common view that stock price changes are generally justified by earnings changes, and that this proves that stock market price movements are not due to any irrational behavior on the part of investors.

As we have noted, there have been only three great bull markets, periods of sustained and dramatic stock price increase, in U.S. history: the bull market of the 1920s, culminating in 1929; the bull market of the 1950s; and the long bull market running from 1982 to 2000. (One might also add the bull market leading to the peak in 1901, but it was not so dramatic. The Ownership-Society Boom 2003–7 and the New-Normal Boom 2009–14 are even less dramatic in comparison.)

The first great bull market, from 1920 to 1929, was a period of rapid earnings growth. Real S&P Composite earnings doubled over this period, and real stock prices increased five-fold. The market change might be viewed as a reaction to the earnings change, albeit an overreaction.

But in the second great bull market, the correspondence between price growth and earnings growth is not so clear. Most of the price growth then occurred in the 1950s, and from January 1950 to December 1959 the real S&P Composite Index almost tripled. But real S&P earnings grew only 16% in total over this entire decade, an earnings performance that was below average by historical standards. In terms of overall economic growth, the 1950s were a little above average, though not as strong as either the 1940s or the 1960s: average real gross domestic product growth was 3.3% a year from 1950 to 1960.

In the third great bull market, real stock prices rose more or less continually from 1982 to 2000, but earnings did not grow at all uniformly. Real S&P Composite earnings were actually lower at the bottom of the recession of 1991 than they were at the bottom of the recession of 1982, but the real S&P Composite Index was almost two and a half times as high. So, for this bull market, price increases cannot be viewed as a simple reaction to earnings increases.

These examples show that earnings growth and price growth do not correspond well at all. One cannot criticize bubble theories by claiming that they do.

A Historical Relation between Price-Earnings Ratios and Subsequent Long-Term Returns

In fact, price movements tend to be large relative to earnings, and price swings relative to the long-trend of earnings have tended, historically, to be reversed later. Figure 11.1 is a scatter diagram showing, on the horizontal axis, for January of each year from 1881 to 2003, the CAPE price-earnings ratio (as discussed in Chapter 1 and plotted in Figure 1.3) for that month, and, on the vertical axis, the annualized real (inflation-corrected) stock market return over the ten years following that month. This scatter diagram allows us to see visually how well price-earnings ratios forecast subsequent long-term (ten-year) returns. Only January data are shown: if all twelve months of each year were shown, there would be so many points that the scatter would be unreadable. The downside of this plotting method, of course, is that by showing only January data, we miss most of the peaks and troughs of the market. For example, we miss the peak of the market in 1929 and also miss the negative returns that followed it.

Figure 11.1 shows how CAPE values have forecast returns, since each CAPE shown on the horizontal axis was known at the beginning of the ten-year period. This scatter diagram was developed by fellow economist John Campbell and me. Plots like it, for various countries, were the centerpiece of our testimony before the board of governors of the Federal Reserve on December 3, 1996, just before Alan Greenspan's irrational exuberance speech.[18] Figure 11.1 differs from a chart we distributed at that meeting only in that we now have data from 17 more years, 1987 through 2003 (endpoints 1997 through 2013), and so 17 new points have been added to the 106 that were on the chart then.

The swarm of points in the scatter shows a definite tilt, sloping down from the upper left to the lower right. The scatter shows that for some dates near the left of the scatter (such as January 1920, January 1949, or January 1982) subsequent long-term returns have been very high. In some years near the right of the scatter (such as January 1929, January 1937, or January 1966) subsequent returns have been very low. There are also some important exceptions, such as January 1899, which still managed to have subsequent ten-year returns as high as 5.5% a year despite a high CAPE of 22.9, and January 1922, which managed to have subsequent ten-year returns of only 8.7% a year despite a low CAPE of 7.4. But the point of this scatter diagram is that, as a rule and on average, years with low CAPEs have been followed by high returns, and years with high CAPEs have been followed by low or negative returns.

The relation between price-earnings ratios and subsequent returns appears to be moderately strong, though there are questions about its statistical significance,

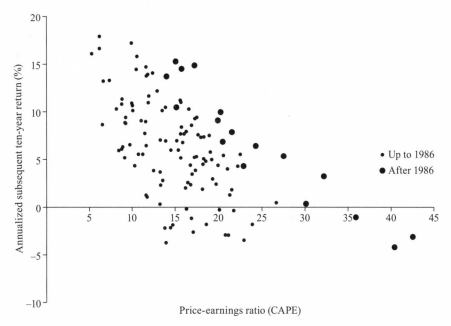

Figure 11.1
Cyclically Adjusted Price-Earnings Ratio (CAPE)
as Predictor of Ten-Year Returns
Scatter diagram of annualized ten-year returns against price-earnings ratios.
Horizontal axis shows the CAPE (as plotted in Figure 1.3) for January of the year.
Vertical axis shows the geometric average real annual return per year on investing
in the S&P Composite Index in January of the year shown, reinvesting dividends,
and selling ten years later. *Source:* Author's calculations using data from sources
given in Figure 1.3. See also Chapter 1, note 3.

since there are only a dozen non-overlapping ten-year intervals in the 123 years'
worth of data. There has been substantial academic debate about the statistical significance of relationships like this one, and some difficult questions of
statistical methodology are still being addressed.[19] We believe, however, that
the relation should be regarded as statistically significant. Figure 11.1 confirms
that long-term investors—investors who could commit their money to an investment for ten full years—did do well when prices were low relative to earnings
at the beginning of the ten years and did do poorly when prices were high at
the beginning of the ten years. Long-term investors would be well advised,
individually, to lower their exposure to the stock market when it is high, other
things equal, and get into the market when it is low.[20] Of course, other things
are not always equal. At the time of this writing, in 2014, the CAPE is very high,

but so too are the prices of alternative investments and long-term bond prices, and short-term interest rates are virtually zero.

The value of the CAPE at the peak of the stock market in 2000, over 40, was far outside the normal historical range of price-earnings ratios, and bond prices and short-term interest rates were not at such extremes. That same year, when the first edition of this book was published, I was careful never to use this chart as a basis for forecasting the stock market. The forecast would have been too extremely pessimistic to be believable. If one were to fit a straight line or a curve to the scatter, and since the 2000 price-earnings ratio was outside the historical range, the shape of the curve would matter a lot. Suffice it to say that the diagram suggested that, measuring from 2000, the forecast would have been for substantially negative returns, on average, to 2010. Measuring from 2014, with a price-earnings ratio in the mid-20s, the figure suggests low positive real returns, a few percent a year, from holding stocks for the ten years ending in 2024, though again that forecast should not be taken as very reliable at all.

Part of the reason to suspect that the relation shown in Figure 11.1 is real, if not highly reliable, is that, historically, when prices have been high relative to earnings as computed here (using a ten-year moving average of earnings), the return in terms of dividends has been low, and when prices have been low relative to earnings, the return in terms of dividends has been high.[21] The year-2000 record-high price-earnings ratios were matched by record-low dividend yields. In January 2000, S&P dividends were 1.2% of prices, far below the 4.7% that was the historical average. By 2004, the market decline and some increases in dividends brought dividends up to 1.7%, higher, but still low, and by 2014, they were up a bit more to 1.9%. It is natural to suppose that when one is getting so much lower dividends from the shares one owns, one ought to expect to earn lower investing returns overall. The dividend is, after all, part of the total return one gets from holding stocks (the other part being the capital gain), and dividends historically represent the dominant part of the average return on stocks. The reliable return attributable to dividends, not the less predictable portion arising from capital gains, is the main reason stocks have on average been such good investments historically.

Returns from holding stocks must therefore be low when dividends are low—unless low dividends themselves are somehow predictors of stock market price increases, so that one can at times of low dividends actually expect stock prices to rise more than usual to offset the effects of the low dividends on returns. As a matter of historical fact, times when dividends have been low relative to stock prices have *not* tended to be followed by higher stock price increases in the subsequent five or ten years. Quite the contrary: times of low dividends relative to stock prices in the stock market as a whole tend to be followed by price *decreases* (or smaller-than-usual increases) over long horizons, and so returns have tended to take a *double* hit at such times, from both low dividend yields and price decreases. Thus, the simple wisdom—that when one is not getting much in dividends relative to the prices one pays for stocks, it is not a good time to buy stocks—turns out to have been right historically.

Interest Rates as Forecasters of Excess Returns of Stocks over Bonds

When interest rates are very low (as they are at the time of this writing), it would seem that the attractiveness of the stock market is enhanced, even if the stock market is looking highly priced by the CAPE, since the alternative to stocks is not looking so good either. Indeed, if long-term interest rates are very low (as when they hit an all-time record low in 2012, around the time that the Fed announced its third round of quantitative easing—see Figure 1.3), then investors in bonds need to have some doubts as to their worthiness as alternatives to the stock market, even if the CAPE is high.

Since the CAPE negatively predicts long-term returns, one might suspect that the *excess* real return between stocks and bonds (that is, the real return on stocks minus the real return on bonds) would be influenced negatively *both* by the CAPE and by an estimated real long-term interest rate. Indeed, this is what we find, with the data shown in Figure 1.1.[22] A strong signal to replace stocks with bonds would be a time with high CAPE and high long-term real interest rates. Such a time was September 1929, when the CAPE was 32.6, when the long-term interest rate was 3.4%, and when, because of deflation in the 1920s, an estimated real interest rate was even higher, 3.7%. The predicted excess returns of stocks over bonds was –2.3% a year for 1929–39. (The actual annualized excess return was –6.3% a year for 1929–39.) It was not so at the time of this writing, in 2014, when the CAPE was around 25, long-term interest rates were around 2.5%, and estimated real long-term interest rates were around a quarter of 1%. The predicted annualized excess return for U.S. stocks over bonds from this simple analysis as of July 2014 for July 2014–July 2024 is 2.4% per year. Any such predictions have to be taken with a good deal of caution, of course.

Dividend Changes and Price Changes

Some economists have claimed that there is a good relation between real stock price movements and, if not real earnings movements, at least real dividend movements.[23] Dividend movements may be regarded as indicators of fundamental value, and so, these economists suggest, there is evidence that stock prices are driven by real fundamentals, not investor attitudes.

I think that these economists overstate their case for co-movements between dividends and prices. The wiggles in stock prices do not in fact correspond very closely to wiggles in dividends. Recall that between the stock market peak in September 1929 and the bottom in June 1932, when the stock market fell 81% as measured by the real S&P Index, real dividends fell only 11%. Between the stock market peak in January 1973 and the bottom in December 1974, when the stock market fell 54% as measured by the real S&P Index, real dividends fell only 6%. And there are many other such examples.

It is also likely that part of the reason for the observed co-movement between real prices and real dividends is the response of dividends to the same factors—possibly including speculative bubbles—that irrationally influence prices. Managers set dividends, and in so doing, they may vary over time the dividend-earnings ratio, that is, the payout rate. The managers are part of the same culture as the investing public, and are therefore probably influenced often enough by the same varying sense of optimism and pessimism that infects the public; they may allow this feeling to influence their decisions on how much of a dividend to pay out. Thus, the mere fact that prices and dividends show some substantial similarity is not inconsistent with the possibility that they are both influenced by fashions and fads.

In sum, stock prices clearly have a life of their own; they are not simply responding to earnings or dividends. Nor does it appear that they are determined only by information about future earnings or dividends. In seeking explanations of stock price movements, we must look elsewhere.

Excess Volatility and the Big Picture

There is indeed a good deal of evidence about market efficiency in academic finance journals, but it is hard to say that it is evidence *for* efficiency rather than against it. A great many anomalies have been discovered over the years within the efficient markets theory. These anomalies include the January effect (stock prices tend to go up between December and January), the small-firm effect (small firms' stocks tend to have higher returns), the day-of-the-week effect (the stock market tends to do poorly on Mondays), and others. How then can we summarize this literature as supporting market efficiency?

One way of arguing that the literature nevertheless supports market efficiency is to claim that many of these have been small effects, not the stuff of bull or bear markets. Another way is to note that many of these effects diminished after they were discovered, as indeed the January effect weakened after 1995 and the small-firm effect disappeared during the Millennium Boom.[24] This makes it tricky to summarize the literature. On the one hand, the fact that these anomalies persisted for a long time shows that markets are inefficient. On the other hand, the fact that many of them have weakened suggests that there is a basic truth to the theory.[25]

Merton Miller, who was a leading advocate of efficient markets theory, recognized that there are indeed many little anomalies, but he argued that they are inconsequential: "That we abstract from all these stories in building our models is not because the stories are uninteresting but because they may be too interesting and thereby distract us from the pervasive market forces that should be our principal concern."[26] But he did not explain his presumption that the pervasive market forces are rational ones.

Abstracting (as Miller urged us to do) from the little details about day-of-the-week effects and the like, what is the basic evidence that stock markets are efficient in the big-picture sense? Do large changes in stock prices over the years really reflect information about important changes in the underlying companies?

The evidence that there is not much short-run momentum or inertia—that there is not much predictability of day-to-day or month-to-month changes in stock price indices—does not tell us anything about efficiency in the big-picture sense. We already know from simple economic reasoning that day-to-day changes in stock prices cannot be very forecastable, since such forecastability would be too good a profit opportunity to be true; it would be too easy to get rich.

One method for judging whether there is evidence in support of the basic validity of the efficient markets theory, which I published in an article in the *American Economic Review* in 1981 (at the same time as a similar paper by Stephen LeRoy and Richard Porter appeared), is to see whether the very volatility of speculative prices, such as stock prices, can be justified by the variability of dividends over long intervals of time. If the stock price movements are to be justified in terms of the future dividends that firms pay out, as the basic version of the efficient markets theory would imply, then under efficient markets we cannot have volatile prices without subsequently volatile dividends.[27]

In fact, my article concluded, no movement of U.S. aggregate stock prices beyond the trend growth of prices has ever been subsequently justified by dividend movements, as the dividend present value with constant discount rate has shown an extraordinarily smooth growth path. This conclusion, coming at a time when the finance profession was much more attached to the efficient markets theory than it is now, produced a strong reaction. I received more attacks on this work than I could hope to answer. No one questioned the observation that stock prices have been more volatile than the dividend present value—only whether the difference between the two was statistically significant or whether my interpretation of this difference was on target.

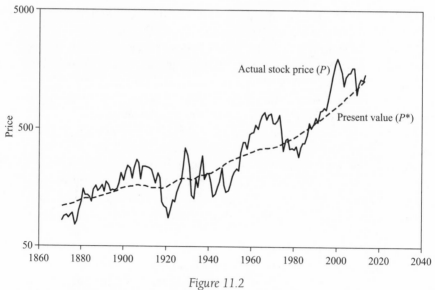

Figure 11.2
Stock Prices and Dividend Present Values, 1871–2013
Real S&P Composite Stock Price Index, 1871–2013 (heavy irregular curve), and present values, 1871–2013, of subsequent real dividends calculated using a constant discount rate (dashed smooth curve). *Source:* Author's calculations using data from sources given in Figure 1.1 and described in Chapter 1, note 3. See text and note 28 of this chapter for a description of the calculations. The vertical axis uses a log scale, in contrast to earlier figures in this book, and also shows only January of each year; hence the real stock price curve, which is otherwise the same as in Figure 1.1, looks different here.

Included in my article was a figure showing the real (inflation-corrected) S&P Composite Stock Price Index for 1871–1979 and, on the same figure, the *dividend present value,* the present value for each year of real dividends paid subsequent to that year on the shares making up the index, computed by making an assumption about dividends after the last year. An updated version of that figure, showing both the stock price and the dividend present value through 2003, is shown in Figure 11.2.[28]

The dividend present value is not known with certainty in the year to which it corresponds, since it is determined entirely by dividends after the year, which have yet to be paid. According to the efficient markets model, the dividend present value subsequent to any given year is the (as yet unknown) true fundamental value of the stock market in that year. The actual level of the real stock market in that same year, the stock price shown in Figure 11.2, is supposed to be the optimal prediction, using information available in that year, of one of the dividend present values shown for the same year.

Looking at this figure, we can get a sense of the extent of big-picture, important evidence for the efficiency of the aggregate stock market in the United States. If the dividend present value moved up and down massively over time, and if the actual stock price appeared to move with these movements as if it were successfully forecasting the changes in the dividend present value, then we could say that there was evidence that stock prices were behaving in accordance with the tenets of the efficient markets theory. But we see that the present-value series has not been more volatile than the price series itself. Moreover, there is little tendency of the stock prices to forecast the dividend present values.[29]

The dividend present value is extremely steady and trend-like, partly because the calculations for present value use data over a range far into the future and partly because dividends have not moved very dramatically. Now that one sees present value plotted over a long range of time, it seems obvious from what some of us (who have thought about it and have good intuitive grasp of quantities) have always known at gut level: the big stock market movements in history were not in fact justified by what actually happened to the businesses of the various companies later. One might try to argue that a little over a century is not a long enough time period to be confident that one *would* expect to see such justification, but the fact still remains that there has been no such justification.

The point I made in 1981 was that stock prices appear to be too volatile to be considered in accord with efficient markets. Assuming that stock prices are supposed to be an optimal predictor of the dividend present value, then they should not jump around erratically if the true fundamental value is growing along a smooth trend. Only if the public could predict the future perfectly should the price be as volatile as the present value, and in that case it should match up perfectly with the present value. If the public cannot predict well, then the forecast should move around a lot less than the present value. But that's not what we see in Figure 11.2.

We learn by considering Figure 11.2 that the common interpretation given in the media for stock market fluctuations in terms of the outlook for the short-run business cycle is generally misguided. The prospect that a temporary recession is on the horizon that will lower future dividends should have virtually no impact on stock prices, if the efficient markets theory is correct. Recessions have just been too short and too small historically to justify the stock price movements that are associated with them. Fluctuations in stock prices, if they are to be interpretable in terms of the efficient markets theory, must instead be due to new information about the *longer-run* outlook for real dividends. Yet in the entire history of the U.S. stock market, we have never seen such longer-run fluctuations, since dividends have closely followed a steady growth path.

As I argued in my 1981 paper, the only way to reconcile the volatility of stock prices with the efficient markets model without relying on ad hoc assumptions about changing stock market discount rates is to suppose that, one way or the other, the historical fluctuations of dividends around their growth path are not representative of the *potential* fluctuations. That is, one would have to say that the fluctuations observed in market prices were the result of people's legitimate concerns with possible major and lasting dividend movements that just did not chance to happen in the century of data we observe. For example, people might have been concerned about a big, rare event, such as a complete nationalization and confiscation of the stock market by the government, or an enormous technological breakthrough that would make existing companies able to pay many times more dividends. They could also be concerned, in pricing stocks, with the movements of future interest rates or of movements in the aggregate economy, possibilities that are considered in the Nobel Lecture in the appendix.[30]

As noted earlier, my work invited the attention of an army of critics. Most notable among them was Robert C. Merton, a brilliant financial theorist who also was to suffer a major financial loss as a principal in the Long Term Capital Management hedge fund. Merton, with Terry Marsh, wrote an article in the *American Economic Review* in 1986 that argued against my results and concluded, ironically, that speculative markets were not too volatile.[31]

John Campbell and I wrote a number of papers attempting to put these claims of excess volatility on a more secure footing, and we developed statistical models to study the issue and deal with some of the problems emphasized by the critics.[32] We felt that we had established in a fairly convincing way that stock markets do violate the efficient markets model.

Our research has not completely settled the matter, however. There are just too many possible statistical issues that can be raised, and the sample provided by only a little over a century of data cannot prove anything conclusively.

It should also be noted that some substantial fraction of the volatility in financial markets *is* justified by news about future dividends or earnings. The very trend-like behavior of U.S. corporate dividends over the past century was probably partly due to luck, not a law saying that dividends must hug a trend. Taking account of uncertainty about the trend, Campbell and I, in interpreting the results of one of our statistical studies, estimated that 27% of the annual return volatility of the U.S. stock market might be justified in terms of genuine information about future dividends.[33] Campbell and John Ammer, using similar methodology and a more recent (postwar) data set, found that 15% of the variability in monthly returns in the U.S. stock market could be attributed to genuine information about future dividends.[34]

There appears to be less evidence of excess volatility in long-term interest rates and little evidence of excess volatility in the spread between stock price indices.[35] Individual stocks, for which the present value of future dividends is much more volatile than with the aggregate market, show less excess volatility than the market as a whole.[36] Excess volatility due to speculative bubbles is probably just one of the factors that drive speculative markets, and the prominence of this factor varies across markets and over time. We are not always in an excess volatility situation.

But we are in such a situation, or recently have been, in many of our stock markets, housing markets, and even commodity markets. Defenders of the recent high price levels of these markets have had a difficult time making an inspiring case that the sudden increases we have seen in these markets can be interpreted as the rational efficient-markets response to genuine new information.

Some of the defenders have therefore moved to a very different explanation of the sudden price increases. To justify the sudden upswings in the market, these defenders abandon the idea that markets have always been efficient. Instead, they say that the markets are only *just now* becoming efficient. They say that people have suddenly learned the truth, after lifetimes of ignorance. This argument is in sharp contradiction to the theory that markets are intrinsically efficient—and yet we cannot dismiss this argument out of hand, given the large number of people who have been advancing it. We turn to an evaluation of this argument in the next chapter.

Twelve

Investor Learning—and Unlearning

At times of apparent speculative over-pricing, such as the time of this writing, a rationalization for the exuberance in the stock market, as well as other speculative markets, is that the public at large has learned that the long-term value of the market is really greater than they had thought it was and is greater than conventional indicators would have suggested it should be. According to this rationalization, the price-earnings ratio in the stock market is higher today than the historical average because the public has now learned some simple facts, facts about historical returns and diversification or about the world situation. This argument differs from the efficient markets argument in supposing that the market was previously priced too low because of public ignorance. The argument is essentially: "The stock market was not efficient for most of its history; it was too low; but (maybe) it is efficient now."

It is potentially plausible, at least at first look, that society may have learned that the market is much more valuable than it once was thought to be. Society as a whole does learn, and the cumulative effect of such learning is the reason that modern society has made such progress when compared with former centuries. But the question remains whether society has really learned something important about the stock market: Is this really true? If so, what have we learned?

"Learning" about Risk

It is commonly said that people have recently learned that the stock market is much less risky than they once thought it was, and that the stock market

214

has always outperformed other investments. Their "learning" is allegedly the result of widespread media coverage over recent years of the historical superiority of stocks as investments. For example, there was the publication in 1994 of the first edition of Jeremy Siegel's book *Stocks for the Long Run*. According to this view, people have realized that, in light of historical statistics, they have been too fearful of stocks. Armed with this new knowledge, investors have now bid stock prices up to a higher level, to their rational or true level, where the stocks would have been all along had there not been excessive fear of them. Stocks, selling now at a higher price, will pay a correspondingly lower yield—but that is all right with investors, since they now know that stocks are not all that risky. In other words, the *equity premium*, the extra return that people require to be compensated for the risk of investing in the stock market, has gone down, because investors have suddenly come to appreciate the historical record of stock market risk.[1]

It is true that the public at times does not appear to perceive much risk in the stock market. In Chapter 5, we saw survey results that showed that, while popular support for the notion that "if there is another stock market crash like October 19, 1987, the market will surely be back up within a couple of years or so" has faded substantially since the peak of the stock market in 2000, most people still believe this. So it is clear that the possibility of major stock market declines does not worry most people very much. But is this because people have acquired some genuinely new knowledge? Or are the new public opinions caused by something altogether different—and ephemeral?

A problem with this "new learning" theory is that the historical fact that investors have supposedly learned is not a new revelation. The observation that the stock market has largely outperformed other investments was made as long ago as 1924 by a best-selling book by Edgar Lawrence Smith. This book made a number of historical comparisons of investments in stocks versus bonds and found that stocks always came out ahead over long holding periods, in both periods of rising general prices (inflation) and periods of declining general prices (deflation).[2] Smith emphasized—as did another author at the time, Kenneth Van Strum—that investing in bonds was risky, too, because, even though the nominal values of bond payments are fixed, their real value fluctuates with the general price level.[3]

According to Professor Irving Fisher, writing in 1929, "These writings threw a bombshell into the investing world." Fisher thought that the bull market of the 1920s had occurred because the public had learned from these books: "It was only as the public came to realize, largely through the writing of Edgar Lawrence Smith, that stocks were to be preferred to bonds during a period of dollar depreciation, that the bull market began in good earnest to cause a proper valuation of common shares."[4]

Others shared Fisher's belief about public learning. Charles Amos Dice wrote in 1929 that "the old prejudice against security markets and the fear of them have been largely dispelled by public education regarding stocks and bonds."[5] A writer for the *New York Herald Tribune* asserted in 1929: "It is gratifying to observe the growth of business. . . . But there is a much larger significance in the growth of understanding among the people who make the growth of business possible. . . . There is nothing to retard the progress of any sound industry when an increasing number of people believe in it, become part owners in the business, and are regularly and reliably informed."[6]

If people did learn during the 1920s that stocks dominated bonds at 1920s prices, they seem to have forgotten the information later, or at least changed their feelings about it. The question before us now is this: Observing the recent stock market, have they really "learned" this time that stocks always outperform bonds, and will they continue to "know" this in the future?

The "fact" that Jeremy Siegel pointed out in his book *Stocks for the Long Run* in 1994, is that in the United States there has been no thirty-year period over which bonds have outperformed stocks. The supposed fact is not really true, since, as Jeremy Siegel himself pointed out in his book, stocks underperformed bonds in the period 1831–61.[7] That may seem like a long time ago until one realizes that there have not been that many non-overlapping thirty-year periods in U.S. stock market history: only five such periods since 1861. There have been many *overlapping* thirty-year periods, but of course these are not independent pieces of evidence. Given the relatively short history of thirty-year periods of stock market returns, we must recognize that there is little evidence that stocks cannot underperform in the future. Siegel himself acknowledges this in the 2014 fifth edition of *Stocks for the Long Run,* published after the post-2000 correction, which brought more thirty-year intervals of U.S. stock market underperformance. The Moody's Aaa Corporate Bond Total Return Index outperformed the S&P 500 Total Return Index in thirty-year periods ending in 2010 and 2011.

I have identified in this book three major peaks of the price-earnings ratio before the 2000 height: peaks in June 1901, September 1929, and January 1966. Note that we are again up around the levels of the price-earnings ratio of the 1966 market. In each of the ten-year periods following the 1929 and 1966 peaks, the stock market return underperformed short-term interest rates.[8] If we take twenty-year periods as our standard, then it is true that, of these three time periods, only in the 1901–21 period did stocks really underperform short-term interest rates.[9] But in each of the twenty-year periods following these peaks, the stock market did badly in real (inflation-corrected) terms. The (geometric) average real return on the S&P Composite Index was –0.2%

a year from June 1901 to June 1921, 0.4% a year from September 1929 to September 1949, and 1.9% a year from January 1966 to January 1986. Despite these puny returns, the stock market still outperformed short-term interest rates during 1929–49 and 1966–86, because inflation brought real average short-term interest rates to very low levels, in fact to negative territory in 1929–49. The inflationary periods associated with World War I, World War II, and the Vietnam War all had the effect of depleting the purchasing power of money earning interest.

Moreover, the United States may itself be the exception rather than the rule in terms of real returns on the stock market. Philippe Jorion and William Goetzmann have studied the real stock market appreciation rates (excluding dividends) for thirty-nine countries for the period 1926–96 and found that the median real appreciation rate was only 0.8% per year for these countries (compared to 4.3% per year for the United States).[10] Thus, if we take the experience of other countries as relevant to our own, we might expect a much poorer performance of the stock market in the future.

The evidence that stocks will *always* out-perform bonds over long time intervals simply does not exist. Moreover, even if history supported this view, we should recognize (and at some level most people must recognize) that the future will not necessarily be like the past. For example, it could be that, with investors buoyed by past successes in the stock market, there is now widespread over-investment. Companies may have hatched too many ambitious plans and spent too much on product development and promotion; therefore, they may not do as well as they have in the past. There was indeed substantial over-investment in the 1990s and 2000s, and this was a major factor in the world economic slowdowns starting in 2001 and 2007.

It could also be that some of the very technological changes that are widely touted as reasons for optimism for existing businesses are in fact reasons their prospects are more uncertain. New technology may diminish the advantage enjoyed by existing companies and cause them to be replaced by upstart newer companies. Thus, these changes could raise, not lower, the probability that stocks will underperform in the next thirty years.

So the "fact" of the superiority of stocks over bonds is not a fact at all. The public has not learned a fundamental truth. Instead, their attention has *shifted away* from some fundamental truths. They seem not to be so attentive to at least one genuine fundamental truth about stocks: that they are residual claims on corporate cash flow, available to stockholders only after everyone else has been paid. Stocks are, therefore, by their very definition, risky. Investors have also lost sight of another truth: that no one is *guaranteeing* that stocks will do well. There is no welfare plan for people who lose in the stock market.

The "Stocks Have Always Outperformed Bonds" Theme in Investing Culture

By the early 1990s, I was already so struck by the ubiquity of the observation that stocks have historically outperformed bonds that I decided to try to learn how common the observation really was. I asked the following in a question-naire survey of U.S. institutional investors in 1991:

> Consider the following argument:
> "Over the past 65 years, stocks have earned much higher returns than bonds and there has been no 20-year period since 1926 that bonds have outperformed stocks. Therefore, anyone with a time horizon of 20 years or more should be investing primarily in stocks."
> [Circle one number]
>   1. I agree with this statement.
>   2. I disagree with this statement.

Of the 172 respondents, 84% chose 1, and only 16% chose 2. This is indeed very solid agreement on a strongly worded statement.

The question as worded did not make it clear how often the respondents had heard that stocks have always outperformed bonds. To clarify this, in the fall of 1993, I asked institutional investors a similar but differently worded question:

> Consider the following claim:
> "There is no 30-year period since 1860 in which U.S. government bonds have outperformed stocks." Have you heard roughly this claim (even if the details, such as the use of 30 years, are different)?
>   1. Yes, often
>   2. Yes, once or twice
>   3. No

Of the 125 respondents, 52% chose "Yes, often," 22% chose "Yes, once or twice," and 26% chose "No." Thus 74% say they remember hearing this statement. Clearly statements like this were already part of our investing culture then.

Knowledge about the long-run historical record, knowledge that dates back at least to 1924 and that clearly was widely remembered in 1991 or 1993, cannot be held directly responsible for the sudden upsurge in stock prices to record levels in the late 1990s. The knowledge was apparently in investors' faces all along. The public confidence that any downturn in the market will be reversed indeed gained remarkable strength in the late 1990s boom years, but this confidence did not derive from a sudden news flash about the historical record. As I have argued, it derives from such things as a feedback mechanism from past price increases (discussed in Chapter 5), driven ultimately by various precipitating factors (discussed in Chapter 4)—not from a sudden discovery of the lessons from long-run historical data.

Learning about Mutual Funds, Diversification, and Holding for the Long Run

James Glassman and Kevin Hassett, in a pair of influential *Wall Street Journal* articles in 1998 and 1999, argued that "investors have become better educated about stocks, thanks in large part to mutual funds and the media. They have learned to hold for the long term and to see price declines as transitory—and as buying opportunities." Thus, Glassman and Hassett concluded that investors have learned that diversified portfolios of stocks are not risky, that stocks are much more valuable as investments than they had formerly thought. Therefore, investors are now willing to pay much more for stocks. Because of this increased investor demand for stocks, the stock market will perpetually remain at a higher level in the future.[11]

Glassman and Hassett followed up these articles in 1999 with a book, *Dow 36,000: The New Strategy for Profiting from the Coming Rise in the Stock Market*. In it they stressed that investors have not finished learning that diversified holdings of stocks are not risky and that they will continue to bid up stock prices in coming years as the lesson really sinks in. They wrote that "a sensible target date for Dow 36,000 is early 2005, but it could be reached much earlier."[12] Any reader who believed this when the book came out in 1999 would have had to conclude that there was an opportunity to make a *lot* of money between 1999 and 2005, or even sooner, by investing in stocks while other investors at large were still gradually learning about the true long-term value of stocks. Despite the ostensible theme of the book—that stocks are so risk-free that they should be thought of as interchangeable with government bonds—the sales pitch for the book (as can be seen in its title) was actually that one could get rich quick on the transition by investing in stocks in 1999, while *other* people would learn later that stocks are risk-free.

We now know that Glassman and Hassett were really totally wrong in their forecast for the market. Glassman and Hassett were, however, right when they said that people were considering the advantages of mutual funds, investing for the long run, and coming to believe the concept that stock price declines are transitory. But one should not infer from this that people had learned or were in the process of learning some essential truths. We have already seen that stock price declines have not been that transitory, that they can persist for decades, and thus that even long-run investors should see risk in stock market investments. There is also reason to believe that much of the enthusiasm for mutual funds is a sort of investor fad that was not caused by any real learning.

Investors show great interest in choosing the right mutual fund, and their interest in mutual funds often takes the form of switching from one to the next. In response to this heightened investor interest, the mutual fund industry has spawned thousands of new funds, with a corresponding proliferation of ads and mailings. Yet studies of mutual fund performance have found that although there has been some tendency for mutual funds that have done well to continue to do so, the tendency is weak and short-lived. People appear to believe that it is smart to pore over rankings of mutual fund performance and constantly shift their investments to the current top performers, but in fact they gain relatively little by doing so.[13]

To assess investors' feelings that they can make money in the stock market, and the role that mutual funds play in this process, I included in a 1996 questionnaire survey of individual investors a sequence of questions about their confidence levels for both investing in general and investing in mutual funds. The questions, along with the percentage responses and the number of respondents n for each answer, were as follows:

Trying to time the stock market, to get out before it goes down and to get in before it goes up, is:
1. A smart thing to try to do; I can reasonably expect to be a success at it.   11%
2. Not a smart thing to try to do; I can't reasonably expect to be a success at it.   83%
3. No opinion.   5%
                                                                                                        [n = 131]

Trying to pick individual stocks, trying to predict, for example, if and when Ford Motor stock will go up or IBM stock will go up, is:
1. A smart thing to try to do; I can reasonably expect to be a success at it.   40%
2. Not a smart thing to try to do; I can't reasonably expect to be a success at it.   51%
3. No opinion.   8%
                                                                                                        [n = 131]

Trying to pick mutual funds, trying to figure out which funds have experts who can themselves pick stocks that will go up, is:
1. A smart thing to try to do; I can reasonably expect to be a success at it.   50%
2. Not a smart thing to try to do; I can't reasonably expect to be a success at it.   27%
3. No opinion.   23%
                                                                                                        [n = 131]

From these results, we see that people effectively believe in the efficiency of the aggregate market and so have given up on timing it; but they often think that they can still pick individual stocks and (particularly) mutual funds. Only 27% say that trying to pick mutual funds that will do well is not a smart thing to do to, compared with 51% who say that trying to pick individual stocks and 83% who say that trying to time the market are not smart things to do.

If one truly believed in efficient markets, then one would reply "not a smart thing to try to do" to *all* these questions. If stock prices are a random walk, then one cannot pick times to enter the market, one cannot pick individual stocks, and one cannot pick others who will pick them.

Since there is only modest evidence that one can in fact be a success at picking mutual funds, what investors have "learned" has little support in fact. And in any case, should it really be easier to pick managers of mutual funds than managers of individual companies?

It is often said that people have learned about the importance of portfolio diversification and are using mutual funds to achieve this.[14] Given well-managed funds with low management fees, this argument makes some sense. But many funds charge such high fees that investors might be better off trying to achieve diversification themselves, if diversification is the primary investment motive. Moreover, when they are investing outside a tax-free environment, by holding stocks directly, investors can avoid capital gains taxes on the gains the mutual fund managers realize when they sell stocks in the funds' portfolios, an important issue with higher-turnover funds. Investors can instead realize, for tax purposes, the losses on the stocks that go down. Mutual funds clearly have their limitations.

Learning and Unlearning

The public is said to have learned that stocks always go right back up after they go down. We have seen evidence that people do largely think this, but that they have gotten their facts wrong. Stocks can go down and stay down for many years. They can become overpriced and underperform for long periods of time.

The public is said to have learned that stocks must always outperform other investments, such as bonds, over the long run, and so long-run investors will always do better in stocks. We have seen evidence that people do largely think this. But again they have gotten their facts wrong. Stocks have not always outperformed other investments over decades-long intervals, and there is certainly no reason to think they must in the future.

And the public is said to have learned about the wisdom of investing in stocks via mutual funds whose management teams have proven track records. We find that people do largely think this, and once more they are wrong. Picking mutual funds that have done well has much smaller benefits than investors imagine.

When the facts are wrong, it can't be called learning. We saw in Figure 5.1 that market events associated with the 2007–9 financial crisis caused investors to unlearn the "fact" that stocks are the "best investment." As high valuations reappear in subsequent peaks, they will relearn this "fact" again. Much of this is not learning at all, but a process of reassessing intuitive ideas about the future based on recent experience, as part of a bubble feedback.

A similar process of investor "learning" appears also to have been going on in connection with other markets besides just the stock market. People spent the aftermath of the 2001 crash "learning" that investments in homes are really not risky, that homes are the "best" investment, as we saw in Figure 5.2. The perception that the public has just learned some important facts lends support to massive market price increases by encouraging the belief that they may be permanent.

The sense that we are all suddenly learning important facts and have arrived at a new enlightenment has appeared so many times in history that it may be regarded as a predictable component of *irrational exuberance*. We must consider how to deal with the change in thinking that leads people to think we have entered a new enlightenment, changes that, through their effects on market prices, impinge on all our lives.

We have to consider what we as individuals and as a society should be doing to offset some of the ill effects of this exuberance. Let us turn to this in the final chapter.

Part Five

A Call to Action

Thirteen

Speculative Volatility in a Free Society

The high valuations that the U.S. and other stock markets attained at the peak in 2000, the relatively high valuations that it showed again in 2007 and once more in 2014, came about for no good reasons. The high valuations that the prices of homes attained in many markets by the opening years of the twenty-first century, peaking around 2006, and then again in many countries after the financial crisis, came about for no better reasons.

The high stock market levels did not, as so many imagine, represent the consensus judgment of experts who have carefully weighed the long-term evidence. The markets have been high because of the combined effect of indifferent thinking by millions of people, very few of whom have felt the need to perform careful research on long-term investment value, and who are motivated substantially by their own emotions, random attentions, and perceptions of conventional wisdom. Their all-too-human behavior has been heavily influenced by news media that are interested in attracting viewers or readers, with limited incentive to discipline their viewers or readers with the type of quantitative analysis that might give them a correct impression of fundamental value.

The housing market levels we saw at the 2006 peak were not, as so many imagined, the outcome only of fundamental forces affecting the rational demand for and supply of housing. Of course, home prices are set by the forces of supply and demand, as homebuyers so often say. The prices have to clear the market. But the factors influencing supply and demand include a lot of social and emotional factors, notably attention to the price increases themselves, a public impression that the experts know they will continue, and a predisposition to believe that they will continue. These factors will change with our changing culture.

Understanding how social forces cause speculative market moves has been the major theme of this book. It is so difficult for most of us to figure out which moves are caused by sensible good reasons and expert opinions and which are caused by human imagination and social psychology. I hope that the argument to this point has made it clear that, as these major markets go, it is often largely the latter that drives prices.

In both the stock market and the housing market, people have only the fuzziest idea what these investments are really worth, what their prices ought to be. They may be able to judge whether one stock is overpriced relative to another, or whether one house is overpriced relative to another, but they just do not know how to judge the overall level of prices. Much more salient in their minds is the rate of increase of the prices, something that they talk and hear about a lot in a time of rapid price change, and that has subtle effects on their demand for speculative assets.

As the price increase during a bubble goes on through time, people constantly reassess their opinions. People who thought there was a bubble, and that prices were too high, find themselves questioning their own earlier judgments, and start to wonder whether fundamentals are indeed driving the price increase. Many people seem to think that if the price increase goes on for years after some experts have called the price increase a bubble, then maybe the experts were wrong. And they then feel that there is no alternative to thinking that it is really fundamentals that are driving the increase, and that these fundamentals will go on forever. These are the phases that individuals who watch these markets go through—different individuals at different times.

The feedback theory that price increases excite investors and lead them to cause more price increases has always been on some people's minds, and most people have at least vaguely heard of the idea, but we have seen that public attention to this theory is on the whole quite weak. The feedback theory stands dimly in the background as a sort of folklore. There are regular newspaper articles that resurrect this theory, but they are not convincing to most people.

People seem to be reassured by the widely cited once-presumed "fact" that there has never been a thirty-year period when stock prices underperformed bonds, and by the "fact" that there has never been a major price decline in homes that has not been quickly reversed. These factoids were part of the psychology that drove bubbles, at least for a while. This psychology has in the past caused dramatic and unsustainable price increases, and it may well continue to do so in the future.

When prices stop increasing for a long while, there is a gradually increasing discontent with this view. This gradually increasing discontent may cause stagnant or declining markets even when fundamentals are increasing. Markets may disappoint for stretches of years or even decades, as the post-bubble dynamics gradually play themselves out.

As of this writing in 2014, we are going through another stock market boom in the United States. This might quite plausibly be followed by another major downward correction, though there is no way to be sure. Historical evidence suggests that stock market prices might also go up a great deal more.

We now have, after the financial crisis, new government agencies to deal with systemic risk, such as the Financial Stability Board created by the G-20 nations in 2009, the Financial Stability Oversight Council created by the Dodd-Frank Act in the United States in 2010, and the European Systemic Risk Board created by the European Parliament in 2010. Still, the problems posed by potential new bubbles and financial crises are not automatically solved by these new agencies. The problems are difficult. Bureaucratic organizations may find it hard to muster the courage and conviction to deal with them. Indeed, even before the recent crisis, every major country of the world had a central bank whose function generally included some form of stabilization mandate, yet they did not prevent the crisis from happening.[1]

When we see any bubble events happening, what should be done about it? Watching bubbles in the stock market, in the housing market, in the oil market, or in any speculative market is like watching an automobile accident happening in slow motion. It sometimes seems that there is nothing at all that can be done. Actually, there are quite a number of things to do.

It is a serious mistake for public figures to acquiesce in the ups and downs of market valuations, to remain silent about the implications of valuations, and to leave all commentary to the market analysts who specialize in the nearly impossible task of forecasting the market over the short term and who may share interests with investment banks, broker-dealers, home builders, or realtors.

Some think that professionals should not talk about the possible overpricing or underpricing of speculative markets, or ever try to predict the markets, since they cannot predict reliably. But that way lies madness, for the efficient markets theory itself, to the extent that it has validity, depends on the aggregate of investors responding to reasoned opinion, and that opinion must be publicly stated if many of them are to hear it. Indeed, it is this kind of madness that probably contributed to the overpricing of the markets at the end of the Millennium Boom, when efficient markets theory was at its highest tide ever.

The valuation of the markets is an important national—indeed, international—issue. All of our plans for the future, as individuals and as a society, hinge on our perceived wealth, and plans can be thrown into disarray if much of that wealth evaporates tomorrow. The tendency for speculative bubbles to grow and then contract can make for a very uneven distribution of wealth.

It may even cause many of us, at times, to question the very viability of our capitalist and free market institutions, as many did after the global financial crisis of 2007–9 and as was manifested a little later in the "Occupy Wall Street" movements of 2011–12 and their variants. It is for such reasons that we must be clear on the prospect for such contractions and on what our individual and national policy regarding this prospect should be.

The trouble with the exercise of moral authority by opinion leaders is that, although views that the market is either very overpriced or very underpriced may become commonplace among some experts, such views are never universally held. The leaders who state such views find themselves doing so based on personal opinion: an intuitive judgment about the state of market fundamentals and psychology, a judgment that is so hard to prove that they probably feel it is an act of courage to make such a statement in the first place.

Of course public figures incur a substantial risk of embarrassment if they go on record saying that stock market or housing market returns might be low or negative in coming years. We have seen in this book that although the markets appear to have substantial long-term forecastability when they are very overpriced, or, alternatively, when they are very underpriced, there is always considerable uncertainty about their outlook. But an observer who remains silent about public over-reliance on the market and overconfidence in future returns because he or she could be wrong about the outlook is no better than a doctor who, having diagnosed high blood pressure in a patient, says nothing because he thinks the patient *might* be lucky and show no ill effects.

Monetary Policy Should Gently Lean against Bubbles

There have been occasions on which tightened monetary policy was associated with the bursting of stock market bubbles. For example, on February 14, 1929, the Federal Reserve raised the rediscount rate from 5% to 6% for the ostensible purpose of checking speculation. In the early 1930s, the Fed continued the tight monetary policy and saw the initial stock market downturn evolve into the deepest stock market decline ever, and a recession evolve into the most serious U.S. depression ever.

In Japan, at the peak of the Japanese stock market between May 1989 and August 1990, the Bank of Japan raised the discount rate from 2.5% to 6%, seemingly to stabilize financial markets (which were thought to have become overpriced because of easy monetary policy) and also to stabilize the yen. It is hard to dismiss the possibility that this action by the bank played some role in the stock market crash and severe recession that followed.[2]

Although the precise causal links are hard to disentangle even in these dramatic episodes, one thing we do know about interest rate policy is that it affects the entire economy in fundamental ways, and that it is not

really big stock price shifts. It is plausible that by concealing a large short-term price change from the public eye, we can head off public overreaction to that price change, and so prevent a longer-term price trend from developing in response to the vivid memory of a really large one-day change. Dramatic one-day changes are attention grabbers, are given tremendous hype by the media, and are remembered long afterward, especially if they set some kind of record. However, we really have very little information about the effects of a policy of closing markets for short periods of time on longer-term price changes. What if an especially large price change is corrected soon after *by the market itself,* as was the October 1987 price change? Perhaps the public's experience of seeing a crash followed by a correction would have a more stabilizing effect than the experience of having a potential crash concealed from it by a market closing.

Another example of a deliberate restraint of trade to prevent bubbles and their bursting are rules regarding short sales. Allowing short sales permits those with negative opinions to express them in the market, thus presumably helping prevent bubbles from ever starting, but such investors also can hasten the collapse of bubbles as they try to short in a falling market. The U.S. Securities and Exchange Commission has long required of exchanges that short sales be allowed only on an uptick, that is, only if the preceding trade was on an increasing price. The uptick rule in the U.S. was eliminated in 2007, on the eve of the financial crisis, then partially reinstated in 2010. Other countries have had complicated histories about the legality of short sales. We have already noted that a number of countries imposed temporary short-sale restrictions on stocks in 2008 and 2009 to try to dampen the falls in their stock markets. China did not allow short sales at all, making its stock markets especially vulnerable to incipient bubbles, until some short selling began to be allowed in 2010.

In the interest of longer-run economic stability, it may be that the best stabilizing influence on markets is to broaden them to allow as many people as possible to trade as often as possible. This will broaden the scope of risks traded on markets.

Given that speculative bubbles are heavily influenced by word-of-mouth effects, by locally perceived values and information, and by patriotic feeling, foreign investors are generally less likely to go along with a bubble than are local investors, and they may even trade in a way that would tend to offset it. For example, in 1989, when the Japanese Nikkei index was at its peak, our questionnaire surveys found that the average Japanese institutional investor expected a 9.5% increase in the Nikkei in the following year, while U.S. institutional investors expected a 7.7% *decrease* in the Nikkei. Something about living in Japan encouraged very different feelings about the market. Had U.S. investors, or other foreign investors, been more prominent in Japanese markets all along, the Japanese stock market overpricing might never have happened.[6] Thus, more generally, broadening of markets by encouraging global participation in them should often have the effect of averaging over these disparate expectations and producing more stable market prices.

We should not assume that any policy that stabilizes markets from day to day is a good policy. Sudden price changes are probably not as bad, in terms of their impact on economic welfare, as long-term continuation of mispricing or, even worse, as the development of a speculative bubble that results in a worse crash in the future.

Given that speculative bubbles tend to occur, their eventual bursting may indeed be on balance a good thing. The Asian financial crisis of 1997–98, sparked by the withdrawal of world investors from Asian markets, may be viewed not as a crisis in the long-term sense but as a sanity check that prevented what might have turned out to be a more disastrous speculative bubble from ever developing. To the extent that this crisis encouraged Asian peoples to rethink their businesses and their economies in light of the criticism they received from abroad, the crisis may have been helpful for the countries.

The expansion of markets can, if done correctly, add salience to information about fundamentals, that is, encourage public attention to long-run fundamentals and deflect attention away from short-run speculation.

Karl Case and I have created home price indices that could be the basis of trade in futures markets. In 2006, Standard & Poor's, working with David Stiff and Linda Ladner at Fiserv, Inc., improved and adopted these as the S&P/Case-Shiller Home Price Indices; and in 2006, the Chicago Mercantile Exchange (CME Group) started futures markets in these indices for ten U.S. cities and for the United States as a whole (see John Dolan's homepricefutures.com). These markets continue today, now with the collaboration of CoreLogic, Inc. Trade in these markets should allow skeptics of home price bubbles to express their views in the markets, and this might tend to stabilize home prices, or at least to prevent the strong momentum we see in these markets. However, as of this date, there has been a disappointing volume of trade in these futures markets.

Michael Brennan has proposed that new markets should be set up for "S&P 500 Strips," that is, a market for the future annual total dividends of the aggregate S&P 500 firms for each year in the future up to some distant horizon. There should thus be, for example, in the year 2005, a market for the 2006 aggregate S&P dividends, another market for the 2007 aggregate S&P dividends, yet another market for the 2008 aggregate S&P dividends, and in fact markets for all subsequent aggregate dividends up to the horizon, say twenty years, and then a market for the terminal index value (say, in 2025). Brennan argued that such markets would "provide an incentive for analysts to concentrate on forecasting those fundamentals [future dividends] . . . rather than to concentrate on simply forecasting the level of the market itself. In addition, since the level of the market index must be consistent with the prices of the future dividend flows, the relation between these will serve to reveal the implicit assumptions the market is making in arriving at its valuation. These assumptions will then be the focus of attention and debate."[7] In recent years, a number of dividend futures have appeared on European markets, though they are not yet influential enough to satisfy Brennan's objectives.

Progress in financial technology may seem at times to be slow, but in fact history shows that major new economic institutions do eventually develop from seemingly slow beginnings. A process of experimentation with new institutional forms encounters many obstacles and setbacks, but we should not interpret these as problems for the long run. Eventually, we learn how to deal with them. The rate of experimentation with, and research on, financial institutions has been increasing over the decades, and advanced information technology that exploits broader databases and reduces the cost of new financial services is being used more extensively.

The Public Should Be Helped to Hedge Risks

To encourage proper risk management, the advice given by public authorities should stress more effective hedging of risks. I have argued in this book that people are ultimately highly influenced by the perceived wisdom of experts—the "they say that . . ." authorities—and they will not carry out risk management well unless experts encourage them to do so.

While financial experts today are typically extolling diversification, they do not stress what genuine risk management really means. Many people still think that they have done all they can if they hold stock in a good number of companies in their own country's stock market. They must invest more broadly than that, and, in fact, to achieve true diversification, they must also pay attention to other existing risks.

In addition, new institutions should be created that would make it easier for individuals to get out of their exposure to the stock market or the housing market. The institutions we have—such as short sales, stock index futures, put options, as well as home price futures—are not particularly user friendly, and most investors do not avail themselves of these. Many investors today feel themselves locked into their holdings because of the capital-gains-tax consequences of selling and their inability to find other ways of reducing their exposure.

People have to be encouraged by experts to understand that true diversification largely means offsetting the risks that they are already locked into.[8] This means investing in assets that help insure their labor incomes, in assets that tend to rise in value when their labor income declines, or at least that do not tend to move in the same direction. This objective can be fulfilled today by taking positions in existing assets that are found to correlate negatively (or at least less positively) with specific labor incomes.[9] It also means investing in assets that help insure the equity in their homes, in assets that tend to rise in value when their home value declines. Since labor income and home equity account for the great bulk of most people's wealth, offsetting the risks to these is the critical function of risk management.

For example, in my 2008 book *Subprime Solution*, I proposed that there should be an alternative mortgage type, that I called a Continuous Workout Mortgage, offering homeowners a preplanned workout (reduction in the principal they owe if home prices fall) that is not one-time-only, but that adapts continuously to changing housing market conditions.[10] Further work with my colleagues Rafał M. Wojakowski, M. Shahid Ebrahim, and Mark B. Shackleton is ironing out some of the details of these possible new mortgages. Issuers of such mortgages can hedge the risks they incur writing them in the home price futures market.[11]

Although hedging is a time-honored practice in business risk management, it is still today foreign to most people's thinking. Few nonprofessionals could even define the term today. Discussion of how investment returns correlate with incomes or with home prices is almost totally absent from public discourse on investments.

It is difficult to change this mindset, since the public has so much invested in the conventional wisdom today and in the notion that one can amass great wealth through stock market or real estate investments. The personal investment media typically feature the opinions of celebrity sources who are apparently already rich and who subtly suggest that their advice might make one rich too. It would be inconsistent with this fantasy to start talking about the mundane task of defending the value of the assets one already has. Those in the media and the investment community often do not want to risk disturbing the get-rich fantasy, which they have learned to exploit to their own advantage. But attitudes can be changed if public opinion leaders take it upon themselves to stress the changes in thinking that must be made. Once it becomes a "they say that . . ." item, people will routinely take proper steps to hedge their existing wealth, much as they routinely buy homeowners insurance today.

Policy Addressing Saving and Retirement Planning Should Be Realistic about Bubbles

There has been an unfortunate tendency for financial advisers to assume that expected returns in major asset classes are constant through time, in accordance with simple efficient markets models, and hence to issue no warnings to those who make saving and retirement plans at times of overvalued markets.

Over much of the course of the Millennium Boom of 1982–2000 and the Ownership-Society Boom from 2003 to 2007, the personal saving rate in the United States declined as the stock market rose, and as, after 1997, the housing market rose, giving people the spurious impression that they did not need to save. The personal saving rate was 12.0% of income at the bottom of the U.S. stock market in July 1982. By November 1996, when the housing boom first showed signs of picking up, it had fallen to 5.8% of income. At the top of the stock market before the financial crisis (near the top of the housing market as well), October 2007, it had fallen to 2.9% of income. Of course, when both stock and housing prices fell sharply, people increased their saving rate sharply, even though, with lower incomes and higher unemployment, it was harder to save. The personal saving rate rose back up to 8.1% by the worst of the financial crisis, May 2009.[12]

Moreover, those in charge of defined benefit pension plans underfunded their plans, thinking that fabulous stock market returns on their investments would provide generously for the retirees they would be responsible for in the future. During the complacency of a boom, it is easy to get away with underfunding pension plans.

We saw the painful consequences of this play out in the years after the bursting of the Millennium Bubble in 2000 and after the bursting of the Ownership-Society Bubble in 2007. Defined benefit pension funds had been grossly underfunded with the blithe assumption that financial markets would do as well as expected despite a very high price-earnings ratio (especially as measured by the CAPE). At a time of complacency during the booms, state and local politicians did not want to address the need to raise taxes to better fund their pension plans. With this complacency, labor unions as well did not bargain aggressively for better funding. The assumption was that further stock market price increases would provide generously for the retiring Baby Boomers, so provisions to fund them well were not needed. The result was disastrous, as state and local governments, facing the need to bolster their retirement funds, cut back on teachers and police officers, and contributed to the depth of the recession by increasing their saving at the worst possible time.

The U.S. Pension Benefit Guaranty Corporation (PBGC), which had been created by an act of Congress in 1974 to accumulate a trust fund to insure workers with private pension plans against losing their pension income when their plan sponsors run out of money, was looking at imminent failure after the Ownership-Society Boom ended, until it was at least temporarily saved by the New-Normal Boom of 2009–2014. But their problems remain unsolved unless the stock market continues to boom. The PBGC, as of its fiscal 2013 Projections Report issued in 2014, was using a Pension Insurance Modeling System (PIMS) with an assumed geometric average rate of return for pension plans of 6.1%, which appears unrealistically high, given the high pricing in the stock market and low bond yields. Even with this optimistic PIMS assumption, in their own 2013 report, the PGBC warned of a likely bankruptcy of their support for multi-employer plans at current premium levels by 2019, and with a 90% probability by 2025.[13]

At the time of this writing, in 2014, with very high stock market valuations and rising real estate valuations, we run the risk of repeating these mistakes again. The U.S. personal saving rate, benefiting from stimulus that is trying to boost it to stimulate the economy, is, at 4.8% with the latest data, still low. It will have to be increased once the economy recovers more fully. Even today, the U.S. government can contribute indirectly to saving by launching public infrastructure investment stimulus programs, which would be very timely, as it can borrow at virtually zero real interest rates to fund them.

Currently (2014), most people are not saving enough for their future, and pension funds are likely not building up enough new funds. The lesson for individual investors at this point of time from very high valuation of the stock market is not to pull investments massively out of the market in favor of bonds, for bond yields are also very low. Rather, the lesson for individuals is to not be lulled into more complacency by past investment successes, to remember that the level of returns we have seen in the past few years is unlikely to continue. The lesson for governments is to promote economic stimulus and infrastructure investments in public goods, taking advantage of their ability to borrow at low rates to invest in the future.

Promoting Good Policy toward Speculative Volatility

The problems posed for policy makers by the tendency for speculative markets to show occasional bubbles are deep ones. They will have to take full account of our evolving understanding of the nature of these bubbles when formulating measures to deal with the problems these bubbles cause. Unfortunately, the nature of the bubbles is sufficiently complex and changeable that experts can never expect to prove the particular role of any given policy in bringing about our objective of long-term economic welfare.

Policies that interfere with markets by shutting them down or limiting them, although under some very specific circumstances apparently useful, probably should not be high on our list of solutions to the problems caused by speculative bubbles. Speculative markets perform critical resource-allocation functions (a point I have taken for granted and have not focused on in this book), and any interference with markets to tame bubbles interferes with these functions as well.

Ultimately, in a free society, the government cannot protect people from all the consequences of their own errors. The government cannot protect people completely without denying them the possibility of achieving their own fulfillment. And, the government cannot completely protect society from the effects of waves of irrational exuberance *or* irrational pessimism—emotional reactions that are themselves part of the human condition.

Policies to deal with speculative volatility are a little like policies to deal with political instability. We worry that a political party appealing to baser instincts or rash judgments will gain control. But we do not deal with this risk by shutting down certain political parties in times of unrest or by taxing their activities. Instead, we rely on the complete freedom of all political parties to express themselves, and we expect that common sense will ultimately prevail among voters. This good outcome is achieved by designing, and continually improving, rules for campaigns and elections.

By analogy, most of the thrust of our national policies to deal with speculative bubbles should take the form of facilitating more free trade, as well as greater opportunities for people to take positions in more and freer markets. A good outcome can be achieved by designing better forms of social insurance and creating better financial institutions to allow the real risks to be managed more effectively. The most important thing to keep in mind whenever we experience tumult in the markets is that we should not let it distract us from such important tasks.[14]

Appendix

Nobel Prize Lecture: Speculative Asset Prices

Iwill start this lecture with some general thoughts on the determinants of long-term asset prices, such as stock prices or home prices: what, ultimately, drives these prices to change as they do from time to time, and how can we interpret these changes? I will consider the discourse in the profession about the role of rationality in the formation of these prices and the growing trend toward behavioral finance and, more broadly, behavioral economics, the increasing acceptance of the importance of alternative psychological, sociological, and epidemiological factors as affecting prices. I will focus on the statistical methods that allow us to learn about the sources of price volatility in the stock market and the housing market, and evidence that has led to the behavioral finance revolution in financial thought in recent decades.

The broader purpose here is to appreciate the promise of financial technology. There is a great deal of popular skepticism about financial institutions afoot these days, after the financial and economic crisis that has dragged on ever since the severest days in 2008. I want to consider the possibilities for the future of finance in general terms, rather than focusing on current stopgap measures to deal opportunistically with symptoms of our current economic crisis. The talk about the rationality of markets is a precursor to this talk of financial technology, for it underpins our notions of the possibilities that new technology offers.

This is a substantial revision (February 19, 2014) of the lecture I gave for the Sveriges Riksbank Prize in Economic Sciences in Memory of Alfred Nobel, on December 8, 2013, www.nobelprize .org/mediaplayer/index.php?id=1996.

I will conclude that the markets have already been "human-factors-engineered" to function remarkably well, and that as we improve our understanding of the kind of psychology that leads to bubbles and related problems, we can further innovate to improve the functioning of these markets.

Price Volatility, Rational Expectations, and Bubbles

The history of thought in financial markets has shown a surprising lack of consensus about a very fundamental question: what ultimately causes all those fluctuations in the price of speculative assets like corporate stocks, commodities, or real estate? One might think that so basic a question would long ago have been confidently answered. But the answer to this question is not so easily found.[1]

At the same time, there has been an equally widespread acceptance in other quarters of the idea that markets are substantially driven by psychology. Indeed, since 1991 Richard Thaler and I have been directors of the National Bureau of Economic Research program in behavioral economics, which has featured hundreds of papers that seem mostly at odds with a general sense of rationality in the markets.[2]

The term "speculative bubble" is often used and applied carelessly. The word "bubble" first became popular at the time of the Mississippi Bubble in European stock markets that came to an end in 1720, a time often mentioned as one of craziness, but whether that period is best described as one of wild irrationality still remains controversial; see Garber (2000) and Goetzmann et al. (2013). I would say that a speculative bubble is a peculiar kind of fad or social epidemic that is regularly seen in speculative markets: not a wild orgy of delusions but a natural consequence of the principles of social psychology coupled with imperfect news media and information channels. In the second edition of my book *Irrational Exuberance* I offered a definition of "bubble" that I thought represents the term's best use:

> A situation in which news of price increases spurs investor enthusiasm, which spreads by psychological contagion from person to person, in the process amplifying stories that might justify the price increases and bringing in a larger and larger class of investors, who, despite doubts about the real value of an investment, are drawn to it partly through envy of others' successes and partly through a gambler's excitement.

---

[1] There is a similarly disconcerting lack of consensus in the economics profession over what drives fluctuations from quarter to quarter in aggregate economic activity, as measured by gross domestic product; see Shiller (1987), Akerlof and Shiller (2009).

[2] http://www.econ.yale.edu/~shiller/behfin/index.htm.

At the center of my definition are the epidemic spread, the emotions of investors, and the nature of the news and information media. Bubbles are not, to my mind, about the craziness of investors. They are rather about how investors are buffeted en masse from one superficially plausible theory about conventional valuation to another. One thinks of how a good debater can take either side of many disputes and, if the debater on the other side has weak skills, can substantially convince the audience of either side. College debate teams demonstrate this phenomenon regularly, and they do it by suppressing certain facts and amplifying and embellishing others. In the case of bubbles, the sides are changed from time to time by the feedback of price changes, with the proliferation, caused by price increases, of reminders of basic facts that a debater might use to defend the bubble. The news media are even better at presenting cases than are typical college debaters.

Investing ideas can spread like epidemics. Economists traditionally have not shown much interest in epidemiology, sociology, social psychology, or communications and journalism, and it takes some effort for them to consider such alien academic traditions.

There is a troublesome split between efficient markets enthusiasts (who believe that market prices accurately incorporate all public information, and so doubt that bubbles even exist) and those who believe in behavioral finance (who tend to believe that bubbles and other such contradictions to efficient markets can be understood only with reference to other social sciences, such as psychology). I suspect that some of the apparent split is illusory, deriving from the problem that there is no widely accepted definition of the term "bubble." The metaphor might suggest that speculative bubbles always burst suddenly and irrevocably, as soap bubbles seem to do, without exception. That would be silly, for history does not generally support the catastrophic burst notion. Though the abrupt ends of stock market booms in 1929, 2000, and 2007 might seem consonant with such a metaphor, these booms were reflated again before long (1933–37, 2003–7, and 2009–present, respectively).

I think that the eventuality of a sudden irrevocable burst is not essential to the general term "speculative bubble" as the phrase is appropriately used. The metaphor may be misleading: it suggests more drama than there in fact is, imparting a sense of uniqueness to current events, which might help explain the popularity of the term with news reporters vying for the attention of readers. Just as reporters like to stir people up by reporting that an index has hit another record high (disregarding the fact that record highs occur quite often, especially since reporters hardly ever correct for inflation), so too they like to suggest the possibility of a collapse in the offing that will be remembered many years later.

I sometimes wish we had a different metaphor. One might consider substituting the term "wind trade" (Dutch *Windhandel*), a term that was used during the tulip mania, the famous boom and bust in tulip prices in the early 1600s. The reference to trading in mere air seems more apt than the evocation of a fragile bubble.

Curiously, in his Nobel Lecture in Medicine during the 2013 Nobel Week in Stockholm, James E. Rothman (2013) invoked soap bubbles too, for their analogy to the cell vesicles that were the focus of his Nobel Prize research. He showed a movie of two soap bubbles being pressed together, and, surprisingly to most of us, they did not burst but merged into a single larger bubble. That's analogous to what cell vesicles can do, he said. It led me to wonder whether we could say that the stock market bubble and the housing bubble of the early 2000s somehow merged into a larger bubble that burst around 2008, touching off widespread financial crisis. Imaginative thinking is fun, and maybe even inspirational, but we cannot let the bubble metaphor, or any simple analogy, guide our models beyond the very beginnings, for any metaphor will break down if we carry it to its absurd conclusions.

Efficient Markets Theory

From the very beginning, in his 1964 PhD dissertation, written under the supervision of Merton Miller and Harry Roberts, Eugene Fama found that stock prices are not very forecastable. He found then that the average correlation coefficient between successive days' log price changes over the thirty Dow Jones Industrial Average stocks between 1957 and 1962 was only 0.03, which he described as "probably unimportant for both the statistician and the investor."[3] The same year saw the appearance of Paul Cootner's *The Random Character of Stock Market Prices*, which reached similar conclusions about market efficiency.

The "efficient markets theory," widely attributed to Fama (1970) and the academic work that he stimulated, maintains that prices have a rational basis in terms of fundamentals like the optimal forecast of earnings, or assessments of the standard deviation of risk factors facing corporations. As the theory went, because they are rationally determined, they are changed from day to day primarily by genuine news, which is by its very nature essentially unforecastable. Fama's work propelled an efficient markets revolution in finance. I was part of the movement then, less than a decade later, with my PhD dissertation (1972) about the efficiency of the long-term bond market.

Alternative Views and Forecastability of Returns

These conclusions came against a backdrop of public interest at the time in speculative bubbles encouraged by the strong bull market in the United

[3] Fama (1964: table 10 and p. 70).

States: real stock prices more than quadrupled in the sixteen years from 1948 to 1964. John Kenneth Galbraith's best-selling 1954 book *The Great Crash: 1929* vividly described the follies of the boom of the 1920s and subsequent collapse, concluding that "the chances for a recurrence of a speculative orgy are rather good."[4]

His book was followed up by another popular work, Charles Poor Kindleberger's *Manias, Panics and Crashes* (1978), which used a similar method, providing an account of human events laced with descriptions of human foolishness. Neither author, writing many years before the behavioral finance revolution, made much use of academic research in psychology or sociology, and so their work came across to some as insubstantial. While both Galbraith and Kindleberger were respected academics, and the stories in their books were often compelling, many felt that their books did not have the scientific credibility of the careful data analysis that was widely taken to support market efficiency—though they were indeed provocative.

Ultimately, reconciling the apparently conflicting views is a matter of constructing the right statistical tests. It turns out that the apparently impressive evidence for market efficiency was not unimpeachable.

Expected Present Value Models and Excess Volatility

The simplest version of the efficient markets model—which maintains that stock price movements can be interpreted entirely as reflecting information about future payouts of dividends, and hence that there is never a good or a bad time to enter the market—has, ever since the efficient markets revolution began, maintained a powerful hold on scholarly imaginations as a worthy approximation to more complex models. This form sets price equal to the expectation, conditional on publicly available information at the time of the present value, of future dividends, discounted at a constant rate through time:

$$P_t = E_t \sum_{k=0}^{\infty} \frac{D_{t+k}}{(1+r)^{k+1}}. \tag{1}$$

One way to test this efficient markets model is to regress the return between t and $t+1$, $t = 1, \ldots, n$ onto information variables known at time t, I_t, $t = 1, \ldots, n$. Often, these tests can be described approximately as tests of the "random walk hypothesis," that price changes are purely random and unforecastable. One accepts the efficient markets model if the coefficients of the information variables used to forecast future returns or price changes are not significantly different from zero. Moreover, even if the model is rejected,

[4]Galbraith (1954: 194).

if the predicted proportion of variance in returns is small, one concludes that the model is a good approximation to reality.

These tests, and various analogues of them, are the kinds of tests of market efficiency that abounded in the literature. But the power of such tests of perpetual unforecastability of returns against an alternative that represents the world as driven entirely by temporary fads and fashions—with no fundamental reason for any change in prices—can be very low, since plausible alternatives of this kind also imply that only a tiny fraction of month-to-month returns is forecastable (Shiller 1984, 1989; Summers 1986).

Many tests of market efficiency use daily observations of prices, and because the observations come so frequently, there may be thousands of observations, even if the span of the data is only a few decades. There is a tendency for many people to think that hundreds of observations must be a lot of data, but it is not necessarily a lot of data from the standpoint of distinguishing an efficient markets model from a relevant alternative.

We might, for example, be trying to determine whether some price time series data is a random walk as against the alternative of a continuous-time first-order autoregressive process.[5] In the former, whether prices are too high or too low has no ability to predict future changes. In the latter, when prices are too high relative to the mean, they should tend eventually to fall (a sort of bursting of the bubble, though not a sudden catastrophic one). But tests may have very little power to distinguish the two models, if the autoregressive parameter is close enough to one, even with a large number of observations, even with day-to-day or minute-to-minute observations. With a fixed span of data, increasing the frequency of observation, even to the limit of continuous observation, does not bring power to one (Shiller and Perron 1985, Phillips and Perron 1988).

The Scientific Background for the 2013 Nobel Prize in Economics (Economic Sciences Prize Committee of the Royal Swedish Academy of Sciences 2013) emphasized the results of this year's laureates as confirming that there is better forecastability (in terms of R-squared) of speculative asset returns for longer time horizons. This accords with long-standing advice that investors should be patient, that they cannot expect to see solid returns over short time intervals. But this is just the opposite of what one would expect in weather forecasting, where experts can forecast tomorrow's temperature fairly well but certainly cannot forecast accurately a year into the future.

It is easy to see why short-term forecastability of price changes in investable assets should in some sense be unlikely: if investment returns were substantially forecastable from day to day, it would be too easy to get rich in

---

[5] In continuous time, we are speaking of distinguishing a Wiener process from an Ornstein-Uhlenbeck process.

a year or so by trading on these forecasts, and we know it cannot be easy to make a lot of money trading. This notion was formalized in a continuous-time framework by Sims (1984), who defined "instantaneous unpredictability" of a speculative asset price by the requirement that the R-squared of the prediction from time t to time $t + s$ goes to zero as s goes to zero. He showed under certain regularity conditions that if prices are not instantaneously unpredictable, then simple rapid-trading schemes could achieve unbounded profits, which of course cannot match reality.

Taking into account these primal reasons to doubt that returns are forecastable over short horizons, we cannot find the low R-squared in many tests of short-run market efficiency either surprising or interesting. The tests tell us only the obvious, and do not tell us about the rationality of markets beyond the fact that people are not missing easy opportunities to get rich very fast.

I proposed that an alternative class of tests, based on the estimated volatility of returns—tests for "excess volatility"—would have more power against the important alternatives to efficient markets theory: first for the bond market, rejecting the expectations model of the term structure of interest rates with U.S. and UK data (Shiller 1979), and then rejecting the simplest efficient markets model for the U.S. stock market (Shiller 1981a).[6] Independent work by Kenneth Singleton (1980) used a variance bounds test to reject the expectations model of the term structure of interest rates with U.S. data, and Stephen LeRoy and Richard Porter (1981) rejected the simple efficient markets theory for the U.S. stock market. Variance bounds tests were also used to test consumption-discount-based efficient markets models (Shiller 1982, Hansen and Jagannathan 1991). Efficient markets models also imply bounds on the covariance between asset prices (Beltratti and Shiller 1993).

These tests may be more powerful than regression tests of the basic efficient markets notions against important alternatives. It is true that under the conventional assumptions of the regression model, the usual t-test for the coefficient of a forecasting variable in a regression with excess return as the dependent variable has well-known optimality properties.[7] But testing market efficiency by regressing excess returns on information variables makes no use of the terminal condition that requires that all movements in prices need to be justified by information about subsequent movements in fundamentals. I showed (1981b) that if we broaden the maintained hypothesis for this condition, then

---

[6] The volatility tests were partly inspired by the work Jeremy Siegel and I did (Shiller and Siegel 1977) involving calculation of ex post rational price series.

[7] Regression tests have pitfalls as well, as when ratios involving price are used in regressions explaining future change in price, creating an endogenous variables problem; see Campbell and Shiller (1989).

a regression test is not optimal. In fact, under certain extreme assumptions about data alignment, a simple variance ratio test, instead of a regression test, may be uniformly most powerful.[8]

Another kind of test of market efficiency is the event study, which is an analysis of the effects of a specified event (such as a stock split) on the price of an asset in the days before and after the event, taking many different examples of a kind of event and showing the average price performance. It is analogous to a test of the significance of coefficients in a regression of a panel of time series of daily returns of many stocks on a dummy variable representing the day of a certain kind of event, and on dummies representing the days after the event became public. The test of market efficiency is a test for significance of the coefficients of the dummies corresponding to days after the event. The first event study in the academic literature has been taken to be Dolley (1933), but, as the Scientific Background for the 2013 Nobel Prize in Economics notes, it was not until the impressive 1969 paper by Eugene Fama, Lawrence Fisher, Michael Jensen, and Richard Roll that it was demonstrated that, conditioning on an event, one tends to see a lack of any consistent and important further price response after the event is public knowledge. Dolley, in his 1933 article, was immersed in all the details of stock splits and of course did not mention efficient markets theory. Fama, Fisher, Jensen, and Roll instead showed evidence for this newly developed and expanded theory, evidence that could be seen visually impressively in a plot of stock returns before and after the event.

But, again, the efficient markets tests, which are essentially the same as regression tests, do not have the power to tell us whether there are also bubbles affecting prices, or even whether the major component of stock price movements comes from bubbles.

The variance bounds test rejections of market efficiency could not be dismissed as correct but unimportant, as were the inefficiencies that the efficient markets literature had discovered, for they suggested that most of the variability of the aggregate stock market was not explainable as related to information about future fundamentals.

Critics of the variance bounds tests became abundant, and I endeavored at first to answer some of them, responding to Marsh and Merton (1986) and Kleidon (1986) (Shiller 1986, 1988). But the volume of the literature expanded beyond my abilities to respond, and significantly changed its direction as well. Sometimes the disagreements turned abstract and seemed to raise deep issues

---

[8]John Cochrane, in his review of my volatility tests (1991, 1992), stressed a sense in which there is an equivalence of volatility tests and regression tests. But this is about the equivalence of null hypotheses, not equivalence of test power. Cochrane later followed this up with a paper (2007) recognizing the importance of the terminal condition; see also Lewellen (2004) and Campbell and Yogo (2006).

about epistemology or the philosophy of logic.[9] I must leave the outcome of this debate to a broader professional consensus.

I collected my papers on the subject and summarized the literatures in my book *Market Volatility* (1989), at which point I largely abandoned my econometric work on excess volatility. Others continued this line of work, and much more has happened since.

Visual Portrayals of Excess Volatility and of the Stock Market as Forecaster

Just as event studies visually convinced many readers of some merits of efficient markets theory by presenting event study plots, showing stock prices before and after an event, so too other simple plots seem to have been convincing, in a different way, that stock markets are really not so efficient.

Figure A.1 is an updated version of one that I showed in my 1981a paper, a third of a century ago, of the real level of the stock market since 1871, as well as the behavior through time of the actual present value of future real dividends discounted at a constant rate. The real stock price series is one published by Standard & Poor's, called the S&P Composite (after 1957 the S&P 500), deflated by the U.S. Consumer Price Index.

The earlier version of this plot turned out to be the centerpiece of that paper, judging from the attention that it drew. Sometimes a simple plot seems to be more disturbing than a formal analysis. Looking at the data is like seeing a photojournalist's account of a historical event rather than reading a chronology: it is more immediate and invites intuitive comparisons.

To produce this figure, the present value of dividends for each date 1871–2013 was computed from the actual subsequent real dividends using a constant real discount rate $r = 7.6\%$ per year, equal to the historical average real return on the market since 1871. For this figure, I was able to make use of the actual dividends, as published by Standard & Poor's since 1926, and extended back to 1871 by Alfred Cowles (1939) as I described in my book (1989). We did not know dividends after 1979 when I published the original version of this figure, and at this writing we do not know dividends after 2013.

For this lecture, in 2013, as I did in 1981, I made some simple assumptions about the as-yet-unseen future dividends, beyond 2013. This time I employed a conventional dividend discount model, the Gordon Model, using the most recent 2013 S&P 500 real dividend as a base for forecasts of dividends after 2013, showing two alternative assumptions about dividends after 2013. In one, I assumed that real dividends will grow forever from the last observed dividend, in 2013, at the same average growth rate as over the most recent

---

[9]Some examples include Flavin (1983), Buiter (1987), and Cochrane (1991).

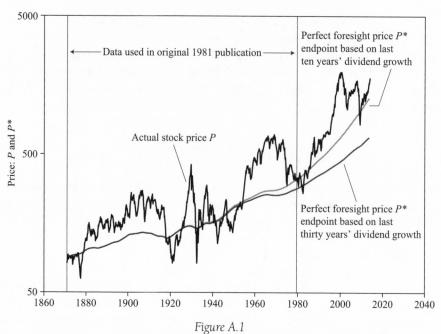

Figure A.1

**Real S&P Composite Stock Price Index with Two Present Values
with Constant Discount Rate of Subsequent Real Dividends
Accruing to the Index, 1871–2013**

The two present values differ in their assumption about dividend growth
after 2013.

ten years, 5.1% per year, which gives a 2013 value of 1,292 for P^*. In another,
the calculations are the same, but the growth rate of dividends after 2013 is
taken as the geometric average growth rate over the last thirty years, 2.5% a
year. This gives a 2013 value of 669 for P^*. Both of these may be contrasted
with real market values of the S&P 500 index over the year 2013 ranging from
1,494 to 1,802.[10]

Should we take the latest ten years' real dividend growth as a guide to
the future, rather than the last thirty years or some other interval? The ten-
year data are more recent, but ten years is a short time historically speaking,

[10] Jeremy Siegel (2005, 2008) has made the point that since the dividend payout rate for earnings
has been trending down since World War II, dividend growth should be higher in the future
than it was. If companies reinvest earnings rather than pay them out, they should have more
dividends to pay in the future. The validity of this theory is not without doubters. Arnott
and Asness (2003) point out that perhaps lower dividend payouts may reflect managers'
decisions in the face of evidence they have that earnings growth will be lower.

and the years 2003 to 2013 were unusual, starting with the aftermath of the 2001 recession, and encompassing the biggest financial crisis, and government stimulus packages, since the Great Depression. Reasonable people will certainly find reasons to differ. Worse than that, there is no objective way to forecast dividends out for decades, which is why I showed both here, as a crude indication of uncertainty today about future dividends, and why it is hard to imagine that the market somehow "knows" the correct optimal forecast.

The point of showing the two different P^* series is that, clearly, there is substantial uncertainty about the present value of dividends after 2013, but there is not so much variability from year to year, as seen today, about the present value of subsequent dividends for earlier years. For earlier years, say before 1980, 2013 is so far in the future, and is discounted so heavily, that over a wide range of possible 2013 dividend values there is not much difference in P^*.

The striking fact is that by either assumption the present value of dividends (on the log scale used in the figure) looks pretty much like a steady exponential growth line, while the stock market oscillates a great deal around it. I asked this question in 1981: If, as efficient markets theory asserts, the actual price is the optimal forecast as of any date of the present value as of that date, why is the stock market so volatile?

Different people have different reactions to this figure, but a common response is that the efficient markets model $P_t = E_t(P_t^*)$ looks implausible here. Why is price jumping around so much if the value it is tracking is just such a simple trend? It is not that P_t should always look smoother through time than P_t^*, for it is consistent with the model that there can be sudden shifts in price when there is important new information about subtle changes in trend. But it would seem that important new information should emerge only rarely, given the smooth nature of dividends.

To see the problem for efficient markets here, imagine that the series labeled P_t^* is not price but air temperature, and that P_t is a meteorologist's forecast of the temperature for that day t. We might be inclined to label this weather forecaster as insane. Even though in the stock market there isn't immediate feedback to forecasters about forecast errors, still they should avoid adjusting forecasts up and down frequently, unless there is actual new information, and clearly there wasn't, not information about something that actually happened in stock market history.

One very basic thing that this figure reveals is that the model that people essentially know the future, a model that is often suggested as an approximation, is wildly wrong in all periods. Sometimes people have suggested that the low stock prices seen in the Great Depression of the 1930s were justified because people rationally saw the damage to future real dividends caused by the Depression. But, in fact, at the worst of the stock market depression, in 1932, subsequent dividends just weren't low enough for long enough to depress P^*_{1932} by much at all. Nothing has ever deflected real dividends for very long from a long-run growth trend of a couple percent a year.

In my original paper (1981a), I detrended the data—as is shown in a reproduction of that plot in the Scientific Background document, posted on the Nobel Foundation website—thinking that it is reasonable to assume that people know the trend. Under that assumption, the efficient markets model implies that the variance around trend should be less for P than for P^*, which is plainly not the case in Figure A.1. But many critics of my paper reacted negatively to the assumption that the trend is essentially known.

Generally, these criticisms held that there was always some reason to think that the path of dividends might eventually depart markedly from its historical growth path, that investors were evaluating constant new information about that possibility, and that they were rational to do so even if the dividend growth path never deviated far for long from a trend. This assumes that all the fluctuations result from genuine information about those "black swan" outlier events that might have happened during a period of more than a century but just didn't happen. Some of the criticism had to do with the possibility that the dividend series might have a unit root, and so the apparent smooth trend was just a chance outcome, one that might not be continued into the future.[11]

The uncertainty about the present value of dividends after 2013 as shown in Figure A.1 does highlight an important problem. At every point in history there must have been some such uncertainty about future dividends. There are always factors or prominent theories that creative minds can invoke that would suggest a higher or lower rate of growth of dividends in the future.

For example, can we tell an efficient markets story about why the stock market was so low in the Great Depression? The present value of actual future dividends was not particularly low in the Depression, but maybe people thought that they would be low, given the extant theories of the time. Or maybe they thought that the government would eventually nationalize the stock market without compensation. One might say that it would not be manifestly irrational, not crazy, to believe such stories. But why, then, do these stories come and go through time, causing the fluctuations in the market?

---

[11] Unit root problems pose potentially serious problems for financial econometrics; see Campbell and Shiller (1987, 1988a); Shiller and Beltratti (1992); Torous, Valkanov, and Yan (2004); Campbell and Yogo (2006); and Cochrane (2007). Campbell and I (1988c) proposed log-differencing to recast excess volatility tests in more robust terms. Fama and French (1988) and Poterba and Summers (1988) showed tests of simple efficient markets models based on ratios of variance of returns of different horizons. West (1988) showed an inequality in terms of variances of innovations in price and present values, which strengthened the evidence for excess volatility.

Variations on the Present Value Model

Of course, as we have noted, the basic notion of efficient markets does not necessarily require that discount rates be constant or that returns not be forecastable. A more general form of efficient markets would allow discount rates to depend on the time-varying one-period rate of interest:

$$P_t = E_t(P_t^{*r}) = E_t \sum_{k=0}^{\infty} \prod_{j=0}^{k} \frac{1}{(1 + r_{t+j} + \varphi)} D_{t+k}. \tag{2}$$

Or, in a model proposed by LeRoy (1973) and Lucas (1978) and developed by Grossman and Shiller (1981) and Hansen and Singleton (1983), it could depend on consumption, using the marginal rate of substitution between consumption in successive periods as a discount rate:

$$P_t = E_t(P_t^{*C}) = E_t \sum_{k=0}^{\infty} \prod_{j=0}^{k} M_{t+j} D_{t+k'} \tag{3}$$

where M_t is the marginal rate of substitution in consumption between t and $t + 1$, which is (assuming constant relative risk aversion A) $\rho(C_t/C_{t+1})^A$, and C_t is real per capita consumption at time t.

Figure A.2 shows the actual stock price in the United States and the perfect foresight stock price corresponding to each of the three measures.[12] One again, the figure reveals that there is little correspondence between any of these measures of ex post rational price and actual stock price. People did not behave, in setting stock prices, as if they knew the future of these variables and reacted rationally to this knowledge. Moreover, if we assume that they did not actually have knowledge of the future, then one is led to wonder why the actual stock prices varied through time as much as, or more than, the perfect foresight prices did.

There are continuing attempts to modify the consumption-based model to improve its fit—see Campbell and Cochrane (1999) and Lars Peter Hansen, in his Nobel Lecture (2013)—but not yet any model that could be set alongside Figure A.2 here as an inspiring vindication of efficient markets theory.

John Campbell and John Ammer (1993) did a variation decomposition (along lines developed in Campbell 1991) of unexpected excess returns using time series methods and U.S. postwar data. The decomposition is based on the log linearization of the present value relation used in Campbell and Shiller (1988b). The time-$t + 1$ innovation $E_{t+1} - E_t$ in the excess return over the risk-free rate

---

[12] The parameter φ was estimated to make the average $r_t + \varphi$ equal the average real return on the stock market 1871–2013. The parameter A was set at four and ρ at one. The one-year interest rate is pieced together from various sources as described in Shiller (1989, 2005) and real per capita consumption is from the U.S. National Income and Product Accounts.

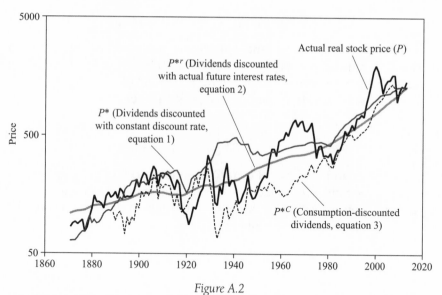

Figure A.2

**Real S&P Composite Stock Price Index along with Three Present Values
of Subsequent Real Dividends Accruing to the Index, 1871–2013**

All three present values assume real dividend growth 2003–13 will continue forever after 2013. The three present values differ from each other only in the assumed time series of discount rates.

e_{t+1} can be shown, with a terminal stationarity condition, as a tautology, to be the sum of three innovations:

$$e_{t+1} - E_t e_{t+1} = (E_{t+1} - E_t)\left\{\sum_{j=0}^{\infty} \rho^j \Delta d_{t+1+j} - \sum_{j=0}^{\infty} \rho^j r_{t+1+j} \right.$$
$$\left. - \sum_{j=1}^{\infty} \rho^j e_{t+1+j} \right\}.$$

Using this decomposition and a vector-autoregressive model in difference form, with post–World War II stock market returns, Campbell and Ammer found that excess returns innovations have a standard deviation that is two or three times greater than the standard deviation of innovations in future dividend growth. Aggregate stock market fluctuations have therefore been dominated by fluctuations in predicted future returns, not by news about future dividends paid to investors.[13]

---

[13] These results have been criticized by Goyal and Welch (2003, 2008); Chen and Zhao (2009); and Chen, Da, and Zhao (2013). They have been rebutted by Campbell, Polk, and Vuolteenaho (2010) and Engsted, Pedersen, and Tanggaard (2012).

Interpretations of Return Predictability

Sociologists offer a possible interpretation of these results, an interpretation reflecting a body of thought that goes back more than a hundred years. The market fluctuates as the sweep of history produces different mindsets at different points of time, different zeitgeists. Émile Durkheim (1893) spoke of the "collective consciousness" that represents the shared beliefs, attitudes, and moral judgments characterizing a historical period. Maurice Halbwachs (1925) spoke of the "collective memory," the set of facts that are widely remembered at any point of time but that are forgotten eventually if word of mouth and active news media do not perpetuate their memory. News media tend to slant their stories toward ideas of current interest, rather than useful facts that readers no longer find interesting.[14] Surely simple forgetting of past experiences affects popular judgments. How many people today could give any account of the financial panic of 1907, or of the housing boom of the late 1940s? One could stop anyone on the street in those times and get a ready account; now almost everyone would betray blank ignorance. When a bubble is building, the suppression of some facts and embellishment of others (as in the strategy of victorious college debaters) occurs naturally through the decay of collective memory, when media and popular talk are no longer reinforcing memories of them, and the amplification of other facts through the stories generated by market events.

It is hardly plausible that speculative prices make effective use of all information about probabilities of future dividends. It is far more plausible that the aggregate stock market price changes reflect inconstant perceptions: changes to which Keynes referred with the term "animal spirits," changes that infect the thinking even of most of the so-called smart money in the market. Keynes anticipated this in his 1921 *Treatise on Probability*, which asserted that probabilities are not precisely measurable in the sense that decision theory supposes, that there are always ambiguities. He said that because of these fundamental ambiguities, there is, in financial transactions, inevitably an "element of caprice."[15] Critical decisions are made on impulse rather than calculation. One may have done calculations of probabilities, but one usually does not fully believe one's own calculations and proceeds on gut feeling.

In an early behavioral finance paper of mine, "Stock Prices and Social Dynamics" (1984), I proposed yet another expected present value model for consideration as a model of stock prices, though it is one that we cannot plot back to 1871 as we did with the three expected present models shown and

---

[14]See Shiller (2000) and Mullainathan and Shleifer (2005).
[15]Keynes (1921: 23).

plotted above, because it depends on a time-varying factor that is not objectively quantifiable, at least for now. I have been attempting to measure a stock market factor like this with survey techniques, of individual and institutional investors, but only since 1989. There are other surveys of investor sentiment as well, but the results are hardly definitive. My surveys of individual and institutional investors starting in 1989,[16] as well as my surveys with Karl E. Case of homebuyers starting in 1988,[17] are being continued by the Yale School of Management.

Thirty years ago I called this as-yet-unmeasured factor the "demand for stocks by ordinary investors," but today let us call it animal spirits, A_t. A_t represents the demand for stocks per outstanding share at time t on the part of everyone who is not smart money, people not really paying attention, not systematic, not engaged in research, buffeted by casually encountered information. They are certainly the majority of investors, and suppose, to take this model to an extreme, that their opinions reflect nothing more than changing fashions and fads, idle talk, and overreaction to irrelevant news stories. A_t is likely to be sluggish through time (usually people don't all change their naive opinions en masse on a dime).

The core idea here was that there are also smart money investors, who are not subject to illusion but have to be wary of investing in the stock market. They must be wary not only because future dividends are not known with certainty, but also because the ordinary investors are somewhat unpredictable, and their erratic behavior could cause price changes that might produce losses in the market for the smart money if they invest too much in it. For these smart money investors, information is constantly coming in about the likely future values of A_t, and, as with all genuinely new information, this new information is uncorrelated and unpredictable through time. I supposed that the demand per share for stocks by the smart money equals their rationally expected excess return on the stock market over and above an alternative riskless return r, which I took for simplicity's sake to be constant through time, the difference divided by a constant risk factor φ. The two demands, the demand of the ordinary investors plus the demand of the smart money, must add up to one for the markets to clear. Solving the resulting rational expectations model forward leaves us with our fourth present value model:[18]

[16] http://som.yale.edu/faculty-research/our-centers-initiatives/international-center-finance/data/stock-market-confidence. Greenwood and Shleifer (2013) examine the relation to stock price data of investor sentiment indices from six different survey sources, including mine.

[17] Case and Shiller (1988, 2003); Case, Shiller, and Thompson (2012).

[18] This is equation (3) in Shiller (1984), with slight changes in notation.

$$P_t = E_t(P_t^{*A}) = E_t \sum_{k=0}^{\infty} \frac{1}{(1+r+\varphi)^{k+1}} (D_{t+k} + \varphi A_{t+k}). \qquad (4)$$

If $\varphi = 0$, smart money dominates; this collapses to equation (1) above. As φ goes to infinity, smart money drops out, it collapses to $P_t = A_t$, and ordinary investors completely determine the price. It is the intermediate case that is interesting. In this intermediate case, price may have low predictability from day to day or month to month, consistent with efficient markets theory, even if animal spirits dominate the broad movements in P_t. Long slow swings in A_t may produce long slow swings in stock prices (perhaps the so-called multiyear "bull" and "bear" markets) even though day-to-day movements in stock prices are nearly uncorrelated through time. The price is responding to news about animal spirits, not just news about future dividends. Event study tests, described above, testing market reaction over time to news about, and subsequently the reality of, such events as stock splits, may come out as beautifully supporting efficient markets, for much of the effect of the event on both dividends and animal spirits will be incorporated into price as soon as the event becomes news to the smart money, not when the event actually happens.

There is another important argument widely used for efficient markets, the argument that a model like (4) with an intermediate φ cannot represent a stable equilibrium because the smart money would get richer and richer and eventually take over the market, and φ would go to zero. In fact this will not generally happen, for there is a natural recycling of investor abilities: the smart money people usually do not start out with a lot of money, and it takes them many years to acquire enough wealth to influence the market; meanwhile they get old and retire, or they rationally lose interest in doing the work to pursue their advantage after they have acquired sufficient wealth to live comfortably on. The market will be efficient enough that advantages to beating the market are sufficiently small, uncertain, and slow to repay one's efforts that most smart people will devote their time to more personally meaningful things, like managing a company, getting a PhD in finance, or some other more enjoyable activity, leaving the market substantially to ordinary investors. Genuinely smart money investors cannot in their normal life cycle amass enough success experience to prove to ordinary investors that they can manage their money effectively: it takes too many years and there is too much fundamental uncertainty for them to be able to do that assuredly, and by the time they prove themselves, they may have lost the will or ability to continue (Shiller 1984, Shleifer and Vishny 1997).

Individual Stocks

These conclusions about the aggregate stock market, however, do not carry over fully to individual stocks. Paul Samuelson has asserted that the market is micro efficient but macro inefficient. That is, individual stock price variations are dominated by actual new information about subsequent dividends, but aggregate stock market variations are dominated by bubbles.[19]

Tuomo Vuolteenaho (2002), using methodology analogous to that of Campbell and Ammer, concluded that for individual stocks the variance of expected return news is approximately one-half of the variance of cash-flow news. For market-adjusted individual stock log returns (log return minus cross-sectional average log return) the variance of the expected return news is only one-fifth of the variance of cash-flow news. Thus bubbles and their bursts cannot have more than a minority impact on the returns of individual stocks, and most of the variation in their returns comes from news about the future payouts the firms will make.

In a 2005 paper I wrote with Jeeman Jung, which looked at long-span data sets of stocks that had survived without significant capital changes for over half a century, we reached similar conclusions. To give a visual impression of how well the efficient markets theory works for individual firms, we felt that we could display how successfully dividend growth could be predicted from the dividend-price ratio. Simple efficient markets theory suggests that firms with relatively low dividend price ratios should eventually, in future years, show higher dividend increases as a fraction of today's price. To make such a visual diagram in such simple terms, we sought out long-lived firms (though such a procedure risks a selection bias).

We found all firms on the Center for Research in Security Prices (CRSP) tape that remained alive and for which there was uninterrupted data from 1926 to 1976. There were only forty-nine such firms, giving us 2,499 firm-year observations 1926–76. Each point on the scatter in Figure A.3 shows $\sum_{k=0}^{24} \frac{\Delta D_{t+k}/P_t}{(1+r)^k}$, the present value of future changes in dividends for the next twenty-five years (measured in dollars, and discounted by the historical average stock market return) divided by current dollar price, against $\frac{D_{t-1}}{P_t}$, the current dividend divided by current price. Efficient markets with a constant discount rate, equation (1), implies, if there is not a problem with our truncation of the present value at twenty-five years, that a regression line through these points should have a slope of minus one and a constant term equal to the constant discount rate. In other words, if markets are efficient,

---

[19]Samuelson went on to say, "Modern markets show considerable *micro* efficiency for the reason that the minority who spot aberrations from micro efficiency can make money from those occurrences and, in doing so, tend to wipe out any persistent inefficiencies. In no contradiction to the previous sentence, I had hypothesized considerable *macro* inefficiency, in the sense of long waves in the time series of aggregate indexes of security prices below and above various definitions of fundamental values" (from a private letter from Paul Samuelson to John Campbell and Robert Shiller).

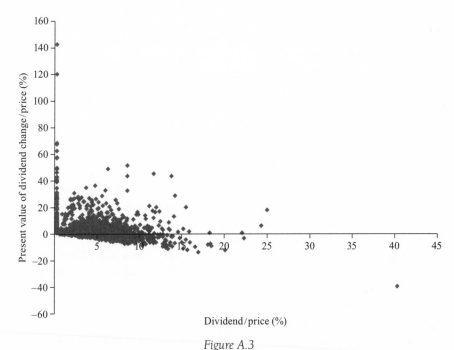

Figure A.3

Present Values of Future Changes in Dividends Plotted against the Dividend Price Ratio for Forty-Nine U.S. Individual Stocks, 1926–76
Source: Jung and Shiller (2005).

then a high dividend price yield for a particular stock today occurs only if people have a real reason to expect dividends to decline, and so demand to be compensated today for that future loss if they are to hold the stock today. Similarly, low dividend yield stocks must be those for which there is genuine evidence that dividends will rise in the future, eventually compensating today's investors for the low dividend return they are receiving.

The estimated slope of a line fitted through this scatter is −0.5, far from the ideal −1.0 but negative as expected. The dividend-price ratio predicts subsequent dividend changes in the right direction for these firms. Zero-dividend firms (which one can see strung out along the vertical axis) tended to have appropriately high subsequent dividend growth relative to price. The rightmost observation, which corresponds to the firm Schlumberger in 1931—a firm that had tried to maintain its dividend despite falling fortunes in the Great Depression—had a dividend payment that was 40% of its current price. People in the market then apparently figured out that the firm could not continue to pay such a dividend, that there would not be another significant dividend for a very long time, and reflected that knowledge in the approximately 40% dividend-price ratio. They were right to do this, as we see after the fact. In individual firms there is sometimes a lot of action in the ratios, and the action in fact often reflects real knowledge about future cash flows. That is an example of the kind of idiosyncratic knowledge about individual firms that makes the efficient markets model a useful approximation of reality for individual firms.[20]

Real Estate Prices

The market for real estate is larger in valuation than that of the entire stock market. According to the Financial Accounts of the United States, in 2013 the value of real estate owned by households and nonprofit organizations was $21.6 trillion, while their holdings of corporate equity shares, whether directly or indirectly, had a market value of only $20.3 trillion.[21]

And yet, when I first collaborated with Karl Case in joint work on real estate prices, in the 1980s, we found that hardly any scholarly research had been done on the efficiency of real estate markets. The state of knowledge about these markets was abysmal. Under the influence of a widely held presumption at that time that all markets must be efficient, many economists, at least in their popular pronouncements, seemed then to assume that real estate markets must be efficient too. This presumption seemed to us quite probably wrong, based on anecdotal evidence suggesting that real estate prices are not at all well approximated by a random walk, as is the case for stocks, but often tend to go in the same direction, whether up or down, again and again for years and years.

Case and I decided to try to test the efficiency of this market for single-family homes, but quickly discovered the importance of a stumbling block that had inhibited research: individual homes sell extremely infrequently, with the interval between sales for individual homes measured not in minutes, as with stocks, but in years or decades. One cannot do any of the most popular tests of efficiency with such data. No runs tests or event studies would ever be possible with individual homes, and so tests of market efficiency would have to be based on indices.

There were some home price indices of sorts available then, but they had serious problems. There was a median sales price of existing homes, published by the National Association of Realtors, but it often appeared to jump around erratically. It was just the median price of whatever homes were selling at the

---

[20] Ang and Bekaert (2007) conclude that the dividend yield's ability to predict dividends is not robust over sample periods or countries, but do not include individual stock data in their study.

[21] U.S. Federal Reserve Board, Z.1, Financial Accounts of the United States, table B.100 (Balance Sheet of Households and Nonprofit Organizations) and table B.100.e (Balance Sheet of Households and Nonprofit Organizations with Equity Detail), December 9, 2013.

moment, and it was not controlled for any change in the composition of sales. Moreover, it appeared that different kinds of homes sold in different months. It had a very strong seasonal component, which we suspected arose because people who sold in the summer, in phase with the academic year and the job market, typically had bigger or higher-quality homes, which had higher prices.

There was also at that time a "Price of New Homes Sold," also called "Constant Quality Index," produced by the U.S. Census Bureau, that was a more sophisticated hedonic index, holding constant such things as square feet of floor space and number of bedrooms, but again it was obviously not trustworthy for testing market efficiency through time, since it was based on different homes every quarter, whatever and wherever homes had just been built that quarter.

So Case and I constructed our own "repeat sales" home price index based on an inspiration of his (Case 1986) and then on a method we devised that inferred price changes only from the change in prices of individual existing homes (Case and Shiller 1987, 1989, 1990). We showed how a quarterly index could be computed even if homes sell much less frequently than quarterly. We discovered that Case's inspiration was largely anticipated by Bailey, Muth, and Nourse (1963), but we had a number of improvements, taking better account of heteroscedasticity. Later, I made the index arithmetic and value weighted, as are the most prominent stock price indices (Shiller 1991). With my former student Allan Weiss we founded Case Shiller Weiss, Inc., in 1991, and we were the first to produce repeat sales indices in real time for regular publication, and we applied these indices to produce automated valuation models for single-family homes (Shiller and Weiss 1999a). Our indices are now produced by CoreLogic, Inc., and the major indices are managed by Standard & Poor's Corporation.

A plot of our quarterly national index corrected for CPI inflation is shown in Figure A.4, along with the Census Constant Quality Index, also converted to real terms.

Simply producing these data and looking at a plot, as shown in Figure A.4, yields some surprises. First of all, the home price data are generally *extremely* smooth through time, except for a small amount of seasonality. Home prices do indeed go through years of price increases and then years of price decreases. So the random walk model of home price behavior is just not even close to being true for home prices (Case and Shiller 1988). Home prices might seem to be described as in accordance with model (4) above, with the parameter φ extremely large, so that the smart money, who might go in and out of the market quickly in response to news, is hardly a factor.

Second, while it was not apparent when we first computed these indices, these data make clear from today's vantage point that there was a huge boom in home prices after 2000 that was not very visible from the Census Constant

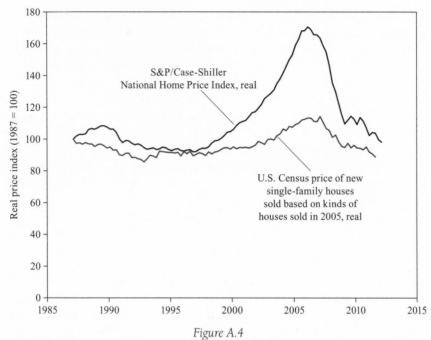

Figure A.4

**Two Indices of U.S. Home Prices Divided by the Consumer Price Index
(CPI-U), 1987–2013**

Both indices are scaled to 1987 = 100.

Quality Index. That boom was unprecedented in scope and magnitude in over one hundred years of U.S. history (Shiller 2005). Why is the boom and bust in home prices after 2000 so much more prominent in our repeat sales index? New homes are built where it is possible and profitable to build them, typically outside congested urban areas where price swings may be most pronounced, and so their level through time may be more nearly determined by simple construction costs. Thus our data collection revealed not only market inefficiencies, but much bigger price swings as well.

The inefficiency that we documented in single-family home prices must be related to market conditions, and so efficiency must be improvable with changes in market institutions. The inefficiency of the market for single-family homes relative to that of the stock market must be partly traced to the relatively much higher cost of trading in that market. It is much more costly for professional traders to trade in and out of the market for single-family homes to profit from predictable price movements. It is difficult to do short sales of overpriced individual homes. Buying and selling individual homes may not work well for professionals for additional reasons: high carrying costs; low rental income;

moral hazard of the renters, who have relatively little incentive to care for the property; and difficulty keeping up with all the local factors that might change the demand for individual houses, so that remote institutional investors would risk being picked off as ignorant losers. Some institutional investors are in the news recently, thinking they can survive and make money in this market. We will see whether they succeed.

We thought that the market efficiency could be improved if an index of home prices could be made tradable (Case, Shiller, and Weiss 1993). Working with Standard & Poor's, and with the people in our company MacroMarkets LLC, we helped the Chicago Mercantile Exchange with plans to set up futures markets based on our indices for ten U.S. cities. These markets were launched in 2006 and are still trading today, albeit with nothing close to the volume of trade that we hoped to see in these markets.[22] We hoped that the creation of these new markets would change the nature of prices in real estate markets, with price discovery that made the price of homes behave more like the random walk that efficient markets theory suggests.

Real estate markets remain wildly inefficient all over the world. We can only look forward to the day when liquid markets support more trade that might permit something rather closer to the efficient markets that theorists have expected.

If we are to achieve such improvements in efficiency, in real estate markets, in stock markets, or in any speculative markets, it is most helpful to understand the causes of market inefficiency, and that requires serious study from the broad perspective afforded by an array of other sciences outside economics.

Behavioral Finance and Behavioral Economics

The behavioral economics revolution, which brings psychology and other social sciences into economics, saw its first beginnings in the 1980s but did not attract public attention until the 1990s. Richard Thaler and I started our behavioral economics workshops at the National Bureau of Economic Research in 1991, and from that beginning behavioral finance played the dominant role.[23] There are a number of surveys of the behavioral finance literature, notably Shleifer (2000), Barberis and Thaler (2003), Shiller (2003), Shefrin (2008), and Baker and Wurgler (2011).

---

[22]See Fabozzi, Shiller, and Tunaru (2009). The market maker John Dolan has a website with up-to-date information about this market, http://homepricefutures.com. Our firm MacroMarkets LLC led by Allan Weiss and Sam Masucci also created paired long and short securities, MacroShares, with ticker symbols UMM (for up major metro) and DMM (for down major metro) based on the S&P/Case-Shiller Ten-City Index that traded on the New York Stock Exchange from August to December 2010.

[23]See http://www.econ.yale.edu/~shiller/behfin/index.htm.

The behavioral finance revolution seemed to take its beginnings from the evidence of market inefficiency that was by then starting to look significant. Once we acknowledge that the efficient markets theory has no special claim to priority for price determination, we can look more sympathetically to other factors to understand market fluctuations. The anomalies literature points indeed to some oddball factors as playing a role. Benos and Jochec (2013) showed that patriotism affects stock prices, in that U.S. stocks with the words "America(n)" or "USA" in their names earn an abnormal return of 6% a year during wartime. Saunders (1993) found that the weather in New York affects stock prices. If such irrelevant things as these affect stock prices, it should be no surprise if more plausible but half-baked theories (about the central bank, fiscal policy, energy prices, the future of capitalism, and on and on) would also affect market prices.

Most stock market investors do not pay much attention to fundamental indicators of value. We might argue that their inattention is in some sense rational, since there is a cost to collecting information. Christopher Sims (2003) has devised a model of rational inattention. But it is hard to believe that their inattention is systematic and thoughtful.

Early History of Behavioral Finance

Behavioral finance until the 1980s was mostly relegated to the community of investment analysts who did not generally attract notice in academia, and who did not generally draw on research from the social sciences. There were, however, some gems from this period. Notable among these analysts were Benjamin Graham and David Dodd, who, in the 1940 edition of their book *Security Analysis,* based their investing method on their observations of "ignorance, of human greed, of mob psychology, of trading costs, of weighting of the dice by insiders and manipulators."[24]

Keynes gave a view of speculative markets that was ahead of its time. In his 1936 book *The General Theory of Employment, Interest and Money,* Keynes described speculative markets as akin to a competition he saw offered by a local newspaper to its readers. His metaphor is widely referred to as Keynes's "beauty contest" theory of the stock market. Each reader was invited to peruse one hundred photos of pretty faces and submit a list of the six he or she thought prettiest. The winner would be the one whose list most closely corresponded to the most popular faces among all the lists of six that readers sent in. Of course, to win this contest a rational person would not choose to be guided by personal preference. Instead one should pick the six faces that one thinks others will think prettiest. Even better, one should pick the faces

[24]Graham and Dodd (2002: 276).

one thinks that others think that others think prettiest, or one should pick the faces one thinks that others think that others think that others think prettiest. The same is true with stock market investing. According to Keynes, "there are some, I believe, who practice the fourth, fifth and higher degrees,"[25] further degrees of removal from reality than were embodied in equation (4) above. That is how speculative markets function, Keynes said. Active participants are trying to buy into their predictions of the conventional valuation of assets in the near future, not the true value.

A key Keynesian idea is that the valuation of long-term assets is substantially a matter of convention, just as it is with judgments of facial beauty. Whatever price people generally have come to accept as the conventional value, and that is embedded in the collective consciousness, will stick as the true value for a long time, even if the actual returns fail for some time to live up to expectations. If an asset's returns are carefully tabulated and disappoint for long enough, people will eventually learn to change their views, but it may take the better part of a lifetime. And many assets, such as owner-occupied homes, do not have unambiguously measured returns, and a mistaken "conventional valuation" based on a faulty popular theory can persist indefinitely. The presumed investment advantages of, say, living in an expensive, land-intensive single-family home near a big city, rather than renting a cheaper and more convenient apartment in an urban high-rise, may just not exist, and most people will never figure that out.

Conventional valuation can be a very subtle phenomenon at any point of time, reflecting popular theories of the time that are perceived by many, who have never studied the theories, to reflect professional wisdom. In a beauty contest, people have even less incentive to consider the validity of this wisdom, since they view it as substantially entrenched in others' thinking. I am reminded, for example, of Modigliani and Cohn's (1979) study showing that inflation-induced biases in conventional accounting practices caused a massive understatement of earnings, a study that allowed them to call roughly, within a few years, the historic bottom of the stock market in 1982. The absence of immediate reaction to their study was just the kind of thing one might expect to see in a beauty contest world, since no one expected anyone else to react much to their paper.

The Blossoming of Behavioral Finance after 1980

The idea that speculative prices are somehow uniquely authoritative, as the best possible judgment of true value, still has its popular appeal even today. But it has lost its unique claim on the attention of economic theorists. Theoretical models of speculative markets that are analogous to Keynes's

---

[25] Keynes (1936: chap. 12, p. 156, Harbinger 1965 edition).

beauty contest theory, and that stress the expectation of reselling to other people who may have optimistic beliefs, have been offered by Harrison and Kreps (1978), Morris (1996), Scheinkman and Xiong (2003), Wu and Guo (2004), Allen, Morris, and Shin (2006), Hong, Scheinkman, and Xiong (2006), Hong and Sraer (2011), Kubler and Schmedders (2012), and Barberis et al. (2013). There are also models that represent bubbles as related to leverage cycles tied in with heterogeneous beliefs: Fostel and Geanakoplos (2008), Geanakoplos (2009), Cao (2010), and He and Xiong (2012). Noise trader models (Kyle 1985, De Long et al. 1990, Campbell and Kyle 1993) have begun to replace models with all rational agents.

Moreover, there are models of financial markets that replace the assumption of rational expected-utility-maximizing agents with alternative models of human behavior, such as prospect theory (Kahneman and Tversky 1979, 2000). Prospect theory, which is a theory of human choice in the face of risk that is based on experimental evidence in the psychology laboratory, is not a theory of rationality in the traditional sense, for it recognizes violations of the basic axioms of rational behavior (Savage 1954). The human behavior that prospect theory describes is vulnerable to the arbitrariness of psychological framing; insignificant changes in context or suggestion can produce profound differences in human behavior.

Barberis, Huang, and Santos (2001) showed that prospect theory with investors who derive direct utility from fluctuations in the value of their wealth can help explain the excess volatility of stock market returns. A "house money effect" can help make bubbles grow even bigger, in analogy to gamblers at casinos, who, after they have won some money, become very risk tolerant with that money because they frame it as somebody else's money that they can afford to lose (Thaler and Johnson 1990). Investors' "narrow framing" (Barberis, Huang, and Thaler 2006) and the disposition to sell winners and hold losers (Shefrin and Statman 1985) can explain other evidence against efficient markets.

The field of psychology offers many other principles of human behavior that have been shown to be relevant for evaluating the efficient markets theory. For example, there is evidence that a general human tendency toward overconfidence causes investors to trade too much (Odean 2000) and CEOs to squander internally generated funds on pet projects (Malmendier and Tate 2005). There is a tendency for investors to be overly distracted by news stories (Barber and Odean 2008) and to overreact to cash dividends (Shefrin and Statman 1984).

Financial theory has also advanced to allow us a better understanding of the effects of the ambiguity regarding probabilities, the fundamental difficulties in placing numerical values for probabilities, that Keynes spoke of (Bewley 2002, Bracha and Brown 2013).

Psychologists have documented a tendency for people to anchor their opinions in ambiguous situations on arbitrary signals that are psychologically salient even if they are obviously irrelevant (Tversky and Kahneman 1974).

Neuroscience has begun to understand how the human brain handles ambiguity. Hsu et al. (2005) and Huettel et al. (2006) use functional magnetic resonance imaging to study brain reactions to situations with clear versus ambiguous probabilities. Huettel et al. concluded that "decision making under ambiguity does not represent a special, more complex case of risky decision making; instead, these two forms of uncertainty are supported by distinct mechanisms."[26] The rapid progress we are now seeing in neuroscience will likely yield new insights into the ambiguity, animal spirits, and caprice that Keynes and others since him have stressed.

Implications for Financial Innovation

The financial institutions that we have today are the product of centuries of experience with the volatility of speculative asset prices, with the important information discovery that these market prices can reveal, as well as the potential for erratic behavior in these markets.[27] The reliability of these markets in revealing genuine information about fundamentals is not terrific, but it is certainly not negligible either, and the reliability might be improved through time with better financial institutions. Efficient markets should be considered a goal, not an established fact. Our present financial institutions are the results of experimentation that has helped people design around this experience; the institutions we will have in the future depend on our continuing experimentation and redesign.

Like mechanical engineering, financial engineering should pay attention to human factors, to make devices that serve people well, with full consideration of human talents and foibles. As this experience accumulates, with each successive financial crisis, and each improvement in information technology, financial innovation can make these institutions work better for humankind.

For example, the very invention, centuries ago, of stock markets, has created an atmosphere for investing that, while it regularly produces the excesses of bubbles, creates an incentive for people to launch exciting new enterprises, to keep up to date on relevant information, and to protect themselves, if they wish, from the inevitable risks of those very bubbles.

As David Moss (2002) has chronicled, a general limited liability statute covering all stock market investors was not such an obviously good idea when

---

[26] Huettel et al. (2006: 765).

[27] For the long history of financial innovation, see Goetzmann and Rouwenhorst (2005).

the world's first such law was passed in New York in 1811, but it turned out to be of fundamental importance for investors' psychology. By clearly forbidding suits against shareholders for a company's sins, it limited the downside risk of investing to psychologically manageable proportions (no more worries that any one of your investments could explode and land you in debtors' prison), and it permitted portfolio diversification to proceed without exhaustive investigation of each company's management.[28] The stock market became an exciting place, like a gambling casino, but tied to business reality rather than mere amusement, and it was a place where investors could diversify and limit their risks. It therefore was highly effective in attracting capital for enterprise.

More recently, people have been experimenting with other details of the stock markets, such as insider trader rules, risk retention rules, capital requirements, and other factors. These interact with human psychology in ways that can improve market functioning, but their effects cannot be accurately foretold on the basis of any received theory.

Much of my work has been involved in considering how both financial theory and human factors need to be considered in the design of new financial structures. I have written a number of books devoted to this: *Who's Minding the Store?* (1992), *Macro Markets* (1993), *The New Financial Order* (2003), *The Subprime Solution* (2008), and *Finance and the Good Society* (2012). Most of the ideas I have expressed in those books are calls for experimentation, not finished ideas. The ideas I discussed are mostly as yet untested, and their final forms, if and when they ever do get implemented—perhaps in the distant future, and with far better information technology—are hard to see in advance.

The ideas in these books, and associated articles, are diverse, go in many directions, and have to be judged as beginnings of ideas. They may look awkward, just as the earliest designs of aircraft did; their later incarnations may look less so.

The overarching theme of this work of mine is that we need to *democratize* and *humanize* finance in light of research on human behavior and the functioning of markets (Shiller 2011). Democratizing finance means making financial institutions work better for real people, dealing with the risks that are most important to them individually, and providing opportunities for inspiration and personal development. Humanizing finance means making financial institutions interact well with actual human behavior, taking account of how people really think and act.

Lionel Robbins, with his 1932 book *An Essay on the Nature and Significance of Economic Science*, has the honor of having invented the most common definition

---

[28]Moss (2002) documents much discussion and experimentation with liability rules in the early nineteenth century, as with "double liability" that limits shareholders' liability to twice their initial investment, or liability that ends when the shares are sold.

today of economic science, articulating the unifying core idea that defines this science. He wrote then:

> The economist studies the disposal of scarce means. He is interested in the way different degrees of scarcity of different goods give rise to different ratios of valuation of them, and he is interested in the way in which changes in conditions of scarcity, whether coming from changes in ends or changes in means—from the demand side or the supply side—affect these ratios.[29]

The importance of prices in allocating scarce resources is an idea whose beginnings go back at least to Adam Smith in the eighteenth century, with his "invisible hand," and there was a certain wisdom in Robbins's framing of the entire field of economics around this idea. Even today, this wisdom is not yet fully apparent to the untrained public. Most people do not appreciate that all of our economic activities and all of our pleasures and satisfactions, and those of subsequent generations, are ultimately guided by prices of scarce resources as formed in the markets.

There is a problem, however, with the interpretation of economics that Robbins so persuasively gave. For his definition appeared to cast the economic problem as being exclusively about scarcity of production resources, like energy and food, rather than also about scarcity of human intellectual and psychological resources. He casts the problem as humans against nature, when in fact much of the economic problem is dealing with humans against themselves.[30]

Long-term asset prices as they are observed today, prices of stocks, bonds, real estate, and commodities, and prices of derivative products such as futures, swaps, and options, and of other institutions like long-term insurance, are especially significant for economics, and especially problematic, since the scarcity that these prices represent is one that is never really objective and directly revealed today. Their levels are influenced by expectations of the distant, and generally nebulous, future. The market prices of speculative assets at any given time reflect, as is commonly asserted, both tastes and technology of that time. But they also reflect expected tastes and technology of the future, the likelihood of discovery of new wellsprings of resources or the technology to develop them. They also reflect sociology and social psychology, and anticipated future changes in these; in government policy such as taxation; and in other primary forces, such as changes in the inequality of incomes and likely social and governmental reactions to these; the potential threat of wars and other catastrophes; and the likely use of, and policy toward, the assets in such times.

---

[29] Robbins (1932: 15).
[30] See, for example, Mullainathan and Shafir (2013).

Fischer Black, in his 1984 presidential address before the American Finance Association, offered a new definition of market efficiency. He redefined an "efficient market" as "one in which price is within a factor of 2 of value, i.e., the price is more than half of value and less than twice value. . . . By this definition, I think almost all markets are efficient almost all of the time."[31]

And yet, even assuming he is somehow right, the existing efficient markets theory remains the fundamental framework from which many economic policy decisions, and decisions to innovate or not, are made. No one would seriously propose the elimination of stock markets even if we all accepted Fischer Black's impression as fact. So why should we not consider other risk markets, markets that have not come into being yet, merely through accidents of history and timing of associated technological breakthroughs?

Institutions can be redesigned so that they reframe people's thinking to the longer term and to things that are better subjects for their attention, by making markets for risks that are better tied to fundamentals people should be thinking about. Institutions that change framing might sometimes qualify as institutions providing a "nudge," as Richard Thaler and Cass Sunstein (2009) have put it, suggesting the right direction for people without being coercive. These authors base their thinking on a philosophy they call "libertarian paternalism," emphasizing the government's providing incentives for appropriate behavior without coercion. Though our groundings in behavioral economics are similar, I wouldn't stress that term, perhaps because it seems to suggest a top-down structure for society, with government at the top. The development of financial capitalism seems to be, or can be, a matter of the voluntary organization of most of society, integrating the activities of people in all walks of life in fulfillment of their diverse purposes. A vision for a better financial capitalism should not be top-down at all.

Some recent examples of financial innovation, examples of new experiments, can help clarify how innovation might help in an imperfect financial world. Consider first the social policy bonds proposed by Ronnie Horesh (2000), which have recently been realized in the social impact bonds first issued with the help of the nonprofit Social Finance, Ltd., in 2010 in the United Kingdom. These redirect speculative impulses into solving social problems over a meaningful horizon that is chosen by the issuer to be neither too short nor too long to allow effective solutions.

Consider also the new crowdfunding initiatives to create websites that allow large numbers of dispersed people each to share information and each to invest a small amount of money directly into new enterprises, without the usual financial intermediaries. These have sprouted in many places around the world,

---

[31] Black (1986: 533).

with websites like kiva.org or kickstarter.com. They are poised, after the U.S. Jumpstart Our Business Startups Act of 2012, to transform venture capital. Such innovations can and certainly will cause some runaway bubbles and abuse of ignorant investors. On the other hand, if designed and regulated right, they could create a new way of arousing animal spirits and focusing informed attention on venture investments. Crowdfunding may be more effective in funding ideas that are hard to prove; whose payoff is not immediate; that have a subtle social, environmental, or inspirational purpose beyond mere profits; and that only a small percentage of the population is equipped to understand.

Consider also the new benefit corporations that are now offered in twenty U.S. states. They are amalgams of for-profit and nonprofit corporations, fundamentally changing the mental framing that investors are likely to have of their investments in them, and encouraging both investors' excitement and more idealistic thinking about these investments.[32] The participation nonprofit business form that I advocated (2012), which makes nonprofits psychologically more similar to equity-financed business, would, if it is ever implemented, increase philanthropy and make it more effective.

These are only the beginning of the financial innovations that we might expect to see in our future, helped along by our improved understanding of behavioral finance and of mathematical economics, and by steadily improving information technology. In particular, it would seem that we can derive great benefit by expanding the scope of our financial markets to allow trading of risks that really matter.

We might further democratize finance from the expansion of trading to include trading of other indices that have only recently come to be measured, but that reflect real and important risks that matter to people. I have already alluded to the futures market for single-family homes that was started at the Chicago Mercantile Exchange in 2006; if that market becomes more successful, it will eventually provide price discovery for a value of great personal importance to individuals, and might lead to a cash market for real estate that is not so woefully inefficient. The home futures market, if it became more successful, would facilitate the creation of many more risk management products, such as home equity insurance (Shiller and Weiss 1999b) or mortgages with preplanned workouts (Shiller 2012, 2014; Shiller et al. 2013).

Had there been a well-developed real estate market before the financial crisis of 2008, it would plausibly have *reduced* the severity of the financial crisis, because it would have allowed, even encouraged, people to hedge their real estate risks. The severity of that crisis was substantially due to the leveraged undiversified positions people were taking in the housing market, sending

---

[32]See http://benefitcorp.net/.

mortgages underwater for over fifteen million U.S. households, and thus reducing their spending. There is no contradiction at all in saying that bubbles occur in the housing market and yet saying that we ought to create better and more liquid markets for housing.

Even further, I along with others have argued that a market for claims on the flow of gross domestic product, or other large macroeconomic aggregates, should be developed to help countries share their risks (Shiller 1993, 2003, 2008; Athanasoulis and Shiller 2000, 2001; Kamstra and Shiller 2009); or that markets should be developed for other significant economic variables, like occupational incomes, to share their livelihood risks (Shiller 1993, Shiller and Schneider 1998, Shiller 2003).

Had the government debts of European countries taken the form of GDP shares, then most likely we would not have had the severe European sovereign debt crisis that started in 2009, for the countries would not have as big a short-run refinancing problem and would find their government obligations cushioned by declining obligations due to declining GDP. Had people sought protection for their own welfare by hedging themselves in occupational income markets, many of them would have suffered less in this crisis.

Examples of innovations that might reframe into better and longer-term thinking about fundamentals include the "perpetual futures" that I have proposed (1993),[33] or the application of the concept of index participations developed by the American Stock Exchange in 1989 to flow indices,[34] or the long-term MacroShares my colleagues and I once strove to launch based on various indices,[35] or the markets for individual future dividend dates on stock price indices that Michael Brennan (1999) argued might "focus investor attention on the fundamentals that determine the value of the index rather than simply on the future resale value of the index."[36]

The development of inflation-indexed bonds, which have gradually grown in importance over the last half century worldwide, are an important past success but as yet an incomplete one. Such markets, and other indexing

---

[33] These are defined in Shiller (1993) in terms of a daily settlement formula involving both the change in settle price and another index representing a cash flow.

[34] See Shiller (1993: 40).

[35] In 2006, our firm MacroMarkets LLC launched paired long and short twenty-year oil MacroShares on the American Stock Exchange, with ticker symbols UCR for Up-Crude and DCR for Down-Crude. The securities traded from November 2006 to June 2008, and at one point reached US$1.6 billion in total value, but were not ultimately a success.

[36] Brennan (1999: 12). Since 2008, dividend futures markets for stock price indices have appeared on a number of European and Asian exchanges, though it is not clear that these new markets have had much of the desired effect of reframing investors' thinking.

institutions, might be enhanced by further deliberate changes in psychological framing. If inflation-indexed units of account, which create an easier way in our language to refer to indexed quantities, were created and widely used, they would help people around their money illusion that inhibits intelligent design of contracts around the real outcomes that really matter. I have been advocating the proliferation of these units of account where they first began in Chile (Shiller 2002), in the United States (Shiller 2003), and in the United Kingdom (Shiller 2009).[37] Their widespread use might have helped prevent the real estate bubble that preceded the current financial woes, a bubble that was likely helped along by the widely held impression that single-family homes have historically shown high real capital gains when in fact over the last century the gains overall have been only nominal and hence illusory (Shiller 2005).

We want such innovations, if not exactly the ones I and others have been advocating to date, because their predecessor innovations, the financial institutions we already have today, have brought such prosperity, despite the occasional big disruptions caused by bubbles and financial crises. No economic system other than financial capitalism has brought the level of prosperity that we see in much of the world today, and there is every reason to believe that further expansion of this system will yield even more prosperity.

The patterns of behavior that have been observed in speculative asset prices are consistent with a view of market efficiency as a half-truth today and at the same time with a view that there are behavioral complexities in these markets that need to be met with properly engineered financial innovations and financial regulations.

Changes in our financial institutions that take the form of creative reinventions in the kinds of risks traded, that change the psychological framing of the things traded, and that change our social relations with business partners and adversaries, can make financial markets less vulnerable to excesses and crashes, and more effective in helping us achieve our ultimate goals.

Acknowledgments

I am grateful to Nicholas C. Barberis, John Y. Campbell, Peter J. Dougherty, and Bengt Holmstrom for help on interpretation of the literature and comments on drafts of this lecture.

---

[37] Chile created its Unidad de Fomento (UF) in 1967; it is still in use there today, http://valoruf .cl/. This innovation helps deal with public resistance to indexation (Shiller 1997).

References

Akerlof, George A., and Robert J. Shiller. 2009. *Animal Spirits: How Human Psychology Drives the Economy and Why This Matters for Global Capitalism.* Princeton, N.J.: Princeton University Press.

Allen, Franklin, Stephen Morris, and Hyun Song Shin. 2006. "Beauty Contests, Bubbles and Iterated Expectations in Financial Markets." *Review of Financial Studies* 19:719–52.

Ang, Andrew, and Geert Bekaert. 2007. "Stock Return Predictability: Is It There?" *Review of Financial Studies* 20:651–757.

Arnott, Robert D., and Clifford S. Asness. 2003. "Surprise! Higher Dividends = Higher Earnings Growth." *Financial Analysts Journal* 59(1):70–87.

Athanasoulis, Stefano, and Robert J. Shiller. 2000. "The Significance of the Market Portfolio." *Review of Financial Studies* 13(2):301–29.

———. 2001."World Income Components: Measuring and Exploiting Risk Sharing Opportunities." *American Economic Review* 91(4):1031–54.

Bailey, Martin J., Richard F. Muth, and Hugh O. Nourse. 1963. "A Regression Method for Real Estate Price Index Construction." *Journal of the American Statistical Association* 58:933–42.

Baker, Malcolm, and Jeffrey Wurgler. 2011. "Behavioral Corporate Finance: An Updated Survey." NBER Working Paper No. 17333.

Barber, Brad, and Terrance Odean. 2008. "All That Glitters: The Effect of Attention on the Buying Behavior of Individual and Institutional Investors." *Review of Financial Studies* 21(2):785–818.

Barberis, Nicholas, and Richard H. Thaler. 2003. "A Survey of Behavioral Finance." In *Handbook of the Economics of Finance*, edited by George M. Constantinides, Milton Harris, and René M. Stulz. Amsterdam: Elsevier.

Barberis, Nicholas, Robin Greenwood, Lawrence Jin, and Andrei Shleifer. 2013. "X-CAPM: An Extrapolative Capital Asset Pricing Model." Working paper, Yale University.

Barberis, Nicholas, Ming Huang, and Tano Santos. 2001. "Prospect Theory and Asset Prices." *Quarterly Journal of Economics* 116(1):1–53.

Barberis, Nicholas, Ming Huang, and Richard H. Thaler. 2006. "Individual Preferences, Monetary Gambles, and Stock Market Participation: A Case for Narrow Framing." *American Economic Review* 96(4):1069–90.

Beltratti, Andrea, and Robert J. Shiller. 1993. "Actual and Warranted Movements in Asset Prices." *Oxford Economic Papers* 45:387–402.

Benos, Evangelos, and Marek Jochec. 2013. "Patriotic Name Bias and Stock Returns." *Journal of Financial Markets* 16(3): 550–70.

Bewley, Truman. 2002. "Knightian Decision Theory. Part I." *Decisions in Economics and Finance* 25(2):79–110.

Black, Fischer. 1986. "Noise." *Journal of Finance* 41:529–43.

Bracha, Anat, and Donald J. Brown. 2013. "(IR)Rational Exuberance: Optimism, Ambiguity and Risk." New Haven, Conn.: Cowles Foundation Discussion Paper No. 1898.

Brennan, Michael. 1999. "Stripping the S&P 500 Index." *Financial Analysts Journal* 54(1):12–22.

Buiter, Willem. 1987. "Efficient 'Myopic' Asset Pricing in General Equilibrium: A Potential Pitfall in Excess Volatility Tests." *Economics Letters* 25(2):143–48.

Campbell, John Y. 1991. "A Variance Decomposition for Stock Returns." *Economic Journal* 101:57–179.

Campbell, John Y., and John Ammer. 1993. "What Moves the Stock and Bond Markets? A Variance Decomposition for Long-Term Asset Returns." *Journal of Finance* 48:3–37.

Campbell, John Y., and John Cochrane. 1999. "By Force of Habit: A Consumption-Based Explanation of Aggregate Stock Market Behavior." *Journal of Political Economy* 107: 205–51.

Campbell, John Y., and Albert S. Kyle. 1993. "Smart Money, Noise Trading, and Stock Market Behavior." *Review of Economic Studies* 60(1):1–34.

Campbell, John Y., Christopher Polk, and Tuomo Vuolteenaho. 2010. "Growth or Glamor? Fundamentals and Systematic Risk in Stock Returns." *Review of Financial Studies* 23:305–44.

Campbell, John Y., and Robert J. Shiller. 1987. "Cointegration and Tests of Present Value Models." *Journal of Political Economy* 95:1062–88.

———. 1988a. "The Dividend-Price Ratio and Expectations of Future Dividends and Discount Factors." *Review of Financial Studies* 1(3):195–228.

———. 1988b. "Interpreting Cointegrated Models." *Journal of Economic Dynamics and Control* 12(2–3):505–22.

———. 1988c. "Stock Prices, Earnings and Expected Dividends." *Journal of Finance* 43(3):661–76.

———. 1989. "The Dividend Ratio Model and Small Sample Bias: A Monte Carlo Study." *Economics Letters* 29:325–31.

Campbell, John Y., and Motohiro Yogo. 2006. "Efficient Tests of Stock Return Predictability." *Journal of Financial Economics* 81(1):27–60.

Cao, Dan. 2010. "Collateral Shortages, Asset Price and Investment Volatility with Heterogeneous Beliefs." Unpublished paper, Department of Economics, Georgetown University.

Case, Karl E. 1986. "The Market for Single Family Homes in Boston." *New England Economic Review*, May/June, 38–48.

Case, Karl E., and Robert J. Shiller. 1987. "Prices of Single-Family Homes since 1970: New Indexes for Four Cities." *New England Economic Review*, September/October, 46–56.

———. 1988. "The Behavior of Home Buyers in Boom and Post-Boom Markets." *New England Economic Review*, November/December, 29–46.

———. 1989. "The Efficiency of the Market for Single Family Homes." *American Economic Review* 79(1):125–37.

———. 1990. "Forecasting Prices and Excess Returns in the Housing Market." *AREUEA Journal* 18(3):253–73.

———. 2003. "Is There a Bubble in the Housing Market?" *Brookings Papers on Economic Activity* 2003(2):299–362.

Case, Karl E., Robert J. Shiller, and Anne Kinsella Thompson. 2012. "What Have They Been Thinking? Homebuyer Behavior in Hot and Cold Markets." *Brookings Papers on Economic Activity* 2:265–98.

Case, Karl E., Robert J. Shiller, and Allan N. Weiss. 1993. "Index-Based Futures and Options Trading in Real Estate," *Journal of Portfolio Management* 19:83–92.

Chen, Long, and Xinlei Zhao. 2009. "Return Decomposition." *Review of Financial Studies* 22(12):5212–49.

Chen, Long, Zhi Da, and Xinlei Zhao. 2013. "What Drives Stock Price Movements?" *Review of Financial Studies* 26(4):841–76.

Cochrane, John H. 1991. "Volatility Tests and Efficient Markets Theory: A Review Essay." *Journal of Monetary Economics* 27:463–85.

———. 1992. "Explaining the Variance of Price-Dividend Ratios." *Review of Financial Studies* 5:243–280.

———. 2007. "The Dog That Did Not Bark: A Defense of Return Predictability." *Review of Financial Studies* 21(4):1533–75.

Cootner, Paul. 1964. *The Random Character of Stock Market Prices.* Cambridge, Mass.: MIT Press.

Cowles, Alfred III, and associates. 1939. *Common Stock Indexes.* 2nd ed. Bloomington, Ind.: Principia Press.

De Long, J. Bradford, Andrei Shleifer, Lawrence Summers, and Robert Waldmann. 1990. "Noise Trader Risk in Financial Markets." *Journal of Political Economy* 98(4):703–38.

Dolley, James C. 1933. "Common Stock Split-Ups—Motives and Effects." *Harvard Business Review* 12(1):70–81.

Durkheim, Émile. 1893. *De la division du travail social.* Paris: Alcan.

Economic Sciences Prize Committee of the Royal Swedish Academy of Sciences. 2013. Scientific Background on the Sveriges Riksbank Prize in Economic Sciences in Memory of Alfred Nobel. 2013. http://www.nobelprize.org/nobel_prizes/economic -sciences/laureates/2013/advanced-economicsciences2013.pdf.

Engsted, Tom, Thomas Q. Pedersen, and Carsten Tanggaard. 2012. "Pitfalls in VAR Based Return Decompositions: A Clarification." *Journal of Banking and Finance* 36(5):1255–65.

Fabozzi, Frank, Robert J. Shiller, and Radu Tunaru. 2009. "Hedging Real Estate Risk." *Journal of Portfolio Management* 35(5):92–103.

Fama, Eugene. 1964. "The Distribution of the Daily Differences of the Logarithms of Stock Prices." PhD diss., University of Chicago. Reprinted in the *Journal of Business* as "The Behavior of Stock Market Prices," 38(1):34–105.

———. 1970. "Efficient Capital Markets: A Review." *Journal of Finance* 25(2):383–417.

Fama, Eugene F., Lawrence Fisher, Michael Jensen, and Richard Roll. 1969. "The Adjustment of Stock Prices to New Information." *International Economic Review* 10:1–21.

Fama, Eugene, and Kenneth R. French. 1988. "Permanent and Temporary Components of Stock Prices." *Journal of Political Economy* 96:(2):246–67.

Flavin, Marjorie. 1983. "Excess Volatility in the Financial Markets: A Reassessment of the Empirical Evidence." *Journal of Political Economy* 96:246–73.

Fostel, Ana, and John Geanakoplos. 2008. "Leverage Cycles in an Anxious Economy." *American Economic Review* 93: 1211–44.

Galbraith, John Kenneth. 1954. *The Great Crash: 1929*. Boston: Houghton Mifflin.

Garber, Peter M. 2000. *Famous First Bubbles: The Fundamentals of Early Manias*. Cambridge, Mass.: MIT Press.

Geanakoplos, John. 2009. "The Leverage Cycle." *NBER Macroeconomics Annual* 24:1–65.

Goetzmann, William N., Catherine Labio, K. Geert Rouwenhorst, and Timothy G. Young, eds. 2013. *The Great Mirror of Folly: Finance, Culture, and the Crash of 1720*. New Haven, Conn.: Yale University Press.

Goetzmann, William N., and K. Geert Rouwenhorst, eds. 2005. *The Origins of Value: The Financial Innovations That Created Modern Capital Markets*. Oxford: Oxford University Press.

Goyal, Amit, and Ivo Welch. 2003. "Predicting the Equity Premium with Dividend Ratios." *Management Science* 49:639–54.

———. 2008. "A Comprehensive Look at the Empirical Performance of Equity Premium Prediction." *Review of Financial Studies* 21:1455–1508.

Graham, David, and David Dodd. 2002. *Security Analysis: The Classic 1940 Edition*. New York: McGraw-Hill.

Greenwood, Robin, and Andrei Shleifer. 2013. "Expectations of Returns and Expected Returns." NBER Working Paper No. 18686.

Grossman, Sanford, and Robert J. Shiller. 1981."The Determinants of the Variability of Stock Market Prices." *American Economic Review* 71:222–27.

Halbwachs, Maurice. 1925. "Les Cadres Sociaux de la Mémoire." In *Les Travaux de L'Année Sociologique*. Paris: Alcan.

Hansen, Lars Peter. 2013. "Uncertainty Outside and Inside Economics Models." Prize Lecture for 2013 Nobel Prize in Economic Sciences. http://www.nobelprize.org/mediaplayer/index.php?id=1994.

Hansen, Lars Peter, and Ravi Jagannathan. 1991. "Implications of Security Market Data for Models of Dynamic Economies." *Journal of Political Economy* 99(2):225–92.

Hansen, Lars Peter, and Kenneth J. Singleton. 1983. "Stochastic Consumption, Risk-Aversion, and the Temporal Behavior of Asset Returns." *Journal of Political Economy* 91(6):929–56.

Harrison, Michael, and David Kreps. 1978. "Speculative Investor Behavior in a Stock Market with Heterogeneous Expectations." *Quarterly Journal of Economics* 92:323–36.

He, Zhiguo, and Wei Xiong. 2012. "Rollover Risk and Credit Risk." *Journal of Finance* 67(2):391–429.

Hong, Harrison, Jose Scheinkman, and Wei Xiong. 2006. "Asset Float and Speculative Bubbles." *Journal of Finance* 61:1073–1117.

Hong, Harrison, and David Sraer. 2011. "Quiet Bubbles." Working paper, Princeton University.

Horesh, Ronnie. 2000. "Injecting Incentives into the Solution of Social Problems: Social Policy Bonds." *Economic Affairs* 20(3):39–42.

Hsu, Ming, Meghana Batt, Ralph Adolphs, Daniel Tranel, and Colin F. Camerer. 2005. "Neural Systems Responding to Degrees of Uncertainty in Human Decision-Making." *Science* 310:1680–83.

Huettel, Scott A., C. Jill Stowe, Evan M. Gordon, Brent T. Warner, and Michael L. Platt. 2006. "Neural Signatures of Economic Preferences for Risk and Ambiguity." *Neuron* 49(5):765–75.

Jung, Jeeman, and Robert Shiller. 2005. "Samuelson's Dictum and the Stock Market." *Economic Inquiry* 43(2):221–28.

Kahneman, Daniel, and Amos Tversky. 1979. "Prospect Theory: An Analysis of Decision under Uncertainty." *Econometrica* 47:236–91.

———. 2000. *Choices, Values and Frames.* Cambridge: Cambridge University Press.

Kamstra, Mark, and Robert J. Shiller. 2009. "The Case for Trills: Giving the People and Their Pension Funds a Stake in the Wealth of the Nation." New Haven, Conn.: Cowles Foundation, Working Paper No. 1717.

Keynes, John Maynard. 1921. *A Treatise on Probability.* London: Macmillan.

———. 1936. *The General Theory of Employment, Interest and Money.* London: Macmillan.

Kindleberger, Charles Poor. 1978. *Manias, Panics and Crashes: A History of Financial Crises.* London: Macmillan.

Kleidon, Allan W. 1986. "Variance Bounds Tests and Stock Price Valuation Models." *Journal of Political Economy* 94:953–1001.

Kubler, Felix, and Karl Schmedders. 2012. "Financial Innovation and Asset Price Volatility." *American Economic Review* 102(3):147–51.

Kyle, Albert. 1985. "Continuous Auctions and Insider Trading." *Econometrica* 53(6):1315–35.

LeRoy, Stephen F. 1973. "Risk Aversion and the Martingale Property of Stock Prices." *International Economic Review* 14(2):436–66.

LeRoy, Stephen F., and Richard D. Porter. 1981. "Stock Price Volatility: Tests Based on Implied Variance Bounds." *Econometrica* 49:97–113.

Lewellen, Jonathan. 2004. "Predicting Returns with Financial Ratios." *Journal of Financial Economics* 74(2):209–35.

Lucas, Robert E. 1978. "Asset Prices in an Exchange Economy." *Econometrica* 46(6):1429–45.

Malmendier, Ulrike, and Geoffrey Tate. 2005. "CEO Overconfidence and Corporate Investment." *Journal of Finance* 60(6):2661–2700.

Marsh, Terry A., and Robert C. Merton. 1986. "Dividend Variability and Variance Bound Tests for the Rationality of Stock Market Prices." *American Economic Review* 76:483–98.

Modigliani, Franco, and Richard Cohn. 1979. "Inflation, Rational Valuation and the Market." *Financial Analysts Journal* 35(2):24–44.

Morris, Stephen. 1996. "Speculative Investor Behavior and Learning." *Quarterly Journal of Economics* 62:1327–47.

Moss, David A. 2002. *When All Else Fails: The Government as Ultimate Risk Manager.* Cambridge, Mass.: Harvard University Press.

Mullainathan, Sendhil, and Eldar Shafir. 2013. *Scarcity: Why Having Too Little Means So Much*. New York: Times Books.

Mullainathan, Sendhil, and Andrei Shleifer. 2005. "The Market for News." *American Economic Review* 95(4):1031–53.

Odean, Terrance. 2000. "Do Investors Trade Too Much?" in *Behavioral Finance*, edited by Hersh Shefrin. Northhampton, Mass.: Edward Elgar.

Phillips, Peter C. B., and Pierre Perron. 1988. "Testing for a Unit Root in Time Series Regression." *Biometrika* 75(2):335–46.

Poterba, James M., and Lawrence H. Summers. 1988. "Mean Reversion in Stock Prices: Evidence and Implications." *Journal of Financial Economics* 22:26–59.

Robbins, Lionel. 1932. *An Essay on the Nature and Significance of Economic Science*. London: Macmillan.

Rothman, James E. 2013. "The Principle of Membrane Fusion in the Cell." Prize Lecture for 2013 Nobel Prize in Medicine. http://www.nobelprize.org/mediaplayer/index .php?id=1975.

Saunders, Edward M. 1993. "Stock Prices and Wall Street Weather." *American Economic Review* 83(5):1337–45.

Savage, Leonard J. 1954. *Foundations of Statistics*. New York: Wiley.

Scheinkman, Jose, and Wei Xiong. 2003. "Overconfidence and Speculative Bubbles." *Journal of Political Economy* 111:1133–1219.

Shefrin, Hersh M. 2008. *A Behavioral Approach to Asset Pricing*. Amsterdam: Elsevier.

Shefrin, Hersh M., and Meir Statman. 1984. "Explaining Investor Preference for Cash Dividends." *Journal of Financial Economics* 13(2):253–82.

———. 1985. "The Disposition to Sell Losers Too Early and Ride Losers Too Long: Theory and Evidence." *Journal of Finance* 40(3):777–90.

Shiller, Robert J. 1972. "Rational Expectations and the Term Structure of Interest Rates." PhD diss., Massachusetts Institute of Technology.

———. 1979. "The Volatility of Long-Term Interest Rates and Expectations Models of the Term Structure." *Journal of Political Economy* 87(6):1190–1219.

———. 1981a. "Do Stock Prices Move Too Much to Be Justified by Subsequent Changes in Dividends?" *American Economic Review* 71(3):421–36.

———. 1981b. "The Uses of Volatility Measures in Assessing Market Efficiency." *Journal of Finance* 36:291–304.

———. 1982. "Consumption, Asset Markets and Macroeconomic Fluctuations." *Carnegie Rochester Conference Series on Public Policy* 17:203–38.

———. 1984. "Stock Prices and Social Dynamics." *Brookings Papers on Economic Activity* 1984(2):457–98.

———. 1986. "The Marsh-Merton Model of Managers' Smoothing of Dividends." *American Economic Review* 76(3):499–503.

———. 1987. "Ultimate Sources of Aggregate Variability." *American Economic Review* 77(2):87–92.

———. 1988. "Portfolio Insurance and Other Investor Fashions as Factors in the 1987 Stock Market Crash." *NBER Macroeconomics Annual* 3:287–97.

Shiller, Robert J. 1989. *Market Volatility*. Cambridge, Mass.: MIT Press.

———. 1991. "Arithmetic Repeat Sales Price Estimators." *Journal of Housing Economics* 1:110–26.

———. 1992. *Who's Minding the Store? The Report of the Twentieth Century Fund Task Force on Market Speculation and Corporate Governance*. New York: The Twentieth Century Fund.

———. 1993. *Macro Markets: Creating Institutions for Managing Society's Largest Economic Risks*. New York: Oxford University Press, 1993.

———. 1997. "Public Resistance to Indexation: A Puzzle." *Brookings Papers on Economic Activity* 1997(1):159–211.

———. 2000. *Irrational Exuberance*, 1st ed. Princeton, N.J.: Princeton University Press.

———. 2002. "Indexed Units of Account: Theory and Analysis of Historical Experience." In *Indexation, Inflation, and Monetary Policy*, edited by Fernando Lefort and Klaus Schmidt-Hebbel. Santiago, Chile: Central Bank of Chile.

———. 2003. *The New Financial Order: Risk in the 21st Century*. Princeton, N.J.: Princeton University Press.

———. 2005. *Irrational Exuberance*, 2nd ed. Princeton, N.J.: Princeton University Press.

———. 2008. *The Subprime Solution: How Today's Global Financial Crisis Happened and What to Do about It*. Princeton, N.J.: Princeton University Press.

———. 2009. *The Case for a Basket: A New Way of Showing the True Value of Money*. London: Policy Exchange.

———. 2011. "Democratizing and Humanizing Finance." In *Reforming U.S. Financial Markets: Reflections before and beyond Dodd-Frank*, edited by Randall S. Kroszner and Robert J. Shiller. Alvin Hansen Symposium on Public Policy at Harvard University. Cambridge, Mass.: MIT Press.

———. 2012. *Finance and the Good Society*. Princeton, N.J.: Princeton University Press.

———. 2014. "Why Is Housing Finance Still Stuck in Such a Primitive Stage?" *American Economic Review*, forthcoming.

Shiller, Robert J., and Andrea Beltratti. 1992. "Stock Prices and Bond Yields: Can Their Comovements Be Explained in Terms of Present Value Models?" *Journal of Monetary Economics* 30(1):25–46.

Shiller, Robert J., and Pierre Perron. 1985. "Testing the Random Walk Hypothesis: Power versus Frequency of Observation." *Economics Letters* 18:381–86.

Shiller, Robert J., and Ryan Schneider. 1998. "Labor Income Indices Designed for Use in Contracts Promoting Income Risk Management." *Review of Income and Wealth* 44(2):163–82.

Shiller, Robert J., and Jeremy J. Siegel. 1977. "The Gibson Paradox and Historical Movements in Real Long Term Interest Rates." *Journal of Political Economy* 85(5):891–98.

Shiller, Robert J., and Allan N. Weiss. 1999a. "Evaluating Real Estate Valuation Systems." *Journal of Real Estate Finance and Economics* 18(2):147–61.

———. 1999b. "Home Equity Insurance." *Journal of Real Estate Finance and Economics* 19(1):21–47.

Shiller, Robert J., Rafal Wojakowski, M. Shahid Ebrahim, and Mark B. Shackleton. 2013. "Mitigating Financial Fragility with Continuous Workout Mortgages." *Journal of Economic Behavior and Organization* 85:269–85.

Shleifer, Andrei. 2000. *Inefficient Markets: A Survey of Behavioral Finance.* New York: Oxford University Press.

Shleifer, Andrei, and Robert Vishny. 1997. "Limits to Arbitrage." *Journal of Finance* 52(1):35–55.

Siegel, Jeremy J. 2005. *The Future for Investors: The Tried and True Beats the Bold and New.* New York: Crown Business.

———. 2008. *Stocks for the Long Run,* 4th ed. New York: McGraw-Hill.

Sims, Christopher A. 1984. "Martingale-Like Behavior of Prices and Interest Rates." Discussion Paper No. 205, Center for Economic Research, Department of Economics, University of Minnesota.

———. 2003. "Implications of Rational Inattention." *Journal of Monetary Economics* 50:665–90.

Singleton, Kenneth J. 1980. "Expectations Models of the Term Structure and Implied Variance Bounds." *Journal of Political Economy* 88:1159–76.

Summers, Lawrence H. 1986. "Does the Stock Market Rationally Reflect Fundamental Values?" *Econometrica* 41:591–601.

Thaler, Richard H., and Eric J. Johnson. 1990. "Gambling with the House Money and Trying to Break Even: The Effects of Prior Outcomes on Risky Choice." *Management Science* 36(6):343–60.

Thaler, Richard H., and Cass R. Sunstein. 2009. *Nudge: Improving Decisions about Health, Wealth and Happiness.* New Haven, Conn.: Yale University Press.

Torous, Walter, Rossen Valkanov, and Shu Yan. 2004. "On Predicting Stock Returns with Nearly Integrated Explanatory Variables." *Journal of Business* 77:937–66.

Tversky, Amos, and Daniel Kahneman. 1974. "Judgment under Uncertainty: Heuristics and Biases." *Science* 185:1124–31.

Vuolteenaho, Tuomo. 2002. "What Drives Firm-Level Stock Returns?" *Journal of Finance* 57(1):233–64.

West, Kenneth D. 1988. "Dividend Innovations and Stock Price Volatility." *Econometrica* 56:37–61.

Wu, Ho-Mou, and Wen-Chung Guo. 2004. "Asset Price Volatility and Trading Volume with Rational Beliefs." *Economic Theory* 23:795–829.

Notes

Preface to the Third Edition

1. Min Zhu (Deputy Managing Director, International Monetary Fund), "Housing Markets, Financial Stability and the Economy" (http://www.imf.org/external/np/speeches/2014/060514.htm), June 5, 2014.

2. "In the countries that have been experiencing outsize financial booms, the risk is that these will turn to bust and possibly inflict financial distress. . . . Based on leading indicators that have proved useful in the past, such as the behaviour of credit and property prices, the signs are worrying." (http://www.bis.org/publ/arpdf/ar2014e1.htm).

3. Eugene Fama, "Two Pillars of Asset Pricing" (Nobel Lecture), *American Economic Review*, 104(6) (2014), p. 1475.

4. Karl E. Case, Robert J. Shiller, and Anne Kinsella Thompson, "What Have They Been Thinking? Homebuyer Behavior in Hot and Cold Markets." *Brookings Papers on Economic Activity*, 2 (2012): 265–98.

Chapter One   The Stock Market in Historical Perspective

1. Alan Greenspan, "The Challenge of Central Banking in a Democratic Society," http://www.federalreserve.gov/BOARDDOCS/SPEECHES/19961205.htm.

2. The Standard & Poor's Composite Index is now called the Standard & Poor's 500; however, I use the older name here, since the historical index did not always contain 500 stocks. The changing composition of the index reflects ongoing choices made by Standard & Poor's. Of course, they have to change the list as companies come and go. Jeremy Siegel reports that of the 500 firms in 1957, only 125 remained in the same corporate form in 2003. An index of the 125 firms surviving since 1957 shows somewhat higher returns than shown by the Standard & Poor's 500 index itself. See Jeremy J. Siegel, *The Future for Investors* (New York: Crown Business, 2005).

3. The price, dividend, and earnings series are from the same sources as described in Chapter 26 of my earlier book *Market Volatility* (Cambridge, Mass.: MIT Press, 1989), although now I use monthly data, rather than annual data. Monthly dividend and earnings data are computed from the S&P four-quarter totals for the quarter since 1926, with linear interpolation to monthly figures. Dividend and earnings data before 1926 are from Cowles and associates (*Common Stock Indexes*, 2nd ed. [Bloomington, Ind.: Principia Press, 1939]), interpolated from annual data. Stock price data are monthly averages of daily closing prices. The CPI-U (Consumer Price Index—All Urban Consumers) published by the U.S. Bureau of Labor Statistics begins in 1913; for years before 1913 I spliced to the CPI Warren and Pearson's price index, by multiplying it by the ratio of the indices in January 1913. December 1999 and January 2000 values for the CPI-U are extrapolated. See George F. Warren and Frank A. Pearson, *Gold and Prices* (New York: John Wiley and Sons, 1935). Data are from their Table 1, pp. 11–14. For the plots, I have multiplied the inflation-corrected series by a constant so that their value in June 2014 equals their nominal value (that is, so that all prices are effectively in June 2014 dollars).

In my older work on stock prices (much of it done jointly with John Campbell), I had used the Producer Price Index (PPI), All Commodities, rather than the CPI, to deflate. In the past, there was not much difference between the PPI and the CPI, except for short-run oscillations, but since the mid-1980s the levels of the series have diverged substantially. Unless otherwise noted, any statistics reported in this book for the U.S. stock market are from the data set described in this endnote. The data used here (as well as Chapter 26 from *Market Volatility*) are currently available on my website, http://www.econ.yale.edu/~shiller.

4. See William H. Gross, "On the 'Course' to a New Normal," http://www.pimco.com/EN/Insights/Pages/Gross%20Sept%20On%20the%20Course%20to%20a%20New%20Normal.aspx.

5. Some have urged that I use a log or ratio scale for the plot, so that the apparent price growth at the end is not "misleading." I do not believe that plotting in levels is misleading. One could as well argue that plots on log scales are misleading. The spike of prices at the end is not an artifact of the plotting procedure. We are not seeing in this figure the "hockey stick" curve of exponential growth with constant high rate of growth. A plot of the same stock price series as in Figure 1.1 also appears on a log scale in Figure 11.2, in Chapter 11.

6. See also for U.S. sector CAPE with a similarly long history Oliver Bunn and Robert J. Shiller, "Changing Times, Changing Values—A Historical Analysis of Sectors within the US Stock Market 1872–2013." New Haven, Conn.: Yale University, Cowles Foundation, 2014, http://cowles.econ.yale.edu/P/cd/d19b/d1950.pdf, and Oliver Bunn, Anthony Lazanas, Robert J. Shiller, Arne Staal, Cenk Ural, and Ji Zhuang, "Es-CAPE-ing from Overvalued Sectors: Sector Selection Based on the Cyclically Adjusted Price-Earnings (CAPE) Ratio," *Journal of Portfolio Management*, 41(1) (2014): 16–33.

7. Graham and Dodd's 1934 "average earnings on common stock price," which is the reciprocal of CAPE without an inflation correction in earnings, seems not to have been much picked up (Benjamin Graham and David Dodd, *Securities Analysis* [New York: McGraw-Hill, 1934]). Even earlier, the *Wall Street Journal* in 1911 published an article

presenting an "Index of Railroad Earnings Covering a Ten-Year Period" and evaluated stock price levels using this index. *Barron's* has published a "ratio price to five-year earnings" for its Barron's 50-Stock Average since the 1950s. Jeremy Siegel of The Wharton School has argued that a better measure of earnings could be used for the denominator of the CAPE ("The Shiller CAPE Ratio: A New Look," paper presented at the Q-Group Conference, 2014). He proposes a denominator of ten-year-average earnings based on a different measure of earnings: National Income and Product Accounts earnings adjusted with a sort of divisor. This is an interesting proposal, which deserves watching, but it is vulnerable to problems associated with the divisor and has a shorter available history, so I did not yet see fit to make the change in the series shown here.

Starting in 1953, the interest rate is the yield of a monthly ten-year Treasury Bond series from the U.S. Board of Governors of the Federal Reserve System. Before 1953, the data are interpolated to monthly from annual average data in Sidney Homer, *A History of Interest Rates* (New Brunswick, N.J.: Rutgers University Press, 1963); for 1871–1900, from Table 38, col. 3, p. 288; for 1901–20, from Table 45, col. 14, p. 341; for 1921–46, from Table 48, col. 1, p. 352; and for 1947–53, from Table 50, col. 1, p. 359. Jeremy Siegel has a very similar government bond yield series (www.jeremysiegel.com) that he has studied in detail in his article "The Real Rate of Interest from 1800–1990: A Study of the U.S. and the U.K.," *Journal of Monetary Economics*, 29 (1992): 227–52.

8. It should be abundantly clear that some smoothing is necessary: consider the possibility of zero earnings in a given year. Annual earnings per share adjusted to the S&P Composite Index have always been strictly greater than zero in every year since the inception of the index in 1871, but they were negative for one quarter, the fourth quarter of 2008, and annual earnings could of course pass below zero in the future. Total after-tax corporate profits were actually negative in the national income accounts for 1931 and 1932. When earnings are zero, the price-earnings ratio would be *infinite* in that year, suggesting that there is no upper bound on the price of the aggregate stock market.

9. The rise in earnings during the stock market's ascent to its peak in 2000 was partly due to the market rise itself, owing to some pension accounting rules that make profits respond to an increase in value of the pension portfolio. It appears that stock market investors did not see through this accounting anomaly. See Julia Lynn Coronado and Steven A. Sharpe, "Did Pension Plan Accounting Contribute to a Stock Market Bubble?" (Washington, D.C.: Board of Governors of the Federal Reserve System, Finance and Economics Discussion Series No. 2003-38, 2003).

10. Scholars have pointed out that since there was no year zero, each new century begins on January 1 of a year ending in 1. In 1900, people were more respectful of such scholarship, and waited a year to celebrate. A celebration of the third millennium, in contrast, happened at the start of 2000.

11. There had been a very slow and gradual growth of price relative to earnings for thirty years (real earnings grew at the rate of 2.3% a year from July 1871 to July 1900, while prices grew at a slightly faster rate of 3.4% a year).

12. These are geometric average real returns using the S&P Composite Index and the Producer Price Index (since the Consumer Price Index begins in 1913) to convert to real values.

13. See also Ibbotson Associates, *Stocks, Bonds, Bills and Inflation: 1999 Yearbook, Market Results for 1926–1998* (Chicago: Ibbotson Associates, 1999), Tables 2-8 through 2-11, pp. 45–51. When comparing the returns shown here with returns given for similar intervals since 1926 in their book, it must be borne in mind that theirs are for calendar years only, and therefore do not generally catch the peaks or troughs of the market.

14. One of John Maynard Keynes's most famous terms, "animal spirits," has some overlap with the concept of irrational exuberance; it has been defined as natural or healthy (rather than necessarily irrational) exuberance. Keynes was probably the most influential economist of the twentieth century; he is famous for his 1936 book *The General Theory of Employment, Interest and Money.* That revolutionary book has been guiding fiscal and monetary policy leaders around the world. He wrote in that book: "Even apart from the instability due to speculation, there is the instability due to the characteristic of human nature that a large proportion of our positive activities depend on spontaneous optimism rather than a mathematical expectation, whether moral or hedonistic or economic. Most, probably, of our decisions to do something positive, the full consequences of which will be drawn out over many days to come, can only be taken as a result of animal spirits—of a spontaneous urge to action rather than inaction, and not as the outcome of a weighted average of quantitative benefits multiplied by quantitative probabilities." John Maynard Keynes, *The General Theory of Employment, Interest and Money* (New York: Harcourt Brace & World, 1961), p. 161. See also George Akerlof and Robert J. Shiller, *Animal Spirits: How Human Psychology Drives the Economy and Why This Matters for Global Capitalism* (Princeton, N.J.: Princeton University Press, 2009).

Chapter Two   *The Bond Market in Historical Perspective*

1. See Annette Vissing-Jorgensen and Arvind Krishnamurthy, "The Effects of Quantitative Easing on Interest Rates: Channels and Implications for Policy," *Brookings Papers on Economic Activity,* 2 (2011): 215–87.

2. See Federal Reserve Board, "Humphrey-Hawkins Report July 22, 1997, Section 2: Economic and Financial Developments in 1997" (http://www.federalreserve.gov/boarddocs/hh/1997/july/ReportSection2.htm); the model is illustrated with a chart titled "Equity Valuation and the Long-Term Interest Rate" showing the ten-year bond yield and the earnings-price ratio from 1982 through 1997.

3. Economic theory suggests that, if anything, there should be a relation between the *real,* not nominal, interest rate and the price-earnings ratio. That there is a relation with the nominal interest rate is an anomaly. We will return to this in Chapter 4. See also Franco Modigliani and Richard A. Cohn, "Inflation, Rational Valuation, and the Market," *Financial Analysts Journal,* 35 (1979): 22–44; reprinted in Simon Johnson (ed.), *The Collected Papers of Franco Modigliani,* Vol. 5 (Cambridge, Mass.: MIT Press, 1989).

4. William H. Gross, "One Big Idea," http://www.pimco.com/EN/Insights/Pages/One-Big-Idea.aspx.

5. See Robert J. Shiller and Jeremy J. Siegel, "The Gibson Paradox and Historical Movements in Real Long Term Interest Rates," *Journal of Political Economy,* 85(5) (1977): 891–98. See also A. H. Gibson, "The Future Course of High Class Investment Values,"

Banker's Magazine (London) 115 (1923): 15–34, and John Maynard Keynes, *A Treatise on Money* (New York: Macmillan, 1930).

6. See "Yield Spreads and Interest Rate Movements: A Bird's Eye View," with John Y. Campbell, *Review of Economic Studies,* 58: 495–514, 1991.

7. John Bates Clark, "The Gold Standard of Currency in the Light of Recent Theory," *Political Science Quarterly,* 10(3) (1895): 383–97.

8. The return is not technically guaranteed to be negative, for if there is sufficient deflation to reduce the inflation-corrected principal below the original nominal principal, the investor receives then the original nominal principal at maturity.

9. "The riskless asset for a long-term investor is an inflation-indexed consol. If this asset is available, it will play some role in the optimal portfolio of any investor who has relative risk aversion greater than one." John Y. Campbell and Luis M. Viceira, *Strategic Asset Allocation: Portfolio Choice for Long-Term Investors,* Oxford University Press, 2002, p. 4. See also Robert J. Shiller, "Can the Federal Reserve Control Real Interest Rates?" in *Rational Expectations and Economic Policy,* ed. Stanley Fischer (Cambridge, Mass.: National Bureau of Economic Research and University of Chicago Press, pp. 117–67, 1980), http://www.nber.org/chapters/c6262.pdf.

10. Michael Ashton in "TIPS and CPI Futures—Practice Makes Perfect," unpublished paper, 2014, describes how changing institutions and rising numbers of professional traders are making the inflation derivatives market more important over the years. See also Michael J. Fleming and John R. Sporn, "Trading Activity and Price Transparency in the Inflation Swap Market," *Economic Policy Review, Federal Reserve Bank of New York,* 19(1):45–58, May 2013.

11. See John Y. Campbell, Robert J. Shiller, and Luis M. Viceira, "Understanding Inflation-Indexed Bond Markets," *Brookings Papers on Economic Activity,* 1 (2009): 79–120.

12. See Robert J. Shiller, "Public Resistance to Indexation: A Puzzle," *Brookings Papers on Economic Activity,* 1 (1997): 159–211.

13. Jeremy Stein, in his speech at the International Monetary Fund, "Incorporating Financial Stability Considerations into a Monetary Policy Framework," March 21, 2014.

14. It is conceivable that an inflation-indexed bond with a negative yield could have a positive real return over its lifetime. This could happen in the United States in the unlikely event that persistent and strong deflation occurs, since the Treasury Inflation Protected Securities promise to pay at least the nominal original value of the principal back on maturity.

Chapter Three   *The Real Estate Market in Historical Perspective*

1. The Bank of International Settlements (BIS) in Basel has pioneered the assembly of home price data around the world (http://www.bis.org/statistics/pp.htm). The *Economist* magazine in London has assembled a list of indices that is similar to the one produced by the BIS (http://www.economist.com/blogs/dailychart/2011/11/global-house-prices).

2. There have been many booming cities in China, but in other parts of China a huge increase in supply has kept home price increases in check: the Chinese government has allowed construction to proceed at a massive rate, without so much of the zoning

and environmental restrictions seen in other countries. In recent years, the Chinese government has sought to temper the rapid increases in home prices.

3. I produced the home price series shown in Figure 3.1 by first linking together various annual home price indices (by multiplying each by a constant so that values in one overlapping year are equalized across indices) to arrive at a nominal home price index. Next, the nominal home price index was deflated by the Consumer Price Index.

Even though there were no regularly published home price indices before the 1960s, some economists were constructing indices of home prices that cover most of the years since 1890. We found home price indices from 1890 to 1934 and from 1953 to the present that used in their construction some device to attempt to hold the quality of the home constant.

The nominal home price index, 1890–1934, is from Leo Grebler, David M. Blank, and Louis Winnick, *Capital Formation in Residential Real Estate: Trends and Prospects* (New York and Princeton, N.J.: National Bureau of Economic Research and Princeton University Press, 1956), Appendix C (http://www.nber.org/chapters/c1339.pdf). It is a repeated-measures index based on a survey of homeowners in twenty-two U.S. cities, who were asked to give the value of their home in 1934 and the date and price of earlier purchase of that home. Since it is based on repeated measures of individual homes, the series is protected, in contrast to the simple median price, from any bias from changes in the mix of houses sold or of the increasing size and quality of newer homes. Its shortcoming is that it depends on memories of the surveyed homeowners for the earlier purchase price.

The nominal home price index that we constructed for 1934–53 is a simple average over five cities of median home prices advertised in newspapers. The cities are Chicago, Los Angeles, New Orleans, New York, and Washington, D.C. My students collected the data from microfilmed newspapers at the Yale University library, collecting approximately thirty prices for each city and year, except that for the fifth city, Washington, D.C., 1934–48, data came from a median price series from E. M. Fisher, *Urban Real Estate Markets: Characteristics and Financing* (New York: National Bureau of Economic Research, 1951). The median series for 1934–53 does not make any attempt to correct for home quality change, as do the indices we use for the other subperiods. Improvement in home size and quality puts an upward bias in median home price, and this is why I avoided using median price as much as possible.

The nominal home price index for 1953–75 is the home purchase component of the U.S. Consumer Price Index (CPI). The Bureau of Labor Statistics collected data on home prices for those years for homes that are held constant in age and square footage. In the 1980s, they discontinued this index when they switched to a rental equivalence basis for housing in the CPI. They made this change to correct what was considered a conceptual flaw in the housing component of the CPI: the CPI is supposed to be a price of consumption goods and services, not of investment assets. For our purposes, however, the old home purchase component is acceptable. There are, however, some shortcomings in the home purchase component, notably that it is based only on homes with certain government-subsidized mortgages, and the procedure that the Bureau of Labor Statistics used to correct for changes in the ceiling on these mortgages was not optimal. See J. S. Greenlees, "An Empirical Evaluation of the CPI Home Purchase Index 1973–8," *American Real Estate and Urban Economics Association Journal,* 10(1) (1982): 1–24. A more detailed discussion of the indices that were used here for years before 1975 can be found in my paper "Consumption, Asset Markets and Macroeconomic Fluctuations," *Carnegie-Rochester Conference Series on Public Policy,* 17 (1982): 203–38.

The nominal home price index for 1975–present is the monthly S&P/Case-Shiller U.S. National Home Price Index produced by CoreLogic, Inc., purchasers of Case Shiller Weiss, Inc. Before 1992, this index relied partly on U.S. Office of Federal Housing Enterprise Oversight (now replaced by the U.S. Federal Housing Finance Agency) indexes to fill in geographic regions for which our own data were missing.

The consumer price index used to deflate nominal series to real is the same as that used in Figure 1.1 and elsewhere in this book.

The building cost index links together two building cost series. The first, for 1890–1915, is taken from Grebler, Blank, and Winnick, *Capital Formation in Residential Real Estate,* Table B-10, col. 1 (Housekeeping), http://www.nber.org/chapters/c1338 .pdf, p. 342. Their index is a weighted average of wages per hour in the building trades and an index of materials prices. The second is the Engineering News Record Building Cost Index. Their index, for 1915–present, based on twenty cities, is the cost of 66.38 hours of skilled labor: bricklayers, carpenters, and structural ironworkers, plus 25 hundredweight of standard structural steel shapes, 1.128 tons of Portland cement, and 1,088 board feet of two-by-four lumber.

From 1890 to 1953 the interest rate series is from Homer, *A History of Interest Rates,* Tables 38 (col. 3), 45 (col. 15), 48 (col. 1), and 50 (col. 1), interpolated from annual to monthly. For April 1953–present it is the monthly ten-year Treasury Bond Yield, from the Federal Reserve. This long rate series is very similar to the one in Jeremy J. Siegel, *Stocks for the Long Run,* 5th ed. (New York: McGraw-Hill, 2014), http:// jeremysiegel.com. Siegel describes the series in Jeremy J. Siegel, "The Real Rate of Interest from 1800–1990."

4. See the Standard & Poor's analysis of costs of buying relative to renting: http:// www.housingviews.com/2013/02/08/charts-of-rent-vs-buy-and-inflation-adjusted -home-prices/. A Federal Reserve study finds no significant evidence from regional data that a high home price–to–income ratio portends future declines in home prices. See Joshua Gallin, "The Long-Run Relation between House Prices and Income: Evidence from Local Housing Markets" (Washington, D.C.: Board of Governors of the Federal Reserve System, Finance and Economics Discussion Paper Series No. 2003.17, 2003). However, this study may not have had sufficient power with its twenty-three years' data, ending in the midst of a national home price boom, to detect such an effect.

5. See Karl E. Case and Robert J. Shiller, "The Efficiency of the Market for Single Family Homes," *American Economic Review,* 79(1) (March 1989): 125–37.

6. According to a Federal Reserve study, the replacement cost of homes from 1970 to 2003 was much more steady than the price of residential land. See Morris A. Davis and Jonathan Heathcote, "The Price and Quantity of Residential Land in the United

States" (Washington, D.C.: Board of Governors of the Federal Reserve System, Finance and Economics Discussion Series No. 2004-37, 2004).

7. Jonathan McCarthy and Richard W. Peach of the Federal Reserve Bank of New York have reached a different conclusion. In a July 2004 article they write: "Home prices have essentially moved in line with increases in family income and declines in nominal mortgage interest rates." See Jonathan McCarthy and Richard W. Peach, "Are Home Prices the Next 'Bubble'?" *Federal Reserve Bank of New York Economic Policy Review,* 2004, p. 1. Part of the reason for their very different conclusion is that they chose to base their analysis on an index of *new* homes, the so-called Constant Quality Index of *new* home prices. The Constant Quality Index has increased much less in the last twenty years than have the repeat sales indices, suggesting that there is no bubble. But new home prices tend to track building costs because new homes tend to be built in areas where land is abundant; we just cannot expect to see a boom in *new* home prices. Nor do we expect to see the burst of a bubble in new home prices: new homes are not built in places where prices have fallen below construction costs. The structural housing market model McCarthy and Peach say explains home price movements in terms of interest rates was fit over their sample period 1981–2003, when interest rates' downtrend inversely matched a home price much better than over a longer period. There is a sense in which they are right, though: there are major areas in the United States where home prices have not risen a lot and there has not been a bubble.

8. See Claudio Borio and Patrick McGuire, "Twin Peaks in Equity and Housing Prices?" *BIS Quarterly Review,* March 2004, pp. 79–93. In the United States fixed-rate long-term mortgages have predominated since the 1930s. It appears that there is greater sensitivity to interest rate changes in countries where floating rate mortgages are more widely used. See Kostas Tsatsaronis and Haibin Zhu, "What Drives Housing Price Dynamics: Cross-Country Evidence," *BIS Quarterly Review,* March 2004, pp. 65–78. Another study of six industrialized countries found an impact on house prices of interest rates, the stock market, and aggregate economic activity. See Gregory D. Sutton, "Explaining Changes in House Prices," *BIS Quarterly Review,* September 2002, pp. 46–55.

9. World War I was a much smaller war than World War II by U.S. standards. The military comprised only 9% of the U.S. male population in World War I, compared with 24% in World War II. U.S. direct involvement in World War I lasted only seven months, whereas U.S. involvement in World War II lasted forty-five months.

10. Our data for the period 1934–53 are based on five large U.S. cities, and each of the five cities shows a sharp increase in home prices after World War II. But it is not clear how much the price increases in these cities correspond to those in the country as a whole. I therefore sought to find other evidence about the country as a whole, particularly regarding the apparently large home price increases after World War II.

The U.S. Census Department has collected data at decadal intervals on home prices since 1940 based on homeowners' estimates. Their data show an increase of 45% between 1940 and 1950 for the median price of a home corrected for inflation; our data show a 30% increase.

A 1951 *New York Times* article reported a survey of 150 cities, a much better representation of the country than just five big cities, made by Myron L. Matthews, vice-president of the Dow Service, Inc. "His report showed that in the typical city the $6000 house of 1941 now has a price tag of $13,860 on it." (Lee E. Cooper, "Effects of Curbs on Building Loans Will Appear Soon," *New York Times,* April 22, 1951, p. 225.) The wording "typical city" is a little vague. But these numbers imply a 131% nominal price increase (28% real increase) in the ten years from 1941 to 1951, not too far from the 154% nominal price increase (41% real increase) that our index shows over that same interval.

However, a 1949 *New York Times* article reported the results of an even bigger study of 276 cities by the National Association of Real Estate Boards. It reported that the median over these cities of the increase in home prices since 1940 was only "about 50%." (Lee E. Cooper, "Realty Men Look for Further Rise in Housing Prices," *New York Times,* May 3, 1949, p. 81.) Since the Consumer Price Index rose 73% from 1940 to 1949, their numbers suggest a *decline* of 13% in real home prices over this interval, rather than the real *increase* of 22% that our numbers show for the same interval. However, the median price increase over 276 cities is likely a downward-biased measure of the national mean price increase, and puts too much emphasis on small cities. That study also said that in some congested areas buyers now had to pay "about 100% more." Our index shows a 111% nominal increase from 1940 to 1949, suggesting that our numbers may show an upwardly biased growth rate relative to prices nationwide after World War II if our five cities were congested areas.

11. President Franklin Roosevelt's statement on signing the GI Bill, June 24, 1944, Franklin D. Roosevelt Presidential Library and Museum, http://www.fdrlibrary .marist.edu.

12. Data are from Japan Real Estate Institute, Shigaichi Urban Land Price Index, Tokyo Metropolitan Area, deflated by consumer price index.

13. Prime Residential Properties, rupees per square foot, deflated by consumer price index, Knight Frank India.

14. See Piet Eichholtz, "A Long Run House Price Index: The Herengracht Index, 1638–1973," unpublished paper, the University of Limburg and the University of Amsterdam, 1996.

15 Karl E. Case, "Measuring Urban Land Values," unpublished paper, Wellesley College, October 26, 1997.

16. Computed from figures shown in his Table XLIV, "Land Values on North–South Streets in the Central Business District of Chicago, 1830–1931," p. 345, in Homer Hoyt, *One Hundred Years of Land Values in Chicago* (Chicago: University of Chicago Press, 1933). I chose the years 1877 and 1931 for comparison because both of them were in the middle of a recession, as defined by the National Bureau of Economic Research, actually both in depressions, and thus in comparable economic conditions.

17. Hoyt, *One Hundred Years of Land Values in Chicago,* p. 279.

18. U.S. Census data show that the average new house rose from 1,500 square feet in 1970 to over 2,200 square feet in 2000, and household size decreased from 3.1 persons per household in 1970 to 2.8 persons in 2002.

19. A search found that the first reference to the median selling price of existing homes in a major newspaper was in the *Washington Post* in 1968. The article said that the survey that had produced the median "was initiated over two years ago." See "Average Sales Price Up $1000 to $20,630," *Washington Post Times Herald,* October 5, 1968. It is clear that there was no well-publicized regularly published index of existing home selling prices before then. An article in the *New York Times* in 1963 about a new government series on median prices of *new* homes noted: "The new study is arousing considerable interest in the housing industry. A reason is that no previous government or industry statistical reports concentrated on sales." See "New Home Study Arouses Interest," *New York Times,* October 13, 1963.

20. Before real estate investment trusts were created by an act of Congress in 1960, there were no publicly traded real estate securities in the United States, and hence no place where speculative attentions to real estate would be recorded in published prices. Even then, the investment performance of real estate investment trusts is not a good indicator of the investment performance of individual owner-occupied homes, because the nature of the homes and of the dividend stream that they yield is fundamentally different.

21. Jennifer Taub, *Other People's Houses: How Decades of Bailouts, Captive Regulators, and Toxic Bankers Made Home Mortgages a Thrilling Business* (New Haven, Conn.: Yale University Press, 2014), p. 141.

22. Atif Mian and Amir Sufi, "Summary of 'the Consequences of Mortgage Credit Expansion,'" *Proceedings, Federal Reserve Bank of Chicago* (May 2008): 129–32.

23. "3 WaMu execs agree to settle FDIC lawsuit for up to $64 million," *Los Angeles Times,* December 3, 2011. http://articles.latimes.com/2011/dec/13/business/la-fi-fdic-wamu-20111214.

24. Gretchen Morgenson, "Lending Magnate Settles Fraud Case," *New York Times,* October 16, 2010. http://www.nytimes.com/2010/10/16/business/16countrywide.html?pagewanted=all&_r=0.

Chapter Four   Precipitating Factors: The Internet, the Capitalist Explosion, and Other Events

1. A number of studies of international data have provided evidence that countries with more highly developed financial markets show higher economic growth or allocate resources more efficiently. See Robert G. King and Ross Levine, "Finance and Growth: Schumpeter May Be Right," *Quarterly Journal of Economics,* 108 (1993): 717–37; Rafael LaPorta, Florencio Lopez-de-Silanes, and Andrei Shleifer, "Corporate Ownership around the World," *Journal of Finance,* 54 (1999): 471–518; and Jeffrey Wurgler, "Financial Markets and the Allocation of Capital," *Journal of Financial Economics,* 58 (2000): 187–214.

2. One study finds that individual investors tend to be less heavily invested in stocks during business cycle troughs, when expected returns tend to be high, while institutional investors tend to do the opposite, and hence to work in the direction of stabilizing the market. See Randolph Cohen, "Asset Allocation Decisions of Individuals and Institutions," Harvard Business School Working Paper Series, No. 03-112, 2003. A Merrill Lynch survey showed that professional fund managers

outside the United States were generally selling U.S. stocks during bull markets from 1994 to 1999, but there was no such clear pattern for U.S. fund managers; see Trevor Greetham, Owain Evans, and Charles I. Clough, Jr., "Fund Manager Survey: November 1999" (London: Merrill Lynch & Co., Global Securities Research and Economics Group, 1999).

3. Some simple economic growth models suggest that a sudden technological advance will have no effect on stock prices; for such models, see Robert Barro and Xavier Sala-i-Martin, *Economic Growth* (New York: McGraw-Hill, 1995); Olivier Blanchard and Stanley Fischer, *Lectures on Macroeconomics* (Cambridge, Mass.: MIT Press, 1989); or David Romer, *Advanced Macroeconomics* (New York: McGraw-Hill, 1996). For example, the theoretical effect of a sudden technological advance might be to spur investment in new capital, which will compete away any extra profits that the technological advance might make for existing capital.

4. On November 1, 1999, Microsoft and Intel were added to the Dow Jones Industrial Average.

5. Survey by Roper-Starch Worldwide, cited in Karlyn Bowman, "A Reaffirmation of Self-Reliance? A New Ethic of Self-Sufficiency?" *Public Perspective,* February–March 1996, pp. 5–8. The plausibility of changes in materialistic values over time is enhanced by evidence of differences in such values across cultures. See Gueliz Ger and Russell W. Belk, "Cross-Cultural Differences in Materialism," *Journal of Economic Psychology,* 17 (1996): 55–77.

6. U.S. Bureau of Justice Statistics, *National Crime Victimization Survey (NCVS),* http://www.ojp.usdoj.gov/bjs/cvict.htm#ncvs. The survey is based on interviews with people in 84,000 households; results are not affected by the trend towards greater reporting of crimes to police.

7. See Joel E. Cohen, "A Global Garden for the Twenty-First Century," *The Key Reporter,* Spring 1998, p. 1.

8. See World Bank, *Averting the Old Age Crisis* (New York: Oxford University Press, 1994).

9. Gurdip S. Bakshi and Zhiwu Chen ("Baby Boom, Population Aging and Capital Markets," *Journal of Business,* 67 [1994]: 165–202) found a substantial correlation between the average age of the U.S. population over age 20 and the real S&P Index, 1950–92. However, Robin Brooks ("Asset Market and Savings Effects of Demographic Transitions," unpublished Ph.D. dissertation, Yale University, 1998) showed that their result was sensitive to the cutoff age (20), and when he extended their analysis to seven other countries, he found that the fit was poorer. Bakshi and Chen are probably on the right track, but the evidence for a relation between the Baby Boom and the level of the stock market is weak.

Possibly the differences in price behavior across asset classes could still be reconciled with a Baby Boom theory by postulating that people in different age groups have different attitudes toward risk because of age-related differences in risk tolerance and that the stock market was relatively high at the peak of the Millennium Boom because the numerous people in their forties today are naturally less risk averse than older people. But such a theory has never been carefully worked out or shown to explain relative price movements. It is also noteworthy that the personal savings rate in the United States was then nearly zero, not significantly positive as the life cycle theory might suggest.

Economists have argued that given the increase in the stock market recently, savings rates are in fact surprisingly high; see William G. Gale and John Sabelhaus, "Perspectives on the Household Saving Rate," *Brookings Papers on Economic Activity,* 1 (1999): 181–224.

10. See Ronald Inglehart, "Aggregate Stability and Individual-Level Flux in Mass Belief Systems," *American Political Science Review,* 79(1) (1985): 97–116.

11. Richard Parker, "The Media Knowledge and Reporting of Financial Issues," presentation at the Brookings-Wharton Conference on Financial Services, Brookings Institution, Washington, D.C., October 22, 1998.

12. James T. Hamilton, *All the News That's Fit to Sell: How the Market Transforms Information into News* (Princeton, N.J.: Princeton University Press, 2004).

13. Data courtesy Mitchell Zacks of Zacks Investment Research. According to a *Business Week* article, the change is even more dramatic: in mid-1983, fully 26.8% were sells, 24.5% were buys, and 48.7% were holds. See Jeffrey Laderman, "Wall Street's Spin Game," *Business Week,* October 5, 1998, p. 148.

14. See Hsiou-Wei Lin and Maureen F. McNichols, "Underwriting Relationships, Analysts' Earnings Forecasts and Investment Recommendations," *Journal of Accounting and Economics,* 25(1) (1998): 101–27.

15. See James Grant, "Talking Up the Market," *Financial Times,* July 19, 1999, p. 12. Nevertheless, the analysts' recommendations are still useful if we take account of this bias. Kent Womack ("Do Brokerage Analysts' Recommendations Have Investment Value?" *Journal of Finance,* 51[1] [1996]: 137–67) shows that when analysts' recommendations are switched from hold to buy, the stock does tend to do well afterward, indicating that analysts do have some ability to predict the stocks' returns. When recommendations are switched from hold to sell, the event is even more accurately predictive (of poorer return). Womack interprets this asymmetric effect as indicating that because analysts are reluctant to issue sell recommendations, they do so only when there is a very good reason.

16. See Steven Sharpe, "Re-examining Stock Valuation and Inflation: The Implications of Analysts' Earnings Forecasts," *Review of Economics and Statistics,* 84(4) (2002): 632–48, Figure 2, p. 637. Earnings forecasts are from I/B/E/S and are aggregated from forecasts for individual firms to forecasts of the S&P 500. Sharpe's results do not give any clear evidence that the bias in earnings forecasts has increased since 1979. Moreover, a relatively small number of failures to predict extreme negative accruals accounts for a good part of the average bias. See Jeffrey Abarbanell and Reuven Lehavy, "Biased Forecasts or Biased Earnings? The Role of Earnings Management in Explaining Apparent Optimism and Inefficiency in Analysts' Earnings Forecasts," *Journal of Accounting and Economics,* 35 (2003): 105–46.

17. Public perception of such a downward bias encouraged in the 1990s the proliferation on the Internet of "whisper numbers": earnings forecasts with no attributed sources from analysts who could freely indulge, due to their anonymity, in their

doubts. On the other hand, the term *whisper numbers* was also applied to some even more extravagant upwardly biased forecasts that firms did not want to go on the record for making, fearing the reputational consequences later of being seen as having made such errors on the optimistic side. The decline in public interest in whisper numbers after 2000 and a renewed public interest in them in 2003 has been interpreted as a sign of the decline of, and then rise in, irrational exuberance. See Matt Kranz, "Earnings Whispers Return," *USA Today,* July 22, 2003.

18. Steven A. Sharpe, "How Does the Market Interpret Analysts' Long-Term Growth Forecasts?" *Journal of Accounting, Auditing and Finance* 20(2) (Spring 2005): 147–66, quote on p. 148.

19. Armen Hovakimian and Ekkachai Saenyasin, "U.S. Analyst Regulation and the Earnings Forecast Bias around the World," *European Financial Management* 20 (3) (June 2014): 435–61.

20. The tax shelter was written into the Internal Revenue Act of 1978 under Section 401(k), but its applicability to company pension plans was not then clear. R. Theodore Benna, executive vice-president of the Johnson Companies, an employee benefits consulting firm, tested the IRS by creating the first 401(k) plan in 1981. The IRS announced in February 1982 that the tax benefits of such plans would be allowed.

21. See New York Stock Exchange, *The Public Speaks to the Exchange Community* (New York, 1955).

22. Shlomo Benartzi and Richard H. Thaler, "Naive Diversification Strategies in Defined Contribution Plans," *American Economic Review,* 91(1) (2001): 79–98. Some faults in the Benartzi-Thaler paper have been identified by Gur Huberman and Wei Jiang "Offering versus Choice in 401(k) Plans: Equity Exposure and Number of Funds," unpublished paper, Columbia University, 2004.

23. Investment Company Institute, *Mutual Fund Fact Book* (Washington, D.C., 1999), http://www.ici.org.

24. See Hugh Bullock, *The Story of Investment Companies* (New York: Columbia University Press, 1959).

25. See Rudolph Weissman, *The Investment Company and the Investor* (New York: Harper and Brothers, 1951), p. 144.

26. Indeed, the flow of investment dollars into mutual funds seems to bear an important relation to market performance, as mutual fund inflows show an immediate and substantial reaction when the stock market goes up. See Vincent A. Warther, "Aggregate Mutual Fund Flows and Security Returns," *Journal of Financial Economics,* 39 (1995): 209–35; and William Goetzmann and Massimo Massa, "Index Fund Investors," unpublished paper, Yale University, 1999.

27. See my article "Why Do People Dislike Inflation?" in Christina D. Romer and David H. Romer (eds.), *Reducing Inflation: Motivation and Strategy* (Chicago: University of Chicago Press and National Bureau of Economic Research, 1997), pp. 13–65.

28. See Modigliani and Cohn, "Inflation, Rational Valuation, and the Market"; see also Robert J. Shiller and Andrea Beltratti, "Stock Prices and Bond Yields: Can Their Comovements Be Explained in Terms of Present Value Models?" *Journal of Monetary Economics,* 30 (1992): 25–46.

29. Modigliani and Cohn also argued (and this is a more subtle point) that people fail to take account of a bias in measured corporate profits due to the fact that corporations deduct from their profits the total interest paid on their debt, and not just the real (inflation-corrected) interest. In inflationary times, part of this interest paid may be viewed merely as a prepayment of part of the real debt, rather than as a cost to the company. Few investors realize this and make corrections for this effect of inflation. Their failure to do so may be described as another example of money illusion. Jay R. Ritter and Richard S. Warr ("The Decline of Inflation and the Bull Market of 1982–1997," *Journal of Financial and Quantitative Analysis* 37[1] [2002]: 29–61) have shown that market misvaluation of individual firms is related both to the level of inflation and to the degree of firm leverage, thus offering evidence in support of the Modigliani-Cohn theory.

30. Public misunderstandings of inflation are described in Eldar Shafir, Peter Diamond, and Amos Tversky, "Money Illusion," *Quarterly Journal of Economics,* 112(2) (1997): 341–74; and Robert J. Shiller, "Public Resistance to Indexation: A Puzzle."

31. *New York Stock Exchange Fact Book* (New York, 1998), http://www.nyse.com. Data on shares traded show an even more dramatic increase, but this increase is substantially due to inflation and the increase in the market value, which together encourage splits and therefore an increase in the total number of shares outstanding.

32. See Gretchen Morgenson, "Investing's Longtime Best Bet Is Being Trampled by the Bulls," *New York Times,* January 15, 2000, p. 1.

33. U.S. Securities and Exchange Commission, "Special Study: On-Line Brokerage: Keeping Apace of Cyberspace," 1999, http://www.sec.gov/pdf/ cybrtrnd.pdf.

34. See Kenneth R. French and Richard Roll, "Stock Return Variances: The Arrival of Information and the Reaction of Traders," *Journal of Financial Economics,* 17 (1986): 5–26; see also Richard Roll, "Orange Juice and Weather," *American Economic Review,* 74 (1984): 861–80.

35. See Shlomo Benartzi and Richard H. Thaler, "Myopic Loss Aversion and the Equity Premium Puzzle," *Quarterly Journal of Economics,* 110(1) (1995): 73–92.

36. As Abbott and Volberg have written, "There can be little doubt that the last two decades of the Twentieth Century have been marked by substantial increases in the availability and acceptability of commercial gambling." Max Wenden Abbott and Rachel A. Volberg, *Gambling and Problem Gambling in the Community: An International Overview and Critique,* Report No. 1 of the New Zealand Gaming Survey, 1999, p. 35.

37. Author's calculations from numbers quoted in Craig Lambert, "Trafficking in Chance," *Harvard Magazine,* 104(6) (July–August 2002): 32.

38. John W. Welte et al. "Gambling Participation in the United States—Results from a National Survey," *Journal of Gambling Studies,* 18(4) (2002): 313–37.

39. Eugene Martin Christiansen and Sebastian Sinclair, *The Gross Annual Wager of the United States, 2000,* Christiansen Capital Advisors, 2000, p. 2.

40. See also William N. Thompson, *Legalized Gambling: A Reference Handbook* (Santa Barbara, Calif.: ABC-CLIO, 1994), pp. 52–53.

41. Quantitative evidence on gambling behavior is hard to come by for the 1920s. I counted the number of articles about gambling in the *Reader's Guide to Periodical Literature* and reported the percentage of all articles on the subject, as follows (where I and II denote the first and second halves of the year 1938, respectively):

1919–21	0%
1922–24	0.004%
1925–28	0.021%
1929–32	0.035%
1933–35	0.006%
1936–38-I	0.003%
1938-II–42	0.008%

These numbers do strongly suggest a sudden and temporary surge in public interest in gambling between 1925 and 1932, but of course they do not convey anything qualitatively about the nature of changed public attitudes toward gambling. For a history of gambling and its relation to speculation, see James Grant, *The Trouble with Prosperity: A Contrarian Tale of Boom, Bust, and Speculation* (New York: John Wiley and Sons, 1996).

42. George W. Bush campaign speech in Onalaska, Wisconsin, October 26, 2004, http://www.presidentialrhetoric.com/campaign/speeches/bush_oct26.html.

43. The idea that private property improves incentives goes back to Adam Smith. That private property creates committed citizens is an ancient tradition. These old ideas are gaining more respectability in recent years. See, for example, William A. Fischel, *The Homevoter Hypothesis: How Home Values Influence Local Government Taxation, School Finance, and Land-Use Policies* (Cambridge, Mass.: Harvard University Press, 2001).

44. On the same questionnaire we asked: "Has this worry about your income encouraged you to buy a house, or to buy a bigger house or a house with more land?" While 81% of the 414 respondents said it had had no effect on their decision to purchase a house, those who said it had encouraged them outnumbered those who said it had discouraged them, by two to one.

45. Data on personal savings are from the U.S. National Income and Product Accounts, Table 5.1. Data on asset growth are from Tables B100 and B100e of the Flow of Funds Accounts of the United States.

46. Nell Henderson, "Greenspan Credits Economy's 'Flexibility'; Federal Reserve Chairman Says Free Market Helps Absorb Shocks" [final edition], *Washington Post*, September 28, 2005.

47. See Adam S. Posen, "It Takes More than a Bubble to Become Japan," Washington, D.C.: Peterson Institute for International Economics, Working Paper No. 03-9, October 2003. http://www.piie.com/publications/wp/03-9.pdf.

48. See question X4 in Survey Research Center, University of Michigan, "Index Calculations," http://www.sca.isr.umich.edu/fetchdoc.php?docid=24770.

49. http://som.yale.edu/faculty-research/our-centers-initiatives/international -center-finance/data/stock-market-confidence-indices/stock-market-confidence -indices. For other stock market confidence indices, see Robert J. Shiller, "Measuring Bubble Expectations and Investor Confidence," *Journal of Psychology and Markets*, 1(1) (2000): 49–60.

50. William H. Gross, "On the 'Course' to a New Normal," http://www.pimco.com/ EN/Insights/Pages/Gross%20Sept%20On%20the%20Course%20to%20a%20New%20 Normal.aspx.

51. Mario Bollini, Jennifer Barry, and Daniela Rus, "BakeBot: Baking Cookies with the PR2," http://web.mit.edu/mbollini/Public/icra/Bakebot.pdf.

52. Robert E. Lucas, "Asset Prices in an Exchange Economy," *Econometrica*, 46 (1978): 1429–45.

53. See, for example, Fareed Zakaria, "Around the World a Dark Nationalism Threatens Peace," http://www.dispatch.com/content/stories/editorials/2014/07/08/around-the-world-a-dark-nationalism-threatens-peace.html.

54. Thomas Piketty, *Capital in the Twenty-First Century* (Cambridge, Mass.: Belknap Press of Harvard University Press), 2014, Figure 8.8, p. 300.

55. See Jeremy J. Siegel, *Stocks for the Long Run*, 5th ed. (New York: McGraw-Hill, 2014), pp. 252–53.

56. The capitalist explosion, cultural changes lending more prestige to business success, expanded media reporting of financial news, analysts' increasingly optimistic forecasts, the decline of inflation, and the expansion of the volume of stock market trades are all factors in Europe, though often not as strongly felt as in the United States. Although Europe had less of a post–World War II Baby Boom than the United States, it did have a pronounced Baby Bust after the mid-1960s. Europe does not appear to show the same increase in gambling opportunities evident in the United States. Nevertheless, even though not all of the precipitating factors are operative in Europe, the strong cultural connections between the United States and Europe, and the effects of U.S. investors' demand for European stocks, should cause a substantial contagion effect.

Chapter Five   Amplification Mechanisms: Naturally Occurring Ponzi Processes

1. Although not explicitly stated there, allusions to the feedback theory can be found in Charles MacKay's *Memoirs of Extraordinary Popular Delusions and the Madness of Crowds* (London: Bentley), written in 1841. MacKay wrote of the tulip mania: "Many individuals suddenly grew rich. A golden bait hung temptingly out before the people, and one after another, they rushed to the tulip marts, like flies around a honey-pot" (p. 146). There is also a suggestion of the feedback theory in an anonymous pamphlet written during the tulip mania in Holland, *Samen-Spraeck tusschen Waermondt ende Gaergoedt nopende de opkomste ende ondergangh van flora* (Haerlem: Adriaen Roman, 1637). This pamphlet describes the contagious enthusiasm spurred by observing others' successes, which brought increasing numbers of people into the market.

2. The sample size *n* varies across questions because of different mailing sizes and response rates. The standard errors for the percentages, for this and other questions reported in this chapter, range from 1% to 4%. Of course, it is conceivable that the results are unreliable for reasons other than sample size; for example, those who chose to answer the questionnaire might be more likely than others to feel confident about the stock market. On the other hand, those who answer the questionnaire are more likely to be the kind of active investors who influence markets, and so the respondents may be more representative of the investors who are behind the stock market boom than would be a truly random group of wealthy respondents.

3. Words that respondents use most often to describe their thoughts about home prices are typically simple, timeless clichés, whose frequency varies through time. See

Karl E. Case Jr. and Robert J. Shiller, "The Behavior of Home Buyers in Boom and Post-Boom Markets," *New England Economic Review,* November–December 1988, pp. 29–46.

4. I did not ask on the questionnaire whether they thought the market would surely go down, but available data on expectations show that most did not think so around the peak of the market in 2000.

5. Frederick Lewis Allen, *Only Yesterday* (New York: Harper and Brothers, 1931), p. 309.

6. David Elias, *Dow 40,000: Strategies for Profiting from the Greatest Bull Market in History* (New York: McGraw-Hill, 1999), p. 8.

7. Dwight R. Lee and Richard B. MacKenzie, "How to (Really) Get Rich in America," *USA Weekend,* August 13–15, 1999, p. 6.

8. Samuel Crowther, "Everybody Ought to Be Rich: An Interview with John J. Raskob," *Ladies Home Journal,* August 1929, pp. 9, 36.

9. Of course, for the majority of people who are saving too little, any encouragement to save more, even if it is couched in terms of exaggerated investment optimism, is generally a good thing.

10. Bodo Schäfer, *Der Weg zur finanziellen Freiheit: In sieben Jahren die erste Million* (Frankfurt: Campus Verlag, 1999); Bernd Niquet, *Keine Angst vorm nächsten Crash: Warum Aktien als Langfristanlage unschlagbar sind* (Frankfurt: Campus Verlag, 1999).

11. See David E. Bell, "Regret in Decision Making under Uncertainty," *Operations Research,* 30(5) (1982): 961–81; and Graham Loomes and Robert Sugden, "Regret Theory: An Alternative Theory of Rational Choice under Uncertainty," *Economic Journal,* 92 (1982): 805–24.

12. Nassim N. Taleb, *Fooled by Randomness: The Hidden Role of Chance in Life and in the Markets,* 2nd ed. (New York: Texere, 2004).

13. See Richard H. Thaler and Eric J. Johnson, "Gambling with the House Money and Trying to Break Even: The Effect of Prior Outcomes on Risky Choice," *Management Science,* 36 (1990): 643–60.

14. John Kenneth Galbraith, *The Great Crash: 1929,* 2nd ed. (Boston: Houghton Mifflin, 1961), p. 79.

15. Data from the National Association of Investors Corporation website, http://www.better-investing.org/member/history.html.

16. "Fun Fades at Investing Clubs," E. S. Browning, *Wall Street Journal,* February 3, 2013, http://search.proquest.com/abicomplete/docview/1283594060/57D6C1EBE49C4575PQ/1?accountid=15172.

17. Brad M. Barber and Terrance Odean, "Online Investors: Do the Slow Die First?" *Review of Financial Studies,* 15(2) (2002): 455–89.

18. A psychological theory rationale for such feedback is offered by Nicholas Barberis, Andrei Shleifer, and Robert Vishny, "A Model of Investor Sentiment," *Journal of Financial Economics,* 49 (1998): 307–43.

19. Economists John Campbell and John Cochrane have proposed a theory of habit formation that may also serve to amplify stock market responses. In their model, people become slowly habituated to the higher level of consumption that they can expect from a more highly valued stock market. After a stock market increase, investors may be newly experimenting with higher consumption levels, but not yet habituated to them.

Investors who have made profits in the market may be willing to take more risks, because they still feel they could give up the higher consumption level if investment losses forced them to do so. Again, their willingness to hold stocks at higher prices may amplify the effects of the precipitating factors. See John Y. Campbell and John H. Cochrane, "By Force of Habit: A Consumption-Based Explanation of Aggregate Stock Market Behavior," *Journal of Political Economy*, 107(2) (1999): 205–51.

20. See Karl E. Case, John M. Quigley, and Robert J. Shiller, "Comparing Wealth Effects: The Stock Market vs. the Housing Market," Working Paper No. 8606 (Cambridge, Mass.: National Bureau of Economic Research, November 2001).

21. See Robert J. Shiller, "Market Volatility and Investor Behavior," *American Economic Review*, 80 (1990): 58–62; and Shiller, *Market Volatility*, pp. 376–77.

22. Some economic theorists claim that negative bubbles cannot occur, since prices have a floor at zero; therefore investors know that price cannot fall forever, and they should figure out by backward induction that a negative bubble cannot even get started. But what they mean to say is that bubbles cannot occur when everyone is rational and calculating—and when everyone assumes that everyone else is rational and calculating.

23. The literature on applications of chaos theory to economics usually does not stress the kind of price feedback model discussed here, but it may nonetheless offer some insights into the sources of complexity in financial markets. See Michael Boldrin and Michael Woodford, "Equilibrium Models Displaying Endogenous Fluctuations and Chaos: A Survey," *Journal of Monetary Economics*, 25(2) (1990): 189–222, for a survey of this literature. See also Benoit Mandelbrot, *Fractals and Scaling in Finance: Discontinuity, Concentration, Risk* (New York: Springer-Verlag, 1997); and Brian Arthur et al., "Asset Pricing under Endogenous Expectations in an Artificial Stock Market," in W. B. Arthur, S. Durlauf, and D. Lane (eds.), *The Economy as an Evolving Complex System II* (Reading, Mass.: Addison-Wesley, 1997). Another related literature sets up experimental markets in which people trade in an environment that is designed so that there is no news or other confounding factors. In these controlled circumstances there tend to be extraneous "bubble" price movements; see Vernon L. Smith, Gary L. Suchanek, and Arlington W. Williams, "Bubbles, Crashes and Endogenous Expectations in Experimental Spot Asset Markets," *Econometrica*, 56 (1988): 1119–51.

24. Lauren R. Rublin, "Party On! America's Portfolio Managers Grow More Bullish on Stocks and Interest Rates," *Barron's*, May 3, 1999, pp. 31–38.

25. Individuals were not surveyed between 1989 and 1996 and between 1996 and 1999. The index is a six-month moving average of monthly surveys starting in 2001.

26. See Joseph Bulgatz, *Ponzi Schemes, Invaders from Mars, and Other Extraordinary Popular Delusions, and the Madness of Crowds* (New York: Harmony, 1992), p. 13.

27. Mike Hinman, "World Plus Pleas: Guilty, Guilty," *Anchorage Daily News*, July 1, 1998, p. 1F; and Bill Richards, "Highflying Ponzi Scheme Angers and Awes Alaskans," *Wall Street Journal*, August 13, 1998, p. B1.

28. John Templeman, "Pyramids Rock Albania," *Business Week*, February 10, 1997, p. 59.

29. Kerin Hope, "Pyramid Finance Schemes," *Financial Times*, February 19, 1997, p. 3; and Jane Perlez, "Albania Calls an Emergency as Chaos Rises," *New York Times*, March 3, 1997, p. A1.

30. Jane Perlez, "Albanians, Cash-Poor, Scheming to Get Rich," *New York Times*, October 27, 1996, p. A9.

31. This willingness to believe may be related to the human tendency for over-confidence discussed in Chapter 9; see also Steven Pressman, "On Financial Frauds and Their Causes: Investor Overconfidence," *American Journal of Economics and Sociology*, 57 (1998): 405–21.

32. Charles P. Kindleberger, *Manias, Panics and Crashes: A History of Financial Crises*, 2nd ed. (London: Macmillan, 1989), p. 90.

33. Rakesh Khurana, *Searching for a Corporate Savior: The Irrational Quest for Charismatic CEOs* (Princeton, N.J.: Princeton University Press, 2002).

34. The term *no-Ponzi condition* has entered the vocabulary of theoretical finance; however, it refers not to feedback loops but instead to an assumption in their models that investors cannot go deeper and deeper into debt forever.

35. See Karl E. Case and Robert J. Shiller ("Is There a Bubble in the Housing Market?" *Brookings Papers on Economic Activity*, 2 [2003]: 299–362) for further discussion.

Chapter Six   The News Media

1. No doubt there were speculative price movements before there were newspapers, but I have found no pre-newspaper accounts of widespread public attention to speculative price movements that are described by contemporaries as wild and inexplicable or as due solely to investors' exuberance.

The first regularly published newspapers appeared in the early 1600s. Once publishers discovered how to generate public interest, increase circulation, and make a profit, papers sprung up rapidly in many European cities.

We might date the beginning of the mass media somewhat earlier, to the invention of printing itself, when publication became no longer dependent on patrons. Innumerable pamphlets, broadsides, and religious and political tracts were printed during the 1500s. Historian of printing David Zaret (*Origins of Democratic Culture: Printing, Petitions, and the Public Sphere in Early-Modern England* [Princeton, N.J.: Princeton University Press, 1999], p. 136) notes that "printing put commerce squarely at the center of textual production. Unlike that of scribal production, the economics of text production increasingly involved calculation, risk taking, and other market behaviors in which printers oriented production to vague estimations of popular demand for printed texts." The advent of printing brought with it an increased incentive for literacy; by the 1600s many if not most urban people in Europe could read.

Histories of speculative manias, such as Kindleberger, *Manias, Panics and Crashes*, give no examples of speculative bubbles before the 1600s, and my polling of local historians provided none either. However, I cannot claim to have researched their history exhaustively.

Indeed there are probably some stories that *could* be regarded as an exception to my generalization about the coincidence of the first manias and the first newspapers, although other interpretations are also possible. Yale historian Paul Freedman offered me the example of pepper as a possible exception: its price in the spice trade seems at times to have been surprisingly high, and in the 1500s it was very volatile. There are ancient and medieval examples of grain prices soaring at times of famine. Land price movements were also remarked in history. For example, in a letter to Nepos around A.D. 95, Pliny the Younger writes, "Have you heard that the price of land has gone up, particularly in the neighborhood of Rome? The reason for the sudden increase in price has given rise to a good deal of discussion." (Pliny the Younger, *Letters and Panegyrics*, trans. Betty Radice [Cambridge, Mass.: Harvard University Press, 1969], Book 6, No. 19, pp. 437–38.) By saying that there was much discussion, he is suggesting word-of-mouth effects, but he really does not tell a mania story.

2. The tulip mania, a speculative bubble in the price of tulips in Holland in the 1630s, was discussed in Chapter 5, note 1.

There were Dutch newspapers by 1618, and Holland, in contrast to other countries at the time, allowed the printing of domestic news, not just foreign news. On these pioneering Dutch newspapers, see Robert W. Desmond, *The Information Process: World News Reporting to the Twentieth Century* (Iowa City: University of Iowa Press, 1978).

The primary surviving source of information about the tulip mania is a pamphlet published in Holland during its peak. The anonymous 1637 document, in the form of a dialogue between two men, gives detailed news of the speculation as it was then unfolding. Numerous other pamphlets about the mania, published just after its end, also survive; see Peter Garber, *Famous First Bubbles: The Fundamentals of Early Manias* (Cambridge, Mass.: MIT Press, 2000). These surviving pamphlets confirm the existence of well-developed print media capable of disseminating information about the tulip mania as it happened.

3. "Why Property Ladder Is Having a Recession Refit," *The Telegraph*, June 4, 2009. http://www.telegraph.co.uk/culture/tvandradio/5446569/Why-Property-Ladder-is -having-a-recession-refit.html.

4. Transcript 3143, *MacNeil/Lehrer NewsHour*, WNET/Thirteen, New York, October 14, 1987, p. 10.

5. Victor Niederhoffer, "The Analysis of World News Events and Stock Prices," *Journal of Business*, 44(2) (1971): 205; see also David Cutler, James Poterba, and Lawrence Summers, "What Moves Stock Prices?" *Journal of Portfolio Management*, 15(3) (1989): 4–12.

6. Robert J. Shiller and William J. Feltus, "Fear of a Crash Caused the Crash," *New York Times*, October 29, 1989, Section 3, p. 3.

7. Cutler, Poterba, and Summers, "What Moves Stock Prices?" p. 10.

8. That is, there is none unless one counts as substantial President Dwight Eisenhower's heart attack on September 26, 1955.

9. "The Tokyo Earthquake: Not 'If' but 'When,'" *Tokyo Business Today*, April 1995, p. 8.

10. David Santry, "The Long-Shot Choice of a Gambling Guru," *Business Week*, May 12, 1980, p. 112; "The Prophet of Profits," *Time*, September 15, 1980, p. 69.

11. Professors Gur Huberman and Tomer Regev of Columbia University wrote a case study of the soaring price of an individual company's stock in response to a newspaper story that, while compellingly written, actually revealed no news. The share price of EntreMed rose from 12 to 85 from the close of the market the day before to its opening on the day of a front-page *New York Times* story that described the potential of the company's drugs to cure cancer. They document that every fact in the story had already been published five months earlier. (See Gur Huberman and Tomer Regev, "Speculating on a Cure for Cancer: A Non-Event That Made Stock Prices Soar," *Journal of Finance*, 56(1) (2001): 387–96.) It is plausible—although the authors do not document

this—that many of the buyers of EntreMed shares on that day knew there was no news in the story, but merely bought thinking that a story that was so well written and featured so prominently would boost the share price.

12. (New Orleans) *Times-Picayune,* October 29, 1929, p. 1, col. 8; *New York Times,* October 29, 1929, p. 1; *Wall Street Journal,* October 29, 1929, p. 1, col. 2.

13. Jude Wanniski, *The Way the World Works,* 2nd ed. (New York: Simon and Schuster, 1983), Chapter 7.

14. Allan H. Meltzer, "Monetary and Other Explanations of the Start of the Great Depression," *Journal of Monetary Economics,* 2 (1976): 460.

15. Rudiger Dornbusch and Stanley Fischer, "The Open Economy: Implications for Monetary and Fiscal Policy," in Robert J. Gordon (ed.), *The American Business Cycle: Continuity and Change* (Chicago: National Bureau of Economic Research and University of Chicago Press, 1986), pp. 459–501.

16. *New York Times,* October 28, 1929, p. 1.

17. *Wall Street Journal,* October 28, 1929, p. 1.

18. O. A. Mather, *Chicago Tribune,* October 27, 1929, p. A1; *New York Times,* October 25, 1929, p. 1, col. 8; *Guaranty Survey* quoted in *New York Times,* October 28, 1929, p. 37, col. 3.

19. The mailing list for individual investors was a list of high-income active investors (active as indicated by such characteristics as subscriptions to investment publications and maintaining accounts with stock brokers) purchased from W. S. Ponton, Inc. The list for institutional investors was compiled from a random sample from the investment managers section of *The Money Market Directory of Pension Funds and Their Investment Managers.* A total of 3,000 questionnaires were sent out during the week of October 19, 1987: 2,000 to the individual investors and 1,000 to the institutional investors. There were no follow-up mailings or reminders. I received 605 completed responses from individual investors and 284 completed responses from institutional investors. See Shiller, *Market Volatility,* pp. 379–402, for the analysis of the results that I wrote in November 1987. We also did a study of Japanese institutional investors in 1987 that confirmed that their stock market action was primarily in response to news from the United States. See Robert J. Shiller, Fumiko Kon-Ya, and Yoshiro Tsutsui, "Investor Behavior in the October 1987 Stock Market Crash: The Case of Japan," *Journal of the Japanese and International Economies,* 5 (1991): 1–13.

20. Of course, since the questionnaire was filled out *after* the crash, part of this reported concern with overpricing may have been due to hindsight bias. Indeed we cannot completely trust even the self-categorization, into buyers versus sellers on October 19, that respondents made on the questionnaire. The anonymity of the questionnaires, the plea for truthfulness, and the stated purpose of the questionnaire as a tool for scientific research on the crash should all have helped to provide us with more nearly objective answers, but of course no survey results can be trusted completely.

21. Presidential Task Force on Market Mechanisms, *Report of the Presidential Task Force on Market Mechanisms* (Brady Commission Report) (Washington, D.C.: U.S. Government Printing Office, 1988), p. v.

22. Mark L. Mitchell and Jeffrey M. Netter ("Triggering the 1987 Stock Market Crash: Antitakeover Provisions in the Proposed House Ways and Means Tax Bill," *Journal of Financial Economics,* 24 [1989]: 37–68) argue that the news did have an immediate impact on some stocks. It is possible that this news served as a trigger for the crash,

as the Brady Commission concludes, by generating initial price decreases, even if the news had been largely forgotten by the day of the crash.

23. Hayne Leland, "Who Should Buy Portfolio Insurance," *Journal of Finance,* 35 (1980): 582.

24. See Robert J. Shiller, "Portfolio Insurance and Other Investor Fashions as Factors in the 1987 Stock Market Crash," in *NBER Macroeconomics Annual* (Cambridge, Mass.: National Bureau of Economic Research, 1988), pp. 287–95.

25. "Repeating the 1920s? Some Parallels but Some Contrasts," *Wall Street Journal,* October 19, 1987, p. 15. This plot was in a box measuring some five inches by ten inches, associated with a story on the same page by Cynthia Crossen, "Market Slide Has Analysts Eating Crow; Justification of Summer Rally Questioned."

26. See Robert K. Merton, *Social Theory and Social Structure.* Glencoe, Ill.: Free Press, 1957.

Chapter Seven   New Era Economic Thinking

1. Dean Foust, "Alan Greenspan's Brave New World," *Business Week,* July 14, 1997, pp. 44–50.

2. Aaron Zitner, "Shhhh, Listen: Could That Be the Ghosts of '29?" *Boston Globe,* June 22, 1997, p. E1; Peter Gosselin, "Dow at 10,000: Don't Laugh Yet," *Boston Globe,* June 22, 1997, p. E1; and Paul Krugman, "How Fast Can the U.S. Economy Grow?" *Harvard Business Review,* 75 (1997): 123–29.

3. A Nexis search on *new era economics* produced forty-eight stories, all of which included the words *stock market.*

4. See George Katona, *Psychological Economics* (New York: Elsevier, 1975).

5. Alexander Dana Noyes, *Forty Years of American Finance* (New York: G. P. Putnam's Sons, 1909), pp. 300–301.

6. *Boston Post,* January 1, 1901, p. 3.

7. Thomas Fleming, *Around the Pan with Uncle Hank: His Trip through the Pan-American Exposition* (New York: Nutshell, 1901), p. 50.

8. "A Booming Stock Market: Strength of the Underlying Conditions," *New York Daily Tribune,* April 6, 1901, p. 3.

9. A. A. Housman, "Reasons for Confidence," *New York Times,* May 26, 1901, p. v.

10. Allen, *Only Yesterday,* p. 315.

11. Tracy J. Sutliff, "Revival in All Industries Exceeds Most Sanguine Hopes," *New York Herald Tribune,* January 2, 1925, p. 1.

12. John Moody, "The New Era in Wall Street," *Atlantic Monthly,* August 1928, p. 260.

13. Charles Amos Dice, *New Levels in the Stock Market* (New York: McGraw-Hill, 1929), pp. 75–183.

14. Irving Fisher, *The Stock Market Crash—and After* (New York: Macmillan, 1930), pp. 101–74.

15. Craig B. Hazelwood, "Buying Power Termed Basis for Prosperity," *New York Herald Tribune,* January 2, 1929, p. 31.

16. Quoted in *Commercial and Financial Chronicle,* March 9, 1929, p. 1444.

17. "Is 'New Era' Really Here?" *U.S. News and World Report,* May 20, 1955, p. 21.

18. "The Stock Market: Onward and Upward?" *Newsweek,* December 12, 1955, p. 59.

19. "The U.S. Prosperity Today," *Time*, November 28, 1955, p. 15.

20. "The Stock Market: Onward and Upward?" p. 59.

21. "Why Businessmen Are Optimistic," *U.S. News and World Report*, December 23, 1955, p. 18.

22. "Is 'New Era' Really Here?" p. 21.

23. "The New America," *Newsweek*, December 12, 1955, p. 58.

24. "Investors Bet on a Kennedy-Sparked Upturn," *Business Week*, February 4, 1961, p. 84; Dean S. Ammer, "Entering the New Economy," *Harvard Business Review* (1967), pp. 3–4.

25. "Investors Bet on a Kennedy-Sparked Upturn," p. 84; "The Bull Market," *Business Week*, March 18, 1961, p. 142.

26. "Battling Toward 900," *Business Week*, January 23, 1965, p. 26; "Year of the White Chips?" *Newsweek*, February 1, 1965, p. 57; "On Toward 1000," *Time*, January 14, 1966, p. 78.

27. E. S. Browning and Danielle Sessa, "Stocks Pass 10,000 before Slipping Back," *Wall Street Journal*, March 17, 1999, p. C1.

28. This is a geometric average real return on the S&P Composite Index.

29. Michael Mandel, "The Triumph of the New Economy," *Business Week*, December 30, 1996, pp. 68–70.

30. See Michael Bruno and William Easterly, "Inflation Crises and Long-Run Growth," *Journal of Monetary Economics*, 41(1) (1998): 2–26. There are of course complicated issues of timing to consider: a stock market might move down on news that inflation is likely to be higher in the future and then move up again gradually as consumer prices increase. Careful thought about such timing issues is too technical for most public discourse, and therefore the issue will most likely never be resolved in the popular mind (or, for that matter, definitively by economists).

31. Roger Bootle, *The Death of Inflation: Surviving and Thriving in the Zero Era* (London: Nicholas Brealey, 1998), pp. 27, 31.

32. Steven Weber, "The End of the Business Cycle?" *Foreign Affairs*, 76(4) (1997): 65–82.

33. See George Hager, "Productivity Rise Not So Stunning after All?" *USA Today*, August 7, 2001.

34. According to the dean of productivity researchers, Robert J. Gordon, U.S. productivity, after abstracting from short-run productivity changes associated with recessions, appears to have gone through one big wave since 1871. Productivity growth rates gradually rose from the late nineteenth century, growth rates peaked in the 1950s and 1960s, and then productivity growth rates gradually declined. Obviously the stock market has not gone through one big wave of this sort. See Gordon, Robert J., "U.S. Productivity Growth since 1879: One Big Wave?" *American Economic Review*, 89(2) (1999): 123–28.

35. "When the Shoeshine Boys Talk Stocks," *Fortune*, April 15, 1996, p. 99; *U.S. News and World Report*, July 14, 1997, p. 57; *Forbes*, May 18, 1998, p. 325; *Fortune*, June 22, 1998, p. 197.

36. See Glenn S. Dumke, *The Boom of the Eighties in Southern California* (San Marino, Calif.: Huntington Library, 1944), p. 49.

37. Dumke (*The Boom of the Eighties*, p. 260), who is in turn quoting Robert Glass Cleland, *History of Occidental College* (Los Angeles: Ward Ritchie Press, 1937, p. 4).

38. See Kenneth Ballinger, *Miami Millions: The Dance of the Dollars in the Great Florida Land Boom of 1925* (Miami, Fla.: Franklin Press, 1936).

39. Data are the home prices of the U.S. FHFA, deflated by the Consumer Price Index.

40. See William A. Fischel, *Regulatory Takings: Law, Economics and Politics* (Cambridge, Mass.: Harvard University Press, 1995).

41. Due-on-sale clauses were provisions that the mortgage had to be repaid when the home was sold, so that the purchaser could not just assume an old mortgage to get its lower rate. When a California savings and loan association in 1969 tried to enforce a due-on-sale clause to force repayment of the low-interest-rate mortgages of two California couples, the couples sued. The California State Supreme Court, in *Tucker v. Lassen Savings & Loan Association* (1974), ruled that due-on-sale clauses in mortgages were not enforceable unless the lender could show impairment of security. Other U.S. states' courts rendered similar decisions. This made it much easier to buy a house, but the other side of this was great stress on mortgage lenders, who strove to get the decisions overturned. This finally happened with the U.S. Supreme Court decision in *Fidelity Federal Saving and Loan Association v. de la Cuesta et al.* (1982).

42. Homeowners were offered "buy-downs" that deferred payment of part of the home purchase price for a few years, after which, many people hoped, mortgage rates would be much lower. High-interest-rate second or third mortgages on homes were sold by mortgage brokers to wealthy investors, many of whom apparently thought that they could cash in on the housing boom by investing in high-yield mortgages. By the early 1980s, when the housing boom faltered, many homeowners defaulted on these mortgages.

43. Karl E. Case, "The Market for Single-Family Homes in the Boston Area," *New England Economic Review*, May–June 1986, p. 47.

44. Economist Edward Glaeser, in his paper "Reinventing Boston: 1640 to 2003" (Working Paper No. 10166, Cambridge, Mass.: National Bureau of Economic Research, 2004), claims that there were some very important changes in the economy that took place then. He points out that Boston had been going through a long period of decline: from 1920 to 1980 Boston's population had fallen from 0.7% of the U.S. population to 0.25%, as its various manufacturing industries were lost to competitors far away. With such population decline, there was a surplus of old housing, some of it now priced below construction costs. As Glaeser argues, when a substantial amount of existing housing is priced in the market below construction costs, there will be relatively little supply response to increased demand, and so prices can rise very rapidly until home prices again surpass construction costs. A solid response in new construction did not come in Boston until well into the 1980s, and then there was overconstruction and a subsequent fall in home prices. See also Karl E. Case and Robert J. Shiller, "A Decade of Boom and Bust in the Prices of Single-Family Homes: Boston and Los Angeles 1983 to 1993," *New England Economic Review*, March–April 1994, pp. 40–51.

45. Quoting Jonathan Rotenberg, in Steven B. Kaufman, "Boston Mixes High Technology with Its Traditional Economy," *Washington Post*, June 30, 1985, p. G3, col. 4.

46. See Edward Glaeser and Albert Saiz, "The Rise of the Skilled City," Working Paper No. 10191 (Cambridge, Mass.: National Bureau of Economic Research, 2004).

47. Albert W. Atwood, "Vanished Millions: The Aftermath of a Great Bull Market," *Saturday Evening Post,* September 1921, p. 51.

48. Christina Romer, "The Great Crash and the Onset of the Great Depression," *Quarterly Journal of Economics,* 105 (1990): 597–624.

49. Oscar Lange, "Is the American Economy Contracting?" *American Economic Review,* 29(3) (1939): 503.

50. See Harvey Klehr, *The Heyday of American Communism: The Depression Decade* (New York: Basic Books, 1984).

51. Okun quoted in *Time,* January 14, 1974, p. 61; Burns quoted in *U.S. News and World Report,* June 10, 1974, p. 20.

52. See Bruno and Easterly, "Inflation Crises."

53. See John Cassidy, *Dot.con: How America Lost Its Mind and Money in the Internet Era* (New York: Perennial Currents, 2003).

54. Quoting Martyn Straw, in Andrew Hill, "Dotcom Fever Fades as Investors Seek Profits," *Financial Times,* April 29, 2000, p. 11.

55. See Jack Willoughby, "Burning Up: Warning: Internet Companies Are Running Out of Cash—Fast," *Barron's,* March 20, 2000, pp. 29–32.

56. By extension, many rituals that our society undertakes have the ultimate purpose of letting everyone know that everyone knows something; in this way the ritual can have fundamental social implications. See Michael Suk-Young Chwe, *Rational Ritual: Culture, Coordination, and Common Knowledge* (Princeton, N.J.: Princeton University Press, 2003).

57. See Hites Ahir and Prakash Loungani, 2014. "There Will Be Growth in the Spring: How Do Economists Predict Turning Points?" *Vox,* April 14, 2014, http://www.voxeu.org/article/predicting-economic-turning-points.

Chapter Eight   New Eras and Bubbles around the World

1. The data for thirty of the countries are from the International Monetary Fund, *International Financial Statistics.* The countries for which data start in January 1957 are Austria, Belgium, Canada, France, Germany, Finland, India, Italy, Japan, the Netherlands, Norway, the Philippines, South Africa, the United States, and Venezuela. The remaining countries from this data source and their starting dates are as follows: Brazil, August 1991; Chile, November 1978; Colombia, October 1963; Denmark, February 1969; Israel, November 1982; Jamaica, July 1969; Korea, January 1978; Luxembourg, January 1980; Mexico, July 1985; Pakistan, July 1960; Peru, September 1989; Portugal, January 1988; Spain, January 1961; Sweden, January 1976; and the United Kingdom, December 1957. The data for the other six countries are taken from Datastream, and their starting dates are as follows: Australia, March 1973; Hong Kong, July 1974; Indonesia, January 1996; Singapore, February 1986; Taiwan, January 1986; and Thailand, January 1984.

For each country, the monthly stock price index was divided by the consumer price index for the same month to produce a real stock price index. Changes in the real stock price index reported are largest month-to-month changes in the real indices over the intervals shown, excluding intervals that occurred within three years of each other. Periods of consumer price index inflation greater than 4% a month were excluded, since in times of high inflation inaccuracies of timing or calculation of the consumer price index could cause spurious jumps in stock price indices.

The tables also show, at the far right, the percentage change in the real stock price index for the period of the same length (twelve months or five years) starting in the month at which the period shown in the table ends. Thus, for example, reading from Table 8.1, we see that the Philippine stock market rose 683.4% in real (inflation-corrected) terms from December 1985 to December 1986, and rose another 28.4% from December 1986 to December 1987. For another example, reading from Table 8.4, we see that the Spanish stock market fell 86.6% in real (inflation-corrected) terms from December 1974 to December 1979 and then rose 0.1% from December 1979 to December 1984.

2. Note from the rightmost column of Table 8.2 that Korea had a stock price increase in 1999 that would have placed it again in Table 8.1 had 1999 fallen within our sample for Table 8.1.

3. "Casino Times: After 280% Increase This Year, Taiwan's Stock Market May Be Poised for a Plunge," *Asian Wall Street Journal Weekly,* October 12, 1987.

4. "Obsessed with Numbers, the Taiwanese Are Forsaking Work, Health and Sanity," *Asian Wall Street Journal Weekly,* September 14, 1987.

5. James Brooke, "Venezuela Isn't Exactly Wild for Another Boom," *New York Times,* September 2, 1990, p. IV.3.

6. Eugene Robinson, "As Venezuela Restructures, Even Gas Prices Must Rise," *Toronto Star,* May 21, 1990, p. C6.

7. "Bonanza for Bombay?" *Far Eastern Economic Review,* May 28, 1992, p. 48.

8. *La Repubblica,* quoted by Ruth Graber, "Milan Stock Market Has Gone to the Bulls," *Toronto Star,* May 25, 1986, p. F1.

9. Alan Friedman, "Milan's Bulls Run Wild: Italy's Stock Market Boom," *Financial Times,* March 25, 1986, p. I.25.

10. David Marsh, "The New Appetite for Enterprise: The French Bourse," *Financial Times,* July 4, 1984, p. I.14.

11. Even though the French bull market in the late 1990s was extraordinary, enthusiasm for the stock market did not seem to have invaded French culture as it did the American way of life. See J. Mo, "Despite Exceptional Performance, the Stock Market Does Not Attract the French," *Le Monde,* November 25, 1999, electronic edition.

12. Werner De Bondt and Richard H. Thaler, "Does the Stock Market Overreact?" *Journal of Finance,* 40(3) (1985): 793–805. See John Y. Campbell, Andrew Lo, and Craig Mackinlay, *The Econometrics of Financial Markets* (Princeton, N.J.: Princeton University Press, 1997), pp. 27–82, 253–89, for a survey of literature on serial correlation of returns.

13. To judge whether a large price increase (or decrease) portends future increases or decreases, it is tempting to try to use the results shown in the tables alone. One notes, for example, from Table 8.3 that of the twenty episodes whose large price increases occurred long enough ago that we can observe the subsequent five-year price change,

thirteen (65%) of the subsequent price changes were down, and the average real price change, averaging over all episodes shown in Table 8.3, was –10%. One notes, too, from Table 8.4, that of the twenty-one episodes whose large price decreases occurred long enough ago that we can observe the subsequent five-year real price change, sixteen (76%) were positive, and the average price increase, averaging over all the episodes shown in Table 8.4, was 130%.

However, there is a problem in interpreting these results as evidence that the markets can be predicted, since we used data subsequent to the five-year intervals shown in the tables to identify the five-year intervals as the largest.

Chapter Nine   *Psychological Anchors for the Market*

1. For a more comprehensive recent survey of the role of psychology in finance, see Hersh Shefrin, *Beyond Greed and Fear: Understanding Behavioral Finance and the Psychology of Investing* (Boston: Harvard Business School Press, 2000); or Andrei Shleifer, *Inefficient Markets: An Introduction to Behavioral Finance* (Oxford: Oxford University Press, 2000).

2. See Amos Tversky and Daniel Kahneman, "Judgment under Uncertainty: Heuristics and Biases," *Science*, 185 (1974): 1124–31.

3. See Robert J. Shiller, "Comovements in Stock Prices and Comovements in Dividends," *Journal of Finance*, 44 (1989): 719–29.

4. See Steven L. Heston and K. Geert Rouwenhorst, "Does Industrial Structure Explain the Benefits of International Diversification?" *Journal of Financial Economics*, 36 (1994): 3–27; John M. Griffin and G. Andrew Karolyi, "Another Look at the Role of the Industrial Structure of Markets for International Diversification Strategies," *Journal of Financial Economics*, 50 (1998): 351–73; and Kenneth Froot and Emil Dabora, "How Are Stock Prices Affected by the Location of Trade?" *Journal of Financial Economics*, 53(2) (1999): 189–216. Investor attention also appears to be attracted to countries with a common language, as anchoring theory would suggest; see Mark Grinblatt and Matti Keloharju, "Distance, Language, and Culture Bias: The Role of Investor Sophistication," *Journal of Finance*, 56(3) (2001): 1053–73.

5. See James D. Petersen and Cheng-Ho Hsieh, "Do Common Risk Factors in the Returns on Stocks and Bonds Explain Returns on REITs?" *Real Estate Economics*, 25 (1997): 321–45.

6. Nancy Pennington and Reid Hastie, "Reasoning in Explanation-Based Decision Making," *Cognition*, 49 (1993): 123–63.

7. See D. W. Bolen and W. H. Boyd, "Gambling and the Gambler: A Review of Preliminary Findings," *Archives of General Psychiatry*, 18(5) (1968): 617–29. Gambling provides stimulation and excitement, and people who are attracted to games of risk tend to be people who have a stronger inclination toward sensation seeking; see Marvin Zuckerman, Elizabeth Kolin, Leah Price, and Ina Zoob, "Development of a Sensation-Seeking Scale," *Journal of Consulting Psychology*, 28(6) (1964): 477–82; William F. Straub, "Sensation Seeking among High- and Low-Risk Male Athletes," *Journal of Sports Psychology*, 4(3) (1982): 243–53; and Helen Gilchrist, Robert Povey, Adrian Dickenson, and Rachel Povey, "The Sensation-Seeking Scale: Its Use in a Study of People Choosing Adventure Holidays," *Personality and Individual Differences*, 19(4) (1995): 513–16.

8. See Gideon Keren, "The Rationality of Gambling: Gamblers' Conceptions of Probability, Chance and Luck," in George Wright and Peter Ayton (eds.), *Subjective Probability* (Chichester, England: John Wiley and Sons, 1994), pp. 485–99.

9. See Shlomo Benartzi, Richard H. Thaler, Stephen P. Utkus, and Cass R. Sunstein, "The Law and Economics of Company Stock in 401(k) Plans," *Journal of Law and Economics,* 501(1) (2007): 45–79. See also Shlomo Benartzi, "Why Do Employees Invest Their Retirement Savings in Company Stock?" unpublished paper, Anderson School, University of California, Los Angeles, 1999. Benartzi finds that employee investment in company stock is strongly influenced by the return on the company stock over the past ten years. He shows that it is extremely rare for companies to offer discount incentives for employees to buy company stock, that employees freely make choices to invest in company stock, and that employee decisions to invest in company stock do not reflect superior employee information about the company, since the level of purchases does not predict returns on the stock in the future. A modest shift away from company stock holdings has been observed since 2006; see the Vanguard Group, Inc., "How America Saves 2013," https://pressroom.vanguard.com/content/nonindexed/2013.06.03_How_America_Saves_2013.pdf.

10. Eldar Shafir, Itamar Simonson, and Amos Tversky, "Reason-Based Choice," *Cognition,* 49 (1993): 11–36.

11. Thomas J. Stanley and William D. Danko, *The Millionaire Next Door: The Surprising Secrets of America's Wealthy* (New York: Pocket Books, 1996).

12. Baruch Fischhof, Paul Slovic, and Sarah Lichtenstein, "Knowing with Uncertainty: The Appropriateness of Extreme Confidence," *Journal of Experimental Psychology: Human Perception and Performance,* 3 (1977): 522–64.

13. See G. Gigerenzer, "How to Make Cognitive Illusion Disappear: Beyond 'Heuristic and Biases,'" *European Review of Social Psychology,* 2 (1991): 83–115.

14. See Gordon W. Pitz, "Subjective Probability Distributions for Imperfectly Known Quantities," in Lee W. Gregg (ed.), *Knowledge and Cognition* (Potomac, Md.: Lawrence Erlbaum Associates, 1975), pp. 29–41.

15. See Allan Collins, Eleanor Warnock, Nelleke Acello, and Mark L. Miller, "Reasoning from Incomplete Knowledge," in Daniel G. Bobrow and Allan Collins (eds.), *Representation and Understanding: Studies in Cognitive Science* (New York: Academic Press, 1975), pp. 383–415.

16. See Dagmar Strahlberg and Anne Maass, "Hindsight Bias: Impaired Memory or Biased Reconstruction," *European Review of Social Psychology,* 8 (1998): 105–32.

17. See E. J. Langer, "The Illusion of Control," *Journal of Personality and Social Psychology,* 32 (1975): 311–28; see also G. A. Quattrone and Amos Tversky, "Causal versus Diagnostic Contingencies: On Self-Deception and the Voter's Delusion," *Journal of Personality and Social Psychology,* 46(2) (1984): 237–48.

18. Tversky and Kahneman, "Judgment under Uncertainty."

19. Economists Nicholas Barberis, Andrei Shleifer, and Robert Vishny have developed the representativeness heuristic into a theory of investors' selective overconfidence and into a psychological theory of an expectational feedback loop. These authors argue that investors, when they see stock prices move in the same direction

for a while, gradually begin to assume that the trend is representative of many trends that they have seen in other economic data. According to a psychological principle of conservatism, people are slow to change their opinions. For this reason, it takes some time before investors begin to conclude that the trend will continue. The interplay between the representativeness heuristic and the principle of conservatism determines the speed at which the speculative feedback progresses. See Barberis, Shleifer, and Vishny, "A Model of Investor Sentiment." For further theoretical discussions about overconfidence and the stock market, see also Nicholas Barberis, Ming Huang, and Tano Santos, "Prospect Theory and Asset Prices," *Quarterly Journal of Economics,* 116 (2001): 1–53; Kent Daniel, David Hirshleifer, and Avanidhar Subrahmanyam, "Investor Psychology and Security Market Over- and Underreaction," *Journal of Finance,* 53(6) (1998): 1839–86; and Harrison Hong and Jeremy C. Stein, "A Unified Theory of Underreaction, Momentum Trading, and Overreaction in Asset Markets," *Journal of Finance,* 54(6) (1999): 2143–84.

20. Such ideas are formalized by Paul Milgrom and Nancy Stokey, "Information, Trade, and Common Knowledge," *Econometrica,* 49 (1982): 219–22; and John Geanakoplos, "Common Knowledge," *Journal of Economic Perspectives,* 6(4) (1992): 53–82.

21. Eldar Shafir and Amos Tversky, "Thinking through Uncertainty: Nonconsequential Reasoning and Choice," *Cognitive Psychology,* 24 (1992): 449–74.

Chapter Ten   Herd Behavior and Epidemics

1. Solomon Asch, *Social Psychology* (Englewood Cliffs, N.J.: Prentice Hall, 1952), pp. 450–501.

2. Morton Deutsch and Harold B. Gerard, "A Study of Normative and Informational Social Influences upon Individual Judgment," *Journal of Abnormal and Social Psychology,* 51 (1955): 629–36.

3. Stanley Milgram, *Obedience to Authority* (New York: Harper and Row, 1974), pp. 13–54.

4. Milgram noted that subjects believed that the experimenter was an expert who knew more than they did. When he tried a variation of the experiment in which the experimenter was clearly not an expert, he found a much-diminished tendency for subjects to administer the shocks (ibid., pp. 89–112). Nevertheless Milgram, like Asch, did not seem to be aware of an information-based interpretation for his results. He thought that they revealed an "instinct for obedience" that had developed from a general evolutionary principle of the "survival of value hierarchy" (ibid., pp. 123–25).

5. See S. D. Bikhchandani, David Hirshleifer, and Ivo Welch, "A Theory of Fashion, Social Custom and Cultural Change," *Journal of Political Economy,* 81 (1992): 637–54; and Abhijit V. Banerjee, "A Simple Model of Herd Behavior," *Quarterly Journal of Economics,* 107(3) (1992): 797–817.

6. See Christopher Avery and Peter Zemsky, "Multidimensional Uncertainty and Herd Behavior in Financial Markets," *American Economic Review,* 88(4) (1998): 724–48; and In Ho Lee, "Market Crashes and Informational Avalanches," *Review of Economic Studies,* 65(4) (1998): 741–60.

7. The respondents were drawn from a random sample of high-income individuals in the United States by Survey Sampling, Inc. We coded their answers into ten categories. The percentages of 131 respondents in each category were as follows: (1) friend or relative (13%), (2) worked for company (21%), (3) someone involved with company (3%), (4) broker (33%), (5) spinoff of successful company (2%), (6) IPO–publicity (2%), (7) periodicals–newspapers (6%), (8) customer of company (2%), (9) stock was inherited or a gift (2%), (10) performance of similar company (0%). The remaining answers could not be placed into categories. See Robert J. Shiller and John Pound, "Survey Evidence on the Diffusion of Interest and Information among Investors," *Journal of Economic Behavior and Organization,* 12 (1989): 47–66. If we repeated this study today, we would of course have to include television (which now has extensive business reporting) and the Internet on the list. In *Psychological Economics,* the psychologist-economist George Katona presented evidence that a process of repeated human interaction is needed to promote the kind of "social learning" that spurs people to take action. Robin Barlow and his colleagues found evidence similar to ours, that individual investors usually make decisions after conversations with others; see Robin Barlow, Harvey E. Brazer, and James N. Morgan, *Economic Behavior of the Affluent* (Washington, D.C.: Brookings Institution, 1966).

8. Amy Feldman and Bill Egbert, "Mess of an Invest: Little People in Big Trouble with 1.3 Million Scam," *New York Daily News,* May 27, 1999, p. 5.

9. See A. A. L. Reid, "Comparing Telephone with Face-to-Face Contact," in Ithiel de Sola Poole (ed.), *The Social Impact of the Telephone* (Cambridge, Mass.: MIT Press, 1977), pp. 386–414.

10. Clarence Day, "Father Lets in the Telephone," in *Life with Father* (New York: Alfred A. Knopf, 1935), p. 178.

11. Regarding securities fraud in the 1920s and contemporary legislation to limit it, see Emmanuel Stein, *Government and the Investor* (New York: Farrar and Reinhart, 1941).

12. See Norman T. Bailey, *The Mathematical Theory of Epidemics* (London: C. Griffin, 1957).

13. The logistic curve is $P = 1/(1 + e^{-rt})$, where P is the proportion of the population infected, r is the infection rate per unit of time, and t is time. This expression is a solution to the differential equation $dP/P = r(1 - P)dt$, and $(1 - P)$ is the proportion of the population that is susceptible to infection.

14. Alan Kirman, "Ants, Rationality and Recruitment," *Quarterly Journal of Economics,* 108(1) (1993): 137–56.

15. See David J. Bartholomew, *Stochastic Models for Social Processes* (New York: John Wiley and Sons, 1967).

16. Giorgio Vasari, *The Life of Leonardo da Vinci* (Longmans Green and Co., 1903), p. 35.

17. "'Mona Lisa' Thief Gets a Year in Jail," *New York Times,* June 6, 1914, p. 3.

18. See Tom Burnam, *More Misinformation* (Philadelphia: Lippincott and Crowell, 1980), pp. 20–21.

19. John Kenneth Galbraith laid to rest the suicide myth. The New York suicide rate did, however, rise during the 1930s with the advent of the Great Depression. See Galbraith, *The Great Crash: 1929*, pp. 132–37.

20. The sample sizes were 30 (control) and 40 (experimental); see Shiller and Pound, "Survey Evidence," p. 54.

21. See N. R. F. Maier, "Reasoning in Humans. II. The Solution of a Problem and Its Appearance in Consciousness," *Journal of Comparative Psychology,* 12 (1931): 181–94; see also Robert E. Nisbett and Timothy DeCamp Wilson, "Telling More than We Can Know: Verbal Reports on Mental Processes," *Psychological Review,* 84(3) (1977): 231–59.

Chapter Eleven   Efficient Markets, Random Walks, and Bubbles

1. See Eugene Fama, "Efficient Capital Markets: A Review of Theory and Empirical Work," *Journal of Finance,* 25 (1970): 383–417.

2. George Gibson, *The Stock Markets of London, Paris and New York* (New York: G. P. Putnam's Sons, 1889), p. 11. For a history of thought on efficient markets theory, see Robert J. Shiller, "From Efficient Markets Theory to Behavioral Finance," *Journal of Economic Perspectives,* 17 (2003): 83–104.

3. Joseph Stagg Lawrence, *Wall Street and Washington* (Princeton, N.J.: Princeton University Press, 1929), p. 179.

4. There does seem to be an advantage to following professional analysts' advice—if one disregards the trading costs associated with following the frequent changes in their opinions. See Womack, "Brokerage Analysts' Recommendations"; and Brad Barber, Reuven Lehavy, Maureen McNichols, and Brett Trueman, "Can Investors Profit from the Prophets? Consensus Analyst Recommendations and Stock Returns," *Journal of Finance,* 56(1) (2001): 531–63. The latter argue that, despite transaction costs, investors "who are otherwise considering buying or selling . . . would be better off purchasing shares in firms with more favorable consensus recommendations and selling shares in those with less favorable ratings" (p. 562).

5. Judith Chevalier and Glenn Ellison, "Are Some Mutual Fund Managers Better than Others? Cross-Sectional Patterns in Behavior and Performance," *Journal of Finance,* 54(3) (1999): 875–99.

6. See, for example, William Goetzmann and Roger Ibbotson, "Do Winners Repeat? Patterns in Mutual Fund Performance," *Journal of Portfolio Management,* 20 (1994): 9–17; Edwin J. Elton, Martin Gruber, and Christopher R. Blake, "Survivorship Bias and Mutual Fund Performance," *Review of Financial Studies,* 9(4) (1996): 1097–1120; and, by the same authors, "The Persistence of Risk-Adjusted Mutual Fund Performance," *Journal of Business,* 69 (1996): 133–37.

7. See Brad M. Barber, Yi-Tsung Lee, Yu-Jane Liu, and Terrance Odean, "Do Individual Day Traders Make Money? Evidence from Taiwan," unpublished paper, University of California, Davis, 2004.

8. Andrew Edgecliffe, "eToys Surges after Listing," *Financial Times,* May 21, 1999, p. 29.

9. Edward M. Miller, "Risk, Uncertainty and Divergence of Opinion," *Journal of Finance,* 32 (1977): 1151–68.

10. Theoretically, the presence of short-sale constraints can also allow for a situation where asset prices exceed fundamental value even when there are no zealots, that is, when everyone is perfectly rational, and even in economic models where everyone knows that the price will come back down by a specified future date. Mathematical economists have demonstrated a theoretical rational expectations model with common knowledge of an asset's overpricing (but not common knowledge of the common knowledge) in which the presence of short-sale constraints thwarts the backward induction from a commonly known terminal value. Everyone knows that the price will fall, but it still can sometimes happen that everyone expects to be able to sell the asset to someone else at a higher price before the price falls. See Franklin Allen, Stephen Morris, and Andrew Postlewaite, "Finite Bubbles with Short Sale Constraints and Asymmetric Information," *Journal of Economic Theory,* 61 (1993): 206–29.

11. See Charles M. Jones and Owen A. Lamont, "Short Sale Constraints and Stock Returns," *Journal of Finance,* 66(2–3) (2002): 207–39.

12. See Owen A. Lamont and Richard H. Thaler, "Can the Market Add and Subtract? Mispricing in Stock Market Carve-Outs," *Journal of Political Economy,* 111 (2003): 227–68.

13. See Stephen Figlewski, "The Informational Effects of Restrictions on Short Sales: Some Empirical Evidence," *Journal of Financial and Quantitative Analysis,* 16 (1981): 463–76. Figlewski's measure of difficulty shorting may not have been an accurate one, and other measures have been proposed that predict subsequent returns better. See Joseph Chen, Harrison Hong, and Jeremy C. Stein, "Breadth of Ownership and Stock Returns," *Journal of Financial Economics,* 66 (2002): 171–205; and Anna Scherbina, "Stock Prices and Differences in Opinion: Empirical Evidence that Prices Reflect Optimism," working paper, Kellogg Graduate School of Management, April 2001.

14. Sanjoy Basu, "The Investment Performance of Common Stocks Relative to Their Price-Earnings Ratios: A Test of the Efficient Markets," *Journal of Finance,* 32(3) (1977): 663–82; Eugene Fama and Kenneth French, "The Cross Section of Expected Stock Returns," *Journal of Finance,* 47 (1992): 427–66. Firms' managers also seem to know when their shares are relatively overpriced by the market and tend to issue new equity more often then. Thus firms' equity financing is a negative signal of future returns; see Malcolm Baker and Jeffrey Wurgler, "The Equity Share in New Issues and Aggregate Stock Returns," *Journal of Finance,* 55(5) (2000): 2219–57.

15. De Bondt and Thaler, "Does the Stock Market Overreact?"; see also James Poterba and Lawrence Summers, "Mean Reversion in Stock Prices: Evidence and Implications," *Journal of Financial Economics,* 22 (1988): 26–59.

16. Jay R. Ritter, "The Long-Run Performance of Initial Public Offerings," *Journal of Finance,* 46(1) (1991): 3–27.

17. The advertisement quoting Lynch appeared in numerous places, for example in *Mutual Funds,* September 1999, p. 37. The ad said that the data were for the S&P 500 Index, but it did not give the sample period. By searching for the interval of greatest earnings growth, and making no correction for inflation, I can roughly replicate the quoted results. To maximize earnings growth, one chooses a start date right after World

War II, when earnings were still depressed by the war, and also at the bottom of the recession in October 1945. Lagging four-quarter-total S&P earnings went up 48-fold from the second quarter of 1946 to the third quarter of 1997. Between June 1946 and April 1998, the S&P Composite Index went up 60-fold. Lynch's basic result is therefore more or less confirmed for these intervals. But if one chooses other intervals the results look very different. Between the fourth quarter of 1947 and the fourth quarter of 1998, earnings went up only 23-fold, while between December 1947 and April 1999 the S&P Composite went up 83-fold. These slightly different sample periods give a very different impression than that created by the ad: these results show price growing far more than earnings.

From 1946 to 1997, the producer-price index went up seven-fold, and so in fact real earnings increased only seven-fold in this period. A seven-fold earnings increase is a growth rate of real earnings of about 4% a year. Between the fourth quarter of 1947 and the fourth quarter of 1998, the growth rate of real earnings was only 3% per year. The growth of inflation-corrected earnings over this entire interval has not been impressive: no more than the current rate of interest on inflation-indexed government bonds. But the ad—by choosing a sample creatively, by reporting changes over very long time intervals, and by not making an inflation correction—fostered the false impression that enormous price increases were warranted by enormous earnings increases.

18. See John Y. Campbell and Robert J. Shiller, "Valuation Ratios and the Long-Run Stock Market Outlook," *Journal of Portfolio Management*, 24 (1998): 11–26; and John Y. Campbell and Robert J. Shiller, "Valuation Ratios and the Long-Run Stock Market Outlook: An Update," in Richard Thaler (ed.), *Advances in Behavioral Finance II* (New York: Sage Foundation, 2005).

19. Some have concluded that the ratios (earnings-price ratios, dividend-price ratios, or ratios of other measures of fundamental value to price) predict returns. In his textbook *Asset Pricing*, John Cochrane asserts flatly, in a display box, "Dividend/price ratios forecast excess returns on stock." See John Cochrane, *Asset Pricing* (Princeton, N.J.: Princeton University Press, 2001), p. 389.

However, the actual academic literature has still not resolved the question of statistical significance. There are unresolved statistical complexities, notably those due to the problem of (near) unit roots in the ratios and the endogenous variable problem of dependency of both independent and dependent variables on price. Campbell and I (1989) concluded that the apparent forecastability of returns like that shown in Figure 11.1 is extremely unlikely to be an artifact of the endogenous variable problem; see John Y. Campbell and Robert J. Shiller, "The Dividend Ratio Model and Small Sample Bias: A Monte Carlo Study." *Economics Letters*, 29 (1989): 325–31. See also Robert Stambaugh, Jianfeng Yu, and Yu Yuan, "The Long of It: Odds that Investor Sentiment Spuriously Predicts Anomaly Returns" (Working Paper No. 18231, Cambridge, Mass.: National Bureau of Economic Research, July 2012). But there are also issues of the relevance of asymptotic distribution theory in small samples, questions about regime change, and measurement issues for the underlying data, as well as difficulty interpreting complex statistical evidence that has been selectively presented by a researcher who may have a preconceived bias.

Jonathan Lewellen, using U.S. data, argued that there should not be a unit root in the ratios, and used this assumption to conclude that the dividend-price ratio, the book-to-market ratio, and the earnings-price ratio are statistically significant in predicting returns. See Jonathan Lewellen, "Predicting Returns with Financial Ratios," *Journal of Financial Economics*, 64 (2004): 209–35.

However, Walter Torous, Rossen Valkanov, and Shu Yan allow for the possibility of unit roots, estimating bounds for the autoregressive parameter, and conclude that with U.S. data there is evidence of predictability based on ratios at short-term horizons but not at long-term horizons. See Walter Torous, Rossen Valkanov, and Shu Yan, "On Predicting Stock Returns with Nearly Integrated Explanatory Variables," *Journal of Business*, 78(1) (2005): 937–66.

John Campbell and Motohiro Yogo derived a more powerful test, also based on estimated bounds for the autoregressive parameter, and concluded that both the dividend-price ratio and the earnings-price ratio are significant in predicting excess stock returns using U.S. stock data back to 1871. See John Y. Campbell and Motohiro Yogo, "Efficient Tests of Stock Return Predictability" (Working Paper No. w10026, Cambridge, Mass.: National Bureau of Economic Research, October 2003).

Amit Goyal and Ivo Welch did out-of-sample tests of predictive regressions using ratios and concluded that the estimated relationships were not stable out of sample. See Amit Goyal and Ivo Welch, "Predicting the Equity Premium with Dividend Ratios," *Management Science*, 49 (2003): 639–54.

Andrew Ang and Geert Bekaert looked at data on five countries and concluded that the predictability of the dividend-price ratio is not robust across countries in predicting returns. See Andrew Ang and Geert Bekaert, "Stock Return Predictability: Is It There?" unpublished paper, Columbia University, 2004.

Rossen Valkanov derived some new results about overlapping observations and long-run predictability regressions, and concluded that the dividend-price ratio is not statistically significant in predicting returns. See Rossen Valkanov, "Long-Horizon Regressions: Theoretical Results and Applications," *Journal of Financial Economics*, 68 (2003): 201–32.

Erik Hjalmarsson was the first to look at the aggregate stock markets of forty countries with pooled regressions, and his results generally, but not always, have been unfavorable to the statistical significance of regressions using ratios to predict returns. See Erik Hjalmarsson, "Predicting Global Stock Returns with New Methods for Pooled and Long-Run Forecasting Regressions," unpublished paper, Yale University, 2004.

The issues that separate these papers are at a high level of subtlety. Years of work will probably be needed before these issues are fully resolved.

20. In addition to this long-run tendency toward reversal of trends, there is a shorter-run weak tendency toward momentum, for stock prices to continue moving in the same direction. See Campbell, Lo, and Mackinlay, *The Econometrics of Financial Markets*; Narasimhan Jegadeesh and Sheridan Titman, "Returns to Buying Winners and Selling Losers: Implications for Stock Market Efficiency," *Journal of Finance*, 48 (1993): 65–91; and Bruce N. Lehmann, "Fads, Martingales, and Market Efficiency," *Quarterly Journal of Economics*, 60 (1990): 1–28.

21. It was shown long ago that dividends tend to behave over time like a long-moving average of earnings. See John Lintner, "The Distribution of Incomes of

Corporations among Dividends, Retained Earnings and Taxes," *American Economic Review,* 46 (1956): 97–113.

22. Using the real data shown in Figure 1.1, an annualized subsequent ten-year real return was constructed both for stocks and bonds for each year from 1881 to 2004 (hence corresponding to returns over ten-year intervals ending from 1891 to 2014). A real long-term interest rate was computed by subtracting the average actual inflation rate over the preceding ten years from the long-term bond yield. A regression of the excess return on both the CAPE and the real interest rate shows a negative coefficient for both and an R-squared of 0.41.

23. Economists Robert Barsky and Brad De Long have argued that stock price movements cannot be considered to have been caused largely by the speculative behavior of investors if they correspond to dividend movements. See Robert Barsky and J. Bradford De Long, "Why Have Stock Prices Fluctuated?" *Quarterly Journal of Economics,* 108 (1993): 291–311. They suggest that perhaps people were rational to suppose that the recent growth of dividends would continue indefinitely into the future—even though in fact this growth rate has never continued for very long in actual historical data.

Kenneth Froot and Maurice Obstfeld, reacting to the same appearance of co-movement between prices and dividends, postulated an "intrinsic bubble" model in which prices respond in an apparently exaggerated fashion, but in fact rationally, to dividend movements. In their theory, stock prices overreact, in a certain sense, to dividends, but yet there are no profit opportunities to trading to take advantage of this overreaction. See Kenneth Froot and Maurice Obstfeld, "Intrinsic Bubbles: The Case of Stock Prices," *American Economic Review,* 81 (1991): 1189–1214. But the fit of their "warranted price" to actual price is not much better than the fit of dividends themselves to actual price, except that their model, by making stock prices more responsive to dividends when dividends are higher, makes warranted price correspond more closely to actual price after 1950.

24. A nice review of the ups and downs of all these anomalies is found in Siegel, *Stocks for the Long Run,* 5th ed., pp. 326, 176, 336, etc. One study looked at ninety-five different stock market anomalies predicting returns published in academic journals and found "an upper bound decline in predictability due to statistical bias of 25%, and a post-publication decline, which [the authors] attribute both to statistical bias and informed trading, of 56%." See R. David McLean and Jeffrey Pontiff, "Does Academic Research Destroy Return Predictability?" unpublished paper, University of Alberta, 2014.

25. The inconstancy of anomalies reported in studies of market efficiency is also due to the varying econometric methodologies employed in the different studies. See Tim Loughran and Jay R. Ritter, "Uniformly Least Powerful Tests of Market Efficiency," *Journal of Financial Economics,* 55 (2000): 361–89.

26. Merton Miller, "Behavioral Rationality in Finance: The Case of Dividends," in Robin M. Hogarth and Melvin W. Reder (eds.), *Rational Choice: The Contrast between Economics and Psychology* (Chicago: University of Chicago Press, 1986), p. 283.

27. Robert J. Shiller, "Do Stock Prices Move Too Much to Be Justified by Subsequent Movements in Dividends?" *American Economic Review,* 71(3) (1981): 421–36; Stephen LeRoy and Richard Porter, "Stock Price Volatility: A Test Based on Implied Variance Bounds," *Econometrica,* 49 (1981): 97–113. See also Sanford J. Grossman and Robert J.

Shiller, "The Determinants of the Variability of Stock Market Prices," *American Economic Review,* 71 (1981): 222–27.

28. To compute the dividend present value for any given month, one sums over each subsequent month the present discounted value for the given year of the real dividends paid in that subsequent year. The present discounted value in the given year of a real dividend paid in a subsequent year is the real dividend divided by $(1 + r)^t$, where r is the annual real discount rate and t is the number of years between the given year and the subsequent year. The dividend present value in Figure 11.2 was drawn with a constant discount rate r equal to the historical geometric average real annual return on the market from 1871 to 2013. The assumption that r is constant through time corresponds to an efficient markets assumption that expected returns on the market are constant through time, that there are no good or bad times to enter the stock market in terms of predictable returns.

Of course, we do not know now what dividends will be after the latest year for which data are available. To compute the dividend present value, I assumed that real dividends after 2013 will grow at their actual average geometric growth rate during 2003–2013. The need to make an assumption about real dividend growth after 2013 means that the more recent values of the dividend present value shown in the figure are unreliable as indicators of actual dividend present value. However, the numbers given for the dividend present value a couple of decades or more before 2013 are most likely fairly accurate, since for these years the subsequent years after 2013 are heavily discounted in the present value calculations.

Concern has been expressed that recent measured dividends may understate cash flow from the firm to investors. Kevin Cole, Jean Helwege, and David Laster ("Stock Market Valuation Indicators: Is This Time Different?" *Financial Analysts Journal,* 52 [1996]: 56–64) estimate that considering share repurchase as a form of dividend would raise dividend-price ratios in the mid-1990s by about 80 basis points. This adjustment would still leave dividend-price ratios on the S&P Composite far below their record historic lows until that time. Liang and Sharpe, in "Share Repurchases and Employee Stock Options," point out that the Cole, Helwege, and Laster assumption that share issues occur at market prices is inaccurate because many issues come about in response to the exercise of employee stock options. Consideration of the fact that issues are made below market price might be interpreted as suggesting lowering the terminal value for the dividend present value below the amount shown in Figure 11.2.

29. It must be stressed that efficient markets theory does not mean that the stock price curve must be more smooth than the dividend present value curve, only that it must be—in a sense that must be carefully defined—less volatile overall. I took great pains to explain this point in my first article on excess volatility; see Robert J. Shiller, "The Volatility of Long-Term Interest Rates and Expectations Models of the Term Structure," *Journal of Political Economy,* 87 (1979): 1062–88. But some critics, overlooking this explanation, thought they were raising a fresh and original idea when they later pointed it out again; see, notably, Allan Kleidon, "Variance Bounds Tests and Stock Price Valuation Models," *Journal of Political Economy,* 94 (1986): 953–1001. No definitive conclusions can be drawn about efficient markets just by looking at this figure.

Nonetheless the figure is, I believe, quite informative about the lack of big-picture evidence for efficient markets in aggregate U.S. stock market data. Looking at this figure can help disabuse us of some possibly erroneous notions about the nature of the evidence for market efficiency.

30. Sanford Grossman and I made much of the possibility that dividend discount rates should vary in response to changing economic conditions, as indicated by changes in real personal consumption expenditures (in "The Determinants of the Variability of Stock Market Prices"), but still described the market overall as excessively volatile.

31. Their argument had to do with firms' setting dividends in response to price, and thereby achieving a certain sort of nonstationarity in dividends; see Terry A. Marsh and Robert C. Merton, "Dividend Variability and Variance Bounds Tests for the Rationality of Stock Market Prices," *American Economic Review*, 76(3) (1986): 483–98. In my reply, I argued that although their model was technically correct, it was hardly relevant to actual U.S. experience over the last century; see Robert J. Shiller, "The Marsh-Merton Model of Managers' Smoothing of Dividends," *American Economic Review*, 76(3) (1986): 499–503. The entire debate is now moot, since econometric work testing for excess volatility no longer relies on assumed stationarity for detrended dividends; see, for example, John Y. Campbell and John Ammer, "What Moves Stock and Bond Markets? A Variance Decomposition for Long-Term Asset Returns," *Journal of Finance*, 48(1) (1993): 3–38.

32. Campbell and I developed a co-integrated log-linear vector-autoregressive model that was capable of representing various forms of the efficient markets model. See John Y. Campbell and Robert J. Shiller, "The Dividend-Price Ratio and Expectations of Future Dividends and Discount Factors," *Review of Financial Studies*, 1 (1988): 195–228; Shiller, *Market Volatility*; and Campbell et al., *Econometrics of Financial Markets*, pp. 253–337.

33. See Campbell and Shiller, "The Dividend-Price Ratio."

34. See Campbell and Ammer, "What Moves Stock and Bond Markets?"

35. See Shiller, *Market Volatility*, pp. 197–214.

36. Paul A. Samuelson once said that stock prices are "micro efficient" and "macro inefficient." That is, there is more truth to the efficient markets hypothesis for individual stocks than there is for the stock market as a whole. There is some evidence that might be construed as supporting Samuelson's dictum; see Jeeman Jung and Robert J. Shiller, "Samuelson's Dictum and the Stock Market," *Economic Inquiry* 43(2) (2005): 221–26. Earlier studies that may be construed as supporting this conclusion are Randolph Cohen, Christopher Polk, and Tuomo Vuolteenaho, "The Value Spread," *Journal of Finance*, 58 (2003): 609–42; and Tuomo Vuolteenaho, "What Drives Firm-Level Stock Returns?" *Journal of Finance*, 57 (2002): 233–64.

Chapter Twelve   Investor Learning—and Unlearning

1. Economists have long puzzled over why the equity premium has been so high historically. How, they wonder, can it be that over the years people haven't invested more in stocks, given that stocks so outperform other investments? See Raj

Mehra and Edward C. Prescott, "The Equity Premium Puzzle," *Journal of Monetary Economics*, 15 (1988): 145–61. According to the learning theory discussed in this chapter, the equity premium puzzle is supposed to be a thing of the past—people have finally wised up.

2. Edgar Lawrence Smith, *Common Stocks as Long-Term Investments* (New York: Macmillan, 1924).

3. Kenneth S. Van Strum, *Investing in Purchasing Power* (Boston: Barron's, 1925).

4. Fisher, *Stock Market Crash*, pp. 202, 99. It is puzzling that he includes the phrase "during a period of dollar depreciation," since he emphasizes elsewhere in the book that the 1920s were a period of exceptionally stable prices. Perhaps he meant to say "even during a period of dollar depreciation" and may have been referring to one of the periods in the 1920s when there was slight inflation. He cannot be referring to the exchange rate of the dollar, since we were then on the gold standard.

5. Dice, *New Levels in the Stock Market*, p. 126.

6. Franklin L. Dame, "Public Interest in Business Is Found Growing," *New York Herald Tribune*, January 2, 1929, p. 30.

7. Siegel, *Stocks for the Long Run*, 1st ed., p. 16.

8. See Ibbotson Associates, *Stocks, Bonds, Bills and Inflation*, Table 2-9, p. 46, or consult the data on my website, http://www.econ.yale.edu/~shiller.

9. According to data shown in Ibbotson Associates, *Stocks, Bonds, Bills and Inflation*, Table 2-11, p. 50, there has been no twenty-year period since 1926 when stocks underperformed short-term interest rates. They do not show data on the 1901–21 time period. My data, from my book *Market Volatility* (updated by using the Consumer Price Index to measure inflation after 1913), actually show a slight underperformance of stocks versus short-term interest rates for 1966–86 as well as 1901–21, and the difference in results between my data and Ibbotson's for 1966–86 can be attributed to a difference in the short-term interest rate (commercial paper versus Treasury bills) and slight differences in timing.

10. See Philippe Jorion and William N. Goetzmann, "Global Stock Markets in the Twentieth Century," *Journal of Finance*, 54(3) (1999): 953–80, and also Stephen J. Brown, William N. Goetzmann, and Stephen A. Ross, "Survival," *Journal of Finance*, 50(3) (1995): 853–73. Jeremy Siegel points out that with financial returns the median is generally much lower than the mean, and the mean appreciation rate over all these countries is not so low. See also Elroy Dimson, Paul Marsh, and Mike Staunton, *Triumph of the Optimists: 101 Years of Global Investment History* (Princeton, N.J.: Princeton University Press, 2002).

11. James K. Glassman and Kevin A. Hassett, "Are Stocks Overvalued? Not a Chance," *Wall Street Journal*, March 30, 1998, p. 18, and "Stock Prices Are Still Far Too Low," March 17, 1999, p. 26; the quote is from the 1999 article.

12. James K. Glassman and Kevin A. Hassett, *Dow 36,000: The New Strategy for Profiting from the Coming Rise in the Stock Market* (New York: Times Business/Random House, 1999), p. 140.

13. See, for example, Goetzmann and Ibbotson, "Do Winners Repeat? Patterns in Mutual Fund Performance"; Elton et al., "Survivorship Bias and Mutual Fund Performance"; and Elton et al., "The Persistence of Risk-Adjusted Mutual Fund Performance."

14. To the extent that mutual funds make better diversification possible for individual investors, they lower the riskiness of stocks, and therefore the proliferation of mutual funds may lower the risk premium that investors require. John Heaton and Deborah Lucas conclude that increased diversification "goes at least half way towards justifying the current high price dividend ratio in the United States." Heaton and Lucas raise a valid and potentially significant issue; nevertheless their theory is a little unsatisfying, as it depicts individuals as completely rational at all times but does not explain why people did not invest that much in mutual funds until recently. See John Heaton and Deborah Lucas, "Stock Prices and Fundamentals," unpublished paper, Northwestern University, 1999.

Chapter Thirteen   *Speculative Volatility in a Free Society*

1. The only countries without central banks are Andorra, Monaco, and the Islamic State (if the last could be called a country).

2. These events are described in Yukio Noguchi, *Baburu no Keizaigaku (Bubble Economics)* (Tokyo: Nihon Keizai Shimbun Sha, 1992). To suppose that the bubble would not have burst even without the monetary policy is also reasonable, and there were changes in speculative expectations that suggest other origins of the Japanese stock market decline; see Robert J. Shiller, Fumiko Kon-Ya, and Yoshiro Tsutsui, "Why Did the Nikkei Crash? Expanding the Scope of Expectations Data Collection," *Review of Economics and Statistics,* 78(1) (1996): 156–64.

3. See Barry Eichengreen, *Golden Fetters: The Gold Standard and the Great Depression: 1919–1939* (New York: Oxford University Press, 1992), Table 12.1, p. 351.

4. "Courtelyou Puts in $25,000,000," *New York Times,* October 24, 1907, p. 1; "Worst Stock Crash Stemmed by Banks," *New York Times,* October 25, 1929, p. 1.

5. "Will History Repeat the '29 Crash?" *Newsweek,* June 14, 1965, p. 78.

6. See Shiller, Kon-Ya, and Tsutsui, "Why Did the Nikkei Crash?"

7. Michael Brennan, "Stripping the S&P 500," *Financial Analysts Journal,* 54(1) (1998): 14.

8. See Marianne Baxter and Urban Jermann, "The International Diversification Puzzle Is Worse than You Think," *American Economic Review,* 87 (1997): 170–80.

9. Athanasoulis and I show, using a theoretical finance model calibrated with real data, that proper management of national income risks alone can have large effects on economic welfare. See Stefano Athanasoulis and Robert J. Shiller, "World Income Components: Discovering and Implementing Risk Sharing Opportunities," *American Economic Review,* 91(4) (2001): 1031–54.

10. Robert J. Shiller, *The Subprime Solution: How Today's Global Crisis Happened and What to Do about It* (Princeton, N.J.: Princeton University Press, 2008).

11. Robert J. Shiller, Rafał M. Wojakowski, M. Shahid Ebrahim, Mark B. Shackleton, "Mitigating Financial Fragility with Continuous Workout Mortgages," *Journal of Economic Behavior and Organization,* 85 (2013): 269–85.

12. U.S. National Income and Product Accounts, Table 2.6, Personal Income and Its Disposition, http://www.bea.gov/iTable/iTable.cfm?ReqID=9&step=1#reqid=9&step=3&isuri=1&904=1960&903=76&906=q&905=2014&910=x&911=0.

13. Fiscal year 2013 PBGC Projections Report, http://www.pbgc.gov/documents/Projections-report-2013.pdf.

14. Ideas for expanding risk markets and social insurance to benefit society are described and analyzed in my recent book *Finance and the Good Society* (Princeton, N.J.: Princeton University Press, 2012).

References

Abarbanell, Jeffrey, and Reuven Lehavy. "Biased Forecasts or Biased Earnings? The Role of Earnings Management in Explaining Apparent Optimism and Inefficiency in Analysts' Earnings Forecasts." *Journal of Accounting and Economics*, 35 (2003): 105–46.

Abbott, Max Wenden, and Rachel A. Volberg. *Gambling and Problem Gambling in the Community: An International Overview and Critique.* Report No. 1 of the New Zealand Gaming Survey, 1999, p. 35.

Advisory Committee on Endowment Management. *Managing Educational Endowments: Report to the Ford Foundation* (Barker Report). New York: Ford Foundation, 1969.

Ahir, Hites, and Prakash Loungani. 2014. "There Will Be Growth in the Spring: How Do Economists Predict Turning Points?" *Vox*, April 14, 2014, http://www.voxeu.org/article/predicting-economic-turning-points.

Akerlof, George A., and Robert J. Shiller. *Animal Spirits: How Human Psychology Drives the Economy and Why This Matters for Global Capitalism.* Princeton, N.J.: Princeton University Press, 2009.

Allen, Franklin, Stephen Morris, and Andrew Postlewaite. "Finite Bubbles with Short Sale Constraints and Asymmetric Information." *Journal of Economic Theory*, 61 (1993): 206–29.

Allen, Frederick Lewis. *Only Yesterday.* New York: Harper and Brothers, 1931.

Ammer, Dean S. "Entering the New Economy." *Harvard Business Review*, September–October 1967, pp. 3–4.

Ang, Andrew, and Geert Bekaert. "Stock Return Predictability: Is It There?" Unpublished paper, Columbia University, 2004.

Arthur, Brian, John H. Holland, Blake LeBaron, Richard Palmer, and Paul Tayler. "Asset Pricing under Endogenous Expectations in an Artificial Stock Market," in W. B.

Arthur, S. Durlauf, and D. Lane (eds.), *The Economy as an Evolving Complex System II*. Reading, Mass.: Addison-Wesley, 1997, pp. 15–44.

Asch, Solomon. *Social Psychology*. Englewood Cliffs, N.J.: Prentice Hall, 1952.

Ashton, Michael. "TIPS and CPI Futures—Practice Makes Perfect," paper presented at the American Economic Association Meetings, Boston, Mass., January 2014.

Athanasoulis, Stefano, and Robert J. Shiller. "World Income Components: Discovering and Implementing Risk Sharing Opportunities." *American Economic Review*, 91(4) (2001): 1031–54.

Avery, Christopher, and Peter Zemsky. "Multidimensional Uncertainty and Herd Behavior in Financial Markets." *American Economic Review*, 88(4) (1998): 724–48.

Bailey, Norman T. *The Mathematical Theory of Epidemics*. London: C. Griffin, 1957.

Baker, Malcolm, and Jeffrey Wurgler. "The Equity Share in New Issues and Aggregate Stock Returns." *Journal of Finance*, 55(5) (2000): 2219–57.

Bakshi, Gurdip S., and Zhiwu Chen. "Baby Boom, Population Aging and Capital Markets." *Journal of Business*, 67 (1994): 165–202.

Ballinger, Kenneth. *Miami Millions: The Dance of the Dollars in the Great Florida Land Boom of 1925*. Miami, Fla.: Franklin Press, 1936.

Banerjee, Abhijit V. "A Simple Model of Herd Behavior." *Quarterly Journal of Economics*, 107(3) (1992): 797–817.

Barber, Brad M., Yi-Tsung Lee, Yu-Jane Liu, and Terrance Odean. "Do Individual Day Traders Make Money? Evidence from Taiwan." Unpublished paper, University of California, Davis, 2004.

Barber, Brad M., Reuven Lehavy, Maureen McNichols, and Brett Trueman. "Can Investors Profit from the Prophets? Consensus Analyst Recommendations and Stock Returns." *Journal of Finance*, 56(1) (2001): 531–63.

Barber, Brad M., and Terrance Odean. "Online Investors: Do the Slow Die First?" *Review of Financial Studies*, 15(2) (2002): 455–89.

Barberis, Nicholas, Ming Huang, and Tano Santos. "Prospect Theory and Asset Prices." *Quarterly Journal of Economics*, 116 (2001): 1–53.

Barberis, Nicholas, Andrei Shleifer, and Robert Vishny. "A Model of Investor Sentiment." *Journal of Financial Economics*, 49 (1998): 307–43.

Barlow, Robin, Harvey E. Brazer, and James N. Morgan. *Economic Behavior of the Affluent*. Washington, D.C.: Brookings Institution, 1966.

Barro, Robert, and Xavier Sala-i-Martin. *Economic Growth*. New York: McGraw-Hill, 1995.

Barsky, Robert, and J. Bradford De Long. "Why Have Stock Prices Fluctuated?" *Quarterly Journal of Economics*, 108 (1993): 291–311.

Bartholomew, David J. *Stochastic Models for Social Processes*. New York: John Wiley and Sons, 1967.

Basu, Sanjoy. "The Investment Performance of Common Stocks Relative to Their Price-Earnings Ratios: A Test of the Efficient Markets." *Journal of Finance*, 32(3) (1977): 663–82.

Batra, Ravi. *The Great Depression of 1990: Why It's Got to Happen, How to Protect Yourself,* rev. ed. New York: Simon & Schuster, 1987.

Baxter, Marianne, and Urban Jermann. "The International Diversification Puzzle Is Worse than You Think." *American Economic Review,* 87 (1997): 170–80.

Bell, David E. "Regret in Decision Making under Uncertainty." *Operations Research,* 30(5) (1982): 961–81.

Benartzi, Shlomo. "Why Do Employees Invest Their Retirement Savings in Company Stock?" Unpublished paper, Anderson School, University of California, Los Angeles, 1999.

Benartzi, Shlomo, and Richard H. Thaler. "Myopic Loss Aversion and the Equity Premium Puzzle." *Quarterly Journal of Economics,* 110(1) (1995): 73–92.

———. "Naive Diversification Strategies in Defined Contribution Plans." *American Economic Review,* 91(1) (2001): 79–98.

———. "Save More Tomorrow: Using Behavioral Economics to Increase Employee Saving." *Journal of Political Economy,* 112(1) (2004): S164–S187.

Benartzi, Shlomo, Richard H. Thaler, Stephen P. Utkus, and Cass R. Sunstein. "The Law and Economics of Company Stock in 401(k) Plans." *Journal of Law and Economics,* 501(1) (2007): 45–79.

Bikhchandani, S. D., David Hirshleifer, and Ivo Welch. "A Theory of Fashion, Social Custom and Cultural Change." *Journal of Political Economy,* 81 (1992): 637–54.

Blanchard, Olivier, and Stanley Fischer. *Lectures on Macroeconomics.* Cambridge, Mass.: MIT Press, 1989.

Boldrin, Michael, and Michael Woodford. "Equilibrium Models Displaying Endogenous Fluctuations and Chaos: A Survey." *Journal of Monetary Economics,* 25(2) (1990): 189–222.

Bolen, D. W., and W. H. Boyd. "Gambling and the Gambler: A Review of Preliminary Findings." *Archives of General Psychiatry,* 18(5) (1968): 617–29.

Bootle, Roger. *The Death of Inflation: Surviving and Thriving in the Zero Era.* London: Nicholas Brealey, 1998.

Borio, Claudio, and Patrick McGuire. "Twin Peaks in Equity and Housing Prices?" *BIS Quarterly Review,* March 2004, pp. 79–93.

Bowman, Karlyn. "A Reaffirmation of Self-Reliance? A New Ethic of Self-Sufficiency?" *Public Perspective,* February–March 1996, pp. 5–8.

Brennan, Michael. "Stripping the S&P 500." *Financial Analysts Journal,* 54(1) (1998): 12–22.

Brooks, Robin. "Asset Market and Savings Effects of Demographic Transitions." Unpublished Ph.D. dissertation, Yale University, 1998.

Brown, Stephen J., William Goetzmann, and Stephen A. Ross. "Survival." *Journal of Finance,* 50(3) (1995): 853–73.

Bruno, Michael, and William Easterly. "Inflation Crises and Long-Run Growth." *Journal of Monetary Economics,* 41(1) (1998): 2–26.

Bulgatz, Joseph. *Ponzi Schemes, Invaders from Mars, and Other Extraordinary Popular Delusions, and the Madness of Crowds.* New York: Harmony, 1992.

Bullock, Hugh. *The Story of Investment Companies.* New York: Columbia University Press, 1959.

Bunn, Oliver, Anthony Lazanas, Robert J. Shiller, Arne Staal, Cenk Ural, and Ji Zhuang. "Es-CAPE-ing from Overvalued Sectors: Sector Selection Based on the Cyclically Adjusted Price-Earnings (CAPE) Ratio." *Journal of Portfolio Management,* 41(1) (2014): 16–33.

Bunn, Oliver, and Robert J. Shiller. "Changing Times, Changing Values—A Historical Analysis of Sectors within the US Stock Market 1872–2013." New Haven, Conn.: Yale University, Cowles Foundation, 2014, http://cowles.econ.yale.edu/P/cd/d19b/d1950.pdf.

Burnam, Tom. *More Misinformation.* Philadelphia: Lippincott and Crowell, 1980.

Campbell, John Y., and John Ammer. "What Moves Stock and Bond Markets? A Variance Decomposition for Long-Term Asset Returns." *Journal of Finance,* 48(1) (1993): 3–38.

Campbell, John Y., and John H. Cochrane. "By Force of Habit: A Consumption-Based Explanation of Aggregate Stock Market Behavior." *Journal of Political Economy,* 107(2) (1999): 205–51.

Campbell, John Y., Andrew Lo, and Craig Mackinlay. *The Econometrics of Financial Markets.* Princeton, N.J.: Princeton University Press, 1997.

Campbell, John Y., and Robert J. Shiller. "The Dividend-Price Ratio and Expectations of Future Dividends and Discount Factors." *Review of Financial Studies,* 1 (1988): 195–228.

———. "The Dividend Ratio Model and Small Sample Bias: A Monte Carlo Study." *Economics Letters,* 29 (1989): 325–31.

———. "Valuation Ratios and the Long-Run Stock Market Outlook." *Journal of Portfolio Management,* 24 (1998): 11–26.

———. "Valuation Ratios and the Long-Run Stock Market Outlook: An Update," in Richard Thaler (ed.), *Advances in Behavioral Finance II.* New York: Sage Foundation, 2005.

Campbell, John Y., Robert J. Shiller, and Luis M. Viceira. "Understanding Inflation-Indexed Bond Markets." *Brookings Papers on Economic Activity,* 1 (2009): 79–120.

Campbell, John Y., and Luis M. Viceira. *Strategic Asset Allocation: Portfolio Choice for Long-Term Investors.* Oxford: Oxford University Press, 2002.

Campbell, John Y., and Motohiro Yogo. "Efficient Tests of Stock Return Predictability." Working Paper No. w10026, Cambridge, Mass.: National Bureau of Economic Research, October 2003.

Case, Karl E. "The Market for Single-Family Homes in the Boston Area." *New England Economic Review,* May–June 1986, pp. 38–48.

———. "Measuring Urban Land Values." Unpublished paper, Wellesley College, October 26, 1997.

Case, Karl E., John M. Quigley, and Robert J. Shiller. "Comparing Wealth Effects: The Stock Market vs. the Housing Market." Cambridge, Mass.: National Bureau of Economic Research Working Paper No. 8606, November 2001.

Case, Karl E., Jr., and Robert J. Shiller. "The Behavior of Home Buyers in Boom and Post-Boom Markets." *New England Economic Review,* November–December 1988, pp. 29–46.

———. "The Efficiency of the Market for Single Family Homes." *American Economic Review,* 79(1) (March 1989): 125–37.

———. "A Decade of Boom and Bust in the Prices of Single-Family Homes: Boston and Los Angeles 1983 to 1993." *New England Economic Review,* March–April 1994, pp. 40–51.

———. "Is There a Bubble in the Housing Market?" *Brookings Papers on Economic Activity,* 2 (2003): 299–362.

Case, Karl E., Robert J. Shiller, and Anne Kinsella Thompson. "What Have They Been Thinking? Homebuyer Behavior in Hot and Cold Markets." *Brookings Papers on Economic Activity,* 2 (2012): 265–98.

Cassidy, John. *Dot.con: How America Lost Its Mind and Money in the Internet Era.* New York: Perennial Currents, 2003.

Chen, Joseph, Harrison Hong, and Jeremy C. Stein. "Breadth of Ownership and Stock Returns." *Journal of Financial Economics,* 66 (2002): 171–205.

Chevalier, Judith, and Glenn Ellison. "Are Some Mutual Fund Managers Better than Others? Cross-Sectional Patterns in Behavior and Performance." *Journal of Finance,* 54(3) (1999): 875–99.

Christiansen, Eugene Martin, and Sebastian Sinclair. *The Gross Annual Wager of the United States, 2000.* Christiansen Capital Advisors, 2000.

Chwe, Michael Suk-Young. *Rational Ritual: Culture, Coordination, and Common Knowledge.* Princeton, N.J.: Princeton University Press, 2003.

Clark, John Bates. "The Gold Standard of Currency in the Light of Recent Theory." *Political Science Quarterly,* 10(3) (1895): 383–97.

Cochrane, John. *Asset Pricing.* Princeton, N.J.: Princeton University Press, 2001.

Cohen, Randolph. "Asset Allocation Decisions of Individuals and Institutions." Harvard Business School Working Paper Series, No. 03-112, 2003.

Cohen, Randolph, Christopher Polk, and Tuomo Vuolteenaho. "The Value Spread." *Journal of Finance,* 58 (2003): 609–42.

Cole, Kevin, Jean Helwege, and David Laster. "Stock Market Valuation Indicators: Is This Time Different?" *Financial Analysts Journal,* 52 (1996): 56–64.

Collins, Allan, Eleanor Warnock, Nelleke Acello, and Mark L. Miller. "Reasoning from Incomplete Knowledge," in Daniel G. Bobrow and Allan Collins (eds.), *Representation and Understanding: Studies in Cognitive Science.* New York: Academic Press, 1975, pp. 383–415.

Consumer Federation of America. "Lower-Income and Minority Consumers Most Likely to Prefer and Underestimate Risks of Adjustable Rate Mortgages." http://www.consumerfed.org/072604_ARM_Survey_Release.pdf. Washington, D.C.

Cooper, John C. B. "Price Elasticity of Demand for Crude Oil: Estimates for 23 Countries." *Opec Review,* 27(1) (2003):1–8.

Coronado, Julia Lynn, and Steven A. Sharpe. "Did Pension Plan Accounting Contribute to a Stock Market Bubble?" Finance and Economics Discussion Series No. 2003-38. Washington, D.C.: Board of Governors of the Federal Reserve System, 2003.

Cowles, Alfred III, and associates. *Common Stock Indexes,* 2nd ed. Bloomington, Ind.: Principia Press, 1939.

Cutler, David, James Poterba, and Lawrence Summers. "What Moves Stock Prices?" *Journal of Portfolio Management,* 15(3) (1989): 4–12.

Daniel, Kent, David Hirshleifer, and Avanidhar Subrahmanyam. "Investor Psychology and Security Market Over- and Underreaction." *Journal of Finance,* 53(6) (1998): 1839–86.

Davis, Morris A., and Jonathan Heathcote. "The Price and Quantity of Residential Land in the United States." Washington, D.C.: Board of Governors of the Federal Reserve System, Finance and Economics Discussion Series No. 2004-37, 2004.

De Bondt, Werner, and Richard H. Thaler. "Does the Stock Market Overreact?" *Journal of Finance,* 40(3) (1985): 793–805.

Dent, Harry S. *The Great Boom Ahead: Your Comprehensive Guide to Personal and Business Profit in the New Era of Prosperity.* New York: Hyperion, 1993.

———. *The Roaring 2000s: Building the Wealth & Lifestyle You Desire in the Greatest Boom in History.* New York: Simon & Schuster, 1998.

———. *The Roaring 2000s Investor: Strategies for the Life You Want.* New York: Simon & Schuster, 1999.

Desmond, Robert W. *The Information Process: World News Reporting to the Twentieth Century.* Iowa City: University of Iowa Press, 1978.

Deutsch, Morton, and Harold B. Gerard. "A Study of Normative and Informational Social Influences upon Individual Judgment." *Journal of Abnormal and Social Psychology,* 51 (1955): 629–36.

Dice, Charles Amos. *New Levels in the Stock Market.* New York: McGraw-Hill, 1929.

Diggins, John Patrick. *The Proud Decades: America in War and in Peace 1941–1960.* New York: W. W. Norton, 1988.

Dimson, Elroy, Paul Marsh, and Mike Staunton. *Triumph of the Optimists: 101 Years of Global Investment History.* Princeton, N.J.: Princeton University Press, 2002.

Dornbusch, Rudiger, and Stanley Fischer. "The Open Economy: Implications for Monetary and Fiscal Policy," in Robert J. Gordon (ed.), *The American Business Cycle: Continuity and Change.* Chicago: National Bureau of Economic Research and University of Chicago Press, 1986, pp. 459–501.

Dumke, Glenn S. *The Boom of the Eighties in Southern California.* San Marino, Calif.: Huntington Library, 1944.

Ehrlich, Paul R. *The Population Bomb.* New York: Ballantine Books, 1968.

Eichengreen, Barry. *Golden Fetters: The Gold Standard and the Great Depression: 1919–1939.* New York: Oxford University Press, 1992.

Eichholtz, Piet A. "A Long Run House Price Index: The Herengracht Index, 1638–1973." Unpublished paper, University of Limburg and University of Amsterdam, 1996.

Elias, David. *Dow 40,000: Strategies for Profiting from the Greatest Bull Market in History.* New York: McGraw-Hill, 1999.

Elton, Edwin J., Martin Gruber, and Christopher R. Blake. "The Persistence of Risk-Adjusted Mutual Fund Performance." *Journal of Business*, 69 (1996): 133–37.

———. "Survivorship Bias and Mutual Fund Performance." *Review of Financial Studies*, 9(4) (1996): 1097–1120.

Fair, Ray C. "How Much Is the Stock Market Overvalued?" Unpublished paper, Cowles Foundation, Yale University, 1999. A revised version of this paper was published as part of Ray C. Fair, "Fed Policy and the Effects of a Stock Market Crash on the Economy: Is the Fed Tightening Too Little and Too Late?" *Business Economics*, April 2000, pp. 7–14. Also available at http://fairmodel.econ.yale.edu/rayfair/pdf/1999c.pdf.

———. "Fed Policy and the Effects of a Stock Market Crash on the Economy: Is the Fed Tightening Too Little and Too Late?" *Business Economics*, April 2000, pp. 7–14. Also available at http://fairmodel.econ.yale.edu/rayfair/pdf/1999c.pdf.

Fama, Eugene. "Efficient Capital Markets: A Review of Theory and Empirical Work." *Journal of Finance*, 25 (1970): 383–417.

———. "Two Pillars of Asset Pricing" (Nobel Lecture), *American Economic Review*, 104(6) (2014): 1467–85.

Fama, Eugene, and Kenneth French. "The Cross Section of Expected Stock Returns." *Journal of Finance*, 47 (1992): 427–66.

Federal Reserve Board. "Humphrey-Hawkins Report July 22, 1997, Section 2: Economic and Financial Developments in 1997." http://www.federalreserve.gov/boarddocs/hh/1997/july/ReportSection2.htm.

Figlewski, Stephen. "The Informational Effects of Restrictions on Short Sales: Some Empirical Evidence." *Journal of Financial and Quantitative Analysis*, 16 (1981): 463–76.

Fischel, William A. *Regulatory Takings: Law, Economics and Politics*. Cambridge, Mass.: Harvard University Press, 1995.

———. *The Homevoter Hypothesis: How Home Values Influence Local Government Taxation, School Finance, and Land-Use Policies*. Cambridge, Mass.: Harvard University Press, 2001.

Fischhof, Baruch, Paul Slovic, and Sarah Lichtenstein. "Knowing with Uncertainty: The Appropriateness of Extreme Confidence." *Journal of Experimental Psychology: Human Perception and Performance*, 3 (1977): 522–64.

Fisher, E. M. *Urban Real Estate Markets: Characteristics and Financing*. New York: National Bureau of Economic Research, 1951.

Fisher, Irving. *The Stock Market Crash—and After*. New York: Macmillan, 1930.

Fleming, Michael J., and John R. Sporn. "Trading Activity and Price Transparency in the Inflation Swap Market." *Economic Policy Review*, Federal Reserve Bank of New York, 19(1) (May 2013): 45–58.

Fleming, Thomas. *Around the Pan with Uncle Hank: His Trip through the Pan-American Exposition*. New York: Nutshell, 1901.

Foot, David K., and Daniel Stoffman. *Boom, Bust & Echo: How to Profit from the Coming Demographic Shift*. Toronto: McFarlane, Walter & Ross, 1996.

French, Kenneth R., and Richard Roll. "Stock Return Variances: The Arrival of Information and the Reaction of Traders." *Journal of Financial Economics*, 17 (1986): 5–26.

Friedman, Benjamin M. *The Moral Consequences of Economic Growth*. New York: Alfred A. Knopf, 2005.

Froot, Kenneth, and Emil Dabora. "How Are Stock Prices Affected by the Location of Trade?" *Journal of Financial Economics*, 53(2) (1999): 189–216.

Froot, Kenneth, and Maurice Obstfeld. "Intrinsic Bubbles: The Case of Stock Prices." *American Economic Review*, 81 (1991): 1189–1214.

Galbraith, John Kenneth. *The Great Crash: 1929*, 2nd ed. Boston: Houghton Mifflin, 1961.

Gale, William G., and John Sabelhaus. "Perspectives on the Household Saving Rate." *Brookings Papers on Economic Activity*, 1 (1999): 181–224.

Gallin, Joshua. "The Long-Run Relation between House Prices and Income: Evidence from Local Housing Markets." Washington, D.C.: Board of Governors of the Federal Reserve System, Finance and Economics Discussion Paper Series No. 2003.17, 2003.

Garber, Peter. *Famous First Bubbles: The Fundamentals of Early Manias*. Cambridge, Mass.: MIT Press, 2000.

Geanakoplos, John. "Common Knowledge." *Journal of Economic Perspectives*, 6(4) (1992): 53–82.

Geanakoplos, John, Olivia S. Mitchell, and Stephen P. Zeldes. "Social Security Money's Worth," in Olivia S. Mitchell, Robert J. Myers, and Howard Young (eds.), *Prospects for Social Security Reform*. Philadelphia: University of Pennsylvania Press, 1999, pp. 79–151.

Ger, Gueliz, and Russell W. Belk. "Cross-Cultural Differences in Materialism." *Journal of Economic Psychology*, 17 (1996): 55–77.

Gibson, A. H. "The Future Course of High Class Investment Values," *Banker's Magazine* (London), 115 (1923): 15–34.

Gibson, George. *The Stock Markets of London, Paris and New York*. New York: G. P. Putnam's Sons, 1889.

Gigerenzer, G. "How to Make Cognitive Illusion Disappear: Beyond 'Heuristic and Biases.'" *European Review of Social Psychology*, 2 (1991): 83–115.

Gilchrist, Helen, Robert Povey, Adrian Dickenson, and Rachel Povey. "The Sensation-Seeking Scale: Its Use in a Study of People Choosing Adventure Holidays." *Personality and Individual Differences*, 19(4) (1995): 513–16.

Glaeser, Edward. "Reinventing Boston: 1640 to 2003." Cambridge, Mass.: National Bureau of Economic Research Working Paper No. 10166, 2004.

Glaeser, Edward, and Albert Saiz. "The Rise of the Skilled City." Cambridge, Mass.: National Bureau of Economic Research Working Paper No. 10191, 2004.

Glassman, James K., and Kevin A. Hassett. *Dow 36,000: The New Strategy for Profiting from the Coming Rise in the Stock Market*. New York: Times Business/Random House, 1999.

Goetzmann, William, and Roger Ibbotson. "Do Winners Repeat? Patterns in Mutual Fund Performance." *Journal of Portfolio Management*, 20 (1994): 9–17.

Goetzmann, William, and Massimo Massa. "Index Fund Investors." Unpublished paper, Yale University, 1999.

Gordon, Robert J. "U.S. Productivity Growth since 1879: One Big Wave?" *American Economic Review*, 89(2) (1999): 123–28.

Goyal, Amit, and Ivo Welch. "Predicting the Equity Premium with Dividend Ratios." *Management Science,* 49 (2003): 639–54.

Graham, Benjamin, and David Dodd. *Securities Analysis.* New York: McGraw-Hill, 1934.

Grant, James. *The Trouble with Prosperity: A Contrarian Tale of Boom, Bust, and Speculation.* New York: John Wiley and Sons, 1996.

Grebler, Leo, David M. Blank, and Louis Winnick. *Capital Formation in Residential Real Estate: Trends and Prospects.* New York and Princeton, N.J.: National Bureau of Economic Research and Princeton University Press, 1956. http://papers.nber.org/books/greb56-1.

Greenlees, J. S. "An Empirical Evaluation of the CPI Home Purchase Index 1973–8." *American Real Estate and Urban Economics Association Journal,* 10(1) (1982): 1–24.

Greenspan, Alan. "The Challenge of Central Banking in a Democratic Society." Speech before the American Enterprise Institute for Public Policy, Washington, D.C., December 5, 1996. Available at http://www.federalreserve.gov/BOARDDOCS/SPEECHES/19961205.htm.

Greetham, Trevor, Owain Evans, and Charles I. Clough, Jr. "Fund Manager Survey: November 1999." London: Merrill Lynch & Co., Global Securities Research and Economics Group, 1999.

Griffin, John M., and G. Andrew Karolyi. "Another Look at the Role of the Industrial Structure of Markets for International Diversification Strategies." *Journal of Financial Economics,* 50 (1998): 351–73.

Grinblatt, Mark, and Matti Keloharju. "Distance, Language, and Culture Bias: The Role of Investor Sophistication." *Journal of Finance,* 56(3) (2001): 1053–73.

Gross, William H. "On the 'Course' to a New Normal," http://www.pimco.com/EN/Insights/Pages/Gross%20Sept%20On%20the%20Course%20to%20a%20New%20Normal.aspx.

Grossman, Sanford J., and Robert J. Shiller. "The Determinants of the Variability of Stock Market Prices." *American Economic Review,* 71 (1981): 222–27.

Gustman, Alan L., and Thomas L. Steinmeier. "Effects of Pensions on Savings: Analysis with Data from the Health and Retirement Survey," *Carnegie Rochester Conference Series on Public Policy,* 50 (1999): 271–324.

Hamilton, James T. *All the News That's Fit to Sell: How the Market Transforms Information into News.* Princeton, N.J.: Princeton University Press, 2004.

Heaton, John, and Deborah Lucas. "Stock Prices and Fundamentals." Unpublished paper, Northwestern University, 1999.

Heston, Steven L., and K. Geert Rouwenhorst. "Does Industrial Structure Explain the Benefits of International Diversification?" *Journal of Financial Economics,* 36 (1994): 3–27.

Hjalmarsson, Erik. "Predicting Global Stock Returns with New Methods for Pooled and Long-Run Forecasting Regressions." Unpublished paper, Yale University, 2004.

Holden, Sara, and Jack VanDerhei. "401(k) Plan Asset Allocation, Account Balances, and Loan Activity in 2003." *Investment Company Institute Perspective,* 10(2) (2004): 1–16.

Homer, Sidney. *A History of Interest Rates.* New Brunswick, N.J.: Rutgers University Press, 1963.

Hong, Harrison, and Jeremy Stein. "A Unified Theory of Underreaction, Momentum Trading, and Overreaction in Asset Markets." *Journal of Finance*, 54(6) (1999): 2143–84.

Hovakimian, Armen, and Ekkachai Saenyasin. "U.S. Analyst Regulation and the Earnings Forecast Bias around the World." *European Financial Management*, 20(3) (June 2014): 435–61.

Hoyt, Homer. *One Hundred Years of Land Values in Chicago: The Relationship of the Growth of Chicago to the Rise in Its Land Values.* Chicago: University of Chicago Press, 1933.

Huberman, Gur, and Wei Jiang. "Offering versus Choice in 401(k) Plans: Equity Exposure and Number of Funds." Unpublished paper, Columbia University, New York, 2004.

Huberman, Gur, and Tomer Regev. "Speculating on a Cure for Cancer: A Non-Event That Made Stock Prices Soar." *Journal of Finance*, 56(1) (2001): 387–96.

Ibbotson Associates. *Stocks, Bonds, Bills and Inflation: 1999 Yearbook, Market Results for 1926–1998.* Chicago: Ibbotson Associates, 1999.

Inglehart, Ronald. "Aggregate Stability and Individual-Level Flux in Mass Belief Systems." *American Political Science Review*, 79(1) (1985): 97–116.

International Monetary Fund. *International Financial Statistics.* Washington, D.C., 1999.

Investment Company Institute. *Mutual Fund Fact Book.* Washington, D.C., 1999.

Jegadeesh, Narasimhan, and Sheridan Titman. "Returns to Buying Winners and Selling Losers: Implications for Stock Market Efficiency." *Journal of Finance*, 48 (1993): 65–91.

Jones, Charles M., and Owen A. Lamont. "Short Sale Constraints and Stock Returns." *Journal of Finance*, 66(2–3) (2002): 207–39.

Jorion, Philippe, and William N. Goetzmann. "Global Stock Markets in the Twentieth Century." *Journal of Finance*, 54(3) (1999): 953–80.

Jung, Jeeman, and Robert J. Shiller. "Samuelson's Dictum and the Stock Market." *Economic Inquiry*, 43(2) (2005): 221–26.

Katona, George. *Psychological Economics.* New York: Elsevier, 1975.

Kennickell, Arthur B. "A Rolling Tide: Changes in the Distribution of Wealth in the U.S., 1989–2001." http://www.federalreserve.gov/pubs/oss/oss2/papers/concentration.2001.10.pdf. Washington, D.C.: Board of Governors of the Federal Reserve System, September 2003.

Keren, Gideon. "The Rationality of Gambling: Gamblers' Conceptions of Probability, Chance and Luck," in George Wright and Peter Ayton (eds.), *Subjective Probability.* Chichester, England: John Wiley and Sons, 1994, pp. 485–99.

Keynes, John Maynard. *A Treatise on Money.* New York: Macmillan, 1930.

———. *The General Theory of Employment, Interest and Money.* New York: Harcourt Brace & World, 1961.

Khurana, Rakesh. *Searching for a Corporate Savior: The Irrational Quest for Charismatic CEOs.* Princeton, N.J.: Princeton University Press, 2002.

Kindleberger, Charles P. *Manias, Panics and Crashes: A History of Financial Crises*, 2nd ed. London: Macmillan, 1989.

King, Robert G., and Ross Levine. "Finance and Growth: Schumpeter May Be Right." *Quarterly Journal of Economics,* 108 (1993): 717–37.

Kirman, Alan. "Ants, Rationality and Recruitment." *Quarterly Journal of Economics,* 108(1) (1993): 137–56.

Klehr, Harvey. *The Heyday of American Communism: The Depression Decade.* New York: Basic Books, 1984.

Kleidon, Allan. "Variance Bounds Tests and Stock Price Valuation Models." *Journal of Political Economy,* 94 (1986): 953–1001.

Kotlikoff, Laurence J., and Scott Burns. *The Coming Generational Storm.* Cambridge, Mass.: MIT Press, 2004.

Krugman, Paul. "How Fast Can the U.S. Economy Grow?" *Harvard Business Review,* 75 (1977): 123–29.

Lambert, Craig. "Trafficking in Chance." *Harvard Magazine,* 104(6) (July–August 2002): 32.

Lamont, Owen A., and Richard H. Thaler. "Can the Market Add and Subtract? Mispricing in Stock Market Carve-Outs." *Journal of Political Economy,* 111 (2003): 227–68.

Lange, Oscar. "Is the American Economy Contracting?" *American Economic Review,* 29(3) (1939): 503–13.

Langer, E. J. "The Illusion of Control." *Journal of Personality and Social Psychology,* 32 (1975): 311–28.

LaPorta, Rafael, Florencio Lopez-de-Silanes, and Andrei Shleifer. "Corporate Ownership around the World." *Journal of Finance,* 54 (1999): 471–518.

Lawrence, Joseph Stagg. *Wall Street and Washington.* Princeton, N.J.: Princeton University Press, 1929.

Lee, In Ho. "Market Crashes and Informational Avalanches." *Review of Economic Studies,* 65(4) (1998): 741–60.

Lehmann, Bruce N. "Fads, Martingales, and Market Efficiency." *Quarterly Journal of Economics,* 60 (1990): 1–28.

Leland, Hayne. "Who Should Buy Portfolio Insurance." *Journal of Finance,* 35 (1980): 581–94.

LeRoy, Stephen, and Richard Porter. "Stock Price Volatility: A Test Based on Implied Variance Bounds." *Econometrica,* 49 (1981): 97–113.

Lewellen, Jonathan. "Predicting Returns with Financial Ratios." *Journal of Financial Economics,* 64 (2004): 209–35.

Liang, J. Nellie, and Steven A. Sharpe. "Share Repurchases and Employee Stock Options and Their Implications for S&P 500 Share Retirements and Expected Returns." Finance and Economics Discussion Series 1999-59. Washington: Board of Governors of the Federal Reserve System, 1999.

Lin, Hsiou-Wei, and Maureen F. McNichols. "Underwriting Relationships, Analysts' Earnings Forecasts and Investment Recommendations." *Journal of Accounting and Economics,* 25(1) (1998): 101–27.

Lintner, John. "The Distribution of Incomes of Corporations among Dividends, Retained Earnings and Taxes," *American Economic Review*, 46 (1956): 97–113.

Loomes, Graham, and Robert Sugden. "Regret Theory: An Alternative Theory of Rational Choice under Uncertainty." *Economic Journal*, 92 (1982): 805–24.

Loughran, Tim, and Jay R. Ritter. "Uniformly Least Powerful Tests of Market Efficiency." *Journal of Financial Economics*, 55 (2000): 361–89.

Lucas, Robert E. "Asset Prices in an Exchange Economy." *Econometrica*, 46 (1978): 1429–45.

Mackay, Charles. *Memoirs of Extraordinary Popular Delusions and the Madness of Crowds.* London: Bentley, 1841.

Maier, N. R. F. "Reasoning in Humans. II. The Solution of a Problem and Its Appearance in Consciousness." *Journal of Comparative Psychology*, 12 (1931): 181–94.

Mandelbrot, Benoit. *Fractals and Scaling in Finance: Discontinuity, Concentration, Risk.* New York: Springer-Verlag, 1997.

Marsh, Terry A., and Robert C. Merton. "Dividend Variability and Variance Bounds Tests for the Rationality of Stock Market Prices." *American Economic Review*, 76(3) (1986): 483–98.

McCarthy, Jonathan, and Richard W. Peach. "Are Home Prices the Next 'Bubble'?" *Federal Reserve Bank of New York Economic Policy Review*, 2004.

McLean, R. David, and Jeffrey Pontiff. "Does Academic Research Destroy Return Predictability?" Unpublished paper, University of Alberta, 2014.

Mehra, Raj, and Edward C. Prescott. "The Equity Premium Puzzle." *Journal of Monetary Economics*, 15 (1988): 145–61.

Meltzer, Allan H. "Monetary and Other Explanations of the Start of the Great Depression." *Journal of Monetary Economics*, 2 (1976): 455–71.

Merton, Robert K. *Social Theory and Social Structure.* Glencoe, Ill.: Free Press, 1957.

Mian, Atif, and Amir Sufi. "Summary of 'the Consequences of Mortgage Credit Expansion.'" *Proceedings, Federal Reserve Bank of Chicago* (May 2008): 129–32.

Milgram, Stanley. *Obedience to Authority.* New York: Harper and Row, 1974.

Milgrom, Paul, and Nancy Stokey. "Information, Trade, and Common Knowledge." *Econometrica*, 49 (1982): 219–22.

Miller, Edward M. "Risk, Uncertainty and Divergence of Opinion." *Journal of Finance*, 32 (1977): 1151–68.

Miller, Merton. "Behavioral Rationality in Finance: The Case of Dividends," in Robin M. Hogarth and Melvin W. Reder (eds.), *Rational Choice: The Contrast between Economics and Psychology.* Chicago: University of Chicago Press, 1986, 267–84.

Mitchell, Mark L., and Jeffrey M. Netter. "Triggering the 1987 Stock Market Crash: Antitakeover Provisions in the Proposed House Ways and Means Tax Bill." *Journal of Financial Economics*, 24 (1989): 37–68.

Modigliani, Franco, and Richard A. Cohn. "Inflation, Rational Valuation, and the Market." *Financial Analysts Journal*, 35 (1979): 22–44. Reprinted in Simon Johnson (ed.), *The Collected Papers of Franco Modigliani*, Vol. 5. Cambridge, Mass.: MIT Press, 1989.

New York Stock Exchange. *The Public Speaks to the Exchange Community.* New York, 1955.

———. *New York Stock Exchange Fact Book.* New York, 1998.

Niederhoffer, Victor. "The Analysis of World News Events and Stock Prices." *Journal of Business*, 44(2) (1971): 193–219.

Niquet, Bernd. *Keine Angst vorm nächsten Crash: Warum Aktien als Langfristanlage unschlagbar sind*. Frankfurt: Campus Verlag, 1999.

Nisbett, Robert E., and Timothy DeCamp Wilson. "Telling More than We Can Know: Verbal Reports on Mental Processes." *Psychological Review*, 84(3) (1977): 231–59.

Noguchi, Yukio. *Baburu no Keizaigaku (Bubble Economics)*. Tokyo: Nihon Keizai Shimbun Sha, 1992.

Nordhaus, William D., and Joseph G. Boyer. "Requiem for Kyoto: An Economic Analysis of the Kyoto Protocol." Cowles Foundation Discussion Paper 1201. New Haven, Conn.: Yale University, November 1998.

Noyes, Alexander Dana. *Forty Years of American Finance*. New York: G. P. Putnam's Sons, 1909.

Orman, Suze. *The 9 Steps to Financial Freedom*. New York: Crown, 1997.

———. *The Courage to Be Rich: Creating a Life of Material and Spiritual Abundance*. Rutherford, N.J.: Putnam, 1999.

Parker, Richard. "The Media Knowledge and Reporting of Financial Issues," presentation at the Brookings-Wharton Conference on Financial Services, Brookings Institution, Washington, D.C., October 22, 1998.

Pennington, Nancy, and Reid Hastie. "Reasoning in Explanation-Based Decision Making." *Cognition*, 49 (1993): 123–63.

Petersen, James D., and Cheng-Ho Hsieh. "Do Common Risk Factors in the Returns on Stocks and Bonds Explain Returns on REITs?" *Real Estate Economics*, 25 (1997): 321–45.

Piketty, Thomas, *Capital in the Twenty-First Century*. Cambridge, Mass.: Belknap Press of Harvard University Press, 2014.

Pitz, Gordon W. "Subjective Probability Distributions for Imperfectly Known Quantities," in Lee W. Gregg (ed.), *Knowledge and Cognition*. Potomac, Md.: Lawrence Erlbaum Associates, 1975, pp. 29–41.

Pliny the Younger. *Letters and Panegyrics*, trans. Betty Radice. Cambridge, Mass.: Harvard University Press, 1969.

Posen, Adam S. "It Takes More than a Bubble to Become Japan." Washington, D.C.: Peterson Institute for International Economics, Working Paper No. 03-9, October 2003. http://www.piie.com/publications/wp/03-9.pdf.

Poterba, James, and Lawrence Summers. "Mean Reversion in Stock Prices: Evidence and Implications." *Journal of Financial Economics*, 22 (1988): 26–59.

Presidential Task Force on Market Mechanisms. *Report of the Presidential Task Force on Market Mechanisms* (Brady Commission Report). Washington, D.C.: U.S. Government Printing Office, 1988.

Pressman, Steven. "On Financial Frauds and Their Causes: Investor Overconfidence." *American Journal of Economics and Sociology*, 57 (1998): 405–21.

Quattrone, G. A., and Amos Tversky. "Causal versus Diagnostic Contingencies: On Self-Deception and the Voter's Delusion." *Journal of Personality and Social Psychology*, 46(2) (1984): 237–48.

Reid, A. A. L. "Comparing Telephone with Face-to-Face Contact," in Ithiel de Sola Poole (ed.), *The Social Impact of the Telephone*. Cambridge, Mass.: MIT Press, 1977, pp. 386–414.

Ritter, Jay R. "The Long-Run Performance of Initial Public Offerings." *Journal of Finance*, 46(1) (1991): 3–27.

———. "Uniformly Least Powerful Tests of Market Efficiency," *Journal of Financial Economics*, 55 (2000): 361–89.

Ritter, Jay R., and Richard S. Warr. "The Decline of Inflation and the Bull Market of 1982–1997." *Journal of Financial and Quantitative Analysis*, 37(1) (2002): 29–61.

Roll, Richard. "Orange Juice and Weather." *American Economic Review*, 74 (1984): 861–80.

———. "Price Volatility, International Market Links, and Their Implication for Regulatory Policies." *Journal of Financial Services Research*, 2(2–3) (1989): 211–46.

Romer, Christina. "The Great Crash and the Onset of the Great Depression." *Quarterly Journal of Economics*, 105 (1990): 597–624.

Romer, David. *Advanced Macroeconomics*. New York: McGraw-Hill, 1996.

Rublin, Lauren R. "Party On! America's Portfolio Managers Grow More Bullish on Stocks and Interest Rates." *Barron's*, May 3, 1999, pp. 31–38.

Schäfer, Bodo. *Der Weg zur finanziellen Freiheit: In sieben Jahren die erste Million*. Frankfurt: Campus Verlag, 1999.

Scherbina, Anna. "Stock Prices and Differences in Opinion: Empirical Evidence That Prices Reflect Optimism." Working paper, Kellogg Graduate School of Management, April 2001.

Shafir, Eldar, Peter Diamond, and Amos Tversky. "Money Illusion." *Quarterly Journal of Economics*, 112(2) (1997): 341–74.

Shafir, Eldar, Itamar Simonson, and Amos Tversky. "Reason-Based Choice." *Cognition*, 49 (1993): 11–36.

Shafir, Eldar, and Amos Tversky. "Thinking through Uncertainty: Nonconsequential Reasoning and Choice." *Cognitive Psychology*, 24 (1992): 449–74.

Sharpe, Steven A. "Re-examining Stock Valuation and Inflation: The Implications of Analysts' Earnings Forecasts," *Review of Economics and Statistics*, 84(4) (2002): 632–48.

———. "How Does the Market Interpret Analysts' Long-Term Growth Forecasts?" *Journal of Accounting, Auditing and Finance*, 20(2) (Spring 2005): 147–66.

Shefrin, Hersh. *Beyond Greed and Fear: Understanding Behavioral Finance and the Psychology of Investing*. Boston: Harvard Business School Press, 2000.

Shiller, Robert J. "The Volatility of Long-Term Interest Rates and Expectations Models of the Term Structure." *Journal of Political Economy*, 87 (1979): 1062–88.

———. "Can the Federal Reserve Control Real Interest Rates?" in *Rational Expectations and Economic Policy*, ed. Stanley Fischer. Cambridge, Mass.: National Bureau of Economic Research and University of Chicago Press, pp. 117–67, 1980. http://www.nber.org/chapters/c6262.pdf.

———. "Do Stock Prices Move Too Much to Be Justified by Subsequent Movements in Dividends?" *American Economic Review*, 71(3) (1981): 421–36.

———. "Consumption, Asset Markets and Macroeconomic Fluctuations." *Carnegie-Rochester Conference Series on Public Policy*, 17 (1982): 203–38.

———. "The Marsh-Merton Model of Managers' Smoothing of Dividends." *American Economic Review,* 76(3) (1986): 499–503.

———. "Portfolio Insurance and Other Investor Fashions as Factors in the 1987 Stock Market Crash," in *NBER Macroeconomics Annual.* Cambridge, Mass.: National Bureau of Economic Research, 1988, pp. 287–95.

———. "Comovements in Stock Prices and Comovements in Dividends." *Journal of Finance,* 44 (1989): 719–29.

———. *Market Volatility.* Cambridge, Mass.: MIT Press, 1989.

———. "Market Volatility and Investor Behavior." *American Economic Review,* 80 (1990): 58–62.

———. "Public Resistance to Indexation: A Puzzle." *Brookings Papers on Economic Activity,* 1 (1997): 159–211.

———. "Why Do People Dislike Inflation?" in Christina D. Romer and David H. Romer (eds.), *Reducing Inflation: Motivation and Strategy.* Chicago: University of Chicago Press and National Bureau of Economic Research, 1997, pp. 13–65.

———. "Social Security and Institutions for Intergenerational, Intragenerational and International Risk Sharing." *Carnegie Rochester Conference Series on Public Policy,* 50 (1999): 165–204.

———. "Measuring Bubble Expectations and Investor Confidence." *Journal of Psychology and Markets,* 1(1) (2000): 49–60.

———. "From Efficient Markets Theory to Behavioral Finance." *Journal of Economic Perspectives,* 17 (2003): 83–104.

———. *The Subprime Solution: How Today's Global Crisis Happened and What to Do about It.* Princeton, N.J.: Princeton University Press, 2008.

———. *Finance and the Good Society.* Princeton, N.J.: Princeton University Press, 2012.

———. "Speculative Asset Prices" (Nobel Lecture). *American Economic Review,* 104(6) (2014): 1486; also appearing here as the appendix to this book.

Shiller, Robert J., and Andrea Beltratti. "Stock Prices and Bond Yields: Can Their Comovements Be Explained in Terms of Present Value Models?" *Journal of Monetary Economics,* 30 (1992): 25–46.

Shiller, Robert J., and John Y. Campbell. "Yield Spreads and Interest Rate Movements: A Bird's Eye View." *Review of Economic Studies,* 58 (1991): 495–514.

Shiller, Robert J., Fumiko Kon-Ya, and Yoshiro Tsutsui. "Investor Behavior in the October 1987 Stock Market Crash: The Case of Japan." *Journal of the Japanese and International Economies,* 5 (1991): 1–13.

———. "Why Did the Nikkei Crash? Expanding the Scope of Expectations Data Collection." *Review of Economics and Statistics,* 78(1) (1996): 156–64.

Shiller, Robert J., and John Pound. "Survey Evidence on the Diffusion of Interest and Information among Investors." *Journal of Economic Behavior and Organization,* 12 (1989): 47–66.

Shiller, Robert J., and Jeremy J. Siegel. "The Gibson Paradox and Historical Movements in Real Long Term Interest Rates." *Journal of Political Economy,* 85(5) (1977): 891–98.

Shiller, Robert J., Rafał M. Wojakowski, M. Shahid Ebrahim, and Mark B. Shackleton. "Mitigating Financial Fragility with Continuous Workout Mortgages." *Journal of Economic Behavior and Organization*, 85 (2013): 269–85.

Shleifer, Andrei. *Inefficient Markets: An Introduction to Behavioral Finance.* Oxford, England: Oxford University Press, 2000.

Siegel, Jeremy J. "The Real Rate of Interest from 1800–1990: A Study of the U.S. and the U.K." *Journal of Monetary Economics*, 29 (1992): 227–52.

———. *Stocks for the Long Run*, 1st ed. Burr Ridge, Ill.: Richard D. Irwin, 1994.

———. *Stocks for the Long Run*, 5th ed. New York: McGraw-Hill, 2014. Also available at http://jeremysiegel.com.

———. *The Future for Investors.* New York: Crown Business, 2005.

———. 2014. "The Shiller CAPE Ratio: A New Look," paper presented at the Q-Group Conference, October 2013 (http://www.q-group.org/wp-content/uploads/2014/01/2013fall_siegelpaper.pdf).

Smith, Edgar Lawrence. *Common Stocks as Long-Term Investments.* New York: Macmillan, 1924.

Smith, Vernon L., Gary L. Suchanek, and Arlington W. Williams. "Bubbles, Crashes and Endogenous Expectations in Experimental Spot Asset Markets." *Econometrica*, 56 (1988): 1119–51.

Stambaugh, Robert, Jianfeng Yu, and Yu Yuan. "The Long of It: Odds that Investor Sentiment Spuriously Predicts Anomaly Returns." Working Paper No. 18231, Cambridge, Mass.: National Bureau of Economic Research, July 2012.

Stanley, Thomas J., and William D. Danko. *The Millionaire Next Door: The Surprising Secrets of America's Wealthy.* New York: Pocket Books, 1996.

Stein, Emmanuel. *Government and the Investor.* New York: Farrar and Reinhart, 1941.

Sterling, William P., and Stephen R. Waite. *Boomernomics: The Future of Your Money in the Upcoming Generational Warfare.* Westminster, Md.: Ballantine, 1998.

Strahlberg, Dagmar, and Anne Maass. "Hindsight Bias: Impaired Memory or Biased Reconstruction." *European Review of Social Psychology*, 8 (1998): 105–32.

Straub, William F. "Sensation Seeking among High- and Low-Risk Male Athletes." *Journal of Sports Psychology*, 4(3) (1982): 243–53.

Sutton, Gregory D. "Explaining Changes in House Prices." *Bank of International Settlements Quarterly Review*, September 2002, pp. 46–55.

Swensen, David. *Pioneering Portfolio Management.* Glencoe, Ill.: Free Press, 2000.

Taleb, Nassim N. *Fooled by Randomness: The Hidden Role of Chance in Life and in the Markets*, 2nd ed. New York: Texere, 2004.

Taub, Jennifer. *Other People's Houses: How Decades of Bailouts, Captive Regulators, and Toxic Bankers Made Home Mortgages a Thrilling Business.* New Haven, Conn.: Yale University Press, 2014.

Thaler, Richard H., ed. *Advances in Behavioral Finance II.* New York: Sage Foundation, 2005.

Thaler, Richard H., and Eric J. Johnson. "Gambling with the House Money and Trying to Break Even: The Effect of Prior Outcomes on Risky Choice." *Management Science*, 36 (1990): 643–60.

Thompson, William N. *Legalized Gambling: A Reference Handbook.* Santa Barbara, Calif.: ABC-CLIO, 1994.

TIAA-CREF Institute. "Participant Asset Allocation Report." http://www.tiaa -crefinstitute.org/Data/statistics/pdfs/AAdec2003.pdf.

Tobias, Andrew. "The Billion-Dollar Harvard-Yale Game." *Esquire,* December 19, 1978, pp. 77–85.

Torous, Walter, Rossen Valkanov, and Shu Yan. "On Predicting Stock Returns with Nearly Integrated Explanatory Variables." *Journal of Business,* 78(1) (2005): 937–66.

Triano, Christine. "Private Foundations and Public Charities: Is It Time to Increase Payout?" http://www.nng.org/html/ourprograms/campaign/payoutppr-table .html#fulltext. National Network of Grantmakers, 1999.

Tsatsaronis, Kostas, and Haibin Zhu. "What Drives Housing Price Dynamics: Cross-Country Evidence." *BIS Quarterly Review,* March 2004, pp. 65–78.

Tversky, Amos, and Daniel Kahneman. "Judgment under Uncertainty: Heuristics and Biases." *Science,* 185 (1974): 1124–31.

U.S. Department of Labor, Pension and Welfare Benefits Administration. "Participant Investment Education: Final Rule." 29 CFR Part 2509, Interpretive Bulletin 96-1. *Federal Register,* 61(113) (1996): 29,585–90. Also available at http://www.dol.gov/ dol/pwba/public/regs/fedreg/final/96–14093.htm.

Valkanov, Rossen. "Long-Horizon Regressions: Theoretical Results and Applications." *Journal of Financial Economics,* 68 (2003): 201–32.

Vanguard Group, Inc. "How America Saves 2013." https://pressroom.vanguard.com/ content/nonindexed/2013.06.03_How_America_Saves_2013.pdf.

Van Strum, Kenneth S. *Investing in Purchasing Power.* Boston: Barron's, 1925.

Vissing-Jorgensen, Annette, and Arvind Krishnamurthy. "The Effects of Quantitative Easing on Interest Rates: Channels and Implications for Policy." *Brookings Papers on Economic Activity,* 2 (2011): 215–87.

Vuolteenaho, Tuomo. "What Drives Firm-Level Stock Returns?" *Journal of Finance,* 57 (2002): 233–64.

Warren, George F., and Frank A. Pearson. *Gold and Prices.* New York: John Wiley and Sons, 1935.

Warther, Vincent A. "Aggregate Mutual Fund Flows and Security Returns." *Journal of Financial Economics,* 39 (1995): 209–35.

Weber, Steven. "The End of the Business Cycle?" *Foreign Affairs,* 76(4) (1997): 65–82.

Weissman, Rudolph. *The Investment Company and the Investor.* New York: Harper and Brothers, 1951.

Welte, John W., et al. "Gambling Participation in the United States—Results from a National Survey." *Journal of Gambling Studies,* 18(4) (2002): 313–37.

Willoughby, Jack. "Burning Up: Warning: Internet Companies Are Running Out of Cash—Fast." *Barron's,* March 20, 2000, pp. 29–32.

Womack, Kent. "Do Brokerage Analysts' Recommendations Have Investment Value?" *Journal of Finance,* 51(1) (1996): 137–67.

World Bank. *Averting the Old Age Crisis.* New York: Oxford University Press, 1994.

Wurgler, Jeffrey. "Financial Markets and the Allocation of Capital." *Journal of Financial Economics*, 58 (2000): 187–214.

Zaret, David. *Origins of Democratic Culture: Printing, Petitions, and the Public Sphere in Early-Modern England*. Princeton, N.J.: Princeton University Press, 1999.

Zuckerman, Marvin, Elizabeth Kolin, Leah Price, and Ina Zoob. "Development of a Sensation-Seeking Scale." *Journal of Consulting Psychology*, 28(6) (1964): 477–82.

Index

Page numbers for entries occurring in figures are followed by an *f*, those for entries occurring in notes by an *n*, and those for entries occurring in tables, by a *t*.